WANTED!

U.S.

CRIMINAL RECORDS

Sources & Research Methodology

RON ARONS

Criminal Research Press
www.ronarons.com

Wanted! U.S. Criminal Records

Copyright © 2009 Ron Arons

ISBN: 978-1-935125-64-8

Printed in the United States of America

Second Edition

Published by:
Criminal Research Press
4012 Whittle Ave.
Oakland, CA 94602
510-530-3975 · www.ronarons.com

To my parents and to Ike, who put me on this path.

Contents

Introduction

Welcome to *WANTED!* U.S. Criminal Records. Whether you have a criminal ancestor in your family or are interested in learning more about a famous gangster or lesser-known felon, you've come to the right place.

The United States has the highest incarceration rate of any nation in the world. That's according to a 2005 report from the Bureau of Federal Statistics. Confirming these results, a 2008 study from the Pew Research Center revealed that "One percent of Americans are incarcerated."

The Pew report showed that American prisons and jails held 2,319,258 adult inmates at the beginning of 2008. In addition to those prisoners currently incarcerated, there are two other groups of criminals to consider: those who have served time and have been released; and lawbreakers who went through a trial, but never served a day behind bars. The total number of criminals in the United States, then, becomes much higher than the figure reported by the Pew Center.

And that's just a snapshot in time. Multiply the current number of criminals by 10 generations, going back to the early 1800s, and the figure climbs to tens or even hundreds of millions of criminals in this country's history. Yet, until now, there has been no comprehensive guide to researching criminals throughout American history.

I became familiar with criminal records via the research I conducted on my own criminal ancestor, writing a book about him and, then, investigating criminals for other projects. Furthermore, I have given hundreds of presentations across the country to groups interested in learning more about criminal history or finding out how to conduct general genealogical research more effectively.

Over the past several years, I have connected with many people who want to research their own criminal relatives. Whenever I give a talk about my research on criminals, people come up to me to tell me their families' stories. Once I relay the story of the personal journey to understand my own ancestor's criminal history, others appear to be quite relieved to know that it's okay to talk about their families as well. There's no longer a stigma attached, no more reason to keep these stories buried under the rug. Sometimes it appears, these same people can't tell me their black sheep stories fast enough. Given my expertise in New York Jewish criminality, I have helped many people, exploring the lives of their relatives who served time in Sing Sing Prison, and hoping to discover more about those incarcerations. With this in mind, I created a database with the names of more than 6,000 Jewish criminals who served time at the famous New York prison and posted it on my Web site, www. ronarons.com. Both for other personal projects and multiple requests from others, I have also researched criminals who committed their crimes in other states, including Illinois, California and Nevada.

I also came to the realization that, just as with genealogy in general, the methodology of researching criminals remains essentially the same across location and, the sources of information you might be looking for also reasonably similar. Yet, there was no reference guide available to help others research more than two centuries of criminals.

WANTED! lists thousands of sets of records concerning incarcerations, criminal court activities, paroles, pardons, executions and police and other organizations' investigations, state by state, across the nation. In short, *WANTED!* provides the best sources of criminal records, to optimize your research.

There are many people to thank. First and foremost, I'd like to thank the professional staff at each of the archives and other repositories listed in this work for not only for granting me permission to print information found on and off their Web sites, but also for helping me to understand their collection. Thanks to Alicia Robertson, of Robertson Publishing, who helped me with the process of self-publishing. Finally, I would like to give my regards to several reviewers of my materials, including Jan Meisels-Allen, Beth Galetto, Rhoda Miller, Rob Gloster, Nina Amir and Jordan Auslander.

I sincerely hope that *WANTED!* jump-starts your research if you are just beginning your genealogical journey, or provides ideas you might not have considered. Wishing you successful sleuthing!

Sources and Research Methodology

To effectively research criminals – a slippery bunch to say the least – you have to understand what sources of information are available and you need guidelines for finding and working with these records.

Family Stories

Before you search for documents about a criminal, try to begin your research by reading or listening to family stories – the strict accuracy of a story is not as important as excavating kernels of truth. Stories have a way of changing (intentionally or not) over time, but some truth can usually be found in the information provided. In my own experience, the family story was kept a deep dark secret; I uncovered the details of my ancestor's transgressions by accidentally finding one document about him and then searching for more records.

General Genealogical Records (Records not covered in WANTED!)

Beginning research about criminals starts out with techniques you would utilize to investigate any other person. In addition to seeking out family stories, you simply look for standard genealogical documents such as census records and newspaper articles. Let's take a look at each of these standard types of documents and sources of information, and discuss their characteristics:

Census Records

U.S. Census records are available for every 10 years beginning in 1790, and all but the 1890 records still exist (1890 was destroyed in a fire). The United States has a 72-year privacy restriction on census records. Therefore, the 1930 census is the most recent set of publicly available census records. The 1940 U.S. Census will become available for public examination in 2012.

The U.S. Census is taken once a decade (years ending with a zero). If your target individual was not incarcerated at the time of the census, you will not be able to find him (or her) in prison through census research. Fortunately, some states also had their own censuses, such as the New York State census taken in 1905, 1915 and 1925.

WANTED! U.S. Criminal Records

You can easily find federal census records online through Ancestry.com, Footnote.com, FamilySearch.org and Heritage Quest (an online service provided at many libraries). Federal censuses are also available on microfilm at the National Archives and Record Administration (NARA) regional offices, The Church of Jesus Christ of Latter Day Saints (LDS) Family History Library in Salt Lake City, various local LDS Family History Centers throughout the world and other libraries, such as the Sutro Library in San Francisco.

In my own research, an index card for the 1900 U.S. Census listed my ancestor as an inmate at Sing Sing Prison. This was my clue that I had a criminal ancestor. (See page 6.)

Newspapers

Newspapers are a wonderful way to get initial information about a criminal. You will, however, need an approximate date and location of the crime and/or the trial. With both the exact date and location, a researcher can look for the more criminal-specific records listed in *WANTED!*

Libraries provide a great resource for local newspapers. For example, the University of California Berkeley Library's Periodical Room has microfilms of newspapers from across the country and even some from around the world, such as the London Times.

More and more newspapers are being digitized and placed online. ProQuest offers online, keyword-searchable access to many of the most popular newspapers, including The New York Times, The Philadelphia Inquirer, The Atlanta Journal-Constitution and the Los Angeles Times. NewspaperArchive.com offers similar online access to hundreds of newspapers from across the country online as does Ancestry.com. Check your local library to determine if it has a subscription to any of these services. The Library of Congress offers articles from a number of turn-of-the-19th-century newspapers: chroniclingamerica.loc.gov.

I found numerous articles regarding my ancestor's criminal activities both online and at various libraries, most notably, the New York Public Library, which has an excellent collection of New York-based newspapers as well as those from other locales. (See one of these articles on page 38.)

Finally, abstracts of newspaper articles can be found absolutely free at the following part of Google's website: news.google.com/archivesearch.

City Directories and Telephone Books

City directories and telephone books are similar to census records in that they allow you to understand where a person lived in a particular year. The good news is that these directories were published year after year, unlike censuses taken every 10 years. These directories are available at local libraries and LDS Family History Centers (via Inter-Library Loan from the LDS Family History Library in Salt Lake City).

Criminal-Specific Records (Found in WANTED!)

Prison Records

Prison records come in all shapes and forms: intake/admission records, discharge records, punishment ledgers, etc. These records usually provide name, age, crime committed, sentence, residential address or location. Infrequently, admission registers include mug shots. A good example of records with photos is the set of Biographical Admission Registers for the New York State Reformatory at Elmira, found at the New York State Archives in Albany, NY. These same registers also list family members, often names of brothers and sisters in addition to the mother's and father's names. Often admission records will list the name of the court where the trial was held. This proves useful in tracking down the docket (calendar) or, better yet, the actual trial transcript. Admission records also typically provide information about other crimes committed by the individual or time served at the same or other correctional facilities. Examples of what type of information can be found in prison records are displayed on pages 14, 114, 156, 178, 216, 230, 274, 280, 312 and 316.

Criminal Court Documents

There are many types of criminal court documents available, including dockets (calendars), court minutes, trial transcripts, etc. Courts involved with criminal cases are named differently depending on: 1) the severity of the crime, 2) the state in which the crime was committed, 3) the time frame in which the crime was committed, and 4) the local customs of naming courts. You might find criminal records from Circuit Courts, Courts of General Sessions, Courts of Oyer and Terminer, etc. If that's not confusing enough, there are federal, state, county and local courts. There is one U.S. Supreme Court, but states also have Supreme Courts and there are layers of appellate courts as well.

If you are lucky enough to track down a trial transcript, you will get to experience the trial as if you were there – through verbatim testimony of the complainant, witnesses and, possibly, the criminal in question. Examples of court records are shown on pages 50, 74, 220 and 270.

Note: the LDS Family History Library (FHL) in Salt Lake City has state and local court records that may not be mentioned in WANTED! To determine if the FHL has court records that suit your purposes, conduct a Place Search at: http://www.familysearch.org/eng/Library/FHLC/frameset_fhlc.asp

Parole Records

A parole record will tell when a criminal was released from prison. It might also provide details of the crime committed. There are parole registers and applications for parole.

Pardon Records

Pardon records are similar to parole records, but they differ in the sense that pardons represent an official excusing of the crime committed. You can find lists of convicts pardoned as well as applications for pardon; the latter provide details about the subjects, whether or not they were subsequently pardoned.

Executions

Some of the worst (usually violent) criminals were put to death via lethal injection, electrocution, the gas chamber or some other method of execution. Every state in the union executed some criminals. Sing Sing Prison, which used the electric chair 614 times, generated various sets of documents about those on death row. The New York State Archives holds separate admission records for Sing Sing inmates scheduled for execution (repeating much of the information found in the admission registers for all Sing Sing inmates) as well as individual case files for those on death row. Examples of what can be found about execution are displayed on pages 156, 178 and 218.

Investigative Files

The Federal Bureau of Investigation, which looked into the activities of some of the more notorious criminals, provides the best known source of these documents. The files can be quite lengthy and sometimes expensive to obtain (because of photocopying charges – ask for a CD with an electronic file, if possible). The FBI Web site has downloadable files for some criminals, such as Bugsy Siegel, Al Capone and John Dillinger. For other criminals, a researcher has to file a Freedom of Information Act (FOIA) request form before receiving a file. FBI files usually have major portions redacted, so don't be surprised if you see pages completely white or completely back, and not worth the money the FBI requests to photocopy them. See page 264 for one page from Bugsy Siegel's FBI file.

Police Files

WANTED! includes a small number of police records. They are similar in nature to investigative files, but have been classified as a separate category. I found a Police "Yellow Sheet" (police report) in the Grand Jury case file for my criminal ancestor. (See page 324.)

Considerations

1. Criminals are difficult to research because they lie about many things, including their name. Many criminals use aliases. Irving Wexler went by the name "Waxey Gordon." Louis Shomberg was called "Dutch Goldberg." Bugsy Siegel's real first name was Benjamin. And so on.

You must understand this when looking for records about a criminal. Very often a prison admission record or trial transcript will list the alias(es), but you have to get to these documents in the fist place to discover the criminal's true name. It really boils down to finding a number of different pieces of the puzzle and then assembling them correctly. The more documents you can collect, the more easily you will see the entire picture so you can arrange the puzzle pieces together in the correct pattern.

2. Criminals frequently commit multiple crimes. These crimes can be all of the same type or quite different from each other. The most notorious gangsters were involved in many different types of illegal endeavors. Many criminals never changed their ways, spending multiple sentences in the same or different prisons.

3. Criminals frequently commit their crimes in multiple jurisdictions, even in multiple states.

4. Records about criminals, even for the same crime, can be located in many different states. As you'll see in WANTED!, records are located in places you'd never expect. Usually this has to do with federal criminal records held at regional National Archives facilities. For example, different sets of federal criminal court records for South Dakota can be found at the Denver and Kansas City branches of the National Archives.

5. Many records have privacy restrictions. It is advisable to contact a repository before you travel there to understand the limits placed on record accessibility.

6. Some files may not be findable at all. Most were not created with maintaining a history in mind. In response to an inquiry I made about a famous gangster, the FBI wrote to me that it previously had four large files about the criminal, but one was "lost." I have heard multiple stories about the destruction or disposal of various New York prison and criminal court records. For example, the criminal court trial transcripts now available at John Jay College of Criminal Justice in Manhattan were found in a dumpster elsewhere in the city.

7. It can take a long time to obtain a file, especially if you are filing a Freedom of Information Act (FOIA) request. I requested a file about a famous gangster and received it only after I waited for more than more than 70,000 earlier inquires (by other researchers) to be handled. The process took two years!

8. You might need to travel a convoluted road to see a particular file. I wanted to see a NY criminal case against Louis Shomberg. To do so, I had to order the case from the National Archives regional facility in Manhattan which, in turn, ordered it from the National Records Center in Missouri. I had to go to the NARA office in Manhattan to view the file. Since I live in California, all of this took quite a bit of coordination.

9. Sometimes repositories do not know what information they have, don't have, or should have. In my research of Irving Wexler and his time at Sing Sing, I learned that he died in Alcatraz (Wexler is the only criminal in American history to have served time in Sing Sing, Leavenworth and Alcatraz). I called the National Archives in Northern California, the repository that holds Alcatraz inmate files, to determine if I could look at Wexler's file. An archivist told me that, since Wexler's name did not appear on the Archives' list of Alcatraz

inmates, he could not possibly have served time at "the Rock." Even after I indicated that I had both a New York Times article and a California death certificate indicating that Wexler died at Alcatraz, the archivist continued to believe that my information was incorrect. Fortunately, I spoke with an archivist in charge of the Leavenworth files in Kansas City, and he told me that I could find a file about Irving Wexler in the Notorious Offender Files found at the National Archives in College Park, MD. After I received this file, I made a copy for the National Archives repository in Northern California.

What to look for first?

I wish I could provide a template that says, "Find the census record first, then the prison record, then the trial transcript, and so on." Unfortunately, researching criminals is not that straightforward. In my research of many different criminals, each investigation has demonstrated different circumstances. The result is that I have not discovered any consistent sequence for seeking documents. The table below should drive this point home. The table shows the order in which I found documents for six different criminals (1=first document found, 2=second document found, etc.)

Record Type	Case 1: Isaac pier	Case 2: Harry Horowitz	Case 3: Louis Buchalter	Case 4: Calman Cooper	Case 5: Mickey Cohen	Case 6: Irving Wexler
Prison Records	3	1	1	1		1
Vital Records	2	4				2
Census	1	5	5			
Court Records	5	3			2	
FBI FOIA			4			
National Archives Materials					1	6
Newspapers	6	2	2		3	3
Other	4		3	2		4

As you can see, I used no consistent pattern for finding documentations about these criminals. I did not, in fact, find all types of document for all of these criminals. You almost never do. My recommendation is to take a shotgun approach, looking for anything and everything.

How to Use This Book

WANTED! lists, state by state (in alphabetical order), repositories and Web sites where you, the researcher, can find prison records, criminal court records, parole records, pardon records, investigation records, police records and information about executions. Following the chapters for all of the 50 states, there is a chapter for the District of Columbia. The final chapter of the book covers Federal prison records and other resources spanning the entire nation. Not all states offer all types of records; for this reason, for example, you will find only a limited number of investigative files and police records listed for some states.

In each chapter, records are listed by repository (such as state archives or a county court) or online resource (Web site). Each set of records is tagged with an icon representing one of seven different types of records:

Icon   **Record Type**

Prison records

Criminal court records

Parole records

Pardon records

Execution records
(the syringe represents executions by all methods: lethal injection, electrocution, gas chamber, firing squad, etc.)

Investigative records

Police records

WANTED! U.S. Criminal Records

Each repository or online resource is listed with address/contact information and/or a URL (Web site address).

At the end of many chapters, there are examples of different kinds of criminal-related documents I have found during the past dozen years. The not are illustrative of what you might find, but are entertaining in their own right. Spend some time exploring the treasures that I've discovered!

Important notes:

1. Most records listed in *WANTED!* are not online, but are available on-site at repositories to which you must travel.

2. Many records have privacy restrictions. It is highly recommended that you contact any repository before you visit to determine what access restrictions might prevent you from looking at certain records.

3. Some repositories require special permission to visit, or that you reserve a table to conduct research. Please call ahead or look at a repository's Web site to determine what restrictions and requirements apply.

4. The fact that *WANTED!* contains more pages for a given state does not necessarily mean the state has more criminal records than another state. States catalog and store their records in different-sized groupings. Some states have many different sets of record groups with fewer records per group than other states. Oregon is one such example.

5. *WANTED!* does not list any information regarding Puerto Rico, the U.S. Virgin Islands, the Panama Canal Zone or any other U.S. territories. Nor does the book include any information regarding extraditions.

Alabama

Alabama State Archives

624 Washington Avenue, Montgomery, AL 36130, (334) 242-4235
www.archives.alabama.gov

Record Type	Location	Title/Description
	Box LGM189, Reel # R03	Henry County Criminal Case Files, 1844-1950
	Box LGM161, Reel # R17	Limestone County Circuit Court Criminal & Civil Docket, 1886-1875
	Box LGM166, Reel # R27	Limestone County Probate Judge Poor Relief Records

ADAHCAT (Alabama Department of Archives & History Catalog)
http://216.226.178.202:81/vwebv/searchBasic
Results for the search term 'corrections'

Record Type	Location/ Call Number	Author	Title/Description
	Housed at Montgomery County Archives	Montgomery County (AL) Sheriff's Dept.	Jail registers, 1878-1935
	SG16,933-16943	Alabama Dept. of Corrections and Institutions	Correspondence concerning corporal punishment, 1928-1945
	SG,7532-7533	Alabama State Board of Administration	County convicts sentenced to hard labor, 1927-1931.
	SG,7484-7508	Alabama Dept. of Corrections and Institutions	Index of state convict record, 1885-1952

	SG,7458-7483	Alabama Dept. of Corrections and Institutions	State convict records, 1889-1952
	Multiple holdings	Alabama Board of Managers of Convicts	Transcripts of convictions, 1885-1894
	SG,7610-7643	Alabama State Board of Administration	Discharge orders for county convicts, 1888-1931
	SG,7509-7524	Alabama Board of Corrections	Index of county convict record, 1931-1954
	SG,7608-7609	Alabama Board of Inspectors of Convicts	Discharge orders for state convicts, 1885-1891
	SG7,435-7449	Alabama Board of Corrections	County convict records, 1931-1954
	SG9,681	Alabama Governor	Correspondence relating to convict paroles, 1916-1943
	SG,14914-14921, 16911-16924	Alabama Dept. of Corrections and Institutions	Weekly conduct reports, 1927-1947
	SG,16427-16430	Alabama Dept. of Corrections and Institutions	Records of punishment, 1928-1951
	SG7,527-7529, 20627, 20633	Alabama Dept. of Corrections and Institutions	Death record of state convicts, 1843-1951
	SG,7525-7526	Alabama Board of Inspectors of Convicts	Death record of county convicts, 1908-1912
	SG,7530-7531	Alabama Board of Inspectors of Convicts	Descriptive record of prisoners, 1910-1913
	SG15,429	Alabama Secretary of State	Convict pardon docket, 1887-1896
	No call number	Alabama Governor	Clemency hearing case files, 1951-1962
	No call number	Alabama Governor (Folsom)	Clemency hearing case files, 1947-1950

	SG013,791	Alabama Governor (Dixon)	Clemency hearing case files, 1939-1942
	No call number	Alabama Governor (Persons)	Clemency hearing case files, 1952-1954
	No call number	Alabama Dept. of Corrections	Psychological case files, 1975-1978
	SG1,9063-019122, 19229-019254, 19663, 20201-020218	Alabama. Attorney General's Office	Prisoner civil rights case files, 1971-1993

Federal Criminal Court Records at the National Archives & Records Admin. (NARA)

NARA Southeast Region
5780 Jonesboro Road, Morrow, Georgia 30260, (770) 968-2100
www.archives.gov/southeast/
atlanta.archives@nara.gov

Record Type	ARC Identifier	Title	Description
	2562228	Criminal Case Files, compiled 1970 - 1983	Textual Records from the U.S. District Court for the Southern (Birmingham) Division of the Northern District of Alabama
	2133127	Criminal Dockets, compiled 1912 - 1962	Textual Records from the U.S. District Court for the Jasper Division of the Northern District of Alabama
	656880	Criminal Case Files, compiled 1887 - 1980	Textual Records from the U.S. District Court for the Mobile Division of the Southern District of Alabama
	2058466	Criminal Case Files, compiled 1912 - 1957	Textual Records from the U.S. District Court for the Middle (Gadsden) Division of the Northern District of Alabama
	1693171	Criminal Dockets, compiled 1886 - 1962	Textual Records from the U.S. District Court for the Southern (Birmingham) Division of the Northern District of Alabama
	1703693	Criminal Case Files, compiled 1903 - 1957	Textual Records from the U.S. District Court for the Eastern (Anniston) Division of the Northern District of Alabama
	656749	Criminal Case Files, compiled 1865 - 1980	Textual Records from the U.S. District Court for the Northern (Montgomery) Division of the Middle District of Alabama

	2133130	Criminal Dockets, compiled 1909 - 1962	Textual Records from the U.S. District Court for the Middle (Gadsden) Division of the Northern District of Alabama
	2565529	Criminal Minutes, compiled 1935 - 1951	Textual Records from the U.S. District Court for the Northern (Montgomery) Division of the Middle District of Alabama
	2133126	Criminal Dockets , compiled 1912 - 1962	Textual Records from the U.S. District Court for the Northwestern (Florence Division) of the Northern District of Alabama
	2363824	Criminal Case Files, compiled 1913 - 1957	Textual Records from the U.S. District Court for the Jasper Division of the Northern District of Alabama
	1890199	Criminal Case Files, compiled 1910 - 1911	Textual Records from the U.S. Circuit Court for the Northwestern (Florence Division) of the Northern District of Alabama
	2565517	Criminal Minutes, compiled 1938 - 1974	Textual Records from the U.S. District Court for the Northwestern (Florence Division) of the Northern District of Alabama
	2619080	Criminal Minutes, compiled 1944 - 1951	Textual Records from the U.S. District Court for the Southern (Dothan) Division of the Middle District of Alabama
	2565511	Criminal Minutes, compiled 1938 - 1974	Textual Records from the U.S. District Court for the Middle (Gadsden) Division of the Northern District of Alabama
	1768097	Criminal Case Files, compiled 1912 - 1957	Textual Records from the U.S. District Court for the Northwestern (Florence Division) of the Northern District of Alabama
	2524667	Criminal Case Files, compiled 1870 - 1911	Textual Records from the U.S. Circuit Court for the Southern (Mobile) Division of the Southern District of Alabama
	2524668	Criminal Case Files, compiled 1920 - 1982	Textual Records from the U.S. District Court for the Eastern (Opelika) Division of the Middle District of Alabama
	2584135	Criminal Case Files, compiled 1909 - 1911	Textual Records from the U.S. Circuit Court for the Middle (Gadsden) Division of the Northern District of Alabama
	1938042	Criminal Dockets, compiled 1910 - 1962	Textual Records from the U.S. District Court for the Northwestern (Florence Division) of the Northern District of Alabama
	1654778	Criminal Case Files, compiled 1885 - 1911	Textual Records from the U.S. Circuit Court for the Southern (Birmingham) Division of the Northern District of Alabama

	1742375	Criminal Dockets, compiled 1912 - 1923	Textual Records from the U.S. District Court for the Eastern (Anniston) Division of the Northern District of Alabama
	2565508	Criminal Minutes, compiled 1938 - 1974	Textual Records from the U.S. District Court for the Eastern (Anniston) Division of the Northern District of Alabama
	2565528	Criminal Minutes, compiled 1938 - 1974	Textual Records from the U.S. District Court for the Northeastern (Huntsville) Division of the Northern District of Alabama
	2565504	Criminal Minutes, compiled 1938 - 1974	Textual Records from the U.S. District Court for the Jasper Division of the Northern District of Alabama
	2305921	Criminal Dockets, compiled 1879 - 1962	Textual Records from the U.S. District Court for the Northeastern (Huntsville) Division of the Northern District of Alabama
	656726	Criminal Case Files, compiled 1893 - 1978	Textual Records from the U.S. District Court for the Southern (Birmingham) Division of the Northern District of Alabama
	2619070	Criminal Dockets, compiled 1887 - 1965	Textual Records from the U.S. District Court for the Mobile Division of the Southern District of Alabama
	2133135	Criminal Dockets, compiled 1911 - 1962	Textual Records
	2565531	Criminal Minutes , compiled 1938 - 1974	Textual Records from the U.S. District Court for the Western (Tuscaloosa) Division of the Northern District of Alabama
	2565503	Criminal Minutes, compiled 1938 - 1974	Textual Records from the U.S. District Court for the Southern (Birmingham) Division of the Northern District of Alabama

Alabama Executions

 http://users.bestweb.net/~rg/execution/ALABAMA.htm

Alabama Department of Corrections Inmate Search

 http://www.doc.state.al.us/inmsearch.asp

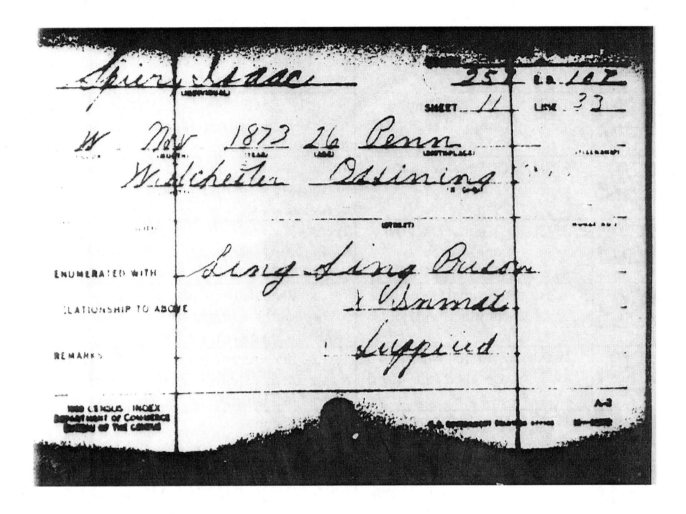

Image 1: Index card for 1900 U.S. Census showing author's great-grandfather, Isaac Spier.

Alaska

Alaska State Archives
141 Willoughby Avenue, Juneau, AK 99811-0525, (907) 465-2270
http://www.archives.state.ak.us/

Record Type	Title/Description
	Prison Records - The Alaska State Archives has "a number of jail records for various towns in the territory. Usually jail registers also served as community police logs."
	Criminal Dockets, Journals & Case Files - 1st Division: SE AK, HQ Juneau, 1900-1950
	Criminal Dockets, Journals & Case Files - 2nd Division: Western AK, HQ Nome, 1900-1959
	Criminal Dockets, Journals & Case Files - 3rd Division: South Central AK, HQ Fairbanks, Valdez, and then Anchorage, 1900-1950
	Criminal Dockets, Journals & Case Files - 4th Division: Interior AK, HQ Fairbanks ca. 1906-1959

Federal Criminal Court Records at the National Archives & Records Admin. (NARA)
NARA's Pacific Alaska Region (Anchorage),
654 West Third Avenue, Anchorage, AK 99501-2145, (907) 261-7820
www.archives.gov/pacific-alaska/anchorage/
alaska.archives@nara.gov

Record Type	ARC Identifier	Title	Description
	617358	Criminal Complaint Files, compiled 1946 - 1960	Textual Records from the Department of Justice. Office of the U.S. Attorney for the Judicial District of Alaska. (ca. 1912 -)

	719573	Civil, Criminal, and Probate Docket, compiled 04/01/1920 - 03/05/1956	Textual Records from the U.S. Territorial Court for the First (Juneau) Division of the District of Alaska. Office of U.S. Commissioners at Hyder. (06/06/1900 - 02/20/1960)
	618023	Significant Civil and Criminal Case Files, compiled 1955 - 1973	Textual Records from the Department of Justice. Office of the U.S. Attorney for the Judicial District of Alaska. (ca. 1912 -)
	618003	Complaint Files, compiled 1946 - 1951	Textual Records from the Department of Justice. Office of the U.S. Attorney for the Judicial District of Alaska. (ca. 1912 -)
	618012	Criminal Case Files, compiled 1947 - 1959	Textual Records from the Department of Justice. Office of the U.S. Attorney for the Judicial District of Alaska. (ca. 1912 -)
	1663377	Transcripts, compiled 1966 - 1973	Textual Records from the U.S. District Court for the Anchorage Division of the District of Alaska. (07/07/1958 -)

Alaska Executions - Inmates Executed, 1927-1994
(via AK Department of Corrections)

 http://www.correct.state.ak.us/corrections/index.jsf

Alaska Executions

 http://users.bestweb.net/~rg/execution/ALASKA.htm

Alaska Inmate Lookup via VineLink

https://www.vinelink.com/vinelink/siteInfoAction.do?siteId=2001

Alaska Trial Court Name Index

http://www.courts.alaska.gov/names.htm

Arizona

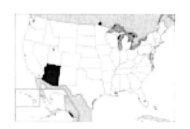

Arizona Department of Corrections
Online database of inmates admitted 1872-1972

 http://www.azcorrections.gov/Historical/Jeff_ADCHistory_HundredYears.aspx

Arizona State Archives
1901 W. Madison, Phoenix, AZ 85009, (602) 926-3720
http://www.lib.az.us/

Record Type	Location/Call Number	Title/Description
	N/A	Criminal court records available at county and territorial level. [Hardcopy finding aid available at the Arizona State Archives.]
	RG 92	Supreme Court Records - Appeals. 1866-1972. (131 boxes and 3 rolls of microfilm). Appeals contain files of cases appealed to the Supreme Court, including civil and criminal cases. Criminal case files, 1871-1912, may include appellee's brief, transcript on appeal, etc. Petitions for pardons, 1924-1936, contain case files.
	COR 1.3:P 16/ 1969 COR 1.3:P 16/ 1970 COR 1.3:P 16/ 1971 COR 1.3:P 16/ 1972 COR 1.3:P 16/ 1973 COR 1.3:P 16/ 1974 COR 1.3:P 16/ 1975 COR 1.3:P 16/ 1976 COR 1.3:P 16/ 1977 COR 1.3:P 16/ 1978	Inmates released by the Arizona Dept. of Corrections. Published by Arizona Department of Corrections. Each year is represented by one book. Books are offsite at a remote location.

Arizona State Law Library

1700 W Washington St # 300, Phoenix, AZ 85007-2812
(602) 542-5297
www.lib.az.us
sll@lib.az.us

Record Type	Call Number	Author	Title/Description
	KFA2445.9 .A62	Arizona Supreme Court	Criminal cases filed by years [microform]
	KFA2448.9 .A12	AZ Court of Appeals, Div. 1	Criminal cases filed numerically by case number
	KFA2448.9 .A22	AZ Court of Appeals, Div. 2	Habeas Corpus Cases; Criminal cases filed numerically by case

Federal Criminal Court Records at the National Archives & Records Admin. (NARA)

NARA Pacific Region (Riverside, CA)
23123 Cajelco Road, Perris, CA, (951) 956-2000
http://www.archives.gov/pacific/frc/riverside/contacts.html
riverside.reference@nara.gov

Record Type	ARC Identifier	Title	Description
	599259	Criminal Dockets, compiled 1882 - 1912	Textual Records from the U.S. Territorial Court for the First Judicial District of Arizona. (1864 - 1912)
	599007	Criminal Final Records, compiled 1882 - 1911	Textual Records from the U.S. Territorial Court for the First Judicial District of Arizona. (1864 - 1912)
	614490	Criminal Case Files, compiled 1891 - 1911	Textual Records from the U.S. Territorial Court for the Fourth Judicial District of Arizona. (1891 - 1912)
	602275	Criminal Dockets, compiled 1913 - 1976	Textual Records from the U.S. District Court for the Tucson Division of the District of Arizona. (1912 -)
	626078	Criminal Case Dockets, compiled 1913 - 1968	Textual Records from the U.S. District Court for the Prescott Division of the District of Arizona. (1912 -)
	600242	Criminal Case Files, compiled 1882 - 1912	Textual Records from the U.S. Territorial Court for the First Judicial District of Arizona. (1864 - 1912)

	609657	Criminal Case Files, compiled 1869 - 1912	Textual Records from the U.S. Territorial Court for the Third Judicial District of Arizona. (1864 - 1912)
	635413	Criminal Case Files, compiled 1914 - 1968	Textual Records from the U.S. District Court for the Globe Division of the District of Arizona. (1912 -)
	635414	Criminal Case Dockets, compiled 1913 - 1968	Textual Records from the U.S. District Court for the Globe Division of the District of Arizona. (1912 -)
	608524	Index to Criminal Case Files, compiled 1864 - 1911	Textual Records from the U.S. Territorial Court for the Third Judicial District of Arizona. (1864 - 1912)
	616756	Criminal Case Files, compiled 1905 - 1911	Textual Records from the U.S. Territorial Court for the Fifth Judicial District of Arizona. (1905 - 1912)
	605266	Criminal Case Files, compiled 1878 - 1912	Textual Records from the U.S. Territorial Court for the Second Judicial District of Arizona. (1864 - 1912)
	600298	Criminal Case Files, compiled 1914 - 1969	Textual Records from the U.S. District Court for the Tucson Division of the District of Arizona. (1912 -)
	611022	Criminal Case Dockets, compiled 1912 - 1986	Textual Records from the U.S. District Court for the Phoenix Division of the District of Arizona (1912 -)
	601681	Dockets, compiled 1894 - 1912	Textual Records from the U.S. Territorial Court for the First Judicial District of Arizona. (1864 - 1912)
	614036	Index to Criminal Case Files, compiled 1946 - 1975	Textual Records from the U.S. District Court for the Phoenix Division of the District of Arizona (1912 -)
	618866	Index to Criminal Case Files, compiled 1957 - 1961	Textual Records from the U.S. District Court for the Prescott Division of the District of Arizona. (1912 -)
	624718	Criminal Case Files, compiled 1913 - 1969	Textual Records from the U.S. District Court for the Prescott Division of the District of Arizona. (1912 -)
	562807	Criminal Case Files, compiled 1912 - 1969	Textual Records from the U.S. District Court for the Phoenix Division of the District of Arizona (1912 -)
	602153	Index Cards to Criminal Cases, compiled 1885 - 1911	Textual Records from the U.S. Territorial Court for the Second Judicial District of Arizona. (1864 - 1912)

	635415	Grand Jury Dockets, compiled 1917 - 1925	Textual Records from the U.S. District Court for the Globe Division of the District of Arizona. (1912 -)
	612939	Index to Criminal Case Files, compiled 1891 - 1912	Textual Records from the U.S. Territorial Court for the Fourth Judicial District of Arizona. (1891 - 1912)
	620185	Grand Jury Dockets, compiled 1917 - 1925	Textual Records from the U.S. District Court for the Phoenix Division of the District of Arizona (1912 -)
	599837	Judgment Books, compiled 1899 - 1911	Textual Records from the U.S. Territorial Court for the First Judicial District of Arizona. (1864 - 1912)
	636357	Civil, Criminal and Equity Judgment Register, compiled 1928 - 1967	Textual Records from the U.S. District Court for the Globe Division of the District of Arizona. (1912 -)

Arizona Executions

 http://users.bestweb.net/~rg/execution/ARIZONA.htm

Arizona Department of Corrections Inmate Search

 http://www.azcorrections.gov/inmate_datasearch/index.aspx

Arizona Judicial Branch Court Case Lookup

 http://apps.supremecourt.az.gov/publicaccess/

Arizona County Courts - Contact Information

Record Type	County	Telephone #	Website
	Apache	(928) 337-4364	www.co.apache.az.us
	Cochise	(520) 432-9200	www.co.cochise.az.us
	Coconino	(928) 774-2011	www.coconino.az.gov

	Gila	(928) 425-3231	www.co.gila.az.us
	Graham	(928) 428-3250	www.graham.az.gov
	Greenlee	(928) 865-2072	www.co.greenlee.az.us
	LaPaz	(928) 669-6115	www.co.la-paz.az.us
	Maricopa	(602) 506-3011	www.maricopa.gov
	Mohave	(928) 753-9141	www.co.mohave.az.us
	Navajo	(928) 524-4000	www.co.navajo.az.us
	Pima	(520) 740-8401	www.pima.gov
	Pinal	(520) 868-6000	www.pinalcountyaz.gov
	Santa Cruz	(520) 375-7800	www.co.santa-cruz.az.us
	Yavapai	(928) 771-3100	www.co.yavapai.az.us
	Yuma	(928) 329-2104	www.co.yuma.az.us

Sing Sing Prison Admission Register entry for author's great-grandfather. Courtesy of NYS Archives and New York Department of Corrections.

Arkansas

Arkansas State Archives

One Capitol Mall, Little Rock, Arkansas 72201, (501) 682-6900
http://www.ark-ives.com/
state.archives@arkansas.gov

Record Type	Location (Microfilm #)	Title/Description
	FHL #: 1302587 Roll #: 39	Circuit Court Records - Criminal, Craighead County, 1883-1892
	FHL #: 1019405 Roll #: 49	Record of Criminal Cases, Woodruff County, 1866-1877

Federal Criminal Court Records at the National Archives & Records Admin. (NARA)

NARA Southwest Region (Fort Worth)
501 West Felix Street, Building 1, Fort Worth, TX 76115-3405, Phone: 817-831-5620
http://www.archives.gov/southwest/
ftworth.archives@nara.gov

Record Type	ARC Identifier	Title	Description
	201532	Defendant Jacket Files for U.S. District Court Western Division of Arkansas, Fort Smith Division, compiled 1866 - 1900	Textual Records from the U.S. District Court for the Fort Smith Division of the Western District of Arkansas. (02/20/1897 -)
	1157520	Sentence Record Books, compiled 1884 - 1909	Textual Records from the U.S. District Court for the Fort Smith Division of the Western District of Arkansas. (02/20/1897 -)

	610941	Criminal Case Files, compiled 1912 - 1977	Textual Records from the U.S. District Court for the Jonesboro Division of the Eastern District of Arkansas. (03/03/1911 -)
	2945948	Criminal Dockets, compiled 1925 - 1981	Textual Records from the U.S. District Court for the El Dorado Division of the Western District of Arkansas. (02/17/1925 -)
	3325363	Criminal Record Books, compiled 06/1904 - 05/1912	Textual Records from the U.S. District Court for the Texarkana Division of the Western District of Arkansas. (02/20/1897 -)
	609757	Criminal Case Files, compiled 1887 - 1975	Textual Records from the U.S. District Court for the Texarkana Division of the Western District of Arkansas. (02/20/1897 -)
	3370927	Criminal and Law Dockets, compiled 1878 - 1879	Textual Records from the U.S. District Court for the Eastern (Helena) Division of the Eastern District of Arkansas. (02/17/1887 -)
	611144	Criminal Case Files, compiled 1964 - 1973	Textual Records from the U.S. District Court for the Pine Bluff Division of the Eastern District of Arkansas. (05/19/1961 -)
	641527	Criminal Case Files, compiled 1914 - 1977	Textual Records from the U.S. District Court for the Northern (Batesville) Division of the Eastern District of Arkansas. (02/20/1897)
	3289465	Criminal Orders, compiled 03/1949 - 01/1962	Textual Records from the U.S. District Court for the Harrison Division of the Western District of Arkansas. (03/18/1902 -)
	3370995	Criminal and Law Bench Dockets, compiled 1912 - 1919	Textual Records from the U.S. District Court for the Jonesboro Division of the Eastern District of Arkansas. (03/03/1911 -)
	3370964	Criminal Records Books, compiled 11/1898 - 03/1957	Textual Records from the U.S. District Court for the Eastern (Helena) Division of the Eastern District of Arkansas. (02/17/1887 -)
	3325382	Dockets, compiled 1926 - 1965	Textual Records from the U.S. District Court for the Texarkana Division of the Western District of Arkansas. Office of U.S. Commissioners. (02/20/1897 - 1968)
	3355805	Index to Judgments, compiled ca. 1920 - 1955	Textual Records from the U.S. District Court for the Western (Little Rock) Division of the Eastern District of Arkansas. (02/17/1887 -)
	609676	Criminal Case Files, compiled 1940 - 1975	Textual Records from the U.S. District Court for the Hot Springs Division of the Western District of Arkansas. (06/11/1940 -)

	3370923	Criminal and Law Records Book, compiled 03/1880 - 11/1898	Textual Records from the U.S. District Court for the Eastern (Helena) Division of the Eastern District of Arkansas. (02/17/1887 -)
	3325364	Criminal Term Dockets, compiled 1889 - 1913	Textual Records from the U.S. District Court for the Texarkana Division of the Western District of Arkansas. (02/20/1897 -)
	3255182	Criminal Dockets, compiled 1901 - 1974	Textual Records from the U.S. District Court for the Fort Smith Division of the Western District of Arkansas. (02/20/1897 -)
	3255179	Indexes to Criminal Defendant Jacket Files, compiled ca. 1866 - 1900	Textual Records from the U.S. District Court for the Fort Smith Division of the Western District of Arkansas. (02/20/1897 -)
	3370966	Criminal Term Docket, compiled 1915 - 1920	Textual Records from the U.S. District Court for the Eastern (Helena) Division of the Eastern District of Arkansas. (02/17/1887 -)
	3370932	Index to Judgments, compiled ca. 1926 - 1951	Textual Records from the U.S. District Court for the Eastern (Helena) Division of the Eastern District of Arkansas. (02/17/1887 -)
	3370931	Records of Law and Criminal Judgments, compiled 1877 - 1899	Textual Records from the U.S. District Court for the Eastern (Helena) Division of the Eastern District of Arkansas. (02/17/1887 -)
	3053989	Index to Criminal Term Dockets, compiled 1889 - 1893	Textual Records from the U.S. District Court for the Western District of Arkansas. Fort Smith Term. (03/08/1871 - 02/20/1897)
	3367714	Criminal and Law Record Books, compiled 1838 - 1938	Textual Records from the U.S. District Court for the Western (Little Rock) Division of the Eastern District of Arkansas. (02/17/1887 -)
	645006	Criminal Case Files, compiled 1866 - 1981	Textual Records from the U.S. District Court for the Western (Little Rock) Division of the Eastern District of Arkansas. (02/17/1887 -)
	647296	Criminal Case Files, compiled 1910 - 1977	Textual Records from the U.S. District Court for the Eastern (Helena) Division of the Eastern District of Arkansas. (02/17/1887 -)
	3370924	Dockets, compiled 1871 - 1889	Textual Records from the U.S. District Court for the Eastern (Helena) Division of the Eastern District of Arkansas. (02/17/1887 -)
	609668	Criminal Case Files, compiled 1907 - 1967	Textual Records from the U.S. District Court for the Harrison Division of the Western District of Arkansas. (03/18/1902 -)

	3292023	Criminal Term Docket, compiled 1902 - 1915	Textual Records from the U.S. District Court for the Harrison Division of the Western District of Arkansas. (03/18/1902 -)
	601760	Criminal Case Files, compiled 1925 - 1969	Textual Records from the U.S. District Court for the El Dorado Division of the Western District of Arkansas. (02/17/1925 -)
	604720	Criminal Case Files, compiled 1901 - 1975	Textual Records from the U.S. District Court for the Fort Smith Division of the Western District of Arkansas. (02/20/1897 -)
	3053993	Criminal Term Dockets, compiled 1883 - 1911	Textual Records from the U.S. District Court for the Fort Smith Division of the Western District of Arkansas. (02/20/1897 -)

Arkansas Executions, 1820-1964

http://users.bestweb.net/~rg/execution/ARKANSAS.htm

Men Executed at Fort Smith, 1873-1896

http://home.nps.gov/fosm/historyculture/
executions-at-fort-smith-1873-to-1896.htm

Outlaws Tried at Fort Smith

http://www.nps.gov/fosm/historyculture/outlaws.htm

Arkansas Department of Corrections Inmate Search

http://www.adc.arkansas.gov/inmate_info/index.html

California

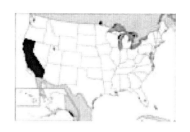

California State Archives

1020 "O" Street, Sacramento, CA 95814, Phone: (916) 653-2246
http://www.sos.ca.gov/archives/

Department of Corrections Records

Record Type	Identifier	Title/Description
	F3717 :987-1012	San Quentin Minute Books, 1874-1943, 27 vols.
	F3717 :1280-1294	Parole Department Files, 1911-1950, 30 ff.
	F3717 :1053-1068	Bertillion Books, San Quentin, 1907-1917, 16 vols.
	F3717 :1208-1251	Advisory Pardon Board Reports, 1931-1944, 45 vols.
	F3717 :1070-1082	San Quentin Minute Books, 1931-1944, 13 vols.
	F3717 :1084-1089	Folsom Minute Books, 1932-1944, 6 vols.
	F3717 :1090-1091	Chino Minute Books, 1941-1942, 2 vols.
	F3717 :1092-1094	San Quentin, Folsom, & Chino Minute Summary Books, 1943-1945, 3 vols.
	F3717	Inmate Commitment Papers, 1867-1900, 26 cf.
	F3750:1-800	Inmate Case Files, 1890-1958

	F3717 :1135-1141	Inmate Indexes, 1851-1940, 7 vols.
	F3717 :1041-1045	Inmate Registers, 1940-1947, 5 vols.
	F3717 :1157-1175	Inmate Received and Discharged Registers, 1859-1864, 1882-1947, 19 vols.
	F3717 :1154-1156	Inmate Transfer Ledgers, 1888-1909, 1917-1934, 1945-1946, 3 vols.
	F3717 :1069	Parolee Ledger, 1893-1940, 1 vol.
	F3717 :1301-1302	Execution Books, 1893-1967, 2 ff.
	F3717 :1142-1143	Death Warrant Books, 1912-1933
	F3717	Identification Photograph Cards, 1907-1946, 16 cf.
	F3717	Folsom Prison Inmate Commitment Papers, 1879-1914, 5 cf.
	F3745:1-587	Folsom Inmate Case Files, 1881-1942, 37 cf.
	F3717 :1114	Folsom Fingerprint Index, 1879-1921, 1 vol.
	F3717 :1046-1052	Folsom Inmate Registers, 1940-1949, 7 vols.
	F3717 :1083	Folsom Parolee Ledger, 1897-1940, 1 vol.
	F3717 :1095-1113	Folsom Inmate Photograph Albums, 1880-1942
	F3717	Folsom Identification Photograph Cards, 1923-1945, 5 cf.
	F3918: 1-415	Execution Files, 1911-1967m 18 cu. ft., restricted files

Department of the Governor's Office: Prison Papers

Record Type	Title
	San Quentin Prison Registers (1851-1942)
	Folsom Prison Registers (1880-1943)
	Applications for Pardon, Historical Case Files (1850-ca. 1935)
	Executive Clemency Case Files (ca. 1930-date)
	Extreme Penalty Case Files (ca. 1948-date)
	Application for Pardon Registers (1876-1944)
	Applications for Pardon, Historical Case Files (1850-ca. 1935)
	Executive Clemency Case Files (ca. 1930-date)
	Pardons (1858-1966)
	Executive Pardons (1872-1903)
	Commutation of Sentence (1876-1907)
	Prison Discharges (1868-1886)
	Executive Orders to Release (1883-1891)

California Executions

 http://users.bestweb.net/~rg/execution/CALIFORNIA.htm

Los Angeles County Archives - Criminal Case Files
222 N. Hill St., Rm. 212, Los Angeles, CA 90012

 http://www.laalmanac.com/_main/LACountyRecords.htm

Los Angeles Superior Court
111 N Hill St., Los Angeles, CA 90189

 http://lasuperiorcourt.org/Criminal/

San Francisco Superior Court
400 McAllister St San Francisco, CA 94102

 http://www.sfgov.org/site/courts_index.asp?id=77500

Pamphlets for Sale
www.rootcellar.org/

Reoord Type	Title
	California State Prison, Folsom, CA, 1879 - 1903
	Folsom Prison, CA - List of Convicts, July 26, 1880 through 1942
	Records of Folsom, CA, Indexes and Extractions 1856-1909 (Vol. 1)
	Records of Folsom, CA, Indexes and Extractions 1863-1880 & 1911-1919
	Sacramento County Justice Court Cases 1850-1877, Defendants & Plaintiffs
	San Quentin Prison, CA - List of Convicts, 1851 through 1939 (Vol. 1, A-L)
	San Quentin Prison, CA - List of Convicts, 1851 through 1939 (Vol. 2, M-Z)
	San Quentin Prison, CA - List of Convicts, Jan. 1, 1940 to Dec. 31, 1944
	San Quentin Prison, CA - List of Convicts, Jan. 1, 1945 - Mar. 22, 1947

Federal Criminal Court Records at the National Archives & Records Admin. (NARA)

NARA Pacific Region (Riverside, CA)
23123 Cajelco Road, Perris, CA, (951) 956-2000
http://www.archives.gov/pacific/frc/riverside/contacts.html
riverside.reference@nara.gov

Record Type	ARC Identifier	Title	Description
	627000	Criminal Dockets, compiled 1888 - 1910	Textual Records from the U.S. Circuit Court for the Southern District of California. (08/05/1886 - 01/01/1912)
	294948	Criminal Case Files, compiled 1888 - 1910	Textual Records from the U.S. Circuit Court for the Southern District of California. (08/05/1886 - 01/01/1912)
	602580	Criminal Dockets, compiled 1929 - 1979	Textual Records from the U.S. District Court for the Southern District of California. (1929 - ?)
	599049	Index to Bankruptcy, Civil, and Criminal Case Files, compiled 1953 - 1954	Textual Records from the U.S. District Court for the Southern District of California. (1929 - ?)
	602582	Index Cards to Criminal Case Files, compiled 1955 - 1962	Textual Records from the U.S. District Court for the Southern District of California. (1929 - ?)
	599513	Index Cards to Civil and Criminal Case Files, compiled 07/1962 - 12/1992	Textual Records from the U.S. District Court for the Southern District of California. (1929 - ?)
	626998	Index to Criminal Case Files, compiled 1888 - 1910	Textual Records from the U.S. Circuit Court for the Southern District of California. (08/05/1886 - 01/01/1912)
	602579	Criminal Case Files, compiled 1929 - 1969	Textual Records from the U.S. District Court for the Southern District of California. (1929 - ?)
	602688	Criminal General Index, compiled 1929 - 1944	Textual Records from the U.S. District Court for the Southern District of California. (1929 - ?)
	294957	Criminal Case Files, compiled 1907 - 1969	Textual Records from the U.S. District Court for the Southern District of California. (1929 - ?)

Records at the National Archives & Records Admin. (NARA)

NARA Pacific Region (San Bruno)
1000 Commodore Drive, San Bruno, CA 94066-2350, (650) 238-3500
http://www.archives.gov/pacific/san-francisco/
sanbruno.archives@nara.gov

Record Type	ARC/ Other Itentifier	Title	Description
	RG 129	Alcatraz Inmate Files	Case files of 1550 men incarcerated at Alcatraz during the prison's operation from 1934 to 63.
	1768480	Criminal Case Files, compiled 1863 - 1911	Textual Records from the U.S. Circuit Court for the Northern District of California. (1886 - 01/01/1912)
	296046	Criminal Cases, compiled 1851 - 1971, documenting the period - ca. 1984	Textual Records from the U.S. District Court for the Southern (San Francisco) Division of the Northern District of California. (1851 - ?)
	1964682	Criminal Case Files, compiled 1916 - 1963	Textual Records from the U.S. District Court for the Northern (Sacramento) Division of the Northern District of California. (05/16/1916 - 09/18/1966)
	296010	Criminal Case Files, compiled 1916 - 1963	Textual Records from the U.S. District Court for the Northern (Sacramento) Division of the Northern District of California. (05/16/1916 - 09/18/1966)
	2387624	Criminal Case Files, compiled 1907 - 1983	Textual Records from the U.S. District Court for the Fresno Division of the Eastern District of California. (09/18/1966 -)
	2517056	Criminal Case Files, compiled 1975 - 1984	Textual Records from the U.S. District Court for the Northern District of California. San Jose Term. (03/18/1966 -)
	2121136	Criminal Case Files, compiled 1903 - 1905	Textual Records from the U.S. Circuit Court for the Northern (Fresno) Division of the Southern District of California. (05/29/1900 - 01/01/1912)
	296040	Criminal Case Files, compiled ca. 1851 - ca. 1971	Textual Records from the U.S. District Court for the Southern (San Francisco) Division of the Northern District of California. (1851 - ?)

California Department of Corrections Inmate Locator Information

 http://www.cdcr.ca.gov/Reports_Research/Inmate_Locator.html

Colorado

Colorado State Archives
1313 Sherman, Room 1B20, Denver, CO 80203, Phone: 303-866-2358
http://www.colorado.gov/dpa/doit/archives/
archives@state.co.us

Record Type	Title
	Record of Convicts for the State Penitentiary, 1871-1973. Includes: name, date convicted, when received, crime, sentence, age, height, where born, & next of kin.
	Reformatory Records, 1887-1939
	Docket Books
	Gilpin County Chancery Cases, 1862-1878
	Prohibition Arrests, 1918-1926

Denver Public Library
10 W. Fourteenth Ave. Pkwy., Denver, CO 80204, (720) 865-1111
http://denverlibrary.org/

Record Type	Title	Description
	Spy Files	Police files re activities of groups that might pose a threat to public safety. Restricted. http://denverlibrary.org/research/government/intelligence.html
	State Reformatory Inmate Index, 1887-1939	http://history.denverlibrary.org/research/reformatory/index.html

Federal Criminal Court Records at the National Archives & Records Admin. (NARA)

NARA Rocky Mountain Region (Denver)
Denver Federal Center, Bldgs 46, 48, Denver, CO 80225, (303) 407-5740
http://www.archives.gov/rocky-mountain/
denver.archives@nara.gov

Record Type	ARC Identifier	Title	Description
	630240	Civil and Criminal Case Files, compiled 1879 - 1900	Textual Records from the U.S. District Court for the District of Colorado. Del Norte Term. (04/20/1880 - 02/16/1903)
	630121	Bankruptcy, Civil, and Criminal Docket, compiled 1879 - 1903	Textual Records from the U.S. District Court for the District of Colorado. Del Norte Term. (04/20/1880 - 02/16/1903)
	628430	Bankruptcy, Civil, and Criminal Case Files, compiled 1862 - 1874	Textual Records from the U.S. Territorial Court for the Second (Central City) District of Colorado. (02/28/1861 - 1876)
	629860	Bankruptcy, Civil, and Criminal Case Files, compiled 1862 - 1876	Textual Records from the U.S. Territorial Court for the Third (Canon City and Pueblo) District of Colorado. (02/28/1861 - 1876)
	1965957	Criminal Dockets, compiled 1923 - 1969	Textual Records from the U.S. District Court for the District of Colorado. Denver Term. Office of the U.S. Magistrate Judge. (1968 - 01/01/1990)
	643593	Civil and Criminal Case Files, compiled 1876 - 1911	Textual Records from the U.S. District Court for the District of Colorado. Denver Term. (04/20/1880 -)
	645222	Index to Record Books, and Civil and Criminal Case Files, compiled 1903 - 1936	Textual Records from the U.S. District Court for the District of Colorado. Denver Term. (04/20/1880 -)
	644975	Criminal Case Files, compiled 1912 - 1968	Textual Records from the U.S. District Court for the District of Colorado. Denver Term. (04/20/1880 -)
	655567	Civil and Criminal Case Files, compiled 1917 - 1935	Textual Records from the U.S. District Court for District of Colorado. Durango Term. (1917 -)
	656354	Civil and Criminal Case Files, compiled 1917 - 1934	Textual Records from the U.S. District Court for the District of Colorado. Grand Junction Term. (1917 -)

	719107	Civil and Criminal Dockets, compiled 1907 - 1949	Textual Records from the U.S. District Court for the Pueblo Division of the District of Colorado. (ca. 1878 -)
	656644	Civil and Criminal Dockets, compiled 1899 - 1932	Textual Records from the U.S. District Court for the District of Colorado. Montrose Term. (ca. 1899 -)
	719168	Criminal Dockets, compiled 1912 - 1947	Textual Records from the U.S. District Court for the Pueblo Division of the District of Colorado. (ca. 1878 -)
	643572	Civil and Criminal Dockets, compiled 1876 - 1911	Textual Records from the U.S. District Court for the District of Colorado. Denver Term. (04/20/1880 -)
	2681548	Civil and Criminal Dockets, compiled 1961 - 1989	Textual Records from the U.S. District Court for the District of Colorado. (1876 - ?)
	719110	Civil and Criminal Case Files, compiled 1907 - 1921	Textual Records from the U.S. District Court for the Pueblo Division of the District of Colorado. (ca. 1878 -)
	657109	Criminal Case Files, compiled 1919 - 1925	Textual Records from the U.S. District Court for the District of Colorado. Montrose Term. (ca. 1899 -)
	656320	Civil and Criminal Dockets, compiled 1917 - 1936	Textual Records from the U.S. District Court for the District of Colorado. Grand Junction Term. (1917 -)
	702560	Bankruptcy, Civil, and Criminal Case Files, compiled 1879 - 1907	Textual Records from the U.S. District Court for the Pueblo Division of the District of Colorado. (ca. 1878 -)
	2802329	Criminal Docket, compiled 1922 - 1952	Textual Records from the U.S. District Court for the Southern District of Florida. Fernandina Term. (02/18/1905 - 1962?)
	655559	Civil and Criminal Dockets, compiled 1917 - 1935	Textual Records from the U.S. District Court for District of Colorado. Durango Term. (1917 -)
	657106	Criminal Docket, compiled 1919 - 1925	Textual Records from the U.S. District Court for the District of Colorado. Montrose Term. (ca. 1899 -)
	656658	Civil and Criminal Case Files, compiled 1908 - 1932	Textual Records from the U.S. District Court for the District of Colorado. Montrose Term. (ca. 1899 -)
	719192	Criminal Case Files, compiled 1918 - 1947	Textual Records from the U.S. District Court for the Pueblo Division of the District of Colorado. (ca. 1878 -)

	3514893	Criminal Case Files, compiled 1981 - 1985	Textual Records from the U.S. District Court for the District of Colorado. Denver Term. (04/20/1880 -)
	702549	Bankruptcy, Civil, and Criminal Dockets, compiled 1879 - 1907	Textual Records from the U.S. District Court for the Pueblo Division of the District of Colorado. (ca. 1878 -)

Colorado Department of Personnel & Administration
CO State Penitentiary Prisoner Index, 1871-1973 Online Index

 http://www.colorado.gov/dpa/doit/archives/pen/

Colorado Executions Online Index

 http://users.bestweb.net/~rg/execution/COLORADO.htm

Colorado Public Records Search (Corrections, Pardons, Docket Books, etc.)

 http://accipiter.state.co.us/archive/publicrecordsearch.do

State of Colorado Criminal and Civil Record Repository

 http://www.cojustice.com/

Colorado Bureau of Investigation records

 https://www.cbirecordscheck.com/CBI_New/CBI_newIndex.asp

Colorado Department of Corrections Inmate Locator

 https://exdoc.state.co.us/inmate_locator/search_form.php

Connecticut

Connecticut State Archives

Connecticut State Library, 231 Capitol Avenue, Hartford, CT 06106, (860) 757-6580
http://www.cslib.org/archives/FAIndexes/

Record Type	Location	Title	Description
	RG 017	Department of Correction, 1800-1974	The materials in this record group pertain mostly to the Wethersfield State Prison (1827-1963) and include inmate records, 1900-53.
	RG 003	Judicial Department, 1636-1991	This record group consists of all types of legal documents relevant to court action, including, but not limited to, dockets, formal decisions, rules, appointments, judges' notes and opinions, indexes, case files, record books, executions, reports, and administrative papers. The bulk of the records are arranged by county and consist of papers of county courts, courts of common pleas, superior courts, and supreme courts of errors.
	RG 043	Board of Parole, 1933-1991	This record group contains minutes of meetings and public information release logs.
	RG 025	Board of Pardons, 1883-1889	This group consists of one book kept by the Board's clerk containing minutes and notes.

Connecticut State Library - Wethersfield Prison Lookup Database

231 Capitol Avenue, Hartford, CT 06106, 860-757-6500

 http://www.cslib.org/wethers.asp

CT Superior Court Records Center

http://www.jud.ct.gov/Publications/es183.pdf

Federal Criminal Court Records at the National Archives & Records Admin. (NARA)

NARA Northeast Region (Boston)

Frederick C. Murphy Federal Center, 380 Trapelo Road, Waltham, MA, 02452-6399

(781) 663-0130

http://www.archives.gov/northeast/

waltham.archives@nara.gov

Record Type	ARC Identifier	Title	Description
	592821	Criminal Case Files, compiled 1913 - 1982	Textual Records from the U.S. District Court for the District of Connecticut. (1789 -)
	2240989	Case Files, compiled 1790 - 1915	Textual Records from the U.S. District Court for the District of Connecticut. (1789 -)
	2240937	Dockets, compiled 11/1789 - 12/1912	Textual Records from the U.S. District Court for the District of Connecticut. (1789 -)
	593465	Case Files, compiled 1790 - 1911	Textual Records from the U.S. Circuit Court for the District of Connecticut. (09/24/1789 - 01/01/1912)
	2657993	Dockets, compiled 04/1790 - 10/1911	Textual Records from the U.S. Circuit Court for the District of Connecticut. (09/24/1789 - 01/01/1912)

Connecticut Executions

 http://users.bestweb.net/~rg/execution/CONNECTICUT.htm

State of Connecticut Judicial Branch - Criminal Case Lookup

 http://www.jud.ct.gov/crim.htm

CT Department of Corrections Inmate Lookup

 http://www.ctinmateinfo.state.ct.us/

Delaware

Delaware State Archives

121 Duke of York Street, Dover, DE 19901, 302-739-5318
http://archives.delaware.gov
http://archives.delaware.gov/collections/guideintro.shtml
archives@state.de.us

Record Type	Location/ Access	Title	Description
⚖	RG 3815, Closed to Public	Court of Common Pleas - Case Files, 1715-1831	The records include information relative to the social and economic conditions of Kent County during the identified periods.
⚖	RG 3805	Court of General Sessions - Quarter Session Docket	Records show court term, case number, name of defendant(s) and witness(es), indictment, type and date of court order issuances, court decision, and court cost.
⚖	RG 4825	Court of Oyer and Terminer - Dockets, 1757-1951	Dockets present a chronological account of cases heard in the Court of Oyer and Terminer. Entries in the dockets generally contain the court term and year; case number; date of trial; names of plaintiff, defendant(s), attorneys, jurors, and witnesses; indictment; disposition of case; and court cost.
🏛	RG 1605, Subgroup 004, Series 028, Closed to Public	Department of Corrections - Inmate Case Files, 19280-2001	Offender case files combining inmate and probations files for all inmates from all prisons statewide. For similar records see also series RG 2847.39
🏛	N/A	United States Prison Record, 1913-1956	Generally shows prisoner number and name, date sentenced, and discharged. Later entries also show why inmate was held, date of hearing and remarks concerning the U.S prison to which sent.

	RG 1914, Confidential	Board of Parole	Files maintained on criminals being considered for and/or granted parole, 1953-2001.
	RG 1315, Subgroup 000, Series 024	Board of Pardon Files, 1889-1992	Files include correspondence from various individuals in support of applicant's pardon, acknowledgement of State Police of individuals application for pardon, Board of Pardons cover sheet, court dockets abstracts, institutional reports. Official pardons are signed by Governor. Files here lack the board's final recommendation, include mostly copies of records submitted to members for review.

Federal Criminal Court Records at the National Archives & Records Admin. (NARA)

NARA Mid Atlantic Region (Philadelphia)

900 Market Street, Philadelphia, PA, 19107-4292, (215) 606-0100

http://www.archives.gov/midatlantic/

philadelphia.archives@nara.gov

Record Type	ARC Identifier	Title	Description
	570387	Criminal Case Files, compiled 1829 - 1981	Textual Records from the U.S. District Court for the District of Delaware. (09/24/1789 -)
	654321	Criminal Dockets, compiled 1795 - 1898	Textual Records from the U.S. Circuit Court for the District of Delaware. (09/24/1789 - 01/01/1912)
	2771443	Criminal Dockets, compiled 1845 - 1979	Textual Records from the U.S. District Court for the District of Delaware. (09/24/1789 -)
	650018	Judgment Index, compiled 1790 - 1979	Textual Records from the U.S. District Court for the District of Delaware. (09/24/1789 -)

Delaware Executions

1662-1946: http://users.bestweb.net/~rg/execution/DELAWARE.htm

Since 1992: http://doc.delaware.gov/information/deathrow_executions.shtml

Delaware Offender Lookup

https://www.vinelink.com/vinelink/initSearchForm.do?searchType=offender&siteId=8000

Florida

Florida State Archives

R.A. Gray Building, 500 South Bronough St., Tallahassee, FL 32399-0250, Phone: (850) 245-6700
http://dlis.dos.state.fl.us/barm/rediscovery/default.asp
archives@dos.state.fl.us

Record Type	Location	Author	Title/Description
	RG J00670, Series .S 500	FL Dept. of Corrections	Prisoner registers, 1875-1959
	RG J00156, Series .S 12	FL Div. of Library & Info. Services	Death warrants, 1869-1972, 1992-2005
	RG J00690, Series .S 270	FL State Board of Pardons	Pardon application dockets and registers, 1874-1917
	RG J00690, Series .S 443	FL State Board of Pardons	Application case files, 1887-1975, 190.50 cubic ft.
	RG J00690, Series .S 158	FL State Board of Pardons	Pardon, commutation, and remission decrees, 1869-1909
	RG 800000, Series .L 60	FL Circuit Court (2nd Circuit: Leon County)	Chancery records, 1825-1945, 200 cubic ft.
	RG 800000, Series .L 61	FL Circuit Court (2nd Circuit: Leon County)	Superior Court and Circuit Court case files, 1825-1944, 107 cubic ft.
	RG 800000, Series .L 337	FL Circuit Court (6th Circuit: Pasco County)	Dockets, 1884-1974, 51 vol.
	RG 800000, Series .L 339	FL Circuit Court (6th Circuit: Pasco County)	Circuit Court and County Court minutes, 1887-1974, 68 vol.
	RG 800000, Series .L 370	FL Circuit Court (8th Circuit: Union County)	Chancery records, 1921-1934, 1 microfilm reel

	RG 000640, Series .S 1091	FL Office of Executive Clemency	Application case files, 1972-2004, 179.00 cubic ft.
	RG 000100, Series .S 1960	Florida Office of the Governor	Capital crimes clemency and execution records, 1973-2008, 127 cubic ft.

Note: many more record sets can be found by using the keywords 'criminal court' for the Series/Collection search found at:
http://dlis.dos.state.fl.us/barm/rediscovery/default.asp?include=wordsearch.htm

Federal Criminal Court Records at the National Archives & Records Admin. (NARA)

NARA Southeast Region
5780 Jonesboro Road, Morrow, Georgia 30260, (770) 968-2100
www.archives.gov/southeast/
atlanta.archives@nara.gov

Record Type	ARC Identifier	Title	Description
	2387576	Criminal Minutes, compiled 1908 - 1952	Textual Records from the U.S. District Court for the Northern District of Florida. Gainesville Term. (02/06/1908 -)
	2443557	Criminal Minutes, compiled 1868 - 1958	Textual Records from the U.S. District Court for the Northern District of Florida. Tallahassee Term. (02/23/1847 -)
	2442241	Criminal Minutes, compiled 1952 - 1953	Textual Records from the U.S. District Court for the Northern District of Florida. Marianna Term. (03/03/1911 -)
	2442493	Criminal Minutes, compiled 1911 - 1972	Textual Records from the U.S. District Court for the Northern District of Florida. Pensacola Term. (02/23/1847 -)
	2443946	Criminal Minutes, compiled 1977 - 1980	Textual Records from the U.S. District Court for the Middle District of Florida. Tampa Term. (1962 -)
	3960433	Index to Criminal Case Files, compiled 1953 - 1965	Textual Records from the U.S. District Court for the Middle District of Florida. Jacksonville Term. (1962 -)
	3960434	Index to Criminal Case Files, compiled 1920 - 1964	Textual Records from the U.S. District Court for the Middle District of Florida. Tampa Term. (1962 -)

	3960436	Index to Criminal Case Files, compiled 1920 - 1935	Textual Records from the U.S. District Court for the Northern District of Florida. Pensacola Term. (02/23/1847 -)
	3960431	Index to Criminal Case Files, compiled 1976 - 1980	Textual Records from the U.S. District Court for the Southern District of Florida. Fort Lauderdale Term. (? -)
	631058	Criminal Case Files, compiled 1916 - 1976	Textual Records from the U.S. District Court for the Miami Division of the Southern District of Florida. (1907 - ?)
	657503	Criminal Case Files, compiled 1928 - 1969	Textual Records from the U.S. District Court for the Northern District of Florida. Marianna Term. (03/03/1911 -)
	1656619	Criminal Case Files, compiled 1908 - 1981	Textual Records from the U.S. District Court for the Northern District of Florida. Gainesville Term. (02/06/1908 -)
	1756115	Criminal Dockets, compiled 1918 - 1979	Textual Records from the U.S. District Court for the Southern District of Florida. Miami Term. (06/09/1906 -)
	2825159	Criminal Trial Docket, compiled 1909 - 1911	Textual Records from the U.S. District Court for the Northern District of Florida. Gainesville Term. (02/06/1908 -)
	657504	Criminal Case Files, compiled 1974 - 1979	Textual Records from the U.S. District Court for the Southern District of Florida. West Palm Beach Term. (1952 -)
	2825165	Criminal Trial Docket, compiled 1879 - 1914	Textual Records from the U.S. District Court for the Southern District of Florida. Key West Term. (02/03/1879 -)
	1756111	Criminal Dockets, compiled 1894 - 1968	Textual Records from the U.S. District Court for the Middle District of Florida. Jacksonville Term. (1962 -)
	1756118	Criminal Dockets, compiled 1907 - 1973	Textual Records from the U.S. District Court for the Northern District of Florida. Pensacola Term. (02/23/1847 -)
	1756108	Criminal Dockets, compiled 1908 - 1954	Textual Records from the U.S. District Court for the Northern District of Florida. Gainesville Term. (02/06/1908 -)
	1756119	Criminal Dockets, compiled 1896 - 1953	Textual Records from the U.S. District Court for the Northern District of Florida. Tallahassee Term. (02/23/1847 -)
	657506	Criminal Case Files, compiled 1860 - 1980	Textual Records from the U.S. District Court for the Northern District of Florida. Pensacola Term. (02/23/1847 -)

	657341	Criminal Case Files, compiled 1976 - 1980	Textual Records from the U.S. District Court for the Southern District of Florida. Fort Lauderdale Term. (? -)
	2102934	Criminal Case Files, compiled 1886 - 1911	Textual Records from the U.S. Circuit Court for the Southern District of Florida. Tampa Term. (02/03/1879 - 01/01/1912)
	657505	Criminal Case Files, compiled 1915 - 1979	Textual Records from the U.S. District Court for the Middle District of Florida. Ocala Term. (1962 -)
	2102943	Criminal Case Files, compiled 1891 - 1911	Textual Records from the U.S. Circuit Court for the Southern District of Florida. Jacksonville Term. (07/23/1894 - 01/01/1912)
	1656616	Criminal Case Files, compiled 1935 - 1952	Textual Records from the U.S. District Court for the Southern District of Florida. Fort Pierce Term. (08/22/1935 -)
	1656615	Criminal Case Files, compiled 1966 - 1980	Textual Records from the U.S. District Court for the Middle District of Florida. Fort Myers Term. (07/30/1962 -)
	1756112	Criminal Dockets, compiled 1917 - 1952	Textual Records from the U.S. District Court for the Southern District of Florida. Key West Term. (02/03/1879 -)
	1756113	Criminal Dockets, compiled 1929 - 1972	Textual Records from the U.S. District Court for the Northern District of Florida. Marianna Term. (03/03/1911 -)
	1756121	Criminal Dockets, compiled 1920 - 1967	Textual Records from the U.S. District Court for the Middle District of Florida. Tampa Term. (1962 -)
	657508	Criminal Case Files, compiled 1900 - 1980	Textual Records from the U.S. District Court for the Middle District of Florida. Tampa Term. (1962 -)
	1656621	Criminal Case Files, compiled 1976 - 1981	Textual Records from the U.S. District Court for the Northern District of Florida. Panama City Term. (1937 -)
	1656613	Criminal Case Files, compiled 1922 - 1923	Textual Records from the U.S. District Court for the Southern District of Florida. Fernandina Term. (02/18/1905 - 1962?)
	1756102	Criminal Dockets, compiled 1922 - 1952	Textual Records from the U.S. District Court for the Southern District of Florida. Fernandina Term. (02/18/1905 - 1962?)

	1756104	Criminal Dockets, compiled 1973 - 1980	Textual Records from the U.S. District Court for the Southern District of Florida. Fort Lauderdale Term. (? -)
	1756107	Criminal Dockets, compiled 1935 - 1955	Textual Records from the U.S. District Court for the Southern District of Florida. Fort Pierce Term. (08/22/1935 -)
	1656620	Criminal Case Files, compiled 1886 - 1953	Textual Records from the U.S. District Court for the Southern District of Florida. Key West Term. (02/03/1879 -)
	2102950	Criminal Case Files, compiled 1862 - 1911	Textual Records from the U.S. Circuit Court for the Northern District of Florida. Pensacola Term. (07/15/1862 - 01/01/1912)
	657343	Criminal Case Files, compiled 1850 - 1980	Textual Records from the U.S. District Court for the Northern District of Florida. Tallahassee Term. (02/23/1847 -)
	657342	Criminal Case Files, compiled 1891 - 1980	Textual Records from the U.S. District Court for the Middle District of Florida. Jacksonville Term. (1962 -)
	657507	Criminal Case Files, compiled 1933 - 1980	Textual Records from the U.S. District Court for the Middle District of Florida. Orlando Term. (07/30/1962 -)
	1756116	Criminal Dockets, compiled 1907 - 1968	Textual Records from the U.S. District Court for the Middle District of Florida. Ocala Term. (1962 -)
	2802329	Criminal Docket, compiled 1922 - 1952	Textual Records from the U.S. District Court for the Southern District of Florida. Fernandina Term. (02/18/1905 - 1962?)

Florida Department of Corrections - Executions

1924-1964: http://www.dc.state.fl.us/oth/deathrow/execlist2.html
1976-present: http://www.dc.state.fl.us/oth/deathrow/execlist.html

Florida Department of Corrections - Inmate Search

http://www.dc.state.fl.us/InmateInfo/InmateInfoMenu.asp
http://www.dc.state.fl.us/ActiveInmates/search.asp

THE BROOKLYN CITIZEN TUESDAY

SPEAR'S MANY WIVES.

Two Were in Court, and There Are Others, the Police Say.

THE SON OF A WELL KNOWN RABBI

How He Was Arrested, and the Pathetic Scene in the Station House— Charged with Abandonment and Bigamy.

A charge of bigamy as well as abandonment confronted Edward Hubert Spear, alias Isaac Speare, a car conductor, when he was arraigned to-day in the Lee Avenue Police Court. He was arrested late yesterday afternoon while running from No. 108 Havemeyer street to catch a car of the Grand street line. Charities Officer James Short made the capture after a several weeks' search for the man.

Spear is 24 years old, and if reports about him are true, he has at least four wives. His father is said to be a well-known rabbi in England. In November, 1894, at Tivoli Hall, this city, Spear, under the name of Isaac Speria, was married to Ida Tarshes. Her parents live at No. 267 Twentieth street. Spear lived with his wife and two children, 2 years and 1 year

When Spear left his family, in February, he evidently went direct to the second wife's abode, at No. 108 Havemeyer street. Spear was married to her under the name of Edward Hubert Spear. Policeman Short, who had the warrant, kept up an incessant search for the fugitive. So did Spear's first wife and her parents. A week ago Spear was located, and yesterday afternoon Short and Mrs. Spear's father waited around the Havemeyer street house for their man. When Spear left the house he ran after a Grand street car going to Newtown. Short went in pursuit and after a lively chase Spear was caught. His second wife had seen Short running after Spear, and when he was taken to the Bedford avenue station she divined something wrong and also went there. There the two wives met, and one of the most dramatic incidents which ever took place in that police station was enacted. Spear repudiated his lawful wife. He declared he had never seen her before. He wilted when his father-in-law held up Spear's 2-year-old boy, who is an exact image of the prisoner. Then the second wife burst out in a paroxysm of grief, and it was thought that she would faint.

IN THE EASTERN DISTRICT.

Brooklyn Citizen newspaper article re the transgressions of the author's great-grandfather.

Georgia

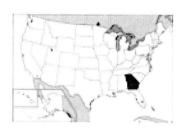

Georgia State Archives

5800 Jonesboro Road, Morrow, GA 30260, (678) 364-3700
http://www.sos.georgia.gov/ARCHIVES/

Record Type	Location	Title/Description
	21/3/27	Prisons - Inmate Administration - Central Register of Convicts, 1817-1976
	31/1/8	Pardons and Parole Board - Board Records - Parole Violator Ledgers, 1943-1975
	78/7/14	Corrections - Offender Rehabilitation - Central Register of Convicts, 1973-1987
	1/4/17	Governor - Convict and Fugitive Records - Paroles, 1913-1943
	1/4/16	Governor - Convict and Fugitive Records - Pardons, 1836-1943
	1/4/11	Governor - Convict and Fugitive Records - Commutations, 1913-1943
	21/1/6	Prisons - State Prison Commission - Convicts At Individual Camps Registers, 1871-1910
	1/4/42	Governor - Convict and Fugitive Records - Applications for Clemency, 1858-1942
	92/1/1	Supreme Court - Clerk of Court - Criminal Appeals Case Files, 1846-1917
	92/1/3	Supreme Court - Clerk of Court - Criminal Appeal Case Fi
	105/4/17	Baldwin County - Justice Court - Criminal Docket, 1869-1958

	111/19/21	Bibb County - City of Macon City Court - Civil and Criminal Case Files, 1885-1955
	116/1/1	Bulloch County - Superior Court - Criminal Dockets, 1889-1936
	116/1/19	Bulloch County - Superior Court - Criminal Subpoena Dockets, 1907-1925
	116/3/21	Bulloch County - County Court - Criminal Docket, 1895-1903
	116/4/9	Bulloch County - Justice of the Peace Court - Criminal Dockets, 1889-1955
	116/20/57	Bulloch County - City Clerk (Statesboro) - Criminal Dockets, 1904-1945
	116/20/61	Bulloch County - City Clerk (Statesboro) - Minutes of Civil and Criminal Cases, 1903-1937
	118/1/10	Butts County - Superior Court - Criminal Dockets, 1876-1909
	118/1/11	Butts County - Superior Court - Criminal Subpoena Dockets, 1900-1943
	118/3/13	Butts County - State / County / City Court - Criminal Dockets, 1866-1902
	118/4/4	Butts County - Justice of Peace Court - Criminal Dockets, 1896-1939
	118/20/63	Butts County - City Clerk / Jackson - Civil and Criminal Subpoena Docket, 1912-1943
	124/1/12	Charlton County - Superior Court - Civil and Criminal Case Files, 1857-1910
	126/1/4	Chattahoochee County - Superior Court - Criminal Docket, 1907-1909
	126/4/23	Chattahoochee County - Justice of the Peace - Criminal Dockets, 1902-1927
	131/1/6	Clayton County - Superior Court - Criminal Subpoena Dockets, 1885-1953
	131/4/1	Clayton County - Justice Court - Criminal Dockets, 1898-1973

	144/1/5	Dekalb County - Superior Court - Criminal Dockets, 1892-1900
	147/1/21	Dougherty County - Superior Court - Criminal Bonds Book, 1854-1881
	156/1/14	Fayette County - Superior Court - Civil and Criminal Case Files, 1822-1945
	159/1/45	Franklin County - Superior Court - Criminal Dockets, 1889-1940
	159/3/46	Franklin County - County Court - Criminal Docket, 1895-1901
	161/1/2	Gilmer County - Superior Court - Criminal Case Files, 1851-1938
	161/2/12	Gilmer County - Probate Court - Civil and Criminal Case Files, 1849-1932
	161/4/51	Gilmer County - Justice Court - Criminal Dockets, 1907-1943
	170/1/61	Hancock County - Superior Court - Criminal Dockets, 1912-1919
	170/3/34	Hancock County - City Court (County Court) - Civil and Criminal Subpoena Dockets, 1875-1935
	175/1/32	Henry County - Superior Court - Criminal Docket, 1913-1921
	179/2/7	Jasper County - Probate Court - Civil and Criminal Case Files, Inferior Court, 1804-1902
	179/3/5	Jasper County - County Court - Civil and Criminal Case Files, 1860-1913
	198/1/1	Mcintosh County - Superior Court - Civil and Criminal Case Files, 1875-1925
	203/1/5	Montgomery County - Superior Court - Criminal Docket, 1830-1849
	204/1/7	Morgan County - Superior Court - Civil and Criminal Court Records, 1800-1900
	204/1/6	Morgan County - Superior Court - Criminal Warrants, 1930-1939

	209/1/8	Oglethorpe County - Superior Court - Civil and Criminal Case Files, 1791-1904
	237/1/1	Tift County - Superior Court - Criminal Case Files (Microfilm), 1976
	247/1/19	Walton County - Superior Court - Cost Or Fi Fa Docket of Civil and Criminal Cases, 1823-1841
	247/1/16	Walton County - Superior Court - Warrant Docket of Criminal Cases, 1885-1895
	255/1/13	Whitfield County - Superior Court - Civil and Criminal Case Files, 1857-1930
	257/1/6	Wilkes County - Superior Court - Civil and Criminal Case Files, 1782-1889
	257/2/3	Wilkes County - Probate Court - Civil and Criminal Case Files, 1776-1856
	257/3/4	Wilkes County - County Court - Civil and Criminal Case Files, 1876-1890
	257/4/5	Wilkes County - Justice of the Peace Court - Civil and Criminal Case Files, 1784-1857

Federal Records at the National Archives & Records Admin. (NARA)

NARA Southeast Region
5780 Jonesboro Road, Morrow, Georgia 30260, (770) 968-2100
www.archives.gov/southeast/
atlanta.archives@nara.gov

Record Type	RG / ARC Identifier	Title	Description
	RG 129.6	Records of the U.S. Penitentiary, Atlanta, GA	Inmate case files, 1902-21
	2205860	Criminal Dockets, compiled 1883 - 1892	Textual Records from the U.S. Circuit Court for the Eastern (Savannah) Division of the Southern District of Georgia. (01/29/1880 - 01/01/1912)
	2205867	Criminal Dockets, compiled 1892 - 1900	Textual Records from the U.S. Circuit Court for the Western (Columbus) Division of the Northern District of Georgia. (03/03/1891 - 12/31/1911)

	1120406	Criminal Dockets, compiled 1870 - 1990	Textual Records from the U.S. District Court for the Atlanta Division of the Northern District of Georgia. (05/28/1926 -)
	2635596	Criminal Dockets, compiled 1958 - 1967	Textual Records from the U.S. District Court for the Waycross Division of the Southern District of Georgia. (05/28/1926 -)
	2190333	Criminal Dockets, compiled 1938 - 1965	Textual Records from the U.S. District Court for the Brunswick Division of the Southern District of Georgia. (08/21/1937 -)
	1105010	Criminal Dockets, compiled 1930 - 1985	Textual Records from the U.S. District Court for the Athens Division of the Middle District of Georgia. (05/28/1926 -)
	1126855	Criminal Dockets, compiled 1900 - 1957	Textual Records from the U.S. District Court for the Rome Division of the Northern District of Georgia. (05/28/1926 -)
	2173116	Criminal Dockets, compiled 1926 - 1954	Textual Records from the U.S. District Court for the Gainesville Division of the Northern District of Georgia. (05/28/1926 -)
	1077402	Criminal Dockets , compiled 1882 - 1981	Textual Records from the U.S. District Court for the Macon Division of the Middle District of Georgia. (05/28/1926 -)
	1208291	Criminal Dockets, compiled 1892 - 1992	Textual Records from the U.S. District Court for the Columbus Division of the Middle District of Georgia. (05/28/1926 -)
	660600	Criminal Case Files, compiled 1956 - 1980	Textual Records from the U.S. District Court for the Atlanta Division of the Northern District of Georgia. (05/28/1926 -)
	660599	Criminal Case Files, compiled 1894 - 1980	Textual Records from the U.S. District Court for the Augusta Division of the Southern District of Georgia. (05/28/1926 -)
	2547466	Criminal Dockets, compiled 1892 - 1900	Textual Records from the U.S. Circuit Court for the Western (Columbus) Division of the Northern District of Georgia. (03/03/1891 - 12/31/1911)
	2658415	Criminal Dockets, compiled 1936 - 1976	Textual Records from the U.S. District Court for the Thomasville Division of the Middle District of Georgia. (06/20/1936 -)
	2205850	Criminal Dockets, compiled 1820 - 1971	Textual Records from the U.S. District Court for the Savannah Division of the Southern District of Georgia. (05/28/1926 -)
	660598	Criminal Case Files, compiled 1882 - 1980	Textual Records from the U.S. District Court for the Macon Division of the Middle District of Georgia. (05/28/1926 -)

	2143039	Criminal Dockets, compiled 1936 - 1975	Textual Records from the U.S. District Court for the Thomasville Division of the Middle District of Georgia. (06/20/1936 -)
	2190334	Criminal Dockets, compiled 1927 - 1958	Textual Records from the U.S. District Court for the Dublin Division of the Southern District of Georgia. (05/28/1926 -)
	2125408	Criminal Dockets, compiled 1935 - 1953	Textual Records from the U.S. District Court for the Newnan Division of the Northern District of Georgia. (08/22/1935 -)
	2190336	Criminal Dockets, compiled 1884 - 1902	Textual Records from the U.S. Circuit Court for the Western (Macon) Division of the Southern District of Georgia. (01/29/1880 - 12/31/1911)
	1433064	Criminal Dockets, compiled 1891 - 1955	Textual Records from the U.S. District Court for the Augusta Division of the Southern District of Georgia. (05/28/1926 -)
	2190335	Criminal Dockets, compiled 1881 - 1911	Textual Records from the U.S. Circuit Court for the Northern (Atlanta) Division of the Northern District of Georgia. (03/03/1891 - 12/31/1911)
	1633380	Criminal Dockets, compiled 1904 - 1975	Textual Records from the U.S. District Court for the Valdosta Division of the Middle District of Georgia. (05/28/1926 -)
	660595	Criminal Case Files, compiled 1900 - 1980	Textual Records from the U.S. District Court for the Savannah Division of the Southern District of Georgia. (05/28/1926 -)
	1633920	Criminal Dockets, compiled 1927 - 1966	Textual Records from the U.S. District Court for the Americus Division of the Middle District of Georgia. (05/28/1926 -)
	1519345	Criminal Case Files, compiled 1926 - 1980	Textual Records from the U.S. District Court for the Albany Division of the Middle District of Georgia. (05/28/1926 -)
	1208117	Criminal Case Files, compiled 1893 - 1980	Textual Records from the U.S. District Court for the Columbus Division of the Middle District of Georgia. (05/28/1926 -)
	1404919	Criminal Case Files, compiled 1909 - 1979	Textual Records from the U.S. District Court for the Valdosta Division of the Middle District of Georgia. (05/28/1926 -)
	1404627	Criminal Case Files, compiled 1936 - 1985	Textual Records from the U.S. District Court for the Thomasville Division of the Middle District of Georgia. (06/20/1936 -)

	2125411	Criminal Case Files, compiled 1935 - 1978	Textual Records from the U.S. District Court for the Newnan Division of the Northern District of Georgia. (08/22/1935 -)
	2642547	Criminal Case Files, compiled 1943 - 1973	Textual Records from the U.S. District Court for the Valdosta Division of the Middle District of Georgia. (05/28/1926 -)
	1253410	Criminal Case Files, compiled 1901 - 1981	Textual Records from the U.S. District Court for the Athens Division of the Middle District of Georgia. (05/28/1926 -)
	1696534	Criminal Case Files, compiled 1949 - 1979	Textual Records from the U.S. District Court for the Swainsboro Division of the Southern District of Georgia. (08/16/1949 - 11/08/1984)
	1120405	Criminal Case Files, compiled 1938 - 1981	Textual Records from the U.S. District Court for the Brunswick Division of the Southern District of Georgia. (08/21/1937 -)
	2635462	Criminal Case Files, compiled 1968 - 1983	Textual Records from the U.S. District Court for the Waycross Division of the Southern District of Georgia. (05/28/1926 -)
	1633897	Criminal Case Files, compiled 1927 - 1981	Textual Records from the U.S. District Court for the Americus Division of the Middle District of Georgia. (05/28/1926 -)
	2141426	Criminal Case Files, compiled 1926 - 1978	Textual Records from the U.S. District Court for the Waycross Division of the Southern District of Georgia. (05/28/1926 -)
	1693174	Criminal Case Files, compiled 1927 - 1982	Textual Records from the U.S. District Court for the Dublin Division of the Southern District of Georgia. (05/28/1926 -)
	1633199	Criminal Case Files, compiled 1968 - 1979	Textual Records from the U.S. District Court for the Rome Division of the Northern District of Georgia. (05/28/1926 -)
	1634174	Criminal Case Files, compiled 1882 - 1912	Textual Records from the U.S. Circuit Court for the Western (Macon) Division of the Southern District of Georgia. (01/29/1880 - 12/31/1911)
	2694578	Criminal Case Files, compiled 1981 - 1983	Textual Records from the U.S. District Court for the Swainsboro Division of the Southern District of Georgia. (08/16/1949 - 11/08/1984)
	2642556	Criminal Case Files, compiled 1979 - 1982	Textual Records from the U.S. District Court for the Valdosta Division of the Middle District of Georgia. (05/28/1926 -)

Georgia Court Cases, 1950-2002

 http://www.lawskills.com/case/ga/

Georgia Department of Corrections - Offender Lookup

 http://www.dcor.state.ga.us/GDC/OffenderQuery/jsp/OffQryForm.jsp

Hawaii

Hawaii State Archives

Kek□uluohi Building, 'Iolani Palace Grounds, 364 S. King Street
Honolulu, Hawai'i 96813, Phone:(808)586-0329
http://hawaii.gov/dags/archives
archives@hawaii.gov

Record Type	Location	Title/Description
	Series 298	Records of Prisoners Received and Discharged, 1863-1916, 24 vol., 3.82 lin. ft.
	Series 299	Records of Prisoners' Descriptions, 1859-1915, 6 vols., .91 lin. ft.
	Series 198	Civil and Criminal Minute Books of the First Circuit Court
	Series 242	Civil and Criminal Minute Books of the Second Circuit Court
	Series 244	Civil and Criminal Minute Books of the Third Circuit Court
	Series 251	Civil and Criminal Minute Books of the Fifth Circuit Court
	Series 002	Criminal Case Files of the First Circuit Court
	Series 010	Criminal Case Files of the Second Circuit Court
	Series 022	Criminal Case Files of the Fourth Circuit Court
	Series 024	Criminal Case Files of the Fifth Circuit Court

	348.048 H31	First Circuit Court criminal case index : 1st series, 1847 to 1900
	3 4 8 . 0 4 8 H37	Indexes of court cases, ca. 1845-1892
	Series 254	Records of the Honolulu District Court Clerk
	Series 243	Records of the Second Circuit Court Clerk
	Series 245	Records of the Third Circuit Court Clerk
	Series 248	Records of the Fourth Circuit Court Clerk
	Series 252	Records of the Fifth Circuit Court Clerk
	Series 203	Paroles and Pardons, 1856-1986, 42.4 cubic ft. Restricted access unless records are more than 80 years old.

Federal Criminal Court Records at the National Archives & Records Admin. (NARA)

NARA Pacific Region (Riverside, CA)

23123 Cajelco Road, Perris, CA, (951) 956-2000

http://www.archives.gov/pacific/frc/riverside/contacts.html

riverside.reference@nara.gov

Record Type	ARC Identifier	Title	Description
	2806111	Criminal Case Files, compiled 1900 - 1980	Textual Records from the U.S. District Court for the District of Hawaii. (1959 -)
	2791140	Criminal Final Record Books , compiled 1901 - 1912	Textual Records from the U.S. District Court for the Territory of Hawaii. (04/30/1900 - 1959)
	2791271	Index to Criminal Case Files, compiled 1900 - 1977	Textual Records from the U.S. District Court for the District of Hawaii. (1959 -)

	2791141	Criminal Dockets , compiled 1900 - 1951	Textual Records from the U.S. District Court for the Territory of Hawaii. (04/30/1900 - 1959)

Hawaii Inmate Lookup via VineLink

 https://www.vinelink.com/vinelink/initSearchForm.do?searchType= offender&siteId=50000

OF THE COUNTY OF KINGS.

THE PEOPLE OF THE STATE OF NEW YORK,

against

ISAAC SPIER, alias
HERBERT EDWARD SPIER.

The Grand Jury of the County of Kings, by this indictment accuse

ISAAC SPIER, alias HERBERT EDWARD SPIER,

of the crime of

BIGAMY

committed as follows:

The said ISAAC SPIER, alias HERBERT EDWARD SPIER, on the 18th day of November, 1894, at the City of Brooklyn, in this County, was lawfully married, under the name of ISAAC SPIER, to one Ida Tarshis, who thereupon became Mrs. Ida Spier, and thereafter did live with the said Ida Spier as her lawful husband, and she, the said Ida Spier, is still living and is still his lawful wife.

AND the said ISAAC SPIER, alias HERBERT EDWARD SPIER, on the 5th day of August, 1896, in the City of New York, in this State, being lawfully married as aforesaid to the said Ida Spier, and then and there knowing the said Ida Spier was still living and was still his lawful wife, feloniously and unlawfully did marry, under the name of HERBERT EDWARD SPIER, one Minnie Ott, and thereafter did live with the said Minnie Ott as her husband.

AND the said ISAAC SPIER, alias HERBERT EDWARD SPIER, was thereafter, to wit: on the 27th day of July, 1897, arrested in the County of Kings upon said charge, and being arraigned in

Grand Jury trial transcript of New York State vs. Isaac Spier.
Courtesy of the New York City Municipal Archives.

Idaho

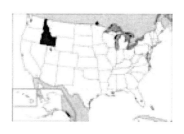

Idaho State Archives

Idaho State Historical Society, 2205 Old Penitentiary Road Boise, Idaho 83712

Phone 208-334-2682

http://www.idahohistory.net/

research@ishs.idaho.gov

Record Type	Location	Title/Description
	AR 42	Idaho Penitentiary Inmate Records, 1864-1947, 185 cubic feet (185 record boxes)
	AR1 / 20042721	Requests for Pardon
	AR1 / 20072453	List of Prisoners in Idaho Penitentiary, 1878-1884
	AR1 /1/ 20042790 / 3	Pardons and Requisitions Book A 1870-1876 (series 1, folio 3)
	AR1 /1/ 20042791 / 9	Register of Applications for Pardons A 1887-1890 (series 1, folio 9)
	AR1 /1/ 20042792 / 6	Pardons and Requisitions Book B 1876-1881 (series 1, folio 6)
	AR42 / 20072454	Register of Prisoners, 1880-1893
	AR42 / 20072455	US Penitentiary Boise City Convict Record, 1878-1893
	AR42 / 20072470	Convict Register 1 Idaho State Penitentiary Boise Idaho, 1884-1917
	AR42 / 20072479	Convict Register 2 Idaho State Penitentiary Boise Idaho, 1917-1942

	AR42 / 20072486	Microfilm: Idaho Penitentiary Inmate Records (incomplete), c1880-1897, Box 1
	AR42 / 20072505	Microfilm: Idaho Penitentiary Inmate Records (incomplete), nos 550 to 1057, Box 2
	AR42 / 20072507	Convict Register 3 Idaho State Penitentiary Boise Idaho, 1942-1957
	AR42 / 20072517	Alphabetical Index of names in Idaho State Penitentiary Registers 1 through 6, 1884-1984
	AR42 / 20072518	Punishment Record Idaho State Penitentiary 1886-1936
	AR42 /2/ 20072497 / 23	Out of State Identification Wanted Circulars and Mug Shots, 1870s-1940s (series 2, box 23)
	AR42 /6/ 20072459 / 4	US Penitentiary Punishment Record, 1878-1893 (series 6, folio 4)
	AR200 / 19973478	Prison Record Alturas County Idaho, 1882-1899
	AR201 / 20017337 / 1	Register of Prisoners Confined in the County Jail of Kootenai County 1890-1904
	AR202 / 20051007	Ada County Criminal Register No 1, 1865-1885
	AR202 / 20072481	Ada County Criminal Record, pages 333 to 450, August 1924 to April 1925
	AR205 / 20040807 / 5	List of Territorial and County Prisoners, 1865
	AR243 / 20019403	Register of Prisoners Confined in the County Jail of Oneida 1885-1913

Inmates of the Idaho Penitentiary, 1864-1947

http://www.idahohistory.net/documents/inmates_1864-1947_008.pdf

Idaho Penitentiary Inmates, 1864-1947, Catalog, Women

http://www.idahohistory.net/documents/inmates_women_1864-1947_005.pdf

Index to Inmates

 http://www.idahohistory.net/documents/inmates_1948-1975_003.pdf

Boise County Criminal and Civil Cases, 1863-1925

 http://www.idahohistory.net/documents/QuarterlyReport-LibraryMarch2004.pdf

Idaho Executions

 http://users.bestweb.net/~rg/execution/IDAHO.htm

Federal Criminal Court Records at the National Archives & Records Admin. (NARA)

NARA's Pacific Alaska Region (Anchorage),
654 West Third Avenue, Anchorage, AK 99501-2145, (907) 261-7820
www.archives.gov/pacific-alaska/anchorage/
alaska.archives@nara.gov

Record Type	ARC Identifier	Title	Description
	572266	Criminal Dockets, compiled 1911 - 1930	Textual Records from the U.S. District Court for the Northern (Coeur d'Alene) Division of the District of Idaho. (1911 -)
	571553	Criminal Case Files, compiled 1892 - 1968	Textual Records from the U.S. District Court for the Northern (Coeur d'Alene) Division of the District of Idaho. (1911 -)
	572201	Criminal Dockets, compiled 1907 - 1929	Textual Records from the U.S. District Court for the Eastern (Pocatello) Division of the District of Idaho. (1911 -)
	572201	Criminal Dockets, compiled 1907 - 1929	Textual Records from the U.S. District Court for the Eastern (Pocatello) Division of the District of Idaho. (1911 -)
	572201	Criminal Dockets, compiled 1907 - 1929	Textual Records from the U.S. District Court for the Eastern (Pocatello) Division of the District of Idaho. (1911 -)
	571419	Criminal Case Files, compiled 1897 - 1910	Textual Records from the U.S. District Court for the Southern (Pocatello) Division of the District of Idaho. (1892 - 1911)
	298169	Criminal Case Files, compiled 1893 - 1968	Textual Records from the U.S. District Court for the Northern (Moscow) Division of the District of Idaho. (1892 - ?)

Idaho Department of Corrections via VineLink

 https://www.vinelink.com/vinelink/initSearchForm.do?searchType=offender&siteId=50000

Illinois

Illinois State Archives

Norton Building, Capitol Complex, Springfield, IL 62756, Phone: (217) 782-4682
http://www.sos.state.il.us/departments/archives/archives.html
https://www.ilsos.gov/ContactFormsWeb/isacontact.html

Record Type	Location	Title/Description
	103.096	Executive Clemency Files, 1835-1973, 522 cu. ft., Index, 1912-1973.
	103.097	Executive Section: Record of Applications for Pardon, 1867-1901, 4 vols., Index
	103.098	Executive Section: Record of Commutations of Sentence, 1877-1927, 1 vol., Index
	103.099	Executive Section: Record of Pardons Granted, 1865-1987, 6 vols. Partial index, 2 vols.
	103.100	Executive Section: Record of Pardons Denied, 1897-1935, 2 vols., Index
	243.001	Register of Prisoners, 1873-1973, 29 vols., No index
	243.002	County Intake Registers, September 1875-January 1970. 8 vols., Partial Index
	243.005	Detailed Register of Prisoners, 1944-1972, 3 vols., No index
	243.006	Conduct Record, 1890-1900; 1920-1938; 1943-1958, 13 vols., No Index
	243.007	Transferred Prisoner Receipt Register, 1933-1951, 1 vol., No Iindex
	243.011	Discharge Registers, 1939-1944; 1953-1964, 2 vols., No Index

	243.012	Discharge Record, 1878-1918; 1922-1970, 7 vols., Partial Index, 1878-1918
	243.013	Parole Register, 1918-1923. 1 vol., Index
	243.016	Electrocution Record, 1930-1950, 0.1 cu. ft., No Index
	243.017	Vandalia State Farm Journal, 1956-1963, 2 vols., No Index
	243.101	Pontiac Correctional Center: Registers of Prisoners, 1895-1975. 96 vols. Index (RS 243.102 and RS 243.103)
	243.102	Pontiac Correctional Center: Master Index, 1896-1954. 3 vols.
	243.103	Pontiac Correctional Center: 1939-1978, 4 vols.
	243.104	Pontiac Correctional Center: County Intake Registers, 1893-1958, 2 vols., No Index
	243.109	Record of Movement of Inmate Population, 1939-1951, 1 vol., No index. All entries include the inmate's registration number and name, county where his crime was committed, description of the crime, and the sentence term. Escapes include the date and occasionally the place where the escape took place.
	243.110	Pontiac Correctional Center: Daily Registers of Prisoners Received and Released, July 1939-November 1955, 3 vols., No Index
	243.200	Alton State Penitentiary and Joliet/Stateville Correctional Center: Registers of Prisoners, August 29, 1833-November 31, 1841; May 15, 1847-June 27, 1975. 172 vols. Index (RS 243.201)
	243.201	Alton State Penitentiary and Joliet/Stateville Correctional Center: Index to Registers of Prisoners, May 1858-July 1975, 18 vols.
	243.203	Alton State Penitentiary and Joliet/Stateville Correctional Center: Discharge Registers, July 10, 1874; December 16, 1884-October 25, 1974, 11 vols., No Index
	243.204	Alton State Penitentiary and Joliet/Stateville Correctional Center: Male and Female Discharge Registers, July 31, 1882-November 18, 1947, 4vols., No Index

	243.206	Alton State Penitentiary and Joliet/Stateville Correctional Center: Movement of Inmate Population Record, 1901-1975, 4 vols., No Index. Record has categories for deaths, pardons, paroles, returned from parole, commutations, released on court writs, escapes, wanted elsewhere, and transfers to other institutions.
	243.207	Alton State Penitentiary and Joliet/Stateville Correctional Center: Daily Register of Prisoners Received and Released, August 1, 1933-September 3, 1973, 11 vols., No Index
	403.002	Institutional Jackets, 1893-1965, 865 cu. ft. and 193 microfilm rolls. Index for microfilm only. Parole Board case files are for inmates of statewide correctional institutions. On the outside of each jacket are listed inmate's name, aliases, register and case numbers, race, age, birthplace and birth date, citizenship status, colors of hair and eyes, nationality, religious affiliation, educational background, marital status and number of children, former occupation, smoking and drinking habits, birthplaces and current address of parents, and age at which inmate left home. Overall, institutional jackets are held for inmates of these institutions: Joliet, 1899-1965; Stateville, Ca.1919-1965; Menard, 1893-1965; Pontiac, 1915-1965; Dwight, 1930-1965; Sheridan, 1950-1959
	403.004	Parole Docket Books, 1910-1924, 9 vols., Index. Docket books are held for these institutions: Joliet, October 1911-November 1924, 4 vols.; Menard, October 1910-November 1924, 3 vols.; Pontiac, September 1918-December 1924, 2 vols.
	403.005	Parole Dockets, January 1919-October 1962, 80 vols., No Index. Parole dockets are held for cases involving inmates of these institutions: Joliet, February 1919-November 1920; January 1923-October 1962, 21 vols.; Stateville, November 1933-October 1962, 14 vols.; Menard, February 1919-October 1962, 21 vols.; Pontiac, January 1919-October 1962, 20 vols.; Dwight, September 1931-October 1962, 2 vols.; Sheridan, 1950-1959; 1961-1962, 1 vol.; St. Charles, 1932-1944; 1946-1950, 1 vol.
	403.010	Orders for Discharge, 1912-1948. 19 vols. Index. Discharge orders are held for inmates of these institutions: Joliet, July 1914-April 1942, 5 vols.; Menard, January 1914-July 1944, 5 vols.; Pontiac, April 1912-May 1948, 8 vols.; Dwight, June 1934-June 1944, 1 vol.
	901.001	Case Files, 1820-1970. 7,314 cu. ft. Index, 1820-1936. Record consists of individual files for every case appealed to the Supreme Court.

Cook County Clerk's Office

Criminal Court Building, 2650 S. California, Rm 526, Chicago, IL 60608, 773-869-3140
http://www.cookcountyclerkofcourt.org/

Files available at the Criminal Division:

- 1893 - present (microfilm, alphabetical listing by defendant)
- 1964 - present (microfilm, Indictment/True bill listing)
- Court files for the current year
- Felony trial matters heard in the City of Chicago for two years
- All remaining Criminal Division Records ordered thru the Record Center

Records Available Through Illinois Regional Archives Depository System

Record Type	Location (Accession #)	Repository	Title/Description
	1/0289/12	Northern Illinois University	Bureau County: Circuit Court Record, Criminal, 1870-1915, 4 microfilm reels
	1/0289/07	Northern Illinois University	Bureau County: County Court Record, Criminal, 1904-1952, .3 linear feet
	3/0135/02	Illinois State University	Champaign County: Sheriff's Process Dockets, Criminal, 1886-1917, 1.1 linear feet, 3 microfilms
	5/0051/04	Eastern Illinois University	Crawford County: Circuit Court Record, Criminal, 1931-1957, 1 microfilm
	3/0075/01	Illinois State University	DeWitt County: County Court Transfer Dockets, Criminal, 1915-1924, .3 linear feet
	5/0114/06	Eastern Illinois University	Effingham County: Circuit Court Record, Criminal, 1868-1972, 5 microfilm reels
	5/0114/09	Eastern Illinois University	Effingham County: County Court Record, Criminal, 1872-1917, 2 microfilm reels
	2/0146/01	Western Illinois University	Fulton County: Circuit Court Case Files, Criminal, 1871-1924, 13 cubic feet
	2/0119/02	Western Illinois University	Fulton County: Circuit Court Record, Criminal, 1869-1938, 8 microfilm reels
	2/0119/01	Western Illinois University	Fulton County: County Court Record, Criminal, 1872-1905, 1 microfilm reel
	2/0148/01	Western Illinois University	Henry County: Circuit Court Case Files, Criminal, 1857-1928, 18 cubic feet

	2/0163/01	Western Illinois University	Henry County: Circuit Court Record, Criminal, 1873-1963, 2.7 linear feet
	2/0163/02	Western Illinois University	Henry County: County Court Record, Criminal, 1872-1961, 2 linear feet
	2/0156/22	Western Illinois University	McDonough County: Circuit Court Record, Criminal, 1870-1937, 2.8 linear feet
	4/0199/01	University of Illinois at Springfield	Macon County: Circuit Court Case Files, Criminal, 1829-1904, 19.5 cubic feet
	4/0299/11	University of Illinois at Springfield	Macon County: County Court Dockets, Criminal, 1899-1909, 2 microfilm reels
	6/0350/04	Southern Illinois University	Madison County: Circuit Court Case Files, Criminal, 1814-1922, 5 cubic feet
	6/0367/04	Southern Illinois University	Madison County: Alton City Court Criminal Dockets, 1897-1929, .8 linear feet, 2 microfilm reels
	6/0367/03	Southern Illinois University	Madison County: Alton City Court Criminal Record, 1897-1929, .3 linear feet, 1 microfilm reel
	1/0268/08	Northern Illinois University	Ogle County: County Court Case Files, Criminal, 1872-1931, 1.2 cubic feet
	3/0125/10	Illinois State University	Piatt County: Circuit Court Dockets, Criminal, 1868-1899, 3 microfilm reels
	6/0156/03	Southern Illinois University	St. Clair County: Circuit Court Order Books, Criminal, 1868-1877, .3 linear feet
	6/0147/01	Southern Illinois University	St. Clair County: County Court Transfer Dockets, Criminal, 1962-1965, .1 linear feet
	4/0169/01	University of Illinois at Springfield	Sangamon County: Circuit Court Record, Criminal, 1885-1896, .2 linear feet
	4/0331/05	University of Illinois at Springfield	Sangamon County: County Court Dockets, Criminal, 1887-1908, .5 linear feet
	3/0015/01	Illinois State University	Vermilion County: Criminal Investigation and Parole Files, 1929-1940, 3 cubic feet
	5/0040/02	Eastern Illinois University	Wayne County: Circuit Court Record, Criminal, 1915-1928, .3 linear feet

	1/0272/01	Northern Illinois University	Will County: Circuit Court Case Files, Criminal, 1838-1931, 27 cubic feet
	1/0254/01	Northern Illinois University	Will County: Circuit Court Record, Criminal, 1862-1938, 3 linear feet
	1/0282/01	Northern Illinois University	Will County: County Court Case Files, Criminal, 1872-1894, 3 cubic feet
	6/0357/09	Southern Illinois University	Williamson County: Sheriff's Process Dockets, Criminal, 1938-1941, 1 microfilm
	1/0267/11	Northern Illinois University	Winnebago County: Circuit Court Record, Criminal, 1883-1922, 2 linear feet

Federal Criminal Court Records at the National Archives & Records Admin. (NARA)

NARA Great Lakes Region (Chicago),
7358 South Pulaski Road, Chicago, IL 60629-5898, (773) 948-9001
http://www.archives.gov/great-lakes/
chicago.archives@nara.gov

Record Type	ARC Identifier	Title	Description
	1126726	Criminal Case Files, compiled 1961 - 1977	Textual Records from the U.S. District Court for the Northern Division of the Southern District of Illinois. Rock Island Term. (08/10/1950 - 10/02/1978)
	1126759	Criminal Case Files, compiled 1906 - 1969	Textual Records from the U.S. District Court for the Western (Freeport) Division of the Northern District of Illinois. (03/03/1905 -)
	1126845	Criminal Case Files, compiled 1924 - 1974	Textual Records from the U.S. District Court for the Southern (Springfield) Division of the Southern District of Illinois. (03/03/1905 - 10/02/1978)
	1126663	Criminal Case Files, compiled 1905 - 1969	Textual Records from the U.S. District Court for the Eastern District of Illinois. East Saint Louis Term. (03/03/1905 - 10/02/1978)
	1125636	Criminal Case Files, compiled 1905 - 05/17/1978, documenting the period 1887 - 1978	Textual Records from the U.S. District Court for the Northern (Peoria) Division of the Southern District of Illinois. (03/03/1905 - 10/02/1978)

	1126834	Criminal Case Files, compiled 1932 - 1976	Textual Records from the U.S. District Court for the Eastern District of Illinois. Danville Term. (03/03/1905 - 10/02/1978)
	1105475	The United States of America v. Alphonse Capone, 03/13/1931 - 04/01/1942	Textual Records from the U.S. District Court for the Eastern (Chicago) Division of the Northern District of Illinois. (03/03/1905 -)
	624785	Criminal Case Files, compiled 1873 - 1969	Textual Records from the U.S. District Court for the Eastern (Chicago) Division of the Northern District of Illinois. (03/03/1905 -)

Homicide in Chicago, 1870-1930

Chicago Police Department Homicide Record Index – chronicling 11,000 homicides in the city during those years

http://homicide.northwestern.edu/

Illinois Genealogy Trails History Group

Transcriptions of the Alton Prison registers up to 1860 and the Joliet Prison registers

http://genealogytrails.com/ill/convicts/convictregister.htm

Illinois Department of Corrections - Inmate Lookup

http://www.idoc.state.il.us/subsections/search/default.asp

Bertillon card. Before fingerprints, photographs and body part measurements were taken to distinguish one suspect from another. Alphonse Bertillon, a French criminologist devised this method of cataloging criminals. The New York City Municipal Archives has a collection of approximately 3,000 Bertillon cards. A few Bertillon cards are on display at the New York City Police Museum.

Indiana

Indiana State Archives

6440 E 30th St, Indianapolis, IN 46219-1007, (317) 591-5222
http://www.fisa-in.org/
http://www.in.gov/icpr/2358.htm
arc@icpr.in.gov

Record Type	Location	Title/Description
	N/A	A database re all prisoners confined at Jeffersonville State Prison from 1822 to 1897.
	N/A	Descriptive Books with information on indivdual prisoners at Jeffersonville State Prison, 1835-?
	N/A	A database re all prisoners confined at Michigan City State Prison from 1860 to approximately 1968
	N/A	Prisoner's Record and Identification Books (Series) provide information on individual prisoners.
	N/A	State Prison at Michigan City Life Prisoner Books
	N/A	Mug shots of Michigan City prisoners from 1880 to approximately 1927
	N/A	Indiana Women's Prison: Admission Books, Prisoner History Books, and Commitment Papers, 1873 to approximately 1960
	N/A	Index to Indiana Reformatory inmates from 1897 to approximately 1950
	N/A	Indiana Reformatory Inmate Record Books
	N/A	Indiana Women's Prison: Admission Books, Prisoner History Books, and Commitment Papers

	N/A	A database re jeuveniles at the Indiana Boys' School (formerly known as the House of Refuge for Jeuvenile Offenders) from 1868 to 1931
	N/A	Indiana Boys' School: Commitment Records, 1883-1928
	N/A	Indiana Boys' School: Inmate Packets, 1869-?
	N/A	A database re jeuvenile girls at the Indiana Girls' School (formerly known as the Indiana Industrial School for Girls) from 1873 to 1945
	N/A	Indiana Girls' School: Inmate Record Books
	N/A	Indiana Girls' School: Commitment Packets
	N/A	Master Card Files for inmates confined at Jeffersonville State Prison, Michigan City State Prison, Indiana Women's Prison, Indiana Reformatory, Indiana Boys' School, and Indiana Girls' School

Federal Criminal Court Records at the National Archives & Records Admin. (NARA)

NARA Great Lakes Region (Chicago),
7358 South Pulaski Road, Chicago, IL 60629-5898, (773) 948-9001
http://www.archives.gov/great-lakes/
chicago.archives@nara.gov

Record Type	ARC Identifier	Title	Description
	1120510	Criminal Case Files, compiled 1928 - 1969, documenting the period 1926 - 1969	Textual Records from the U.S. District Court for the New Albany Division of the Southern District of Indiana. (04/21/1928 -)
	1124628	Criminal Case Files, compiled 1928 - 1969, documenting the period 1925 - 1969	Textual Records from the U.S. District Court for the South Bend Division of the Northern District of Indiana. (04/21/1928 -)
	1120495	Criminal Case Files, compiled 1956 - 1969	Textual Records from the U.S. District Court for the Lafayette Division of the Northern District of Indiana. (02/10/1954 -)

	1112367	Criminal Case Files, compiled 1928 - 1969, documenting the period 1879 - 1969	Textual Records from the U.S. District Court for the Indianapolis Division of the Southern District of Indiana. (04/21/1928 -)
	1124626	Criminal Case Files, compiled 1928 - 1969, documenting the period 1925 - 1969	Textual Records from the U.S. District Court for the Hammond Division of the Northern District of Indiana. (04/21/1928 -)
	1124647	Criminal Case Files, compiled 1928 - 1969, documenting the period 1925 - 1969	Textual Records from the U.S. District Court for the Fort Wayne Division of the Northern District of Indiana. (04/21/1928 -)
	1112355	Criminal Case Files, compiled 1928 - 1969, documenting the period 1925 - 1969	Textual Records from the U.S. District Court for the Evansville Division of the Southern District of Indiana. (04/21/1928 -)
	722104	Case Files, compiled 1945 - 1980	Textual Records from the U.S. Court of Appeals for the Seventh Circuit. (1948 -)

Online Searchable Index to Prisoner's Statements: State Prison at Michigan City

 http://www.in.gov/icpr/2810.htm

Indiana Courts System

 http://www.in.gov/judiciary/

Online searchable access to criminal court records

 http://mycase.in.gov/

Indiana Historical Court Cases

Doxpop provides access to over 10,436,233 current and historical cases from 141 courts in 48 Indiana counties in the Doxpop Network.

 https://www.doxpop.com/prod/court/

Indiana Death Row, 1977-2008

 http://www.clarkprosecutor.org/html/death/rowold.htm

Indiana Executions Since 1900

 http://www.clarkprosecutor.org/html/death/executions.htm

Indiana Executions, 1841-1981

 http://users.bestweb.net/~rg/execution/INDIANA.htm

Indiana Department of Corrections - Inmate Lookup

 http://www.in.gov/apps/indcorrection/ofs/ofs

Iowa

Iowa State Archives

600 E Locust St, Des Moines, IA 50319-1006, (515) 281-3007
www.iowahistory.org/archives/index.html
http://infohawk.uiowa.edu/ (online catalog)
dm.library@iowa.gov

Record Type	Location	Title	Description
	N/A	Governor's Records	Criminal Records

Anamosa State Penitentiary - Historical Database Lookup

 http://www.asphistory.com/

Iowa Executions

http://users.bestweb.net/~rg/execution/IOWA.htm

Iowa City Historical Library

402 Iowa Ave
Iowa City, IA 52240-1809
(319) 335-3916
www.iowahistory.org

Record Type	Location	Title/Description
	F627.L4 I7 1991	Index, criminal docket and fee book

University of Iowa College of Law Library

200 Boyd Law Building, Iowa City, IA 52242-1166

http://www.law.uiowa.edu/library/

Record Type	Location	Title/Description
	KFI4792 .L815	Parole violations in Iowa, 1950-62. Prepared for the Iowa Board of Control and the Iowa Board of Parole

Federal Criminal Court Records at the National Archives & Records Admin. (NARA)

NARA Central Plains Region (Kansas City),

400 West Pershing Road, Kansas City, MO 64108, (816) 268-8000

http://www.archives.gov/central-plains/kansas-city/

kansascity.archives@nara.gov

Record Type	ARC Identifier	Title	Description
	583465	Criminal Case Files, compiled 1891 - 1962, documenting the period 1890 - 1962	Textual Records from the U.S. District Court for the Cedar Rapids Division of the Northern District of Iowa. (02/24/1891 -)
	583473	Criminal Case Files, compiled 1874 - 1969	Textual Records from the U.S. District Court for the Western (Council Bluffs) Division of the Southern District of Iowa. (07/30/1882 -)
	583560	Criminal Case Files, compiled 1913 - 1965	Textual Records from the U.S. District Court for the Ottumwa Division of the Southern District of Iowa. (02/20/1907 -)
	583563	Criminal Case Files, compiled 1904 - 1969	Textual Records from the U.S. District Court for the Davenport Division of the Southern District of Iowa. (04/28/1904 -)
	583492	Criminal Case Files, compiled 1901 - 1966	Textual Records from the U.S. District Court for the Southern (Creston) Division of the Southern District of Iowa. (06/01/1900 -)
	583426	Criminal Case Files, compiled 1883 - 1980	Textual Records from the U.S. District Court for the Western (Sioux City) Division of the Northern District of Iowa. (07/30/1882 -)

	583432	Criminal Case Files, compiled 1882 - 1968	Textual Records from the U.S. District Court for the Central (Fort Dodge) Division of the Northern District of Iowa. (07/30/1882 -)
	583346	Criminal Case Files, compiled 1863 - 1962	Textual Records from the U.S. District Court for the Eastern (Dubuque) Division of the Northern District of Iowa. (07/30/1882 -)
	1103573	Chancery, Criminal, and Habeas Corpus Case Files, compiled 1858 - 1864	Textual Records from the U.S. District Court for the Southern (Keokuk) Division of the District of Iowa. (03/03/1859 - 07/30/1882)
	1065460	All Divisions Criminal Docket, compiled 05/15/1920 - 04/26/1922	Textual Records from the Department of Justice. Office of the U.S. Attorney for the Northern Judicial District of Iowa. (07/20/1882 -)
	583279	Criminal Case Files, compiled 1865 - 1966	Textual Records from the U.S. District Court for the Eastern (Keokuk) Division of the Southern District of Iowa. (07/30/1882)
	583281	Criminal Case Files, compiled 1871 - 1969	Textual Records from the U.S. District Court for the Central (Des Moines) Division of the Southern District of Iowa. (07/30/1882 -)
	3164755	Criminal Dockets, compiled 1886 - 1949	Textual Records from the U.S. District Court for the Eastern (Dubuque) Division of the Northern District of Iowa. (07/30/1882 -)
	2922400	Criminal Dockets, compiled 07/17/1891 - 12/27/1949	Textual Records from the U.S. District Court for the Cedar Rapids Division of the Northern District of Iowa. (02/24/1891 -)
	2897163	Judgment Index, compiled 1891 - 1932	Textual Records from the U.S. District Court for the Cedar Rapids Division of the Northern District of Iowa. (02/24/1891 -)

Iowa Bureau of Identification

Wallace State Office Building, Des Moines, IA 50319, (515) 281-5138

www.dps.state.ia.us/DCI/index.shtml

To obtain a copy of a criminal record in Iowa, one must submit a Criminal Record Request form and billing form. Both documents are available at the web site listed above or at the Iowa Department of Public Safety. There is a $13 fee per request

Iowa Court Case Search

 http://www.iowacourts.state.ia.us/ESAWebApp/SelectFrame

Iowa Department of Corrections - Offender Lookup

 http://www.doc.state.ia.us/OffenderInfo.asp

Kansas

Kansas State Archives/Kansas State Historical Society

6425 SW 6th Ave, Topeka, KS 66615-1099, (785) 272-8681
www.kshs.org
email: http://www.kshs.org/contact/emailref.php

Record Type	Location	Title	Description
	N/A	Penitentiary (state only) Records, 1864-1958	Prisoner files, ledgers, and indexes; parole and pardon records; maximum sentence expiration registers. The indexes to these records are available on microfilm in our reading room. Use of some records is restricted.
	N/A	Supreme Court	Case files containing briefs, petitions, transcripts of evidence, decisions, bonds, correspondence, and other documents; dockets; journals; mandates; final records; correspondence of justices; and records of the board of law examiners.
	N/A	State Appellate Courts	Case files, dockets, and briefs exist from 1861 on for civil and criminal cases. Name indexes include "Hatcher's Kansas Digest" and the Kansas Supreme Court dockets. The Archives also has a small collection of territorial court records, 1854-1860. The State Archives is not the repository for case records from the State District Courts, but appellate court case files sometimes include transcripts from the District Court proceedings.

	N/A	Governor	Correspondence; reports; proclamations; investigations petitions; appointments and resignations of officeholders; records of pardons, paroles, commutations, requisitions, and extraditions; and miscellaneous records. The papers of all Kansas governors, with the exception of George Docking, Robert Docking and Robert Bennett, are in the state archives

Kansas State Historical Society – Local Records

 http://www.kshs.org/genealogists/localgovt/lrguide.pdf

Kansas District Court Search

 https://www.accesskansas.org/districtcourt/

National Achives & Records Admin. (NARA) - Index to Leavenworth Prison Inmate Files

 http://www.archives.gov/central-plains/kansas-city/finding-aids/leavenworth-penitentiary/

Federal Records at the National Archives & Records Admin. (NARA)

NARA Central Plains Region (Kansas City),
400 West Pershing Road, Kansas City, MO 64108, (816) 268-8000
http://www.archives.gov/central-plains/kansas-city/
kansascity.archives@nara.gov

Record Type	Location/ ARC Identifier	Title	Description
	RG 129	Leavenworth Prison Inmate Files	The records document individual inmates. The are primarily case files, 1895-1920, but also include account books and ledgers, annual reports, correspondence, and journals. Nontextual records include photographs.
	583082	Criminal Case Files, compiled 1959 - 1974	Textual Records from the U.S. District Court for the Kansas City Division of the District of Kansas. (1903 -)
	582992	Criminal Case Files, compiled 1861 - 1974	Textual Records from the U.S. District Court for the First (Topeka) Division of the District of Kansas. (06/09/1890 -)

	583081	Criminal Case Files, compiled 1892 - 1961	Textual Records from the U.S. District Court for the Third (Fort Scott) Division of the District of Kansas. (05/03/1892)
	583048	Criminal Case Files, compiled 1890 - 1974	Textual Records from the U.S. District Court for the Second (Wichita) Division of the District of Kansas. (06/09/1890 -)
	573453	Criminal Case Files, compiled 1879 - 1980	Textual Records from the U.S. District Court for the Western (Kansas City) Division of the Western District of Missouri. (01/21/1879 -)
	283623	District of Kansas: Wichita: Criminal Cases, compiled 1890 - 1968	Photographs and other Graphic Materials and Textual Records from the U.S. District Court for the Second (Wichita) Division of the District of Kansas. (06/09/1890 -)

Kansas Bureau of Investigation - Criminal History Check

 http://www.accesskansas.org/kbi/criminalhistory/

Kansas Executions

 http://users.bestweb.net/~rg/execution/KANSAS.htm

Kansas Department of Corrections Inmate Search

 http://www.doc.ks.gov/kasper

COURT OF GENERAL SESSIONS OS THE PEACE

IN AND FOR THE COUNTY OF NEW YORK

PART II.

- x

THE PEOPLE OF THE STATE OF NEW YORK : B e f o r e :-

      -against-   : HON. THOMAS C. O'SULLIVE,J

  E L I S E   H O F F M A N,   :   and a Jury.
      (Two cases)

                        :

- x

New York, Tuesday, April 25th, 1911.

THE DEFENDANT IS INDICTED OFOR ABORTION.

INDICTMENT FILED MARCH 8TH, 1911.

A p p e a r a n c e s :-

    T. Channon Press, Esq., Assistant District Attorney

        for the people.

    Max Steinert, Esq.,

    Abraham Levy, Esq. and

    Murray M. Simon, Esq.,

        for the Defendant.

       - - - - - - - - - -

(Twelve talesmen are duly called and take their

seats in the jury box)

       - - - - - - - - - -

                      Amos C. Russell,
                    Official Stenographer.

Trial transcript. Courtesy of Lloyd Sealy Library, Special Collections
John Jay College of Criminal Justice/CUNY

Kentucky

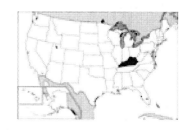

Kentucky Department for Libraries and Archives

300 Coffee Tree Road, Frankfort, Kentucky 40601, (502) 564-8300
http://www.kdla.ky.gov/
http://www.kdla.ky.gov/research.htm
http://kdla.kyvl.org/vwebv/searchBasic

Note: The criminal court records listed in the following table are culled from just the first-five pages of 87 results pages for the search terms 'criminal court' in the KDLA search page: http://kdla.kyvl.org/vwebv/searchBasic (There are many more records to be found at the Kentucky Archives)

Record Type	Title/Description
	Inmate file-duplicate, 1972-1988 Blackburn Correctional Complex (Lexington, Ky.), 1972
	Offender record, 1889- . Kentucky. Corrections Cabinet. Office of Administrative Services, 1889
	Persistent felony offenders, [microform] 1985 Kentucky. Legislative Research Commission, 1985
	Inmate file-duplicate, 1973-1988 Bell County Forestry Camp (Pineville, Ky.), 1973
	Subject files, 1954-1970 Kentucky. Corrections Cabinet. Dept. of Adult Institutions, 1954
	Punishment record books, 1880-1921 Kentucky State Penitentiary (Frankfort, Ky.), 1880
	Register of prisoners by county, 1894-1950 Kentucky State Penitentiary (Frankfort, Ky.) , 1894
	Prisoner's account books, 1910-1913 Kentucky State Penitentiary (Frankfort, Ky.), 1910

	Admission and discharge record, 1938-1952 Kentucky Correctional Institution for Women (Pewee Valley, Ky.), 1938
	Inmate education folders, 1961-1967 Kentucky Correctional Institution for Women (Pewee Valley, Ky.), 1961
	Inmate file-duplicate, 1928-1988, Kentucky Correctional Institution for Women (Pewee Valley, Ky.), 1928
	Inmate work cards, 1901-1937 Kentucky State Reformatory (La Grange, Ky.), 1901
	Inmate file-duplicate, 1904-1988 Kentucky State Reformatory (La Grange, Ky.), 1904
	Prisoners admitted/discharged register, 1891-1912 Kentucky State Penitentiary (Eddyville, Ky.), 1891
	Offenses and punishment register (indexed), 1891-1916 Kentucky State Penitentiary (Eddyville, Ky.), 1891
	Inmate file-duplicate, 1947-1982 Kentucky State Penitentiary (Eddyville, Ky.), 1947
	Alias name register, 1893-1939 (bulk 1893-1894, 1930-1939) Kentucky State Penitentiary (Eddyville, Ky.), 1893
	Prisoner description books (indexed), 1889-1910. Kentucky State Penitentiary (Eddyville, Ky.), 1889
	Register of prisoners, 1890-1929. Kentucky State Penitentiary (Eddyville, Ky.), 1890
	Inmate file-duplicate, 1953-1983. Western Kentucky Farm Center (Fredonia, Ky.), 1953
	Inmate file-duplicate, 1983. Northpoint Training Center (Burgin, Ky.), 1983
	Inmate file-duplicate, 1900-1988. Roederer Farm Center (La Grange, Ky.), 1900
	Prisoner description books, 1887-1909. Kentucky State Penitentiary (Frankfort, Ky.), 1887
	Crime register, 1891-1926 (bulk 1891-1901, 1921-1926). Kentucky State Penitentiary (Frankfort, Ky.), 1891
	Cell house register, 1907-1909. Kentucky State Penitentiary (Frankfort, Ky.), 1907
	Register of prisoners, 1827-1938. Kentucky State Penitentiary (Frankfort, Ky.), 1827

	Prisoner court record books (indexed), 1896-1919 (bulk 1918-1919). Kentucky State Penitentiary (Frankfort, Ky.), 1896
	Master card file on probationers, parolees, misdemenant, and pre-trial. Kentucky. Corrections Cabinet. Office of Community Services.
	Master card on probationers and parolees. Kentucky. Corrections Cabinet. Office of Community Services.
	List of inmates on death row. Kentucky. Corrections Cabinet. Dept. of Adult Institutions.
	Inmate file-duplicate, 1973-1988. Bell County Forestry Camp (Pineville, Ky.), 1973
	General indexes to civil and criminal cases, 1842-1899 [microform]. Kentucky. Circuit Court (Ballard County), 1842
	Criminal order books (indexed), 1902-1979 [microform]. Kentucky. Circuit Court (Allen County), 1902
	Criminal judgment books (indexed), 1910-1977 (bulk 1910-1938, 1973-1977). Kentucky. Circuit Court (Allen County), 1910
	Criminal execution book (indexed), 1903-1977. Kentucky. Circuit Court (Allen County), 1903
	Criminal Order Books (with Index), [microform] 1876-1967. Adair County (Ky.). Circuit Court., 1876
	Criminal Case Files, 1894-1964. Adair County (Ky.). Circuit Court., 1894
	Case files, 1854-1976. Kentucky. Court of Appeals (1792-1975), 1854
	Case files, 1976-1984. Kentucky. Court of Appeals (1976-), 1976
	Criminal case files, 1907-1960 (bulk 1907, 1914-1960). Kentucky. Circuit Court (Bell County), 1907
	Civil and criminal case files, 1876-1949. Kentucky. Circuit Court (Bell County), 1876
	Criminal order books (indexed), 1886-1977 [microform]. Kentucky. Circuit Court (Bath County), 1886
	Criminal case files, 1848-1977 (bulk 1848-1849, 1875-1905, 1907-1916, 1970-1977). Kentucky. Circuit Court (Bath County), 1848
	Civil and criminal case files, 1886-[1977?]. Kentucky. Circuit Court (Bath County), 1886

	General indexes to civil and criminal cases, 1879-1977 [microform]. Kentucky. Circuit Court (Bath County), 1879
	General index to civil and criminal cases, 1867-1897 [microform]. Kentucky. Court of Common Pleas (Ballard County), 1867
	Criminal Case Files - General Indexes, [microform] 1917-1963. Breathitt County (Ky.). Circuit Court., 1917
	Appealed Criminal Case Files, 1964-1975. Boyle County (Ky.). Circuit Court, 1964
	Criminal Order Books (Indexed), [microform] 1876-1973 Boyd County (Ky.). Circuit Court., 1876
	Order Books (Indexed), [microform] 1860-1876. Boyd County (Ky.). Circuit Court., 1860
	Criminal Case Files, 1911-1946. Boyd County (Ky.). Circuit Court., 1911
	Criminal Case Files - General Index, [microform] 1911-1940 Boyd County (Ky.). Circuit Court., 1911
	Criminal Order Books (with Indexes), [microform] 1884-1977, (bulk 1884-1901, 1928-1977). Boone County (Ky.). Circuit Court., 1884
	Order Books (with Indexes), 1804-1936. Boone County (Ky.). Circuit Court., 1804
	Criminal Case Files, 1871-1952. Boone County (Ky.). Circuit Court., 1871
	Criminal Case Files Off-Docket - General Index, 1914-1963 Boone County (Ky.). Circuit Court., 1914
	Case Files - Defendant Index, 1851-1871. Boone County (Ky.). Circuit Court., 1851
	General index to civil and criminal cases, 1888-1897 [microform]. Kentucky. Court of Common Pleas (Bell County), 1888
	Governor's official correspondence file - commutations, 1899. Kentucky. Governor (1899-1900 : Taylor) 1899
	Governor's official correspondence file - commutations, 1924-1927. Kentucky. Governor (1923-1927 : Fields)
	Governor's official correspondence file - paroles, 1923-1927. Kentucky. Governor (1923-1927 : Fields)
	Governor's official correspondence file - commutations, 1916-1919. Kentucky. Governor (1915-1919 : Stanley)

	Governor's commutation of sentence : Governor A. B. Chandler, 1956-1959. Kentucky. Secretary of State.
	Governor's commutation of sentence : Governor Earle C. Clements, 1948-1950. Kentucky. Secretary of State.
	Governor's commutation of sentence : Governor Bert T. Combs, 1960-1963. Kentucky. Secretary of State.
	Governor's official correspondence file - recommendations for parole, 1920-1923. Kentucky. Governor (1919-1923 : Morrow)
	Governor's official correspondence file - parole violation warrants, 1920-1922 (bulk 1920, 1922). Kentucky. Governor (1919-1923 : Morrow)
	Governor's official correspondence file - parole lists, 1915-1918. Kentucky. Governor (1915-1919 : Stanley)
	Governor's official correspondence file - parole violation warrants, 1914-1915. Kentucky. Governor (1911-1915 : McCreary)
	Parole Records, 1934-1941. Laurel County (Ky.). Circuit Court.
	Governor's official correspondence file - petitions for pardons and remissions, 1820-1824. Kentucky. Governor (1820-1824 : Adair)
	Governor's official correspondence file - petitions for pardons and remissions, 1816-1820. Kentucky. Governor (1816-1820 : Slaughter)
	Governor's official correspondence file - petitions for pardons, 1804-1808. Kentucky. Governor (1804-1808 : Greenup)
	Governor's official correspondence file - petitions for pardons and remissions, 1799-1804 (bulk 1799, 1801-1804). Kentucky. Governor (1796-1804 : Garrard)
	Official Correspondence - Pardons Correspondence 1987-1991. Kentucky. Governor (1987-1991 : Wilkinson)
	Governor's official correspondence file - petitions for pardons and remissions, 1841-1844. Kentucky. Governor (1840-1844 : Letcher)
	Governor's official correspondence file - petitions for pardons and remissions, 1837-1839. Kentucky. Governor (1836-1839 : Clark)
	Governor's official correspondence file - petitions for pardons, 1831-1833. Kentucky. Governor (1832-1834 : Breathitt)
	Governor's official correspondence file - petitions for pardons, 1829-1832. Kentucky. Governor (1828-1832 : Metcalfe)
	Governor's official correspondence file - petitions for pardons and remissions, 1824-1828. Kentucky. Governor (1824-1828 : Desha)

	Governor's official correspondence file - petitions for pardons and remissions, 1859-1862. Kentucky. Governor (1859-1862 : Magoffin)
	Governor's official correspondence file - petitions for pardons, remissions, and respites 1855-1859. Kentucky. Governor (1855-1859 : Morehead)
	Governor's official correspondence file - petitions for pardons, remissions, and respites, 1848-1850. Kentucky. Governor (1848-1850 : Crittenden)
	Governor's official correspondence file - petitions for pardons, 1850-1851. Kentucky. Governor (1850-1851 : Helm)
	Governor's official correspondence file - petitions for pardons and remissions, 1839-1840. Kentucky. Governor (1839-1840 : Wickliffe)
	Governor's official correspondence file - petitions for pardons and remissions, 1844-1848. Kentucky. Governor (1844-1848 : Owsley)
	Governor's official correspondence file - petitions for pardons, 1851-1855. Kentucky. Governor (1851-1855 : Powell)
	Governor's official correspondence file - petitions for pardons, remissions, and respites, 1871-1875. Kentucky. Governor (1871-1875 : Leslie)
	Governor's official correspondence file - petitions for pardons, remissions, and respites, 1875-1879. Kentucky. Governor (1875-1879 : McCreary)
	Governor's official correspondence file - petitions for pardons, remissions, and respites, 1867-1871. Kentucky. Governor (1867-1871 : Stevenson)
	Governor's official correspondence file - petitions for pardons, remissions, and respites, 1867. Kentucky. Governor (1867 : Helm)
	Governor's official correspondence file - petitions for pardons, remissions, and respites 1863-1867. Kentucky. Governor (1863-1867 : Bramlette)
	Governor's official correspondence file - petitions for pardons, remissions, and respites, 1862-1863. Kentucky. Governor (1862-1863 : Robinson)
	Governor's official correspondence file - petitions for remissions, 1895-1899. Kentucky. Governor (1895-1899 : Bradley)
	Governor's official correspondence file - petitions for pardons, remissions and respites, 1895-1899. Kentucky. Governor (1895-1899 : Bradley)
	Governor's official correspondence file - petitions for pardons, remissions, and respites, 1891-1895. Kentucky. Governor (1891-1895 : Brown)
	Governor's official correspondence file - petitions for pardons, remissions, and respites, 1883-1887. Kentucky. Governor (1883-1887 : Knott)
	Governor's official correspondence file - register of petitions for pardons, remissions, and respites, 1883-1887. Kentucky. Governor (1883-1887 : Knott)

	Governor's official correspondence file - rejected petitions for pardons, remissions, and respites, 1879-1883. Kentucky. Governor (1879-1883 : Blackburn)
	Governor's official correspondence file - petitions for pardons, remissions, and respites, 1879-1883. Kentucky. Governor (1879-1883 : Blackburn)
	Governor's official correspondence file - rejected petitions for pardons, remissions, and respites, 1851-1855. Kentucky. Governor (1851-1855 : Powell)
	Governor's official correspondence file - rejected petitions, 1916-1919. Kentucky. Governor (1915-1919 : Stanley)
	Governor's official correspondence file - rejected petitions for pardons, 1912-1915. Kentucky. Governor (1911-1915 : McCreary)
	Governor's official correspondence file - petitions for pardons, remissions, and respites, 1919. Kentucky. Governor (1919 : Black)
	Governor's official correspondence file - commutations, 1919-1923. Kentucky. Governor (1919-1923 : Morrow)
	Governor's official correspondence file - rejected petitions for pardons, 1919-1923. Kentucky. Governor (1919-1923 : Morrow)
	Governor's official correspondence file - petitions for pardons, 1919-1923. Kentucky. Governor (1919-1923 : Morrow)
	Governor's official correspondence file - rejected petitions, 1895-1899. Kentucky. Governor (1895-1899 : Bradley)
	Governor's official correspondence file - miscellaneous petitions for pardons records, [1895?-1899?]. Kentucky. Governor (1895-1899 : Bradley)
	Governor's official correspondence file - pardons, 1916-1919. Kentucky. Governor (1915-1919 : Stanley)
	Governor's official correspondence file - petitions for pardons and respites, 1899-1900. Kentucky. Governor (1899-1900 : Taylor)
	Governor's official correspondence file - commutations, 1899. Kentucky. Governor (1899-1900 : Taylor)
	Governor's official correspondence file - pardons, 1924-1927. Kentucky. Governor (1923-1927 : Fields)
	Governor's official correspondence file - commutations, 1924-1927. Kentucky. Governor (1923-1927 : Fields)
	Governor's official correspondence file - petitions, 1916-1919. Kentucky. Governor (1915-1919 : Stanley)
	Governor's official correspondence file - commutations, 1916-1919. Kentucky. Governor (1915-1919 : Stanley)

	Records Pertaining to Petitions for Pardons, Remissions, and Respites, 1887-1891. Kentucky. Governor (1887-1891 : Buckner)
	Governor's official correspondence file - rejected petitions for pardons, remissions, and respites, 1887-1891. Kentucky. Governor (1887-1891 : Buckner)
	Governor's official correspondence file - respites, 1919-1923. Kentucky. Governor (1919-1923 : Morrow)
	Governor's official correspondence file - petitions for pardons, remissions, and respites, 1887-1891. Kentucky. Governor (1887-1891 : Buckner)
	Governor's official correspondence file - petitions for pardons and remissions of fines, [microform] 1887-1890. Kentucky. Governor (1887-1891 : Buckner)

Federal Criminal Court Records at the National Archives & Records Admin. (NARA)

NARA Southeast Region
5780 Jonesboro Road, Morrow, Georgia 30260, (770) 968-2100
www.archives.gov/southeast/
atlanta.archives@nara.gov

Record Type	ARC Identifier	Title	Description
	657553	Criminal Case Files, compiled 1906 - 1980	Textual Records from the U.S. District Court for the Western District of Kentucky. Louisville Term. (02/12/1901 -)
	2564190	Criminal Orders, compiled 1901 - 1961	Textual Records from the U.S. District Court for the Western District of Kentucky. Bowling Green Term. (02/12/1901 -)
	1544734	Criminal Case Files, compiled 1884 - 1982	Textual Records from the U.S. District Court for the Eastern District of Kentucky. Covington Term (02/12/1902 -)
	719117	Criminal Case Files, compiled 1885 - 1969	Textual Records from the U.S. District Court for the Eastern District of Kentucky. Frankfort Term. (02/12/1901 -)
	2581086	Criminal Dockets, compiled 1901 - 1974	Textual Records from the U.S. District Court for the Eastern District of Kentucky. London Term. (02/12/1901 -)
	2581085	Criminal Dockets, compiled 1920 - 1978	Textual Records from the U.S. District Court for the Eastern District of Kentucky. Lexington Term. (01/19/1920 -)
	2564194	Criminal Orders, compiled 1901 - 1918	Textual Records from the U.S. District Court for the Eastern District of Kentucky. Richmond Term. (02/12/1901 -)

	1983027	Criminal Dockets, compiled 1888 - 1983	Textual Records from the U.S. District Court for the Eastern District of Kentucky. Covington Term (02/12/1902 -)
	1155048	Criminal Case Files, compiled 1936 - 1981	Textual Records from the U.S. District Court for the Eastern District of Kentucky. Pikeville Term. (06/22/1936 -)
	1145967	Criminal Case Files, compiled 1901 - 1969	Textual Records from the U.S. District Court for the Eastern District of Kentucky. Richmond Term. (02/12/1901 -)
	2564201	Criminal Orders, compiled 1901 - 1920	Textual Records from the U.S. District Court for the Eastern District of Kentucky. London Term. (02/12/1901 -)
	2629235	Criminal Final Records, compiled 1885 - 1914	Textual Records from the U.S. District Court for the Eastern District of Kentucky. Frankfort Term. (02/12/1901 -)
	1148092	Criminal Case Files, compiled 1920 - 1981	Textual Records from the U.S. District Court for the Eastern District of Kentucky. Lexington Term. (01/19/1920 -)
	2564206	Criminal Orders, compiled 1879 - 1915	Textual Records from the U.S. District Court for the Eastern District of Kentucky. Frankfort Term. (02/12/1901 -)
	2564192	Criminal Orders, compiled 1912 - 1961	Textual Records from the U.S. District Court for the Western District of Kentucky. Louisville Term. (02/12/1901 -)
	2564193	Criminal Orders, compiled 1889 - 1936	Textual Records from the U.S. District Court for the Western District of Kentucky. Owensboro Term. (02/12/1901 -)
	2564204	Criminal Orders, compiled 1908 - 1919	Textual Records from the U.S. District Court for the Eastern District of Kentucky. Jackson Term. (05/22/1908 -)
	2871062	Index of Bankruptcy, Civil, and Criminal Case Files, compiled 1928-1974	Textual Records from the U.S. District Court for the Eastern District of Kentucky. Jackson Term. (05/22/1908 -)
	2581084	Criminal Dockets, compiled 1908 - 1963	Textual Records from the U.S. District Court for the Eastern District of Kentucky. Jackson Term. (05/22/1908 -)
	2126665	Criminal Dockets, compiled 1936 - 1976	Textual Records from the U.S. District Court for the Eastern District of Kentucky. Pikeville Term. (06/22/1936 -)
	2887111	Index to Criminal Case Files, compiled 1928 - 1967	Textual Records from the U.S. District Court for the Eastern District of Kentucky. Frankfort Term. (02/12/1901 -)

	2887110	Index to Criminal Case Files, compiled 1936 - 1976	Textual Records from the U.S. District Court for the Eastern District of Kentucky. Pikeville Term. (06/22/1936 -)
	1544870	Criminal Case Files, compiled 1901 - 1977	Textual Records from the U.S. District Court for the Western District of Kentucky. Bowling Green Term. (02/12/1901 -)
	2581087	Criminal Dockets, compiled 1901 - 1968	Textual Records from the U.S. District Court for the Eastern District of Kentucky. Richmond Term. (02/12/1901 -)
	2581359	Criminal Dockets, compiled 1902 - 1962	Textual Records from the U.S. District Court for the Western District of Kentucky. Bowling Green Term. (02/12/1901 -)
	2125182	Criminal Case Files, compiled 1911 - 1982	Textual Records from the U.S. District Court for the Western District of Kentucky. Paducah Term (02/12/1901 -)
	2887112	Index to Criminal Case Files, compiled 1928 - 1969	Textual Records from the U.S. District Court for the Eastern District of Kentucky. Catlettsburg Term. (03/10/1902 -)
	1150937	Criminal Case Files, compiled 1902 - 1981	Textual Records from the U.S. District Court for the Eastern District of Kentucky. London Term. (02/12/1901 -)
	1542517	Criminal Case Files, compiled 1902 - 1982	Textual Records from the U.S. District Court for the Eastern District of Kentucky. Catlettsburg Term. (03/10/1902 -)
	2581088	Criminal Dockets, compiled 1888 - 1967	Textual Records from the U.S. District Court for the Eastern District of Kentucky. Frankfort Term. (02/12/1901 -)
	1150847	Criminal Case Files, compiled 1909 - 1964	Textual Records from the U.S. District Court for the Eastern District of Kentucky. Richmond Term. (02/12/1901 -)
	2581083	Criminal Dockets, compiled 1907 - 1976	Textual Records from the U.S. District Court for the Eastern District of Kentucky. Catlettsburg Term. (03/10/1902 -)

Kentucky Executions

http://users.bestweb.net/~rg/execution/KENTUCKY.htm

Kentucky Department of Corrections Offender Lookup

http://www.corrections.ky.gov/kool.htm

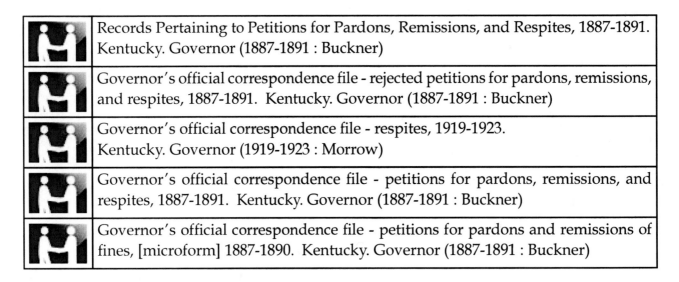

http://www.corrections.ky.gov/kool.htm

Louisiana

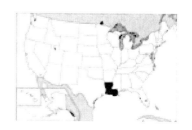

Louisiana Department for Libraries and Archives

3851 Essen Lane, Baton Rouge, LA 70809, 225-922-1208
http://www.sos.louisiana.gov/tabid/53/Default.aspx
library@sos.louisiana.gov

Record Type	Location	Title/Description
	Cabinet 398 - Drawer 7 P1980-353	Louisiana State Penitentiary – Angola / State Penitentiary Records 1866-1960. Collection is convict records with indexes, registers and records of convicts at the Louisiana State Penitentiary. Closed to researchers without written permission from the Department of Corrections. After 50 years, no permission is needed. (43 Volumes, 13505-13564)
	P1977-123	State Penitentiary Records: 1901-1912, 1928
	P1980-345	State Penitentiary Records: 1929-1932
	P1980-353	State Penitentiary Records: 1866-1960(?)
	P1981-451	Louisiana State Penitentiary Records: 1911-1940
	P1981-495	State Penitentiary Records: 1952-1964
	P1985-261	Dept. of Corrections Probation & Parole Records: 1968-1973
	P1988-143	Pardons and Denied Pardons: 1936-1958
	P1991-90	Department of Corrections: 1989
	P1992-14	Department of Corrections: 1983-1984

	P1994-17	Pardons: 1944-1972
	P1975-21	Pardons issued by the Governor: 1879-1940
	P2004-9	Pardons issued by Governor Mike Foster: 2002-2004
	701 - Drawers 3-4 N1997-14	French Superior Council Records: 1679-1803 Microfilm of original records housed in the Louisiana Historical Center, Old Mint Building, New Orleans. Includes various types of court records such as civil and criminal suits, probates, land transactions, settlements of debts, etc. of the French Superior Council dated 1679-1803. Inventory available.
	701 - Drawers 4-7 N1997-22	Judicial Records of the Spanish Cabildo, 1769-1804. Microfilm of original records housed in the Louisiana Historical Center, Old Mint Building, New Orleans. Includes various types of court records such as civil and criminal suits, probates, land transactions, settlements of debts, etc. of the Spanish Cabildo dated 1769-1804
	Cabinet 457 - Drawer 5 P1987-166	St. Landry Parish, Ward 1 Criminal Dockets: 1950-1970 Collection consists of St. Landry Parish criminal & civil court dockets. Also contains affidavits, warrants, guidelines for issuing traffic citations, and misc. court records. See inventory detailed listing.
	Cabinet 438 - Drawers 8-10 P2002-33	East Baton Rouge Parish Clerk of Court Records: 1811-1977 Tax assessment rolls, tax exempt books, judicial record books, criminal records, docket books, probate minute books, etc.
	Cabinet 398 - Drawer 2 P1987-166	St. Landry Parish, Ward 1 Criminal Dockets: 1950-1970 Collection consists of St. Landry Parish criminal & civil court dockets. Also contains affidavits, warrants, guidelines for issuing traffic citations, and misc. court records. See inventory detailed listing.

Louisiana Executions

http://users.bestweb.net/~rg/execution/LOUISIANA.htm

Federal Criminal Court Records at the National Archives & Records Admin. (NARA)

NARA Southwest Region (Fort Worth)

501 West Felix Street, Building 1, Fort Worth, TX 76115-3405, Phone: 817-831-5620

http://www.archives.gov/southwest/

ftworth.archives@nara.gov

Record Type	ARC Identifier	Title	Description
	593252	Criminal Case Files, compiled 1916 - 1971	Textual Records from the U.S. District Court for the Baton Rouge Division of the Eastern District of Louisiana. (08/13/1888 - 12/18/1971)
	595022	Criminal Case Files, compiled 1882 - 1977	Textual Records from the U.S. District Court for the Shreveport Division of the Western District of Louisiana. (1881 -)
	592767	Criminal Case Files, compiled 1912 - 1978	Textual Records from the U.S. District Court for the New Orleans Division of the Eastern District of Louisiana. (1806 -)
	593645	Criminal Case Files, compiled 1974 - 1979	Textual Records from the U.S. District Court for the Baton Rouge Division of the Middle District of Louisiana. (12/18/1971 -)
	3440946	Index to Case Files, compiled ca. 1806 - 1981	Textual Records from the U.S. District Court for the New Orleans Division of the Eastern District of Louisiana. (1806 -)
	3440943	Index to Defendants, compiled ca. 1962 - 1982	Textual Records from the U.S. District Court for the Baton Rouge Division of the Middle District of Louisiana. (12/18/1971 -)

Louisiana Department of Corrections Inmate locator

 http://www.corrections.state.la.us/view.php?cat=10&id=64

Louisiana Offender Lookup (Dept of Corrections and Many Parishes)

 https://www.vinelink.com/vinelink/initSearchForm.do?searchType=offender&siteId=19000

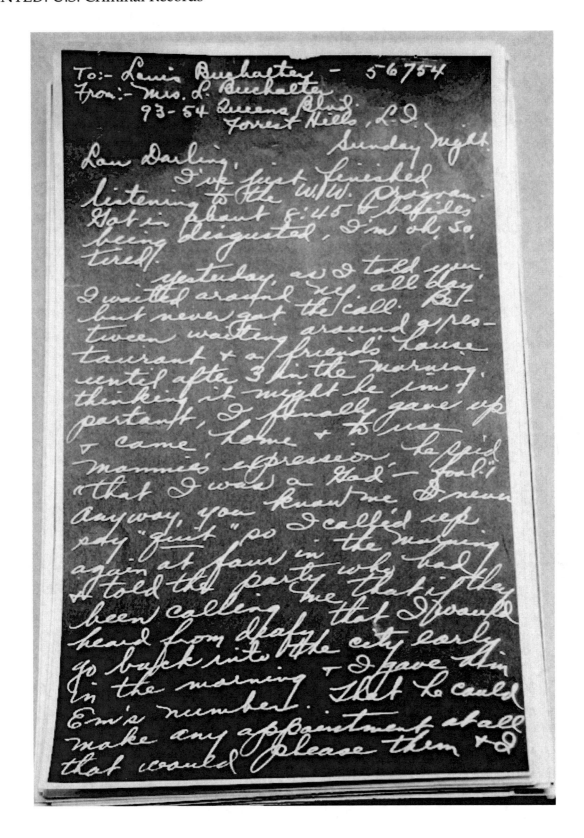

Photo stat of letter to Louis "Lepke" Buchalter from his wife Betty.
Courtesy of:
Lloyd Sealy Library, Special Collections
John Jay College of Criminal Justice/CUNY
BURTON B. TURKUS PAPERS

Maine

Maine State Archives

84 State House Station, Augusta, Maine 04333, (207) 287-5790
www.maine.gov/sos/arc/
https://www.maine.gov/online/archives/index.html

Record Type	Title	Description
	Inmate File Case Records (Charleston Correctional Facility)	Supervisor's Recommendation For Pre-Release, Disipline Reports, Prisoner Furlough Permission Reports, Inmate Seat-Belt Rule, Classification Board Reports, Request For Furlough Investigation, Case History Outline, Weekly Inmate Evaluation. Date Range: 01/01/1980 to 12/31/1985
	Inmate Case Files - Maine State Prison	Commitment Papers, Indictments, Prison Filing, Writs, Photo, Fingerprints, SBI & FBI Records, Case History, Classification Material And Institutional Progress. Date Range: 01/01/1920 to 12/31/1939
	Inmate Case Files - Maine State Prison	Commitment Papers, Indictments, Prison Filing, Writs, Photo, Fingerprints, SBI & FBI Records, Case History, Classification Material And Institutional Progress. Date Range: 12/01/1966 to 08/31/1973
	Inmate Case Files - Maine State Prison	Commitment Papers, Indictments, Prison Filing, Writs, Photo, Fingerprints, SBI & FBI Records, Case History, Classification Material And Institutional Progress. Date Range: 06/01/1979 to 07/31/1979
	Pardons - Corporations Elections Commissions	Action Taken By Governor Of Maine Voiding A Decision Of Maine Courts. Includes Petition For Clemency, Information Sheet From Governor\'S Board On Exectutive Clemency, Warrant Of Conditional Pardon, Related Correspondence.
	Parole Records	Probation And Parole : Individual Case Folders Contain Material On Either Probationers Or Parolees.

	Court Records	Courts 1696-1854. Downloadaable MS-Access 97 database indexes early cases from the York County Court of Common Pleas (1696-1760), the Kennebec County Supreme Court (1799-1854), and the Washington County District Court (1839-1846), including depositions and decisions. Inclusive Dates: 1696-1854. Records: 27,525 cases, and 55,254 plaintiffs or defendants. URL for Downloadable Access database: www.maine.gov/sos/arc/databases/COURTS99.ZIP

Notes:

Typing in the keyword 'prison' at: https://www.maine.gov/online/archives/index.html yields 123 matches to the keyword 'prison', even though clearly there are many duplicate matches.

Typing in the keywords 'criminal court' into https://www.maine.gov/online/archives/index.html yields 9,020 results (although, presumably there are many duplicates.) The results include criminal dockets, criminal case files, etc.

Federal Criminal Court Records at the National Archives & Records Admin. (NARA)

NARA Northeast Region (Boston)
Frederick C. Murphy Federal Center, 380 Trapelo Road, Waltham, MA, 02452-6399
(781) 663-0130
http://www.archives.gov/northeast/
waltham.archives@nara.gov

Record Type	ARC Identifier	Title	Description
	592882	Criminal Case Files, compiled 1907 - 1982	Textual Records from the U.S. District Court for the Southern Division of the District of Maine. (1916 -)
	592883	Criminal Case Files, compiled 1917 - 1961	Textual Records from the U.S. District Court for the Northern Division of the District of Maine. (1916 -)
	2675020	Criminal Dockets, compiled 06/05/1913 - 11/06/1943	Textual Records from the U.S. District Court for the Northern Division of the District of Maine. Office of U.S. Commissioners. (ca. 1916 - 1968)

⚖	2788867	Dockets , compiled 05/1820 - 12/1906	Textual Records from the U.S. Circuit Court for the District of Maine. (03/30/1820 - 01/01/1912)
⚖	2771406	Dockets, compiled 1789 - 1906	Textual Records from the U.S. District Court for the District of Maine. (1789 - 1916)
⚖	2839187	Case Files, compiled 1820 - 1906	Textual Records from the U.S. Circuit Court for the District of Maine. (03/30/1820 - 01/01/1912)
⚖	2675024	Judgement Dockets, compiled 1914 - 1935	Textual Records from the U.S. District Court for the Southern Division of the District of Maine. (1916 -)

Maine Executions

http://users.bestweb.net/~rg/execution/MAINE.htm?Maine=

Maine Department of Corrections Inmate Lookup

http://www.maine.gov/corrections/FAQ.htm#findInmate

	ART NELSON	180
39.	DUTCH	175
40.	"PICKLES" LIEBMAN	160
41.	JIM SCARPA	200
42.	"JIM"	155
43.	"LUCKY" EISEMAN, Captain	180
44.	"BOB"	200
45.	AL DAVEY	160
46.	MALAVASI	175
47.	"JOIE" HAYES	170
48.	"BUCK" O'NEILL	180
49.	"BLINK" WEISBERG	175
50.	TED BIELEFELD	180
51.	"MICKEY"	160
52.	"SWEDE" OLSEN	160
53.	BROWN	165
54.	BERNSTEIN	160
55.	DUANE	145
56.	"ED"	195
57.	"KNUTE" DILLON	185
58.	"WINK" WINKLER	150
59.	"RED"	200
60.	PETE MAURIELLO	205
61.	"MOON" BYRD	195
62.	"WHITEY" HAND	190
63.	NELSON	145
64.	MASTRELLI	185
65.	"FLASH" PINE	190
66.	MC LAUGHLIN	170
67.	SEELEY	150
68.	KESSLER	185
69.	STOKES	170

GERALD F. CURTIN—ATHLETIC DIR

COACHES

JOHN LAW   RICHARD
V. P. KENNARD   GEORGE "J
DR. G. K. MC CRACKEN—PHYSICI

Quarter	1st	2nd	3rd
Sing Sing Black Sheep			

Program for football game between Sing Sing (Prison) "Black Sheep"
and the Kingston Yellow Jackets, October 27, 1933. Courtesy of:
Lloyd Sealy Library, Special Collections
John Jay College of Criminal Justice/CUNY
LEWIS E. LAWES PAPERS (1883-1947)

Maryland

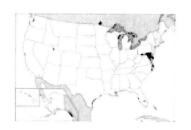

Maryland State Archives

350 Rowe Blvd, Annapolis, MD 21401-1686, (410) 260-6400
www.msa.md.gov
ref@mdsa.net

Record Type	Location	Title	Description
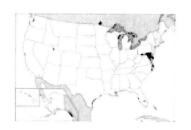	N/A	Maryland Penitentiary Prisoners Records	The entries in the Prisoners Records list the prisoner's name, birth place, age, complexion, hair type, stature, eye color, usual place of residence, occupation, distinguishing marks, county where convicted, crime, date and length of sentence, release date, occupation in prison, and when and how discharged.
	N/A	Maryland Penitentiary Prisoners Records Indices	Prisoners Records after 1839 are indexed.
	N/A	Maryland House of Correction Prisoners Records	The entries in the Prisoners Records list the prisoner's name and number, former occupation, crime, sentence length, age, education, Sunday school attendance, at what age orphaned, whether bound to a trade, temperance, religion, race, sex, marital status, number of convictions, place of birth, county where convicted, date incarcerated, and expiration of sentence.
	N/A	Maryland House of Correction Prisoners Records Index	Prisoners Records are indexed from 1879 to 1905
	MSA T875, Boxes 1-2	Parole Records Index	Paroles are indexed from 1907 to 1959

District Court Records Held at the Maryland State Archives

Record Type	District/County/ Designator	Records or Indices	Location	Title
	Allegany County (12/01/AL/W)	Records	T1090	Criminal Docket, 1927-1939, 1954-1971 (Docket books only)(All files at District Court Record Center)
	Allegany County (12/01/AL/W)	Records	T3304	Natural Resources Docket, 1991-1995 HF & 1996-1997
	Allegany County (12/01/AL/W)	Records	T3491	Citations, 1996-1997
	Allegany County (12/01/AL/W)	Records	T3490	Special Proceedings Docket, 1987-1988
	Allegany County (12/01/AL/W)	Indices	S1754	Criminal Docket, Index, 1971-1983
	Allegany County (12/01/AL/W)	Indices	T3518	Special Proceedings Docket, Index, 1984-1991
	Anne Arundel Cty. (07/AA/A)	Records	C107	Trial Magistrate Docket, 1939-1942, 1950-1951
	Anne Arundel Cty. (07/AA/A)	Records	C66	People's Court Docket, 1964-1971
	Anne Arundel Cty. (07/AA/A)	Records	C105	Justice of the Peace Docket, 1833-1939
	Anne Arundel Cty. (07/AA/A)	Records	T1080	Criminal Docket, 1917-1918 OR, 1939-1964, 1990-1992, 1994 (All District Court Dockets from 1971 - 1989, 1993, 1995-? are at District Court Record Center.)
	Anne Arundel Cty. (07/AA/A)	Records	S464	Criminal Docket, 1971-1975
	Anne Arundel Cty. (07/AA/A)	Records	T1174	Docket, 1875-1899, 1902-1906, 1920-1933
	Anne Arundel Cty. (07/AA/A)	Records	T3670	Natural Resources Docket, 1995
	Anne Arundel Cty. (07/AA/A)	Records	T2840	Special Proceedings Docket, 1972-1987, 1990 OR, 1981-1986, 1991 MSA, 1995-1996 HF

	Anne Arundel Cty. (07/AA/A)	Indices	S1175	Criminal Docket, Index, 1971-1981
	Anne Arundel Cty. (07/AA/A)	Indices	T3391	Special Proceedings Docket, Index, 1985-1995
	Baltimore City (01/BC/B)	Records	C2110	Police Department Criminal Docket, Northeastern District, 1900-1959
	Baltimore City (01/BC/B)	Records	T231	Docket, 1955-1956, 1959-1971
	Baltimore City (01/BC/B)	Records	T1072	Criminal Docket, All files have been returned to District Court Record Center except for one box for 1971-1973.
	Baltimore City (01/BC/B)	Records	C2111	Police Department Criminal Docket, Eastern District, 1863-1961
	Baltimore City (01/BC/B)	Records	T1765	Criminal Docket, Housing, 1974-1980
	Baltimore City (01/BC/B)	Records	T2099	Fugitive Docket, 1983-1986
	Baltimore City (01/BC/B)	Records	T2821	Domestic Violence Docket,1980-1985 at MSA
	Baltimore City (01/BC/B)	Records	T3492	Special Proceedings Docket, 1980-1985 MSA
	Baltimore City (01/BC/B)	Records	C2112	Police Department Criminal Docket, Northwestern District, 1876-1959
	Baltimore City (01/BC/B)	Records	SM66	Criminal Papers, 1971-1976 (The Baltimore City District Court possesses the indices for these records.
	Baltimore City (01/BC/B)	Records	C2113	Police Department Criminal Docket, Southern District, 1867-1960
	Baltimore City (01/BC/B)	Records	C2114	Police Department Criminal Docket, Western District, 1959-1961
	Baltimore City (01/BC/B)	Records	C2115	Police Department Criminal Docket, Southeastern District, 1959-1961
	Baltimore City (01/BC/B)	Records	C2117	Police Department Criminal Docket, Central District, 1893-1960
	Baltimore County (08/BA/C)	Records	T1081	Criminal Docket, 1963-1971

Baltimore County (08/BA/C)	Records	C372	Justice of the Peace Docket, 1815-1886, 1900-1935
Baltimore County (08/BA/C)	Records	C1630	Trial Magistrate Criminal Docket, 1939-1970
Baltimore County (08/BA/C)	Records	C1632	Trial Magistrate Criminal Appeal Docket, 1962-1963
Baltimore County (08/BA/C)	Records	C373	Police Justice Criminal Docket, 1922-1927, 1935-1939
Baltimore County (08/BA/C)	Records	T3305	Special Proceedings Docket, 1986 HF, 1987 CW, 1988-1990 OR
Calvert County (04/01/CV/O)	Records	T1648	Criminal Docket, 1990-1994; (1971-1989 at District Court Record Center)
Calvert County (04/01/CV/O)	Records	T3306	Natural Resources Docket, 1990, 1996 OR, 1991-1995 HF
Calvert County (04/01/CV/O)	Records	T3392	Municipal Docket, 1996 (OR)
Calvert County (04/01/CV/O)	Records	C447	Justice of the Peace Docket, 1868-1933
Calvert County (04/01/CV/O)	Records	T3595	Special Proceedings Docket, 1977-1990 OR
Calvert County (04/01/CV/O)	Indices	S1770	Criminal Docket, Index, 1971-1985
Caroline County (03/01/CA/J)	Records	C531	Trial Magistrate Docket, 1939-1971
Caroline County (03/01/CA/J)	Records	T2587	Criminal Docket, 1990, 1993, 1995
Caroline County (03/01/CA/J)	Records	T2968	Natural Resources Docket, 1991-1992 MSA, 1996, 1999, 2001 CW
Caroline County (03/01/CA/J)	Records	C530	Justice of the Peace Docket, 1813-1869, 1914-1939
Caroline County (03/01/CA/J)	Indices	S1791	Criminal Docket, Index, 1971-1981ff
Carroll County (10/02/CR/S)	Records	T1084	Criminal Docket; all files returned to District Court Record Center

	Carroll County (10/02/CR/S)	Records	T2969	Natural Resources Docket, 1991-1994 MSA, 1995-1998 OR, 1999-2000 CW
	Carroll County (10/02/CR/S)	Records	T2837	Special Proceedings Docket 1981-1984, 1986-1987 MSA, 1985, 1988-1998 OR
	Carroll County (10/02/CR/S)	Records	T3781	Criminal Docket, 1837-1967 CW (These appear to be magistrates dockets that were in the possession of the Carroll County Circuit Court
	Carroll County (10/02/CR/S)	Indices	S1751	Criminal Docket, Index, 1971-1981
	Carroll County (10/02/CR/S)	Indices	T3440	Special Proceedings Docket, Index 1983-1991 OR
	Cecil County (03/02/CE/K)	Records	T1075	Criminal Docket,1971-1995
	Cecil County (03/02/CE/K)	Records	T2582	Natural Resources Docket, 1981-1994 at MSA, 1995-1999 OR, 2000-2001 CW
	Cecil County (03/02/CE/K)	Records	T2583	Special proceedings Docket, 1981-1985 MSA , 1986-1989 OR (Contains Domestic Violence Dockets)
	Cecil County (03/02/CE/K)	Records	T2584	Criminal Docket, Fugitive, 1981-1990
	Cecil County (03/02/CE/K)	Indices	S1756	Criminal Docket, Index, 1971-1983
	Cecil County (03/02/CE/K)	Indices	T3300	Criminal Docket, Index to Special Proceedings (index to Domestic Violence and Fugitive Dockets) 1986-1991
	Charles County (04/02/CH/P)	Records	T1078	Criminal Docket, 1948-1971, 1992-1993 (1971-1991 at District Court Record Center)(includes PCM 4 Justice of the Peace Docket 1952-1973)
	Charles County (04/02/CH/P)	Records	T2819	Natural Resources Docket, 1975-1994 MSA, 1995-1996 HF, 1996-1997, 1999-2000 CW
	Charles County (04/02/CH/P)	Records	T234	Docket, 1880-1948
	Charles County (04/02/CH/P)	Records	T2841	Special Proceedings Docket 1980-1985

WANTED! U.S. Criminal Records

Charles County (04/02/CH/P)	Indices	S1766	Criminal Docket, Index,1971-1990
Dorchester County (02/01/DO/F)	Records	T1740	Criminal Docket, 1908-1927 OR, 1971-1979 MSA (1979-1983 returned to District Court Record Center)
Dorchester County (02/01/DO/F)	Records	T1952	Justice of the Peace Docket), 1833-1955
Dorchester County (02/01/DO/F)	Records	T3596	Special Proceedings Docket, 1985-1987, 1989 OR, 1990-1991 CW
Dorchester County (02/01/DO/F)	Indices	S1767	Criminal Docket, Index, 1971-1983
Frederick County (11/01/FR/U)	Records	T237	Docket, 1812-1971
Frederick County (11/01/FR/U)	Records	T1085	Criminal Docket, 1971-1985, 1987-1991, 1993
Frederick County (11/01/FR/U)	Records	T2816	Natural Resources Docket, 1991-1992, 1994 MSA, 1997 OR
Frederick County (11/01/FR/U)	Records	T2975	Domestic Violence Docket, 1980-1985 OR
Frederick County (11/01/FR/U)	Records	T2842	Fugitive Warrants, 1989-1991
Frederick County (11/01/FR/U)	Records	T3493	Special Proceedings Docket, 1987-1988, 1990, 1995 OR, 1989 CW
Frederick County (11/01/FR/U)	Records	S1753	Criminal Docket, Index, 1971-1983
Garrett County (12/02/GA/X)	Records	T239	Docket, 1857-1971
Garrett County (12/02/GA/X)	Records	T1091	Criminal Docket, All Records returned to District Court Record Center
Garrett County (12/02/GA/X)	Records	T3307	Natural Resources Docket, 1991-1996 HF, 1997 OR
Garrett County (12/02/GA/X)	Records	T3494	Special Proceedings Docket, 1980-1988 OR
Garrett County (12/02/GA/X)	Indices	S1755	(Criminal Docket, Index), 1971-1987

	Garrett County (12/02/GA/X)	Indices	T3504	Special Proceedings Docket, Index, 1988-1991 OR
	Harford County (09/HA/R)	Records	T1082	Criminal Docket, 1951-1971, 1990, 1992, 1994-1995 (1971-1989, 1991, 1993 files at District Court Record Center)
	Harford County (09/HA/R)	Records	T3178	Natural Resources Docket, 1991-1994
	Harford County (09/HA/R)	Records	T3190	Special Proceedings Docket, 1980-1986 MSA, 1989, 1995-1996 OR
	Harford County (09/HA/R)	Indices	S1750	Criminal Docket, Index, 1971-1981
	Howard County (10/01/HO/T)	Records	C997	Trial Magistrate Docket, 1939-1964
	Howard County (10/01/HO/T)	Records	T1083	Criminal Docket, All Files returned to District Court Record Center
	Howard County (10/01/HO/T)	Records	C996	Justice of the Peace Docket, 1854-1939
	Howard County (10/01/HO/T)	Records	T2095	Special Proceedings Docket, 1976-1985 MSA, 1986-1990 OR
	Howard County (10/01/HO/T)	Indices	S1752	Criminal Docket, Index, 1971-1982
	Howard County (10/01/HO/T)	Indices	T3443	Special Proceedings Docket, Index, 1980-1991 OR
	Kent County (03/03/KE/L)	Records	T1076	Criminal Docket, 1971-1977, 1990-1992, 1995
	Kent County (03/03/KE/L)	Records	T2817	Natural Resources Docket, 1991-1994 MSA, 1995-1998 OR, 2000-2001 CW
	Kent County (03/03/KE/L)	Records	T3597	Municipal Docket, 1995-1996 OR, 2001 CW
	Kent County (03/03/KE/L)	Records	C1078	Justice of the Peace Docket, 1823-1922
	Kent County (03/03/KE/L)	Records	T2994	Special Proceedings Docket, 1981-1990 OR
	Kent County (03/03/KE/L)	Indices	T3825	Special Proceedings Docket, Index, 1986-1990 CW

	Kent County (03/03/KE/L)	Indices	S1794	Criminal Docket, Index, 1971-1984 September
	Montgomery County (06/O/D)	Records	T1079	Criminal Docket, 1963-1972, 1991 (1973-1990 files at District Court Record Center)
	Montgomery County (06/O/D)	Records	T1678	Stet Docket, 1972-1975
	Montgomery County (06/O/D)	Records	T2245	Municipal Docket, 1983-1991
	Montgomery County (06/O/D)	Records	T2284	Natural Resources Docket, 1983-1984
	Montgomery County (06/O/D)	Records	T2845	Fugitive Warrants, 1985-1990
	Montgomery County (06/O/D)	Records	T2488	Docket, 1876-1900, 1935-1939 MSA, 1902-1911 HF
	Montgomery County (06/O/D)	Indices	S1749	Criminal Docket, Index, 1971-1983
	Montgomery County (06/O/D)	Indices	C2874	Peoples Court Criminal Docket, Index, 1963-1971
	Prince George's County (05/PG/E)	Records	T241	Criminal Docket, 1927-1971, 1980-1983, 1988-1990, 1992-1993 MSA, 1927-1928 OR (1969-1971 no index for files)
	Prince George's County (05/PG/E)	Records	T243	Stet Docket, 1971
	Prince George's County (05/PG/E)	Records	T247	Docket, 1847-1852, 1941-1958
	Prince George's County (05/PG/E)	Records	T250	Criminal Docket, Municipal, 1947-1964
	Prince George's County (05/PG/E)	Records	T2844	Domestic Violence Docket, 1980-1987, 1989 MSA, 1981-1985, 1987-1990, 1998 OR
	Prince George's County (05/PG/E)	Records	T2099	Fugitive Docket, 1983-1986
	Prince George's County (05/PG/E)	Records	T2577	(Fugitive Warrants), 1985-1991
	Prince George's County (05/PG/E)	Records	T2818	Natural Resources Docket, 1980-1989, 1992 OR, 1991 Warrant Invalidations MSA

	Prince George's County (05/PG/E)	Records	C1257	Justice of the Peace Docket, 1815-1939
	Prince George's County (05/PG/E)	Records	T3394	Municipal Docket, 1985-1991 OR
	Prince George's County (05/PG/E)	Records	T2843	Special Proceedings Docket, 1981-1985 Health & Housing, 1987-1988 MSA, 1986-1988, 1990, 1998 OR
	Prince George's County (05/PG/E)	Indices	S1757	Criminal Docket, Index, 1971-1981
	Prince George's County (05/PG/E)	Indices	T3387	Natural Resources Docket, Index, 1975-1983
	Prince George's County (05/PG/E)	Indices	T3386	Special Proceedings Docket, Index 1989
	Queen Anne's County (03/04/QA/M)	Records	T2448	Criminal Docket, 1989-1991, 1993, 1995
	Queen Anne's County (03/04/QA/M)	Records	T2970	Natural Resources Docket, 1991-1994, 1997 MSA, 1995-1996, 1998 OR, 1999-2001 CW
	Queen Anne's County (03/04/QA/M)	Records	T3338	Special Proceedings Docket, 1988 MSA, 1980-1987 OR
	Queen Anne's County (03/04/QA/M)	Records	T3212	Fugitive Warrants, 1981-1991
	Queen Anne's County (03/04/QA/M)	Records	C1442	Trial Magistrate Criminal Docket, 1871-1930
	Queen Anne's County (03/04/QA/M)	Records	C1443	Police Justice Criminal Docket, 1929-1939
	Queen Anne's County (03/04/QA/M)	Records	C1444	Criminal Docket, 1939, 1951-1959
	Queen Anne's County (03/04/QA/M)	Records	C1445	Justice of the Peace Docket, 1811-1939
	Queen Anne's County (03/04/QA/M)	Records	T3795	Stet Docket, 1971-1987 CW

	Queen Anne's County (03/04/QA/M)	Indices	S1792	Criminal Docket, Index, 1971-1984
	Queen Anne's County (03/04/QA/M)	Indices	T3794	Special Proceedings Docket, Index, 1987 CW
	St. Mary's Cty. (04/03/SM/Q)	Records	C1643	Justice of the Peace Docket, 1819-1939
	St. Mary's Cty. (04/03/SM/Q)	Records	T2971	Natural Resources Docket, 1992-1994 MSA, 1995 OR, 1996-1997 CW
	St. Mary's Cty. (04/03/SM/Q)	Records	T1093	Criminal Docket, 1950-1971 Docket Books, 1971-1985, 1990-1995
	St. Mary's Cty. (04/03/SM/Q)	Records	T1094	Motor Vehicle Stet Docket, 1966-1970
	St. Mary's Cty. (04/03/SM/Q)	Records	T3495	Special Proceedings Docket, 1983-1988 OR
	St. Mary's Cty. (04/03/SM/Q)	Indices	S1768	Criminal Docket, Index, 1971-1983
	St. Mary's Cty. (04/03/SM/Q)	Indices	T3514	Special Proceedings Docket, Index, 1989 OR
	Somerset Cty. (02/02/SO/G)	Records	C1787	Trial Magistrate Docket, 1957
	Somerset Cty. (02/02/SO/G)	Records	T255	Criminal Docket, 1947-1965 (Docket Books), 1977-1984
	Somerset Cty. (02/02/SO/G)	Records	T2972	Natural Resources Docket, 1991-1994 MSA, 1995-1997 OR, 1998-2000 CW
	Somerset Cty. (02/02/SO/G)	Indices	S1771	Criminal Docket, Index 1971-1991
	Talbot County (03/05/TA/N)	Records	T1077	(Criminal Docket), 1939-1959 MSA, 1959-1971 OR (Docket Books), 1971-1984, 1989-1994 MSA
	Talbot County (03/05/TA/N)	Records	T1982	(Docket), 1843-1939
	Talbot County (03/05/TA/N)	Records	T3339	(Municipal Docket), 1996 MSA, 1997 OR
	Talbot County (03/05/TA/N)	Records	T2973	(Natural Resources Docket), 1991-1994, 1996 MSA, 1995, 1997-1999 OR, 2001 CW

	Talbot County (03/05/TA/N)	Records	T2993	Special Proceedings Docket, 1993 MSA, 1987-1990, 1995 OR
	Talbot County (03/05/TA/N)	Records	T3799	Stet Docket, 1973-1979 CW
	Talbot County (03/05/TA/N)	Indices	T3798	Special Proceedings Docket, Index, 1986 CW
	Talbot County (03/05/TA/N)	Indices	S1793	Criminal Docket, Index, 1971-1984
	Washington Cty. (11/02/WA/V)	Records	C1941	Trial Magistrate Criminal Docket, Municipal), 1963-1971
	Washington Cty. (11/02/WA/V)	Records	C1975	Trial Magistrate Criminal Docket, 1963-1971
	Washington Cty. (11/02/WA/V)	Records	T257	Criminal Docket, Municipal, 1952-1965
	Washington Cty County (11/02/WA/V)	Records	T1087	Criminal Docket, 1951-1965 (Docket Books), 1988-1990, 1993-1995 (1971-1987, 1991-1992 at District Court Record Center)
	Washington Cty. (11/02/WA/V)	Records	T2820	Natural Resources Docket, 1991-1993 MSA, 1996 OR, 1999-2001 CW
	Washington Cty. (11/02/WA/V)	Records	T3668	Domestic Violence Docket, 1989 OR
	Washington Cty. (11/02/WA/V)	Records	T3671	Special Proceedings Docket, 1985-1990 OR
	Washington Cty. (11/02/WA/V)	Indices	S1769	Criminal Docket, Index 1971-1983, A-K only (L-Z at court)
	Wicomico Cty. (02/03/WI/H)	Records	T1073	Criminal Docket, 1971-1983, 1985-1989 (1984 at District Court Record Center)
	Wicomico Cty. (02/03/WI/H)	Records	T3340	Domestic Violence Docket, 1985-1986 MSA, 1980-1985, 1987-1989 OR
	Wicomico Cty. (02/03/WI/H)	Records	T3598	Fugitive Docket, 1992-1994 OR
	Wicomico Cty. (02/03/WI/H)	Records	T3496	Special Proceedings Docket, 1981-1993 OR
	Wicomico Cty. (02/03/WI/H)	Indices	T3814	Natural Resources Docket, 1996-1997, 2000 CW

	Worcester Cty. (02/04/WO/I)	Records	T260	Docket, 1932-1971
	Worcester Cty. (02/04/WO/I)	Records	T1074	Criminal Docket, 1971-1988, 1990-1991, 1993
	Worcester Cty. (02/04/WO/I)	Records	T3308	Natural Resources Docket, 1991-1993, 1995 HF, 1997 CW
	Worcester Cty. (02/04/WO/I)	Records	T3213	Special Proceedings Docket, 1980-1987 MSA, 1988-1990 OR
	Worcester County (02/04/WO/I)	Indices	S1780	Criminal Docket, Index, 1971-1983 PLEASE NOTE: there are separate indices for Ocean City (1977-1983) and Snow Hill (1979-1983).

Circuit Court Records at the Maryland Archives

Record Type	County	Records or Indices	Location	Title
	Allegany	Records	T3844	Criminal Appeals, 1958-1993 CW
	Allegany	Records	T3815	Criminal Papers, 1958-1994 CW
	Allegany	Records	T2036	Stet Docket, 1920-1952
	Allegany	Records	T1784	Court Papers, 1792-1954 January Term
	Allegany	Records	T2035	Stet Papers, 1875-1953
	Anne Arundel	Records	C65	Docket,1852-1910
	Anne Arundel	Records	T1105	Criminal Continuance Docket, 1904-1944
	Anne Arundel	Records	T1101	Criminal Docket, 1934-1981 (Volumes through GTC 10 indexed)
	Anne Arundel	Records	T2868	District Court Criminal Appeal Docket, 1967-1983

	County	Type	ID	Description
	Anne Arundel	Records	T1167	Stet Docket, 1890-1944 OR
	Anne Arundel	Records	T1066	Criminal Papers, 1946-1947
	Anne Arundel	Records	T1157	Grand Jury Docket, 1948-1950 OR
	Anne Arundel	Records	T1169	Parole Docket, 1935-1944 OR
	Anne Arundel	Indices	T1103	Criminal Docket, Index, 1894-1951
	Baltimore City	Records	T3372	Criminal Papers, 1983 MSA,1984 Criminal Appeals ONLY MSA, 1985-1987 Criminal Appeals ONLY, 1988 HF, 1990-1993 OR ,1984-1987, 1994-1997 CW (Criminal Appeals (3)and Change of Venue files(8) are listed after the other types of Criminal Files for 1990-1997) (SEE T495 for earlier years)
	Baltimore City	Records	C1849	Criminal Court Docket, 1852-1959
	Baltimore City	Records	T59	Criminal Court Docket, (does not circulate--see CM1299) 1960-1974 May Term
	Baltimore City	Records	CM1299	Criminal Court (Criminal Docket), 1960-1974 May Term
	Baltimore City	Records	T487	Criminal Court (Appeal Docket), 1865-1867, 1922-1974 May Term
	Baltimore City	Records	T486	Criminal Court (Special Docket), 1921-1925, 1940-1964, 1967-1977
	Baltimore City	Records	T1666	Criminal Court (Special Investigations), 1956-1982 (SEALED RECORDS FOR JUVENILES IN THIS SERIES)
	Baltimore City	Records	T1670	Criminal Court (Stet Docket), 1965-1976
	Baltimore City	Records	T496	Criminal Court (Transcripts), 1890-1982 (SEE T3657 for later dates) , (FILES PRIOR TO 1969 MAY NEED TRANSCRIPT NUMBER FOUND IN CM1299 OR C1849), Files at MSA, OR, HF(see inventory)

	Baltimore City	Records	T1667	Criminal Court (Warrant Docket), 1969-1974
	Baltimore City	Records	T1668	Criminal Court (Criminal Information Docket), 1968, 1971-1974
	Baltimore City	Records	T3657	Baltimore City Circuit Court (Criminal Transcript) 1983-1993 MSA, OR, HF, CW (Earlier Transcripts in T496)
	Baltimore City	Records	T481	Criminal Court (Bastardy Information Docket), 1940-1963
	Baltimore City	Records	T495	Criminal Court, (Criminal Papers), 1872-1982 (Criminal Appeals ONLY 1981), (See T3372 for Later years) MSA, HF, OR
	Baltimore City	Records	T494	Criminal Court (Grand Jury Docket), 1868-1973 January Term
	Baltimore City	Records	T497	Baltimore City Criminal Court (Post Conviction Papers), 1957-1974, 1976 MSA (To Find Post Conviction number use C1849 or CM1299), SEE T3372 FOR ADDITIONAL POST CONVICTION PAPERS STORED AT CW
	Baltimore City	Records	T1372	Bastardy Information Papers, 1937, 1939-1950 HF, 1951-1963 MSA
	Baltimore City	Records	T491	Domestic Information Docket, 1931-1970 MSA, 1971-1979, 1981 OR
	Baltimore City	Records	T2406	Domestic Information Papers, 1931-1950 HF, 1951-1964, 1973-1982 MSA, 1964-1972 OR (See T3646 for later years)
	Baltimore City	Records	T3646	Domestic Information Papers, 1983-1990 MSA, 1991 HF (See T2406 for earlier years)
	Baltimore City	Indices	T2260	Criminal Court Docket, Index, 1964-1968
	Baltimore County	Records	T2137	Criminal Docket, 1944-1960 (Also see CM142)
	Baltimore County	Records	T692	Criminal Docket, Removals, 1873-1926
	Baltimore County	Records	C315	Criminal Docket, 1854-1938

	Baltimore County	Records	C423	Stet Docket, 1874-1933
	Baltimore County	Records	T1769	Criminal Papers, 1969-1976 MSA, 1985-1989 OR (See Also C2896), 1990-1991 CW
	Baltimore County	Records	CM142	Criminal Docket, 1854-1964
	Baltimore County	Records	C2896	Criminal Papers, 1985-1987
	Baltimore County	Records	CE1	Criminal Papers, 1985-1989
	Baltimore County	Indices	T1472	Criminal Docket, Index, 1970 December 10-1985 June
	Calvert County	Records	T1850	Criminal Docket, 1947-1961
	Calvert County	Records	T1856	District Court Appeal Record, 1971-1978
	Calvert County	Records	T2226	Stet Docket, 1954-1972
	Calvert County	Records	C438	Docket, 1882-1948
	Caroline County	Records	C503	Docket, 1853-1947 (Also see T2460)
	Caroline County	Records	T2460	Docket, 1837-1893, 1918-1933 (Also see C503)
	Carroll County	Records	T3765	Criminal Appeals, 1953-1983 CW
	Carroll County	Records	T3766	Criminal Papers, 1953-1993 CW
	Carroll County	Records	T3788	Criminal Papers, Court Reporters Notes, 1992 CW
	Carroll County	Records	T3781	Criminal Docket, 1837-1967 CW (These are magistrates dockets that have been in the possession of the Circuit Court),
	Cecil County	Records	T2955	Criminal Docket, 1861-1937 HF

	Cecil County	Records	T3123	Appeal Docket, 1896, 1902, 1918-1936 HF
	Cecil County	Records	T3122	Stet Docket, 1870-1947, 1960-1963 HF
	Cecil County	Records	T3111	Trial Docket, 1850-1898, 1904-1907, 1930-1934, 1943, 1961 HF
	Cecil County	Records	T1836	Court Papers, 1884-1971
	Cecil County	Records	T1225	Criminal Papers, 1964-1965 (files 1040 & 1390 only)
	Cecil County	Records	T3757	Criminal Transcripts, 1959-1992 (Name and File number listed on inventory) OR
	Cecil County	Records	T3108	Pardon Record, 1936-1941
	Cecil County	Indices	T3103	Criminal Docket, Index, 1976-1985
	Charles County	Records	T399	Docket, 1833-1946
	Charles County	Records	T2178	Stet Docket, 1897-1977
	Charles County	Records	T2663	Criminal Papers, 1950-1990 MSA, 1955-1993 OR, 1966-1996 CW(These are Repeat Offender cases involving Drugs and Violent Crimes only)
	Charles County	Records	T396	Court Papers, 1867-1949, 1955-1964
	Dorchester County	Records	T2091	Criminal Papers, 1949-1960, 1970 (see also CE201 & CE206) The 1970 file consists of court records relating to the criminal proceeding against H. Rap Brown in connection with the Cambridge riots of 1968. There are portions of this file that are sealed and cannot be circulated without a judges' order.
	Dorchester County	Records	T1955	Docket, 1792-1871, 1900-1914, 1933 MSA, OR (Please check Inventory)
	Dorchester County	Records	T3465	Stet Docket, 1876, 1916-1917, 1924, 1934, 1942, 1960-1967 (OR)

	Dorchester County	Records	T1955	Docket, 1792-1871, 1900-1914, 1933 MSA, OR (Please check Inventory)
	Dorchester County	Records	T3465	Stet Docket, 1876, 1916-1917, 1924, 1934, 1942, 1960-1967 (OR)
	Dorchester County	Indices	CE206	Criminal Docket, Index, 1949-1993
	Frederick County	Records	T193	Criminal Papers, 1900-1964 MSA, 1982-1991 CW
	Frederick County	Records	T174	Criminal Appeal Docket, 1916-1955
	Frederick County	Records	T104	Criminal Appeals, 1916-1937
	Frederick County	Records	T176	Court Papers, 1750-1929 (please try T193 first. The inventory is not very descriptive for most of these records)
	Frederick County	Records	T138	Criminal Docket, 1892-1960
	Frederick County	Records	T125	Stet Docket, 1866-1969
	Garrett County	Records	T2265	Docket, 1873-1953 MSA, Some scattered volumes at OR
	Garrett County	Records	T2268	Stet Docket, 1873-1952
	Garrett County	Records	T3630	Criminal Docket, 1928-1959 OR
	Garrett County	Records	T1033	Criminal Papers, 1873-1970 MSA, 1970-1985 OR
	Garrett County	Records	T3752	Criminal Appeals, 1970-1999 OR
	Garrett County	Records	T2658	Court Papers, 1873-1953 MSA, 1896-1997 OR
	Harford County	Records	T2248	Criminal Appeals 1961-1987 CW
	Harford County	Records	T3734	Criminal Papers, 1960-1990, recognizances 1996-2003 CW

Howard County	Records	T1032	Stet Docket, Criminal, 1912-1948
Howard County	Records	T3237	Criminal Papers, 1965-1979 HF
Howard County	Records	T1037	Criminal Docket, 1891-1922 HF, 1923-1970 OR
Howard County	Records	T461	Criminal Docket Sheets, 1948-1971
Howard County	Indices	T3611	Criminal Docket, Index, 1971-1986
Montgomery County	Records	T961	Docket, 1779-1952
Montgomery County	Records	T962	Stet Docket, 1892-1952
Montgomery County	Records	T2185	Criminal Papers, Transcripts and Exhibits, 1953-1985 MSA, 1973-1993 OR
Montgomery County	Records	CM1274	Criminal Appeals, 1993- no inventory
Prince George's County	Records	T760	Criminal Appeals, 1945-1966
Prince George's County	Records	T761	Criminal Papers, 1939-1976 (Mostly Transcripts, Large gaps between case numbers), 1962-1992 CW
Prince George's County	Records	C2930	Grand Jury Docket, 1955-1975
Prince George's County	Records	T726	Stet Docket, 1892-1947
Queen Anne's County	Records	C1385	Criminal Docket, 1851-1905
Prince Mary's County	Records	T3034	Stet Docket, 1918-1966 HF
Prince Mary's County	Records	T2241	Docket, 1905 MSA, 1951-1958
Prince Mary's County	Records	T2236	Court Papers, 1882-1972 HF

	Somerset County	Records	T770	Stet Docket, 1913-1931 MSA, 1931-1976 CW
	Somerset County	Records	T776	Docket, 1900-1949
	Somerset County	Records	T778	Grand Jury Docket, 1939-1946, 1965-1967
	Somerset County	Records	T836	Criminal Papers, 1947-1979 MSA, 1985-1991 CW (see T779 for cases prior to 1947)
	Somerset County	Records	T779	Court Papers, 1869-1885, 1900-1949
	Somerset County	Indices	T830	Docket, Index, 1947-1949
	Talbot County	Records	T1798	Criminal Docket, 1882-1897, 1935-1947, 1953-1956
	Talbot County	Records	T1790	Docket, 1780-1948, 1969-1972
	Talbot County	Records	T1787	Stet Docket, 1874-1945
	Talbot County	Records	T1961	Criminal Papers, 1956-1984 HF, 1956-1961 MSA,1949-1952, 1978, 1982-1983, 1986-1998 CW
	Talbot County	Records	T1800	Grand Jury Docket, 1866-1947
	Talbot County	Records	T1625	Court Papers, 1800-1994 MSA, HF, OR (See inventory, mostly civil records)
	Talbot County	Records	T1786	Parole Docket, 1910-1916 MSA, 1948-1964 OR
	Washington County	Records	T3334	Criminal Appeals Docket, 1953-1983 HF
	Washington County	Records	T3046	Stet Docket, 1852-1952
	Washington County	Records	T3065	Bastardy Papers, 1953-1964
	Washington County	Indices	T3050	Criminal Docket, Index, 1956-1967

	Wicomico County	Records	CM1072	Criminal Docket, 1900-1973 (Not Indexed)
	Wicomico County	Records	CM743	Docket, 1868-1903
	Wicomico County	Records	T460	Court Papers, 1868-1918
	Worcester County	Records	T3540	Criminal Docket, 1947-1961 OR
	Worcester County	Records	T3538	Court Docket, 1901-1949 OR
	Worcester County	Records	T3555	Stet Docket, 1876-1968 OR
	Worcester County	Records	CM1091	Criminal Papers, 1968-1969
	Worcester County	Records	T2551	Court Papers, 1852-1970 OR
	Worcester County	Indices	T3541	Criminal Docket, Index, 1925-1949 OR
	Worcester County	Indices	T3539	Court Docket, Index, 1810-1922 OR

Federal Criminal Court Records at the National Archives & Records Admin. (NARA)

NARA Mid Atlantic Region (Philadelphia)

900 Market Street, Philadelphia, PA, 19107-4292, (215) 606-0100

http://www.archives.gov/midatlantic/

philadelphia.archives@nara.gov

Record Type	ARC Identifier	Title	Description
	655566	Criminal Dockets, compiled 1864 - 1903	Textual Records from the U.S. Circuit Court for the District of Maryland. Baltimore Term. (03/21/1892 - 01/01/1912)
	278841	Criminal Case Files, compiled 1795 - 1903	Textual Records from the U.S. Circuit Court for the District of Maryland. Baltimore Term. (03/21/1892 - 01/01/1912)

	278859	Criminal Case Files, compiled 1841 - 1981	Textual Records from the U.S. District Court for the District of Maryland. (ca. 1952 - 10/1994)
	570403	Criminal Case Files, compiled 1907 - 1933	Textual Records from the U.S. District Court for the District of Maryland. Cumberland Term. (03/21/1892 - ca. 1952)
	655562	Criminal Dockets, compiled 1907 - 1933	Textual Records from the U.S. District Court for the District of Maryland. Cumberland Term. (03/21/1892 - ca. 1952)
	3318897	Criminal Dockets, compiled 1867 - 1909	Textual Records from the U.S. District Court for the District of Maryland. Office of U.S. Commissioners. (1896 - 1968)
	654306	Criminal Dockets, compiled 1841 - 1969	Textual Records from the U.S. District Court for the District of Maryland. (ca. 1952 - 10/1994)
	2945845	Civil and Criminal Dockets, compiled 1790 - 1877	Textual Records from the U.S. District Court for the District of Maryland. (09/24/1789 - 03/21/1892?)
	3060124	Rough Criminal Docket, compiled 1905 - 1908	Textual Records from the U.S. District Court for the District of Maryland. Baltimore Term. (03/21/1892 - ca. 1952)
	3179974	Criminal Docket, compiled 1877 - 1886	Textual Records from the Department of Justice. Office of the U.S. Marshal for the District of Maryland. (07/01/1870 - 12/17/1956)

Maryland Executions

http://users.bestweb.net/~rg/execution/MARYLAND.htm

Maryland Department of Corrections Inmate Lookup

http://www.dpscs.state.md.us/inmate/

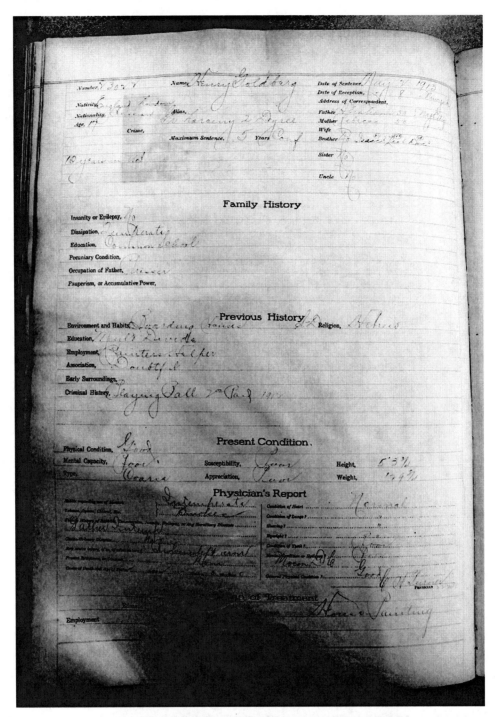

Entry for Henry Goldberg (Louis Shomberg) in the Biographical registers and receiving blotters, 1879-1957, Elmira Reformatory, RG 0141, New York State Archives. Courtesy of the New York State Archives and the New York Department of Corrections.

Massachusetts

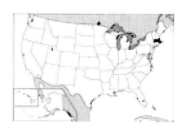

Massachusetts State Archives

220 Morrissey Blvd., Boston, MA 02125, (617) 727-2816

www.sec.state.ma.us/arc/

archives@sec.state.ma.us

Record Type	Title	Description
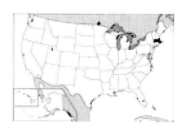	Records of State Institutions	Many of the human services agency records held by the Archives document the activities of state institutions, including prisons. Case histories, records of admissions and dismissals, and other registers provide detail on the lives and families of people at these institutions. Records may be restricted to preserve the privacy of individuals at the institution. Researchers should contact the Archives before planning a visit to use these records in order to determine what restrictions will apply.

Judicial Archives

Supreme Judicial Court Archives, 16th Floor, Highrise Court House, 3 Pemberton Square
Boston, MA 02108, Phone: 617-557-1082

http://www.sec.state.ma.us/arc/arccol/colidx.htm

Record Type	Title	Description
	Court and Judicial Records at the MA State Archives	The Judicial Archives contains the pre-1860 records of the predecessor courts of the Superior Court (Court of General Sessions of the Peace and Inferior Court of Common Pleas) for 9 counties. Other records include Supreme Judicial Court and Superior Court of Judicature; a limited number of County Court records; records of some Justices of the Peace, and records of a small number of special courts. As some collections of court records may still remain in original court houses, the public is encouraged to contact the Archives prior to beginning research utilizing court records. Detailed inventories, finding aids and guides are available at the Archives.

Federal Criminal Court Records at the National Archives & Records Admin. (NARA)

NARA Northeast Region (Boston)

Frederick C. Murphy Federal Center, 380 Trapelo Road, Waltham, MA, 02452-6399

(781) 663-0130

http://www.archives.gov/northeast/

waltham.archives@nara.gov

Record Type	ARC Identifier	Title	Description
	592786	Criminal Case Files, compiled 1917 - 1983	Textual Records from the U.S. District Court for the District of Massachusetts. (1789 -)
	2953531	Dockets, compiled 10/1800 - 05/1874	Textual Records from the U.S. Circuit Court for the District of Massachusetts. (1789 - 01/01/1912)
	610796	Case Files, compiled 1790 - 1911	Textual Records from the U.S. Circuit Court for the District of Massachusetts. (1789 - 01/01/1912)
	2827638	Judgment Docket, compiled 1912 - 1949	Textual Records from the U.S. District Court for the District of Massachusetts. (1789 -)
	2953580	Final Record Books, compiled 05/1790 - 12/1911	Textual Records from the U.S. Circuit Court for the District of Massachusetts. (1789 - 01/01/1912)
	2826597	Judges' Opinion Books, compiled 06/09/1915 - 12/31/1944	Textual Records from the U.S. District Court for the District of Massachusetts. (1789 -)

Executions in Massachusetts

 http://users.bestweb.net/~rg/execution/MASSACHUSETTS.htm

Massachusetts Department of Corrections Offender Lookup

 http://www.mass.gov/?pageID=eopsmodulechunk&L=3&L0=Home&L1=Public +Safety+Agencies&L2=Massachusetts+Department+of+Correction&sid=Eeops&b= terminalcontent&f=doc_locate_an_offender&csid=Eeops

Michigan

Michigan State Archives

702 W Kalamazoo St, Lansing, MI 48915-1609, (517) 373-1408

www.michigan.gov/archivesofmi

email: https://www.sos.state.mi.us/forms/request_frm.html

Record Type	Location	Title	Description
	RG 83-86	Department of Corrections, Prisoner index card catalog dated ca. 1839-1980.	Offers the names of prisoners serving in Michigan's correctional institutions providing length of sentences, dates of sentence, registration identification number, and counties where crimes occurred. Includes any parole or discharge dates. A few index cards include photographs of inmates. Arranged alphabetically by prisoner names (series 1).
	RG 76-97	Marquette Branch Prisons, Inmate record books dated 1889-1925.	Lists prisoner's name and alias, number, date of entrance to prison, county of conviction and date of sentence, term, nature of crime, measurements, physical description, age, remarks, and in most instances photographs. Arranged numerically (series 1).
	RG 82-112	Marquette Branch Prisons, Record of convicts dated 1922-1937.	Ledger format lists prisoner number, name, term of sentence, county or court, sentence and receipt dates, date of discharge, and crime. Arranged numerically (series 1). Description of prisoners dated 1927-1938. Includes photographs, name, crime, general description, relatives, physical markings, Bertillion measurements, number of children, years in school, personal habits (i.e., drinking or smoking), plus discharge and transfer information. Arranged numerically (series 2).
	RG 87-138	Marquette Branch Prisons, Prisoner registers dated ca. 1937-1957.	Offers name, identification number, county where prisoner was born, date of birth, date of transfer, aliases, length of sentence, crime committed as well as any ownership of real estate. Arranged numerically by prisoner number (series 1).

	RG 64-53	Ionia Prison, Description of inmates, 1874-1892.	Offers date, registration number, nativity, offense, sentence, residence, race, height, and personal description. Entry is chronological (series 7). Record of prisoners, ca. 1885-1944. Gives inmate number, name, county of residence, dates received, sentence, education, and physical description (series 8).
	RG 80-27	Ionia Prison, Register of inmates dated 1874-1883, 1925, 1926, 1928.	Offers date of sentence, registration number, name, term, date and kind of discharge. Arranged chronologically by date of sentence and numerically by registration number (series 14). Alphabetical register of inmates dated 1919-1922; 1926-1935. Offers date of sentence, registration number, name, term of assignment, "lock, cell, ward," expiration of sentence, plus kind and date of discharge (series 15). Register of residents dated 1888-1960. Offers name, alias, registration number, date of sentence, physical description, when received, age, past occupation, marital status, nationality, citizenship, nature of crime, as well as criminal history. Arranged chronologically by date received (series 16). Index to register of residents dated ca. 1883-1908; ca. 1940. Offers name, register number, and date of expiration. Arranged alphabetically by first letter of surname (series 17).
	RG 64-50	State Prison of Southern Michigan at Jackson, Record of commitment dated 1839-1937.	Offers number, name, age, term, date received, occupation, offense, date of sentence, county, physical description, detention record, date of discharge, and remarks about parole, return, transfer and discharge. Arranged as received (series 7). Record of prisoners dated 1900-1926. Offers inmate's number, name, county of residence, dates received, sentenced, escaped, returned, transferred, dead, pardoned, and discharged. Gives physical description, offense, summary of convictions as well as use of tobacco. Photographs of prisoners are included. Arranged numerically (series 10). Indexes to convict registers, ca. 1875-1960. Offers number and name of prisoner. Arranged alphabetically (series 11).
	RG 56-27	State Prison of Southern Michigan at Jackson, Convict identifications dated 1875-1884.	Offers name, identification number, age, nativity, charge and sentence. Arranged chronologically (series 16).

	RG 77-7	State Prison of Southern Michigan at Jackson, Record of inmates dated 1925-1926.	Offers inmate's name, number, term of sentence, birth place, race, educational level, parent's name, employment history, previous criminal record, and military service. Arranged chronologically (series 1).

Circuit Court Records at the Michigan Archives

Record Type	Location (Record Group)	Series	County	Title/Date
	2008-30	6	Alger	Circuit Court Calendars & Journals, 1885-1975
	2008-30	7	Alger	Chancery Court Calendars & Journals, 1886-1972
	2008-30	8	Alger	Criminal Court Calendars & Records, 1887-1958
	71-19	15	Bay	Docket, 1900-1922
	67-24	18	Berrien*	Chancery Rule Book, 1847-1886
	67-24	19	Berrien*	Common Rule Book, 1843-1907
	67-109	16	Berrien*	Proceedings, 1839-1841
	67-48	1	Berrien*	Communist Party Exhibits, 1921-1922
	76-74	1	Branch	Journals, 1833-1886
	76-75	1	Branch	Chancery Orders, 1847-1886
	91-452	1	Calhoun	Court Records, 1838-1839, 1847-1959
	91-453	2	Calhoun	Case Files, 1913-1957

	75-35	1	Cass*	Common Rule Book, 1839-1864
	77-15	1	Charlevoix	Chancery Files, 1884-1913
	77-15	2	Charlevoix	Criminal Files, 1890-1913
	77-15	3	Charlevoix	Law Files, 1883-1913
	77-15	4	Charlevoix	Journals, 1869-1957
	93-123	1	Chippewa	Chancery Case Files, 1840-1882
	98-148	1	Clinton	Case Files (No Index), c. 1883-1871
	71-95	2	Dickinson	Jurors Time Table, 1892-1907
	80-15	2	Eaton	Case Files, 1931-1941
	81-44	3	Genesee	Court Records, 1837-1889
	81-44	4	Genesee	Case Files, 1841-1870
	2007-19	1	Gratiot	Law & Criminal Calendars/Dockets, 1857-1949
	2007-19	2	Gratiot	Chancery Calendars, 1858-1963
	2007-19	3	Gratiot	Divorce Calendars, 1899-1949
	2007-19	16	Gratiot	Chancery Case Files, 1858-1940
	2007-19	18	Gratiot	Criminal Case Files, 1857-1940
	2007-19	21	Gratiot	Justice of the Peace Records, 1904-1976

	85-10	2	Hillsdale	Chancery Records, 1847-1939
	85-10	7	Hillsdale	Criminal Records, 1885-1932
	85-10	16	Hillsdale	Criminal Case Files, 1835-1903
	85-10	17	Hillsdale	Chancery Case Files, 1840-1910
	89-465	1-3	Houghton**	Case Files, 1849-1953
	97-343	1-3	Houghton**	Case Files, 1849-1953
	89-284	1	Ingham	Chancery Records, 1903-1950
	89-284	2	Ingham	Criminal Calendar, 1922-1952
	89-284	10	Ingham	Criminal Case Files, 1921-1949
	79-51	1	Ionia	Chancery Record, 1848-1894
	78	2	Isabella	Chancery Proceedings, 1867-1952
	78	3	Isabella	Criminal Proceedings, 1914-1957
	84-75	1	Kalamazoo*	Criminal Case Files, 1857-1931
	84-75	3	Kalamazoo*	Chancery Case Files, 1821-1847
	84-75	4	Kalamazoo*	Criminal Calendars, 1857-1931
	84-75	6	Kalamazoo*	Chancery Case Files, 1831-1847
	84-75	7	Kalamazoo*	Chancery Calendars, 1836-1850
	84-75	22	Kalamazoo*	Indexes, 1860-1920

	84-76	2	Kalamazoo*	Sheriff Records, 1931-1972
	71-44	10	Kent	Chancery Cases, 1859-1861
	71-49	11	Kent	Journal of Proceedings, 1875-1926
	78-77	1	Lake	Case Files, 1871-1963
	89-458	1	Lenawee	Transcripts, 1902-1908
	76-68	3	Livingston	Judgment Books, 1841-1898
	71-116	1	Mackinac	Case Files, 1817-1879
	72-136	1	Mackinac	Case Files, 1820-1894
	79-94	1-2	Macomb	Case Files, 1818-1856
	75-70	3	Manitou	Common Rule Book, 1872-1894, Journal, 1870-1894, Calendar, 1857-1892
	69-54	11	Mecosta	Chancery Orders, 1859-1874
	77-91	5	Midland***	Common Rule Book, 1857-1924
	62-55	2	Monroe	Docket, 1826-1833
	84-87	2	Monroe	Court Records, 1805-1881
	84-31	3	Muskegon	Chancery Calendars, 1850-1931
	84-31	9	Muskegon	Criminal Calendars, 1873-1931
	84-31	17	Muskegon	Criminal Case Files, 1876-1931
	84-31	18	Muskegon	Chancery Case Files, 1858-1939

	67-56	1	Oakland	Testimony and Statements, 1943-1946
	67-56	2	Oakland	Selected Cases, 1943-1960
	67-56	3	Oakland	Selected Complaints, 1940-1943
	67-21	11	Saginaw	Rules, 1956
	67-7	16	St. Clair	Civil and Criminal Accounts Received, 1877-1883
	80-64	3	St. Clair	Chancery Calendars, 1847-1870
	80-64	8	St. Clair	Criminal Docket, 1840-1883
	80-64	9	St. Clair	Criminal Case Files, 1840-1884
	80-64	12	St. Clair	Chancery Case Files, 1835-1871
	67-53	1	Van Buren*	Case Files, 1871-1929
	68-28	1	Van Buren*	Case Files, 1845-1887
	68-28	3	Van Buren*	Chancery Cases, 1848-1880
	70-54	1	Van Buren*	Chancery Cases, 1855-1885
	96-178	1	Washtenaw	Criminal Case Files, 1836-1876
	96-178	2	Washtenaw	Chancery Case Files, 1834-1876
	96-226	4	Washtenaw	Criminal Journal/Calendar, 1835-1880
	96-226	5	Washtenaw	Chancery Journal/Calendar, 1838-1870
	85-34	3	Wayne	Chancery Court Records, 1847-1903

	85-34	4	Wayne	Superior Court Records, 1873-1889
	85-34	5	Wayne	Circuit Court Records, 1833-1909

Notes: additional records can be found at:

http://www.michigan.gov/documents/mhc_sa_circular37_49972_7.pdf

* Western Michigan University Archives

*** Central Michigan University Archives

Pardon and Parole Records at the Michigan Archives

Record Type	Location (Record Group)	Lot/Box	Agency	Title
	66-44	4/	Corrections	Paroles, 1948-1951
	79-36	20/1	Corrections	Parole and Pardon Board, 1953-1968
	80-27	22/V14	Corrections	Paroled Convicts, 1947-1950
	80-38	23/4	Corrections	Parole Board, 1965-1971
	80-38	23/7	Corrections	Paroles, 1968-1969
	80-38	23/8	Corrections	Parole and Probation, 1954-1956
	80-38	23/17	Corrections	Parole Board, 1972
	80-38	23/24	Corrections	Parole Board, 1973
	80-38	23/31	Corrections	Parole Board, 1974
	80-38	23/41	Corrections	Parole Board, 1975

	80-38	23/56	Corrections	Parole Board, 1976
	81-55	26/6	Corrections	Parole Board, 1977
	82-01	27/7	Corrections	Parole Board, 1978
	82-112	28/104	Corrections	Paroled Prisoners, 1911-1926
	83-16	30/5	Corrections	Parole Board, 1979
	83-92	33/2	Corrections	Parole Board, 1974
	83-92	33/8	Corrections	Parole Board, 1975
	84-03	36/2	Corrections	Parole Board, 1980
	84-66	39/3	Corrections	Probation and Parole, 1972-1973
	84-66	39/4	Corrections	Staff Meeting Parole Board, 1972
	85-66	43/4	Corrections	Paroles, 1972-1974
	85-66	43/5	Corrections	Parole Board, 1972-1974
	86-17	44/4	Corrections	Parole Board, 197501977
	87-02	45/16	Corrections	Parole Board, 1982-1983
	88-01	49/5	Corrections	Parole Board, 1984
	88-266	51/13	Corrections	Parole Board, 1984-1985
	92-440	74/5	Corrections	Parole Board, 1990
	85-52	27/113-127	Executive	Pardons and Commutations, 1961-1982

	RG	Box/Folder	Branch	Description
	RG44	1/59	Executive	Pardon Board, 1873-1909
	RG44	1/84	Executive	Pardon Board, 1901
	RG44	1/185	Executive	Pardon Board, 1885-1910
	RG44	1/244	Executive	Pardon Board Reports, 1909
	RG50	1/20	Executive	State Pardon Board, 1920
	RG50	1/21	Executive	Pardons and Paroles, 1921-1922
	RG45	1/6	Executive	Pardon Board, 1911
	RG45	1/8	Executive	Pardon Board, 1912
	RG48	1/14	Executive	Probation and Parole, 1922
	RG48	1/22	Executive	Paroled Prisoners, 1922
	RG48	1/30	Executive	Pardons and Paroles, 1923
	RG49	1/15-16	Executive	Pardons and Paroles, 1927
	RG49	1/77-79	Executive	Pardons and Paroles, 1928
	RG49	1/138-141	Executive	Pardons and Paroles, 1929
	RG49	1/181-190	Executive	Pardons and Paroles, 1930
	RG42	1/5-6	Executive	Pardons and Paroles, 1943
	RG42	1/21-22	Executive	Pardons and Paroles, 1944
	RG42	1/36-38	Executive	Pardons and Paroles, 1945

	RG42	1/130-131	Executive	Pardons and Paroles, 1946
	RG43	1/9	Executive	Pardons and Paroles, 1947
	RG43	1/39	Executive	Pardons and Paroles, 1948
	RG43	1/95	Executive	Parole Board, 1947
	RG43	1/100	Executive	Parole Board, 1948
	RG43	1/110-112	Executive	Pardons and Paroles, 1947-1948
	88-269	36/13	Executive	Pardons and Paroles, 1969
	88-269	36/45	Executive	Pardons and Paroles, 1970
	88-269	36/86	Executive	Pardons and Paroles, 1971
	88-269	36/120	Executive	Pardons and Paroles, 1972
	88-269	36/155-156	Executive	Pardons and Paroles, 1973
	88-269	36/204-205	Executive	Pardons and Paroles, 1974
	88-269	36/251-252	Executive	Pardons and Paroles, 1975
	88-269	36/296	Executive	Pardons and Paroles, 1976
	88-269	36/336-337	Executive	Pardons and Paroles, 1977
	88-269	36/439	Executive	Pardons and Paroles, 1980
	88-269	36/481	Executive	Pardons and Paroles, 1981
	88-269	36/523	Executive	Pardons and Paroles, 1982

	88-269	36/1652	Executive	Pardons and Paroles, 1976
	56-26	3/139-148	State	Pardons, 1841-1942
	56-26	3/149-163	State	Paroles, 1895-1921
	84-54	139/V10	State	Commutations, 1906-1944
	84-54	139/V11	State	Pardons, 1862-1942
	84-54	139/V12-13	State	Paroles, 1895-1921
	64-50	3/V38-39	State Prison	Paroles, 1889-1904

Note: additional records can be found at:
http://www.michigan.gov/documents/mhc_sa_circular48_50005_7.pdf

Criminal Justice Information Center (CJIC)

http://www.michigan.gov/msp/0,1607,7-123-1589_1878_8311-16223--,00.html

The Criminal Justice Information Center (CJIC) is the state repository for all arrests, charges, and convictions of serious crimes committed in Michigan. All law enforcement agencies, prosecutors, and courts send information that is matched together and forms the criminal history record database. Here is the Criminal Records Reporting Manual.

Criminal history background checks are performed either through a search by name or a search using fingerprints. Fingerprints are done only if a state or federal statute or executive order or rule requires such a search. A criminal history record includes personal descriptors regarding the person and information on misdemeanor convictions and felony arrests and convictions.

A record is built from reports provided by Michigan law enforcement, prosecutors, courts and prisons. Michigan law enforcement agencies are required to provide fingerprints and arrest information when a person is charged with an offense punishable by over 92 days, which includes all felony and the serious misdemeanor offenses. Other misdemeanor offenses are reported with fingerprints after the person is convicted of the charge and if the sentence includes imprisonment with fines and costs totaling more than $100.00.

Criminal convictions are public information, therefore, anyone can request a search of criminal histories. The search does not include a search of any other state or national criminal record system; nor is a warrant search included. There will be a "no record meeting dissemination criteria" statement provided when there is no record located. If the search locates a criminal history record, the record provided is considered a possible match (common names, aliases, reporting/entry errors or the defendant use of names other than their own could result in a response for the name searched). The decisions affected by the record should be reserved until the subject of the search has an opportunity to review the information and verify its content.

Federal Criminal Court Records at the National Archives & Records Admin. (NARA)

NARA Great Lakes Region (Chicago),
7358 South Pulaski Road, Chicago, IL 60629-5898, (773) 948-9001
http://www.archives.gov/great-lakes/
chicago.archives@nara.gov

Record Type	ARC Identifier	Title	Description
	1112286	Criminal Case Files, compiled 1878 - 1965	Textual Records from the U.S. District Court for the Northern (Marquette) Division of the Western District of Michigan. (06/19/1878 -)
	1107016	Criminal Case Files, compiled 1963 - 1969	Textual Records from the U.S. District Court for the Northern (Flint) Division of the Eastern District of Michigan. (02/10/1954 -)
	1127014	Criminal Case Files, compiled 1894 - 1911, documenting the period 1837 - 1911	Textual Records from the U.S. Circuit Court for the Southern (Detroit) Division of the Eastern District of Michigan. (04/30/1894 - 01/01/1912)
	1112213	Criminal Case Files, compiled 1878 - 1969, documenting the period 1863 - 1969	Textual Records from the U.S. District Court for the Southern (Grand Rapids) Division of the Western District of Michigan. (06/19/1878 -)
	1087335	Criminal Case Files, compiled 1894 - 1971, documenting the period 1851 - 1971	Textual Records from the U.S. District Court for the Southern (Detroit) Division of the Eastern District of Michigan. (04/30/1894 -)
	722103	Case Files, compiled 1924 - 1976	Textual Records from the U.S. Court of Appeals for the Sixth Circuit. (1948 -)

	281838	Criminal Case Files, compiled 1863 - 1969	Photographs and other Graphic Materials from the U.S. District Court for the Southern (Grand Rapids) Division of the Western District of Michigan. (06/19/1878 -)

Michigan Court Records

 http://www.mymichigangenealogy.com/mi_records.htm

Records at the county level are the responsibility of different offices-office of the county clerk: birth, death, and marriage; register of deeds: land records; office of the probate judge: probate files; and circuit court office or office of the county clerk: circuit court records.

County circuit court records are kept by the county clerk or the circuit court clerk in the appropriate county office. There are no state indexes to these records.

Michigan Executions

 http://users.bestweb.net/~rg/execution/MICHIGAN.htm

Michigan Offender Lookup Facility

http://www.state.mi.us/mdoc/asp/otis2.html

Minnesota

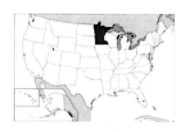

Minnesota State Archives
345 W. Kellogg Blvd., St. Paul, MN 55102-1906, (651-259-3000)
http://www.mnhs.org/preserve/records/index.htm
reference@mnhs.org

Record Type	Location	Author	Title	Description
	MN Hist. Soc., Manuscripts Notesbooks: Call #: ALPH	Maccabee, Paul, 1955-	St. Paul gangster history research collection, 1981-1995	Maccabee's book focuses on the personalities, places, and events which made St. Paul a haven for criminals of the 1920s and 1930s gangster era. 7.0 cu. ft. (7 boxes)
	MN Hist. Soc., See State Archives Notebooks	MN State Reformatory for Men	Inmate case files, Willow River Camp, [ca. 1952]-1972	Case files for youths remanded to the Willow River Camp correctional facility by the Youth Conservation Commission, following physical and psychological testing at the commission's reception canter located at the St. Cloud Reformatory.
	MN Hist. Soc., See State Archives Notebooks	MN State Reformatory for Women, Shakopee	Inmate case files (minors), 1948-1977	Discharged inmate case files, for minors admitted to the reformatory under the supervision of the Youth Conservation Commission.
	MN Hist. Soc., See State Archives Notebooks	MN State Reformatory for Men	Inmate case files, Annex for Defective Delinquents, 1945-1961.	Files DD5 - DD288 (incomplete).

	MN Hist. Soc., See State Archives Notebooks	MN Home School for Girle	Inmate records, 1937-1998.	Records containing information on individual inmates, including Pioneer Cottage isolation reports (1937-1946); Youth Conservation Commission numerical admission record (1948-1966); runaway activity log (1965-1997); more
	MN Hist. Soc., See State Archives Notebooks	MN State Prison (Stillwater, MN)	Photographs of inmates (negatives), [1930s]-[1970s].	Both a side and front view of each inmate are included on each negative. Each negative shows a case file number on a "menu board" below the inmate
	MN Hist. Soc., See State Archives Notebooks	MN State Reformatory for Women, Shakopee	Inmate case files, 1919-1977	Discharged inmate case files, nos. 1-1707, for inmates admitted from 1919 to 1977.
	MN Hist. Soc., See State Archives Notebooks	MN State Prison (Stillwater, MN) Custody Office	Inmate files, 1910-1962 (bulk 1940-1962).	Files containing inmates' records, primarily requests for changes in custody status, job assignment, or various privileges.
	MN Hist. Soc., See State Archives Notebooks	MN State Prison (Stillwater, MN)	Convict record, 1876-1915.	Admission (registration) data and details on the inmates' time in prison, including a record of solitary confinement, good time lost, and parole and discharge.
	MN Hist. Soc., See State Archives Notebooks	MN State Prison (Stillwater, MN)	Record of sentences, 1856-1926.	Information recorded may include the individual inmate's name and number and data on the crime; sentence; parole, pardon, or commutation; and transfer, release, or death.
	MN Hist. Soc., See State Archives Notebooks	MN State Training School for Boys	Inmate case files, [1915] - [1963].	In three sections, each separately box-numbered: 1915-1955 A-K; 1915-1955 K-Z; 1955-1963 A-Z.
	MN Hist. Soc., See State Archives Notebooks	MN State Reformatory for Men	Inmate photograph scrapbooks, 1896-[ca.1898].	Fairly complete for inmate numbers 160-498

	MN Hist. Soc., See State Archives Notebooks	MN State Prison (Stillwater, MN)	Photographs of inmates (glass plate negatives), 1895-1919 and 1926-1929.	Both a side and front view of each inmate are included on each plate. Some negatives are missing.
	MN Hist. Soc., See State Archives Notebooks	MN State Reformatory for Men	Inmate registers, 1893-1927 (bulk 1898-1927).	Essentially an intake record, apparently compiled at the time of admission to the reformatory, containing summary descriptive and background information about individual prisoners, many of whom were juveniles.
	MN Hist. Soc., See State Archives Notebooks	MN State Reformatory for Men	Trial transcripts, 1891-1970.	Transcripts of proceedings from inmates' district court jury trials. Transcripts were created for only a small proportion of the inmate case files.
	MN Hist. Soc., See State Archives Notebooks	MN State Prison (Stillwater, MN)	Case files (discharged inmate files), [1890s] - 1978.	Correspondence, reports, administrative forms, and related papers documenting the incarceration, parole, and discharge of prisoners at the Minnesota state prison. A prisoner's file may include the admittance record; correspondence with the sentencing court and with relatives; record of the inmate's work, discipline, and other activities while in prison; physician's reports; correspondence with criminal justice agencies in other states; photograph (in later files); and parole reports.
	MN Hist. Soc., See State Archives Notebooks	MN State Training School for Boys	Admission and discharge records, 1890-1993.	Daily records of admissions and discharges from the school; information recorded includes inmate number, name, where received from or sent to, and summary statistics for each month.
	MN Hist. Soc., See State Archives Notebooks	MN State Reformatory for Men	Indexes to inmate records, 1889-1910 [microform].	Two indexes to case files (nos. 1-2614) of inmates who entered the St. Cloud State Reformatory during the years 1889-1910.

	MN Hist. Soc., See State Archives Notebooks	MN State Reformatory for Men	Indexes to inmate records, 1889-1979.	Photocopy of a Cardex index to the reformatory's "base files" (general inmate case files).
	MN Hist. Soc., See State Archives Notebooks	MN State Reformatory for Men	Inmate case files, 1889-1978.	File numbers 1-30,281, constituting the institution's "base files" (general inmate case files) for inmates discharged prior to July 1, 1978.
	MN Hist. Soc., See State Archives Notebooks	MN State Reformatory for Men	Misconduct records, 1889-1902.	Volumes 1 and 2 (1889-1897) contain a record of inmate name, number, maximum sentence, minimum sentence, date received, and a weekly tabular record of misconduct reports (if any). Volumes 3 and 4 (1892-1902) are labeled "Register of Vital Statistics and Misconduct Record" and contain, besides a tabular record of conduct, substantial data regarding each inmate's background, appearance, and health.
	MN Hist. Soc., See State Archives Notebooks	MN State Prison (Stillwater, MN)	Punishment records, 1887-1972.	Daily logs of punishment given inmates for violating prison rules. The volumes list name of inmate and officer involved, register (inmate) number, violation, punishment, and general remarks.
	MN Hist. Soc., See State Archives Notebooks	MN State Reformatory for Men	Inmate history and record, 1887-1935.	The volumes for 1896-1935 contain two-page records of descriptive and background data on each inmate.
	MN Hist. Soc., See State Archives Notebooks	MN State Prison (Stillwater, MN)	Inmate register sheets, 1880-1978 (bulk 1915-1978).	Admission (registration) data and details of each inmate's background and behavior in prison, including information about his crime and trial, prior arrests, family background, misconduct in prison, visitors while in prison, and parole.
	MN Hist. Soc., See State Archives Notebooks	MN State Prison (Stillwater, MN)	Indexes to inmates, 1876-1979.	Indexes of inmates, listing register (inmate) number, name, and scattered information on the inmate's background, crime, and date of parole, discharge, or transfer.

	MN Hist. Soc., See State Archives Notebooks	MN State Training School for Boys	Inmate history records, 1868-1923.	Variously titled as "History Book," "Record of Commitment and History of Inmates," and "Statistical Record," with some overlap for 1868-1884, and no record at all for 1893-1897.
	MN Hist. Soc., See State Archives Notebooks	MN State Training School for Boys	Inmate case files and commitment papers, 1868-1917.	By case file number.
	MN Hist. Soc., Microfilm Call #: SAM 245	MN State Prison (Stillwater, MN)	Indexes to inmate records, 1862-1924 [microform].	In most volumes, names are grouped alphabetically by the first letter of the inmate's surname, and within each group are listed in the order in which the inmates entered the prison.
	MN Hist. Soc., See State Archives Notebooks	MN State Prison (Stillwater, MN)	Record of sentences, 1856-1926.	Information recorded may include the individual inmate's name and number and data on the crime; sentence; parole, pardon, or commutation; and transfer, release, or death.
	MN Hist. Soc., See State Archives Notebooks	MN State Prison (Stillwater, MN)	Convict registers, 1854-1902.	Registration (admission) data on inmates upon entering the prison. Each entry lists inmate's name, register (inmate) number, county of admission (where the trial was held and sentence imposed), date of admission (in some early records this may be the sentencing date instead), crime, age, state or country of birth, and date of discharge.
	MN Hist. Soc., See State Archives Notebooks	MN Home School for Girls	Discharged resident cards, [ca. 1911] - [ca. 1998].	The master index cards (bulk 1930s-mid 1990s) may provide data on the following areas: name, OID number, birth date, date of nineteenth or twenty-first birthday, date received at the school, home county and town, religious affiliation, residence cottage as the school, offense, names and addresses of relatives, and discharge or parole date.

	MN Hist. Soc., See State Archives Notebooks	Minnesota. County Court (Wright County).	Criminal registry and judgment books, 1972-1981.	The volumes are indexed; each volume may contain documents that pre- or post-date the individual volume ranges.
	MN Hist. Soc., See State Archives Notebooks	Minnesota. District Court (Otter Tail County).	Criminal case files index, 1969-1983.	A file-by-file list of microfilmed criminal case files 3325-5189 (1969-1983).
	MN Hist. Soc., See State Archives Notebooks	Pope County (MN) Probate Court. Municipal Division.	Register of criminal actions and judgment book 2, 1969-1977.	Volume is indexed.
	MN Hist. Soc., See State Archives Notebooks	Lyon County (MN) Probate Court	Criminal action registry and judgment book, 1968-1971.	This volume covers the transition period between the abolition of the justice and municipal courts and the establishment of the county court, which in Lyon County was handled via the probate court.
	MN Hist. Soc., See State Archives Notebooks	Minnesota. County Court (Anoka County). Municipal Court Division.	Criminal docket, 1968-1972.	Physical Details 1 v.
	MN Hist. Soc., See State Archives Notebooks	Roseau (MN) Municipal Court.	Civil and criminal docket, 1962-1972.	Physical Details 6 folders in partial box.

	MN Hist. Soc., See State Archives Notebooks	Aitkin County (MN) Probate Court. Municipal Court Division.	Civil, criminal, and traffic registry and judgment books, 1960-1981.	Criminal action registry and judgment books (1960-1981).
	MN Hist. Soc., See State Archives Notebooks	Pennington County (MN) Probate Court.	Criminal dockets, 1960-1975.	The docket entries give the parties involved, nature of the case, and actions taken.
	MN Hist. Soc., See State Archives Notebooks	Wright County (MN) Probate Court.	Civil, criminal, and traffic registry and judgment books, 1960-1972.	Criminal action registry and judgments (1960-1972).
	MN Hist. Soc., See State Archives Notebooks	Hopkins (MN) Municipal Court.	Records, 1959-1964.	Judgment index and register (1959-1964), criminal docket (1961-1964), and civil dockets (1960-1964).
	MN Hist. Soc., See State Microfilm Call # SAM 441	Duluth (MN) Municipal Court.	Criminal records, 1958-1960, 1962-1973 [microform].	These books include a summary record, usually consisting of one page, noting the defendant, the charge, names of attorneys, sentence imposed, and sentence completed (fine paid, time served, etc.).
	MN Hist. Soc., See State Archives Notebooks	MN Dept. of Corrections	Probation case registers, 1947-1979.	Three series of probation case registers, giving case number, name of individual, county, judge, offense, and data on sentence or probation. One volume lists probation date, county of residence, court, and name of probation supervisor, and is believed to represent probations granted and supervised directly by the district, probate, or juvenile courts.

	MN Hist. Soc., See State Archives Notebooks	MN State Training School for Boys	Parole records, 1895-1962.	Record of parolees and returns (1895-1942) and parole calendars (1920-1935), both with detailed information on inmates paroled each month. Also parole and discharge papers (1909-1951)
	MN Hist. Soc., See State Archives Notebooks	MN State Prison (Stillwater, MN)	Parole records, 1892-1973.	The parole record books (1892-1920) give name, prison register number, information on the crime and sentence, date of parole, employer and type of work, and a synopsis of reports to the parole officer. After 1920, there are only summary lists of parolees and monthly statistics.
	MN Hist. Soc., See State Archives Notebooks	MN Board of Pardons	Pardon Calendars, 1897-1992	Minutes (titled "calendars" by the board) of the Board of Pardons, largely comprising a record of actions on individual pardon applications, although other actions of the board are also mentioned. The pardon applications are often discussed in some detail.
	MN Hist. Soc., See State Archives Notebooks	MN Board of Pardons	Pardon Applications	Application forms or letters formally requesting a pardon or commutation of sentence; letters, petitions, and/or affidavits in support and/or opposition; recommendations of the prosecuting attorney, trial judge, and/or trial jury; and sometimes trial transcripts, other background items, additional documentation submitted by the requestor, or other supporting papers.
	MN Hist. Soc., See State Archives Notebooks	MN Board of Pardons	Pardon application registers, 1897-1934.	Registers of applications for pardon or commutation of sentence submitted to the Pardon Board by inmates of state, and some county and local, correctional institutions.

	MN Hist. Soc., See State Archives Notebooks	MN State Prison (Stillwater, MN)	Case files: Pardons extraordinary, [undated].	Files removed from the main series of inmate case files upon the inmate's receipt of a pardon extraordinary, which restores all civil rights and, in effect, nullifies the conviction and purges the criminal record.
	MN Hist. Soc., See State Archives Notebooks	MN State Reformatory for Men	Inmate case files: pardons extraordinary, [undated].	Files removed from the main series of inmate case files upon the inmate's receipt of a pardon extraordinary.
	MN Hist. Soc., See State Archives Notebooks	MN State Reformatory for Women, Shakopee	Inmate case files: pardons extraordinary, [undated].	Files removed from the main series of inmate case files upon the inmate's receipt of a pardon extraordinary.

Federal Records at the National Archives & Records Admin. (NARA)

NARA Central Plains Region (Kansas City),
400 West Pershing Road, Kansas City, MO 64108, (816) 268-8000
http://www.archives.gov/central-plains/kansas-city/
kansascity.archives@nara.gov

Record Type	ARC Identifier	Title	Description
	582973	Criminal Case Files, compiled 1907 - 1957	Textual Records from the U.S. District Court for the First (Winona) Division of the District of Minnesota. (04/26/1890 - ca. 1951)
	582969	Criminal Case Files, compiled 1907 - 1965	Textual Records from the U.S. District Court for the Fourth (Minneapolis) Division of the District of Minnesota. (04/26/1890 -)
	1096606	Criminal Case Files, compiled 1966 - 1969	Textual Records from the U.S. District Court for the Fourth (Minneapolis) Division of the District of Minnesota. (04/26/1890 -)
	1101834	Criminal Case Files, compiled 1955 - 1969	Textual Records from the U.S. District Court for the Fifth (Duluth) Division of the District of Minnesota. (04/26/1890 -)

	582970	Criminal Case Files, compiled 1907 - 1955	Textual Records from the U.S. District Court for the Fifth (Duluth) Division of the District of Minnesota. (04/26/1890 -)
	1096602	Criminal Case Files, compiled 1966 - 1969	Textual Records from the U.S. District Court for the Third (St. Paul) Division of the District of Minnesota. (04/26/1890 -)
	582968	Criminal Case Files, compiled 1875 - 1965	Textual Records from the U.S. District Court for the Third (St. Paul) Division of the District of Minnesota. (04/26/1890 -)
	2284295	Criminal Case Files, compiled 1862 - 1900	Textual Records from the U.S. Circuit Court for the Third (St. Paul) Division of the District of Minnesota. (04/26/1890 - 01/01/1912)
	2284300	Indictments, compiled 1862 - 1873	Textual Records from the U.S. Circuit Court for the Third (St. Paul) Division of the District of Minnesota. (04/26/1890 - 01/01/1912)
	2290615	Indictments, compiled 1861 - 1906	Textual Records from the U.S. District Court for the Third (St. Paul) Division of the District of Minnesota. (04/26/1890 -)
	582971	Criminal Case Files, compiled 1907 - 1957	Textual Records from the U.S. District Court for the Sixth (Fergus Falls) Division of the District of Minnesota. (04/26/1890 - ca. 1978)
	582972	Criminal Case Files, compiled 1907 - 1957	Textual Records from the U.S. District Court for the Second (Mankato) Division of the District of Minnesota. (04/26/1890 - ca. 1951)
	283640	District of Minnesota: Minneapolis: Criminal, compiled 1907 - 1969	Photographs and other Graphic Materials and Textual Records from the U.S. District Court for the Fourth (Minneapolis) Division of the District of Minnesota. (04/26/1890 -)

Minnesota Executions

http://users.bestweb.net/~rg/execution/MINNESOTA.htm

Minnesota Department of Corrections – Offender Lookup

http://www.doc.state.mn.us/search/default.htm

Mississippi

Mississippi Department of Archives and History

William F. Winter Archives and History Building, 200 North St.
Jackson, MS 39201, (601) 576-6876
http://mdah.state.ms.us
refdesk@mdah.state.ms.us (for MS residents only)

Record Type	Location	Author	Title/Description
	Series 1565	MS Department of Corrections	Probation and Parole Board Case Files,1936-1976.
	Series 1567	MS State Penitentiary	Convict Registers,1874-1981. The earlier volumes (Books D through M) are arranged in rough alphabetical order by last name of prisoner. There is no order to the convict numbers in these volumes. The later volumes (Books N through A-R) are arranged by convict number.
	Series 1572	MS State Penitentiary	Microfilm copies of bound ledgers containing detailed personal information about convicts. The ledgers from 1898 to 1909 give the convict's name, number, physical description, birth date, date of sentence, term received, county of conviction, religion, nationality, education, family history, and more. These ledgers are indexed by last name of prisoner. The ledgers from 1948 to 1950 contain a bit less information than the earlier ones, and are not indexed, but entries are arranged by convict number.
	Series 1572	MS State Penitentiary	Index to Convict Registers,1878-1902;1904-1930.
	Series 1570	MS State Penitentiary	Outgoing Register,1973-1975.

	Series 54	MS Office of the Governor	Probation and Parole Records,1945-1975.
	Series 26	MS Supreme Court	Dockets - Criminal,1892-1986.

Federal Criminal Court Records at the National Archives & Records Admin. (NARA)

NARA Southeast Region

5780 Jonesboro Road, Morrow, Georgia 30260, (770) 968-2100

www.archives.gov/southeast/

atlanta.archives@nara.gov

Record Type	ARC Identifier	Title	Description
	1065742	Criminal Case Files, compiled 1889 - 1981	Textual Records from the U.S. District Court for the Southern Division of the District of Mississippi. Biloxi Term. (1967? -)
	1065740	Criminal Case Files, compiled 1908 - 1981	Textual Records from the U.S. District Court for the Eastern (Meridian) Division of the Southern District of Mississippi. (07/18/1894 -)
	2635616	Criminal Dockets, compiled 1960 - 1966	Textual Records from the U.S. District Court for the Greenville Division of the Northern District of Mississippi. (08/07/1950 -)
	2873739	Index to Bankruptcy, Civil, and Criminal Case Files, compiled 1952 - 1992	Textual Records from the U.S. District Court for the Eastern (Meridian) Division of the Southern District of Mississippi. (07/18/1894 -)
	719118	Criminal Case Files, compiled 1871 - 1976	Textual Records from the U.S. District Court for the Jackson Division of the Southern District of Mississippi. (07/18/1894 -)
	2375456	Criminal Dockets, compiled 1853 - 1968	Textual Records from the U.S. District Court for the Western (Oxford) Division of the Northern District of Mississippi. (06/15/1882 -)

	2263054	Criminal Case Files, compiled 1903 - 1965	Textual Records from the U.S. District Court for the Western (Vicksburg) Division of the Southern District of Mississippi. (02/28/1887 - ca. 12/31/1997)
	2375452	Criminal Dockets, compiled 1907 - 1967	Textual Records from the U.S. District Court for the Western (Vicksburg) Division of the Southern District of Mississippi. (02/28/1887 - ca. 12/31/1997)
	2619166	Criminal Dockets , compiled 1871 - 1994	Textual Records from the U.S. District Court for the Jackson Division of the Southern District of Mississippi. (07/18/1894 -)
	2658488	Criminal Dockets, compiled 1901 - 1931	Textual Records from the U.S. District Court for the Eastern (Meridian) Division of the Southern District of Mississippi. (07/18/1894 -)
	2406660	Criminal Dockets, compiled 1867 - 1964	Textual Records from the U.S. District Court for the Jackson Division of the Southern District of Mississippi. (07/18/1894 -)
	2876644	Index to Bankruptcy, Civil, and Criminal Case Files, compiled 1898 - 1991	Textual Records from the U.S. District Court for the Western (Vicksburg) Division of the Southern District of Mississippi. (02/28/1887 - ca. 12/31/1997)
	2642034	Index of Criminal Cases, compiled 1916 - 1928	Textual Records from the U.S. District Court for the Eastern (Meridian) Division of the Southern District of Mississippi. (07/18/1894 -)
	2642031	Index of Criminal Cases, compiled 1889 - 1893	Textual Records from the U.S. Circuit Court for the Western (Oxford) Division of the Northern District of Mississippi. (02/06/1889 - 12/31/1911)
	2875070	Index to Bankruptcy, Civil, and Criminal Case Files, compiled 1950 - 1992	Textual Records from the U.S. District Court for the Southern Division of the District of Mississippi. Biloxi Term. (1967? -)
	2375454	Criminal Dockets, compiled 1889 - 1983	Textual Records from the U.S. District Court for the Southern Division of the District of Mississippi. Biloxi Term. (1967? -)

	2619167	Criminal Dockets, compiled 1901 - 1993	Textual Records from the U.S. District Court for the Eastern (Meridian) Division of the Southern District of Mississippi. (07/18/1894 -)
	2642029	Index of Criminal Cases, compiled 1882 - 1926	Textual Records from the U.S. District Court for the Western (Oxford) Division of the Northern District of Mississippi. (06/15/1882 -)
	719119	Criminal Case Files, compiled 1867 - 1980	Textual Records from the U.S. District Court for the Western (Oxford) Division of the Northern District of Mississippi. (06/15/1882 -)
	2619168	Criminal Dockets, compiled 1907 - 1994	Textual Records from the U.S. District Court for the Western (Vicksburg) Division of the Southern District of Mississippi. (02/28/1887 - ca. 12/31/1997)
	2658486	Criminal Dockets, compiled 1913 - 1969	Textual Records from the U.S. District Court for the Delta (Clarksdale) Division of the Northern District of Mississippi. (05/27/1912 -)
	2642036	Index of Criminal Cases, compiled 1905 - 1908	Textual Records from the U.S. Circuit Court for the Jackson Division of the Southern District of Mississippi. (04/04/1888 - 01/01/1912)
	2375450	Criminal Dockets, compiled 1882 - 1963	Textual Records from the U.S. District Court for the Eastern (Aberdeen) Division of the Northern District of Mississippi. (06/15/1882 -)
	279292	Criminal Cases, compiled 1913 - 1973	Textual Records from the U.S. District Court for the Eastern (Aberdeen) Division of the Northern District of Mississippi. (06/15/1882 -)
	279291	Criminal Cases, compiled 1885 - 04/1969	Textual Records from the U.S. District Court for the Eastern (Aberdeen) Division of the Northern District of Mississippi. (06/15/1882 -)
	279293	Criminal Cases, compiled 01/17/1951 - 1969	Textual Records from the U.S. District Court for the Eastern (Aberdeen) Division of the Northern District of Mississippi. (06/15/1882 -)

Mississippi Executions

 http://users.bestweb.net/~rg/execution/MISSISSIPPI.htm

Mississippi Department of Corrections – Inmate Locator

 http://www.mdoc.state.ms.us/inmatetest.asp

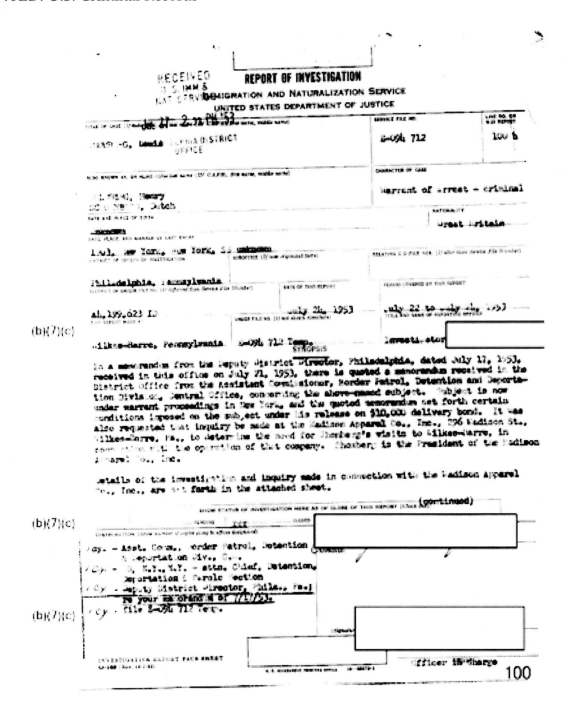

"A(lien)" File for Louis Shomberg from the USCIS (formerly INS) re the federal government's attempt to deport Shomberg. Obtained via a Freedom of Information Act (FOIA) request to the National Records Center in Lee's Summit, MO. Note: with more than 70,000 FOIA requests ahead of it, this request took two years to process.

Missouri

Missouri State Archives

600 W Main St # 119, Jefferson City, MO 65101-1592, (573) 751-3280
http://www.sos.mo.gov/archives/
http://msa.library.net/ Catalog
archref@sos.mo.gov

Record Type	Author	Title	Description
	Jefferson City Correctional Center	Register of inmates received and discharged, 1866-1961 (bulk 1866-1875, 1943-1961)	Inmates received contains: inmate number; date received; offense; sentence; county; occupation; nativity; age; training (church); education; marital status; soldier or citizen; and remarks (parents' residence, etc.)
	Jefferson City Correctional Center	Register of inmates received by county 1880-1967.	Registers provide: inmate number; inmate name; "color;" age; offense; sentence; date sentence begins; and remarks, such as institutional assignments, transfers and discharges.
	Jefferson City Correctional Center	Individual index, 1875-1892	Indexes provide: date received; name; crime; county; sentence (years); register number; cell assignment; place of work (if any); and remarks (usually date of discharge).
	Jefferson City Correctional Center	Index to register of inmates received, 1836-1967.	Indexes, 1836-1902, contain: name; "color"; register volume and page; county; register number (1876-1902); and remarks (usually final disposition). Indexes, 1902-1967, contain: name; "color"; county; number; and remarks.

	Chillicothe Correctional Center	Register, 1892-1981	
	Boonville Correctional Center	Commitment registers, 1888-1983	Records include: name; address; physical description (scars, tatoos, etc.); age; parents' names; additional children within family; and date and crime.
	Jefferson City Correctional Center	Criminal identification record 1908-1969	A system of inmate identification, giving: inmate number; date; name; residence; alias; age; date and place of birth; physical description, including marks and scars; emergency address; prison record summary; and previous criminal record. This series was known as Bertillion measurement records from 1908-1931.
	Jefferson City Correctional Center	Inmates executed files, 1938-1965	Case files of inmates executed at the Jefferson City Correctional Center, 1938-1965
	Boonville Correctional Center	Index to numerical record, 1960-1983	Index provides: name; age; date admitted; county; and register number.
	Jefferson City Correctional Center	Discharge registers, 1881-1987	Register provides: date discharged; name; "color;" age; nativity; occupation; county; crime; sentence; and remarks (i.e., pardon, death)
	Jefferson City Correctional Center	Parole dockets, 1915-1937	Record of parole meetings of the Missouri State Penitentiary, including: name of inmate; original charges; sentence; list of those involved in hearing; and conditions of parole. Each volume contains an index to specific individuals' names.
	Chillicothe Correctional Center	Personal inmate histories, 1889-1918	
	Chillicothe Correctional Center	Discharge record, 1933-1959	

	Jefferson City Correctional Center	Parole dockets, 1915-1937	Record of parole meetings of the Missouri State Penitentiary, including: name of inmate; original charges; sentence; list of those involved in hearing; and conditions of parole. Each volume contains an index to specific individuals' names.

Finding Aid to Pardon Records at the Missouri State Archives

 http://www.sos.mo.gov/archives/resources/findingaids/rg005-20.pdf

Federal Criminal Court Records at the National Archives & Records Admin. (NARA)

NARA Central Plains Region (Kansas City),
400 West Pershing Road, Kansas City, MO 64108, (816) 268-8000
http://www.archives.gov/central-plains/kansas-city/
kansascity.archives@nara.gov

Record Type	ARC Identifier	Title	Description
	572482	Law, Equity, and Criminal Case Files, compiled 1838 - 1912	Textual Records from the U.S. Circuit Court for the Eastern (St. Louis) Division of the Eastern District of Missouri. (02/28/1887 - 01/01/1912)
	582694	Criminal Case Files, compiled 1864 - 1980	Textual Records from the U.S. District Court for the Eastern (St. Louis) Division of the Eastern District of Missouri. (02/28/1887 -)
	573455	Criminal Case Files, compiled 1862 - 1972	Textual Records from the U.S. District Court for the Central (Jefferson City) Division of the District of Missouri. (01/21/1879 -)
	573454	Criminal Case Files, compiled 1928 - 1960	Textual Records from the U.S. District Court for the Chillicothe Division of the Western District of Missouri. (1910 - ca. 1963)

![]	573458	Criminal Case Files, compiled 1887 - 1971	Textual Records from the U.S. District Court for the Southern (Springfield) Division of the Western District of Missouri. (01/21/1879 -)
![]	573456	Criminal Case Files, compiled 1902 - 1964	Textual Records from the U.S. District Court for the Southwestern (Joplin) Division of the Western District of Missouri. (1901 -)
![]	573457	Criminal Case Files, compiled 1890 - 1982	Textual Records from the U.S. District Court for the Northern (St. Joseph) Division of the Western District of Missouri. (02/28/1887 -)
![]	573453	Criminal Case Files, compiled 1879 - 1980	Textual Records from the U.S. District Court for the Western (Kansas City) Division of the Western District of Missouri. (01/21/1879 -)
![]	583672	Criminal Case Files, compiled 1887 - 1965	Textual Records from the U.S. District Court for the Northern (Hannibal) Division of the Eastern District of Missouri. (02/28/1887 -)
![]	583677	Criminal Case Files, compiled 1905 - 1975	Textual Records from the U.S. District Court for the Southeastern (Cape Girardeau) Division of the Eastern District of Missouri. (1905 -)
![]	1807713	Criminal Dockets, compiled 1907 - 1981	Textual Records from the U.S. District Court for the Eastern (St. Louis) Division of the Eastern District of Missouri. (02/28/1887 -)
![]	1965853	Criminal Record Book, compiled 02/10/1834 - 09/29/1835	Textual Records from the U.S. District Court for the District of Missouri. (03/16/1822 - 03/03/1857)

Missouri Executions

http://users.bestweb.net/~rg/execution/MISSOURI.htm

Missouri Department of Corrections – Inmate Locator

https://web.mo.gov/doc/offSearchWeb/search.jsp

Montana

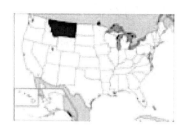

Montana State Archives/Montana Historical Society

225 North Roberts, Helena, MT 59620-1201, (406) 444-2694
http://www.his.state.mt.us/
http://nwda-db.wsulibs.wsu.edu/nwda-search/
mhslibrary@mt.gov

Record Type	Location	Author	Title	Description
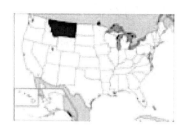	RS 197	Montana State Prison	Montana State Prison records, 1869-1974	This collection consists of records of the Montana State Prison (1869-1974), the Board of Pardons (1890-1965), the Board of Prison Commissioners (1890-1962), and the United States Penitentiary, Montana Territory, including materials such as prisoner description sheets, prisoner receipt and discharge registers, minutes, etc.
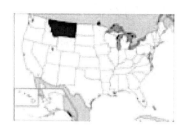	SMF 36	Montana State Prison	Montana State Prison records, 1871-1981	These Montana State Prison records (1871-1981) consist of convict registers, descriptive lists of prisoners, personal descriptions, including name, birth date, physical description, nature of crime, previous convictions, etc. There is a prisoner card index covering the years 1892-2000 in the Archives offices.

	RS 235	MT Dept. of Institutions	MT Department of Institutions Records, 1894-1991	These Department of Institutions records consist of four subgroups: the State Reform School/State Industrial School (Miles City), the State Vocational School for Girls (Helena), the Swan River Youth Forest Camp, and the Women's Correctional Center (Warm Springs). The records (1894-1964) of the State Industrial School consist of correspondence, financial records, minutes, organizational materials, reports and subject files. The State Vocational School for Girls records (1930-1948) include correspondence and annual and quarterly reports. The Swan River Youth Forest Camp records (1976) consist of architectural specifications for remodeling the facility. The Women's Correctional Center records (1989-1991) include correspondence, financial records, legislative materials, and reports primarily concerning remodeling on the Warm Springs campus, and planning for a new facility. [Photographs and printed material have been transferred to the Photo Archives and the Library, respectively.]
	RS 76	Montana Attorney General's Office	Montana Attorney General's Office Records, 1893-1969	These records consist of general correspondence (1905-1920); subject files (1900-1962); informal opinions (1897-1915); docket registers (1893-1963); docketed and undocketed case files (1902-1968); financial ledgers (1905-1969); and an abstract register (1921-1941).

	MC 35	Montana Governor	Montana Governors Records, 1889-1962	Records consist of legislative files (1893-1935), including correspondence, bills, vetos, governors messages, petitions, etc.; general correspondence (1902-1962) for individual administrations; and subject files (1889-1962) arranged by state agency and topic.

Federal Criminal Court Records at the National Archives & Records Admin. (NARA)

NARA Pacific Alaska Region (Seattle),

6125 Sand Point Way NE, Seattle, WA 98115-7999, (206) 336-5134

http://www.archives.gov/pacific-alaska/seattle/

seattle.archives@nara.gov

Record Type	ARC Identifier	Title	Description
	571793	Criminal Case Files, compiled 1948 - 1968	Textual Records from the U.S. District Court for the District of Montana. Missoula Term. (1889? -)
	568150	Civil, Criminal and Bankruptcy Case Files, compiled 1865 - 1889	Textual Records from the U.S. Territorial Court for the First (Bozeman) District of Montana. (1864 - 1889)
	568166	Criminal Case Files, compiled 1924 - 1968	Textual Records from the U.S. District Court for the District of Montana. Billings Term. (1889? -)
	571301	Criminal Case Files, compiled 1892 - 1900	Textual Records from the U.S. District Court for the District of Montana. Butte Term. (1889? -)
	569287	Civil and Criminal Case Files, compiled 1885 - 1888	Textual Records from the U.S. Territorial Court for the Fourth (Miles City) District of Montana. (1884 - 1889)
	569281	Civil, Criminal, and Bankruptcy Case Files, compiled 1865 - 1889	Textual Records from the U.S. Territorial Court for the Second (Deer Lodge) District of Montana. (1864 - 1889)
	569285	Civil, Criminal, and Bankruptcy Case Files, compiled 1865 - 1889	Textual Records from the U.S. Territorial Court for the Third (Helena) District of Montana. (1864 - 1889)
	567592	Criminal Case Files, compiled 1890 - 1911	Textual Records from the U.S. Circuit Court for the District of Montana. Helena Term. (ca. 1889 - 01/01/1912)

	570236	Criminal Case Files, compiled 1956 - 1967	Textual Records from the U.S. District Court for the District of Montana. Billings Term. (1889? -)
	570066	Criminal Case Files, compiled 1900 - 1947	Textual Records from the U.S. District Court for the District of Montana. Butte Term. (1889? -)
	573058	Criminal Dockets, compiled 1923 - 1954	Textual Records from the U.S. District Court for the District of Montana. Great Falls Term. (1889? -)
	298174	Criminal Case Files, compiled 1889 - 1961	Textual Records from the U.S. District Court for the District of Montana. Helena Term. (1889 -)

Federal Criminal Court Records at the National Archives & Records Admin. (NARA)

NARA Rocky Mountain Region (Denver)
Denver Federal Center, Bldgs 46, 48, Denver, CO 80225, (303) 407-5740
http://www.archives.gov/rocky-mountain/
denver.archives@nara.gov

Record Type	ARC Identifier	Title	Description
	1136560	Criminal Case Files, compiled 1967 - 1973	Textual Records from the U.S. District Court for the District of Montana. Billings Term. (1889? -)
	1136443	Criminal Case Files, compiled 1966 - 1977	Textual Records from the U.S. District Court for the District of Montana. Butte Term. (1889? -)
	1136686	Criminal Case Files, compiled 1952 - 1973	Textual Records from the U.S. District Court for the District of Montana. Great Falls Term. (1889? -)
	1142528	Dockets, compiled 1920 - 1966	Textual Records from the U.S. District Court for District of Montana. Office of U.S. Commissioners. (07/10/1890 - 1968)
	3514890	Criminal Case Files, compiled 1970 - 1983	Textual Records from the U.S. District Court for the District of Montana. Butte Term. (1889? -)
	3514892	Criminal Case Files, compiled 1974 - 1979	Textual Records from the U.S. District Court for the District of Montana. Billings Term. (1889? -)
	3514888	Criminal Case Files, compiled 1978 - 1982	Textual Records from the U.S. District Court for the District of Montana. Great Falls Term. (1889? -)

Madison County, Montana – List of Known Outlaws & Vigilantes

 http://www.rootsweb.ancestry.com/~mtmadiso/OutlawVigilanteList.htm?cj=1&o_xid=0001177077&o_lid=0001177077

Montana Executions

 http://users.bestweb.net/~rg/execution/MONTANA.htm

Montana Department of Corrections – Offender Lookup

 http://app.mt.gov/conweb/

NEW YORK — DEPARTMENT OF CORRECTION

SING SING PRISON

AUTOPSY REPORT

CASE NO.

No. 110-139   NAME COOPER,Calman

AGE 48   DATE 9 July,1955

DATE OF ADMISSION 9 July,1955

DATE OF DEATH 9 July,1955

PHYSICIAN Harold W. Kipp,M.D.,Chief of Staff

HOUR OF AUTOPSY 11:35 P.M.

CLINICAL DIAGNOSIS

CAUSE OF DEATH   LEGAL ELECTROCUTION

FINDINGS:

EXAMINATION OF THE BODY: The body is that of a well nourished white male of the stated age of 48 years. Well developed and weighing approximately 230 lbs. The body lies on the table in the usual position after execution: Head back: Eyes staring: Mouth open: and the right leg drawn up in about a half-flexion. There are the usual seared marks over the nape of the neck and on the right leg just below the knee.

VENTRAL INCISION: The body is opened through a mid-line ventral incision and the thorax is opened by removal of the breast plate. The subcutaneous tissue and muscle in the line of section present the usual appearance.

LUNGS: The right lung shows adhesions on the anterior wall and weighs 350 grams. The left lung is normal in size, shape and position, and weighs 340 grams.

SPLEEN: The spleen weighs 400 grams and appears normal in size,shape and position.

COLON: There is a diverticulum in the transverse colon,but the remainder of the colon and intestines appear normal .

KIDNEYS: On cut section the left and right kidneys appear normal in size,shape and position. The left kidney weighs 200 grams. and the right kidney weighs 200 grams.

HEART: The heart appears normal in size,shape and position and weighs 500 grams.

LIVER: The liver appears normal in size, shape and position and weighs 3100 grams.

ADRENALS: The adrenals appear normal in size, shape and position.

GALL BLADDER: The gall bladder appeared normal in size and appearance, color and texture. No stones were found in the gall bladder.

TESTES: Both testes appear normal in size,shape and position.

BRAIN: Not done.

H.W.Kipp,M.D.Sr.Physician

HWK/as

Autopsy report of Calman Cooper, death row inmate at Sing Sing Prison. From New York State Archives, RG B0145, Case files of inmates sentenced to electrocution, 1939-1963. Courtesy of the New York State Archives and the New York Department of Corrections.

Nebraska

Nebraska State Historical Society: Library & Archives

1500 R St, Lincoln, NE 68508-1651, (402) 471-4751

www.nebraskahistory.org

Record Type	Location	Subgroup	Title/Description
	RG034	Roll #1MP3263, Vol 1.	Criminal Record, September 1870 - March 28, 1882
	RG034	Vol 2.	Inmate Register, 1882-1887
	RG034	Vol 3.	Inmate Register, 1887-1892 #1276 (Sept. 1887) thru #2334 (Dec. 1892)
	RG034	Vol 4.	Index to Prisoners, 1919 Alphabetical Index giving prisoners names and numbers, #2655 (c.1895) thru #7500 (1919)
	RG034	Vol 5.	Inmate Register, 1893-1897
	RG034	Vol 6.	Inmate Register, 1897-1908 #3187 (May 1897) thru #4978 (Jan. 1908)
	RG034	Vol 7.	Inmate Register, 1908-1915 #4979 (Feb. 1908) thru #6570 (May 1915)
	RG034	Vol 8.	Inmate Register - Penitentiary, 1915-1921 #6571 (May 1915) thru #8119 (Feb. 1921)
	RG034	Vol 9.	Inmate Register - Women's Reformatory #1 (8171), September 14, 1920 thru #414 (8585), March 25, 1931
	RG034	Vol 10.	Inmate Register - Men's Reformatory Oversize #1 (September 22, 1921) thru #2001 (December 3, 1930)
	RG034	Vol 11.	Inmate Register - Men's Reformatory Oversize #2002 (November 29, 1930) thru #5338 (November 29, 1948)

	RG034	Roll #1	Index Cards, 1876-1990, 10,236 cards

Finding Aid for Pardon and Parole Records at the Nebraska State Archives

http://www.nebraskahistory.org/lib-arch/research/public/state_finding_aids/
pardons_paroles_bd.pdf

NSHS Library/Archives, Nebraska Court Records

(Results for keyword search 'criminal court' at www.nebraska.gov/search/search.cgi)

Finding Aids Found for Nebraska County Court Records:

Record Type	County	Finding Aid URL
	Adams	http://www.nebraskahistory.org/lib-arch/research/public/county_finding_aids/adams.pdf
	Alliance	http://www.nebraskahistory.org/lib-arch/research/public/municipal_finding_aids/alliance_ne.pdf
	Antelope	http://www.nebraskahistory.org/lib-arch/research/public/county_finding_aids/antelope.pdf
	Ashland, Saunders	http://www.nebraskahistory.org/lib-arch/research/public/municipal_finding_aids/ashland_ne.pdf
	Blaine	http://www.nebraskahistory.org/lib-arch/research/public/county_finding_aids/blaine.pdf
	Blair	http://www.nebraskahistory.org/lib-arch/research/public/municipal_finding_aids/blair_ne.pdf
	Buffalo	http://www.nebraskahistory.org/lib-arch/research/public/county_finding_aids/buffalo.pdf
	Burt	http://www.nebraskahistory.org/lib-arch/research/public/county_finding_aids/burt.pdf
	Butler	http://www.nebraskahistory.org/lib-arch/research/public/county_finding_aids/butler.pdf
	Cass	http://www.nebraskahistory.org/lib-arch/research/public/county_finding_aids/cass.pdf

	Clay	http://www.nebraskahistory.org/lib-arch/research/public/county_finding_aids/clay.pdf
	Cuming	http://www.nebraskahistory.org/lib-arch/research/public/county_finding_aids/cuming.pdf
	Dakota	http://www.nebraskahistory.org/lib-arch/research/public/county_finding_aids/dakota.pdf
	Dawson	http://www.nebraskahistory.org/lib-arch/research/public/county_finding_aids/dawson.pdf
	Dixon	http://www.nebraskahistory.org/lib-arch/research/public/county_finding_aids/dixon.pdf
	Fillmore	http://www.nebraskahistory.org/lib-arch/research/public/county_finding_aids/fillmore.pdf
	Gosper	http://www.nebraskahistory.org/lib-arch/research/public/county_finding_aids/gosper.pdf
	Hall	http://www.nebraskahistory.org/lib-arch/research/public/county_finding_aids/hall.pdf
	Hamilton	http://www.nebraskahistory.org/lib-arch/research/public/county_finding_aids/hamilton.pdf
	Harlan	http://www.nebraskahistory.org/lib-arch/research/public/county_finding_aids/harlan.pdf
	Holt	http://www.nebraskahistory.org/lib-arch/research/public/county_finding_aids/holt.pdf
	Jefferson	http://www.nebraskahistory.org/lib-arch/research/public/county_finding_aids/jefferson.pdf
	Keith	http://www.nebraskahistory.org/lib-arch/research/public/county_finding_aids/keith.pdf
	Keya Paha	http://www.nebraskahistory.org/lib-arch/research/public/county_finding_aids/keya_paha.pdf
	Kimball	http://www.nebraskahistory.org/lib-arch/research/public/county_finding_aids/kimball.pdf
	Lancaster	http://www.nebraskahistory.org/lib-arch/research/public/county_finding_aids/lancaster.pdf
	Lincoln	http://www.nebraskahistory.org/lib-arch/research/public/county_finding_aids/lincoln.pdf
	Nance	http://www.nebraskahistory.org/lib-arch/research/public/county_finding_aids/nance.pdf

	Nemaha	http://www.nebraskahistory.org/lib-arch/research/public/county_finding_aids/nemaha.pdf
	Otoe	http://www.nebraskahistory.org/lib-arch/research/public/county_finding_aids/otoe.pdf
	Phelps	http://www.nebraskahistory.org/lib-arch/research/public/county_finding_aids/phelps.pdf
	Platte	http://www.nebraskahistory.org/lib-arch/research/public/county_finding_aids/platte.pdf
	Red Willow	http://www.nebraskahistory.org/lib-arch/research/public/county_finding_aids/red_willow.pdf
	Richardson	http://www.nebraskahistory.org/lib-arch/research/public/county_finding_aids/richardson.pdf
	Rock	http://www.nebraskahistory.org/lib-arch/research/public/county_finding_aids/rock.pdf
	Sarpy	http://www.nebraskahistory.org/lib-arch/research/public/county_finding_aids/sarpy.pdf
	Saunders	http://www.nebraskahistory.org/lib-arch/research/public/county_finding_aids/saunders.pdf
	Seward	http://www.nebraskahistory.org/lib-arch/research/public/county_finding_aids/seward.pdf
	Sheridan	http://www.nebraskahistory.org/lib-arch/research/public/county_finding_aids/sheridan.pdf
	Territorial Courts	http://www.nebraskahistory.org/lib-arch/research/public/state_finding_aids/territorial_courts.pdf
	Thurston	http://www.nebraskahistory.org/lib-arch/research/public/county_finding_aids/thurston.pdf
	Valley	http://www.nebraskahistory.org/lib-arch/research/public/county_finding_aids/valley.pdf
	Washington	http://www.nebraskahistory.org/lib-arch/research/public/county_finding_aids/washington.pdf
	Wayne	http://www.nebraskahistory.org/lib-arch/research/public/county_finding_aids/wayne.pdf

Federal Criminal Court Records at the National Archives & Records Admin. (NARA)

NARA Central Plains Region (Kansas City),
400 West Pershing Road, Kansas City, MO 64108, (816) 268-8000
http://www.archives.gov/central-plains/kansas-city/
kansascity.archives@nara.gov

Record Type	ARC Identifier	Title	Description
	1105112	Chancery, Criminal, Equity, and Law Case Files, compiled 03/30/1867 - 12/26/1911	Textual Records from the U.S. Circuit Court for the Omaha Division of the District of Nebraska. (1867 - 01/01/1912)
	583664	Criminal Case Files, compiled 1908 - 1955	Textual Records from the U.S. District Court for the McCook Division of the District of Nebraska. (1907 - ca. 1957)
	582637	Criminal Case Files, compiled 1867 - 1983	Textual Records from the U.S. District Court for the Omaha Division of the District of Nebraska. (1867 -)
	583668	Criminal Case Files, compiled 1908 - 1955	Textual Records from the U.S. District Court for the North Platte Division of the District of Nebraska. (1907 -)
	583667	Criminal Case Files, compiled 1908 - 1955	Textual Records from the U.S. District Court for the Hastings Division of the District of Nebraska. (1907 - 1955)
	583635	Criminal Case Files, compiled 1907 - 1955	Textual Records from the U.S. District Court for the Grand Island Division of the District of Nebraska. (1907 - 1955)
	583620	Criminal Case Files, compiled 1907 - 1955	Textual Records from the U.S. District Court for the Chadron Division of the District of Nebraska. (1907 - 1955)
	583666	Criminal Case Files, compiled 1907 - 1955	Textual Records from the U.S. District Court for the Norfolk Division of the District of Nebraska. (1907 - 1955)
	1151233	Criminal Dockets, compiled 1907 - 1955	Textual Records from the U.S. District Court for the Norfolk Division of the District of Nebraska. (1907 - 1955)
	1151243	Criminal Dockets, compiled 1921 - 1955	Textual Records from the U.S. District Court for the North Platte Division of the District of Nebraska. (1907 -)
	1142865	Criminal Dockets, compiled 1908 - 1955	Textual Records from the U.S. District Court for the Hastings Division of the District of Nebraska. (1907 - 1955)

⚖	1150837	Criminal Dockets, compiled 1908 - 1954	Textual Records from the U.S. District Court for the McCook Division of the District of Nebraska. (1907 - ca. 1957)
⚖	1151067	Criminal Dockets, compiled 1907 - 1955	Textual Records from the U.S. District Court for the Grand Island Division of the District of Nebraska. (1907 - 1955)
⚖	1145987	Criminal Case Files, compiled 1927 - 1960	Textual Records from the Department of the Interior. Bureau of Indian Affairs. Pine Ridge Agency. (09/17/1947 - 09/09/9999)
⚖	582967	Criminal Case Files, compiled 1907 - 1983	Textual Records from the U.S. District Court for the Lincoln Division of the District of Nebraska. (1907 -)

Nebraska Executions

http://users.bestweb.net/~rg/execution/NEBRASKA.htm

Nebraska Department of Corrections – Inmate Lookup

http://dcs-inmatesearch.ne.gov/Corrections/COR_input.html

Nevada

Nevada State Library and Archives

100 North Stewart Street, Carson City, Nevada 89701-4285, (775) 684-3360
http://nevadaculture.org/nsla/
nslref@nevadaculture.org

Record Type	Location	Title	Description
		Name Index to the Nevada State Prison Inmate Case Files	Covers files dating from 1863 to 1972
		Inmate Case Files	Early files usually contain very little information; more contemporary files can be voluminous. Nineteenth century case files may contain correspondence and records of the Board of Parole and Pardons Commissioners. Twentieth century case files became more detailed after the creation of the Nevada State Police in 1908, who introduced the Bertillon system of physical description and photographs in 1909. There may be summaries of the crime, applications for parole and/or pardons, and correspondence to the Parole Board. Files dated after 1908 may contain information obtained from the Federal Bureau of Investigation (FBI), including arrest, conviction and incarceration in other states. There may be personal correspondence received by an inmate and inquiries from out-of-state law enforcement agencies about an inmate's criminal activity. Beginning in the 1970s there are some health records and psychological evaluations.

	29-P93/1: year	Biennial Reports to the Legislature, 1865-1917	These reports, specifically those of the Warden of the Nevada State Prison, enumerated all the prisoners by name, age, nativity, occupation, crime, county received from, sentence, date of receipt and date of discharge.
	In paper form or on microfilm	The first volume of each Appendix to the Journals of the Nevada State Senate and Assembly	Pardons granted by the Board of Pardons Commissioners were listed in the Governors' messages to the Legislature from 1865 until 1959.
	29-Su7/5: year	Reports of Cases Determined by the Supreme Court of the State of Nevada	Some criminal court cases were appealed to the Nevada State Supreme Court and were indexed indexed in the Alphabetical List of Nevada Supreme Court Cases. The cases were reported in the Reports of Cases Determined by the Supreme Court of the State of Nevada.
	29-Su7/12: year	Nevada Supreme Court Cases	

County Court Records

Criminal court cases are on file with the county clerk of the county where trials were held. NSLA has nineteenth century district court criminal case files for Douglas, Storey and Washoe Counties on microfilm.

Record Type	Nevada Court	Address
	Beatty Justice Court	426 C Ave S, Beatty, NV 89003
	Boulder City Municipal Court	501 Avenue G, Boulder City, NV 89005
	Carlin Municipal Judge	101 S 8th St, Carlin, NV 89822
	Carson City Dist Court Clerk	885 E Musser St #3031, Carson City, NV 89701
	Carson City District Judge	885 E Musser St, Carson City, NV 89701

	Carson City Justice Court	885 E Musser St #2007, Carson City, NV 89701
	Churchill County Justice Court	71 N Maine St, Fallon, NV 89406
	Clark County District 12 Judge	200 S 3rd St, Las Vegas, NV 89155
	Clark County District 9 Judge	200 S 3rd St, Las Vegas, NV 89155
	Clark County District Court	200 S 3rd St, Las Vegas, NV 89155
	Clark County District Judge	601 N Pecos Rd, Las Vegas, NV 89101
	Clark County Justice Court	200 S 3rd St, Las Vegas, NV 89155
	Clark County Justice Court	243 S Water St, Henderson, NV 89015
	Clark County Justice Court	505 Avenue G, Boulder City, NV 89005
	Dayton Justice Court	235 Main St, Dayton, NV 89403
	District Court Dept 1 Judge	200 S 3rd St, Las Vegas, NV 89155
	District Court Jury Info	75 Court St, Reno, NV 89501
	District Court Reporter	885 E Musser St, Carson City, NV 89701
	District Court-Discovery Comm	75 Court St #121, Reno, NV 89501
	District Court-Filing Office	75 Court St, Reno, NV 89501
	Douglas County District Court	1625 8th St, Minden, NV 89423
	Eastline Justice Court	935 W Wendover Blvd West Wendover, NV 89883

	Elko County District Court	571 Idaho St Fl 3, Elko, NV 89801
	Ely Municipal Court	154 Pioche Hwy, Ely, NV 89301
	Eureka County Court House	10 S Main St, Eureka, NV 89316
	Fallon Municipal Court	55 W Williams Ave, Fallon, NV 89406
	Fernley Justice Court	565 E Main St, Fernley, NV 89408
	Gabbs Municipal Court	501 Brucite, Gabbs, NV 89409
	Henderson Municipal Court	243 S Water St, Henderson, NV 89015
	Humboldt County District Court	25 W 5th St, Winnemucca, NV 89445
	Jackpot Justice Court	1120 Snyder Way, Jackpot, NV 89825
	Jean Justice Court	1 Main St, Jean, NV 89019
	Justice Court	Highway 95, Schurz, NV 89427
	Justice Court	190 W Virgin St, Bunkerville, NV 89007
	Justice Court	1090 Cottonwood Cove Rd, Searchlight, NV 89046
	Justice Court	1625 8th St, Minden, NV 89423
	Justice Court Clerk	935 W Wendover Blvd, West Wendover, NV 89883
	Justice Court Clerk	571 Idaho St, Elko, NV 89801

	Justice Court-Civil Div	630 Greenbrae Dr, Sparks, NV 89431
	Lake Township Justice Court	400 Main St, Lovelock, NV 89419
	Las Vegas Municipal Court	400 Stewart Ave, Las Vegas, NV 89101
	Laughlin Justice Court	101 Civic Way, Laughlin, NV 89029
	Lovelock Municipal Court	400 14th St, Lovelock, NV 89419
	Lund Justice Court	80 E 1st S, Lund, NV 89317
	Lyon County Justice Court	565 E Main St, Fernley, NV 89408
	Meadow Valley Justice Court	1 Main St, Pioche, NV 89043
	Mesquite Justice Court	500 Hillside Dr, Mesquite, NV 89027
	Mesquite Municipal Court	500 Hillside Dr, Mesquite, NV 89027
	Mina Twp Justice Court	945 Front St, Mina, NV 89422
	Mineral County District Judge	105 S A St #1, Hawthorne, NV 89415
	Moapa Justice Court	1340 E Highway 168, Moapa, NV 89025
	Moapa Valley Justice Court	320 N Moapa Valley Blvd, Overton, NV 89040
	Montello Justice Court	4th & A St, Montello, NV 89830
	Municipal Court	571 Idaho St, Elko, NV 89801
	Nye County District Judge	101 Radar Rd, Tonopah, NV 89049
	Pershing County District Judge	400 Main St, Lovelock, NV 89419

	Reno City Municipal Court	33 High St, Reno, NV 89502
	Searchlight Justice Court	1090 Cottonwood Cove Rd, Searchlight, NV 89046
	Sixth Judicial District Judge	315 S Humboldt St, Battle Mountain, NV 89820
	Smith Valley Justice Court	PO Box 141, Smith, NV 89430
	Wadsworth Justice Court	390 Main, Wadsworth, NV 89442
	Washoe County District Court	75 Court St, Reno, NV 89501
	Washoe County Justice Court	865 Tahoe Blvd #301 Incline Village, NV 89451
	Washoe County Justice Court	740 2nd, Verdi, NV 89439
	Washoe County Justice Court	390 W Main St, Wadsworth, NV 89442
	Wells City Judge	1510 Lake Ave, Wells, NV 89835
	White Pine County Dist Judge	875 Clark St, Ely, NV 89301

Federal Criminal Court Records at the National Archives & Records Admin. (NARA)

NARA Pacific Region (San Bruno, CA),
1000 Commodore Drive, San Bruno, CA 94066-2350, (650) 238-3500
http://www.archives.gov/pacific/san-francisco/
sanbruno.archives@nara.gov

Record Type	ARC Identifier	Title	Description
	2839210	Criminal Case Files, compiled 1865 - 1982	Textual Records from the U.S. District Court for the District of Nevada. Reno Term. (11/15/1945 -)

Federal Criminal Court Records at the National Archives & Records Admin. (NARA)

NARA Pacific Region (Riverside, CA)
23123 Cajelco Road, Perris, CA, (951) 956-2000
http://www.archives.gov/pacific/frc/riverside/contacts.html
riverside.reference@nara.gov

Record Type	ARC Identifier	Title	Description
	603764	Criminal Case Dockets, compiled 1954 - 1983	Textual Records from the U.S. District Court for the District of Nevada. Las Vegas Term. (ca. 06/24/1930 -)
	608450	Criminal Case Dockets of Commissioner William G. Ruymann, compiled 1970 - 1972	Textual Records from the U.S. District Court for the District of Nevada. Las Vegas Term. (ca. 06/24/1930 -)
	608414	Magistrate Criminal Case Dockets, compiled 1979 - 1983	Textual Records from the U.S. District Court for the District of Nevada. Las Vegas Term. (ca. 06/24/1930 -)
	608446	Criminal Case Dockets of Commissioner G. Russell Pike, compiled 1968 - 1970	Textual Records from the U.S. District Court for the District of Nevada. Las Vegas Term. (ca. 06/24/1930 -)
	603763	Criminal Case Files, compiled 1954 - 1969	Textual Records from the U.S. District Court for the District of Nevada. Las Vegas Term. (ca. 06/24/1930 -)
	608456	Petty Offense Dockets of Commissioner William G. Ruymann, compiled 1968 - 1970	Textual Records from the U.S. District Court for the District of Nevada. Las Vegas Term. (ca. 06/24/1930 -)
	608457	Petty Offense Dockets of Commissioner Elton M. Garrett, compiled 1965 - 1970	Textual Records from the U.S. District Court for the District of Nevada. Las Vegas Term. (ca. 06/24/1930 -)
	608453	Petty Offense Dockets of Commissioner G. Russell Pike, compiled 1970 - 1971	Textual Records from the U.S. District Court for the District of Nevada. Las Vegas Term. (ca. 06/24/1930 -)
	608500	Petty Offense Dockets of Commissioner Roy L. Nelson II, compiled 1969 - 1971	Textual Records from the U.S. District Court for the District of Nevada. Las Vegas Term. (ca. 06/24/1930 -)

Nevada Executions

 http://users.bestweb.net/~rg/execution/NEVADA.htm

Nevada Department of Corrections – Inmate Lookup

 http://www.doc.nv.gov/notis/search.php

New Hampshire

New Hampshire State Archives

71 S Fruit St, Concord, NH 03301-2410, (603) 271-2236

www.sos.nh.gov/archives/

Record Type	Location	Title
	V23	Register of Convicts, 1812-1912
	V24 / B-1, 29, 49	Punishments Reports, 1917
	V24 / B-1, 59, 81, 98, 99	Punishments Reports, 1918
	V24 / B-1, 13, 23, 28, 48	Parole Reports, 1917
	V24 / B-1, 58, 67, 94, 95, 105, 121	Parole Reports, 1918
	V24 / B-1, 122, 129, 131, 147	Parole Reports, 1919
	V24 / B-1, 153, 155, 162, 173	Parole Reports, 1920
	V24 / B-1, 181, 187	Parole Reports, 1921

Court Records at the New Hamshire State Archives

Record Type	Location	County / Court	Title
	V39	Hillsborough	Case Records c.1772
	V32, V33	Hillsborough	Docket Books 1794-c.1836
	V31, V32	Hillsborough	Judgment Books, 1783-c.1900
	V39	Merrimack	County Records, 1 Vol
	V39	Merrimack	Second District Court, 1870-1874
	V31	Merrimack	Superior Court of Judicature [S.C.J.], Index by Plaintiff 1824-1880, 1 Vol
	V40	Merrimack	Superior Court of Judicature [S.C.J.], Docket Books, 1824-1855, 12 Vols
	V40	Merrimack	Superior Court of Judicature [S.C.J.], Docket Book, 1916-1921, 1 Vol
	V39	Merrimack	Superior Court of Judicature [S.C.J.], Judgments 1840-1858, 2 Vols
	V31	Merrimack	Court of Common Pleas [C.C.P.], Index by Plaintiff 1825-1872, 3 Vols
	V31	Merrimack	Court of Common Pleas [C.C.P.], General Index 1872-1883
	V40	Merrimack	Court of Common Pleas [C.C.P.], Docket Books, Oct. 1823-Mar. 1859, 46 Vols
	V40	Merrimack	Court of Common Pleas [C.C.P.], Judgments 1840-1859, 11 Vols
	V31	Merrimack	Sessions Court (part of Supreme Judicial Court), Index 1823-1864, 1 Vol
	V41	Merrimack	Sessions Court (part of Supreme Judicial Court), Docket Books, Feb. 1834, 1 Vol
	V40	Merrimack	Sessions Court (part of Supreme Judicial Court), 1845-1878, 8 Vols

	V41	Merrimack	Sessions Court (part of Supreme Judicial Court), Judgments, 1841-1867, 3 Vols
	V41	Merrimack	Sessions Court (part of Supreme Judicial Court), Judgments, 1869-1874, 1 Vol
	V40	Merrimack	Supreme Court, Dockets, 1878-1895, 25 Vols
	V41	Merrimack	Supreme Court, Judgments, 1890-1899
	V41	Merrimack	Supreme Court, Sessions, Oct 1876-Oct 1889, 1 Vol
	V41	Merrimack	Supreme Court, State, Oct 1876-Oct 1892, 3 Vols
	V41	Merrimack	Supreme Court, Trial Terms, Apr. 1877-Oct. 1880, 9 Vols
	V41	Merrimack	Supreme Court, Equity Terms, Oct. 1876-Oct 1889, 5 Vols
	RA	Rockingham	Index Volumes
	V29-30	Rockingham	Docket Books
	V76	Rockingham	Docket Books, 1924-1932 20 Vols
	MT	Rockingham	Index Cards for 1920s Cases
	V75	Rockingham	Road Records, 1795-1888, 3 Vols
	942084/ 951013	Rockingham	Superior Court, Civil & Equity, Index, 1920s
	V28	Provincial	Case Records, 1659-1696, 11 Vols
	RA	Provincial	Card Index to Case Records, c.1679-c.1772; Case Records, c.1679-c.1772, #1 - #14853 V6
	V77	Provincial	Case Records, c.1679-c.1772 #14854 - #16219

![icon]	V76	Provincial	Case Records, c.1679-c.1772, #16220 - #20179
![icon]	V78	Provincial	Case Records, c.1679-c.1772, #20180 - #21560
![icon]	V61	Provincial	Case Records, c.1679-c.1772, #21561 - #30429
![icon]	Unpro-cessed	Strafford	Court Records (1780-1859; 1870-1874)
![icon]	V33	Strafford	Docket Books 1820-1874 (Not Conclusive)
![icon]	V28	Superior Court	Superior Court, 1699-1773
![icon]	V31	Supreme Court	Docket Books

Federal Criminal Court Records at the National Archives & Records Admin. (NARA)

NARA Northeast Region (Boston)

Frederick C. Murphy Federal Center, 380 Trapelo Road, Waltham, MA, 02452-6399

(781) 663-0130

http://www.archives.gov/northeast/

waltham.archives@nara.gov

Record Type	ARC Identifier	Title	Description
![icon]	592842	Criminal Case Files, compiled 1907 - 1983	Textual Records from the U.S. District Court for the District of New Hampshire. (1789 -)
![icon]	2997087	Judgement Docket, compiled 1925 - 1955	Textual Records from the U.S. District Court for the District of New Hampshire. (1789 -)

New Hampshire Executions

 http://users.bestweb.net/~rg/execution/NEW%20HAMPSHIRE.htm

New Hampshire Department of Corrections – Inmate Lookup

 http://www4.egov.nh.gov/Inmate_Locator/

New Jersey

New Jersey State Archives

2300 Stuyvesant Ave, Ewing, NJ 08618-3226, (609) 292-4756
www.state.nj.us/state/darm/links/archives.html
archives.reference@sos.state.nj.us

Record Type	Location (Control #)	Title/Description
	SINTR001	Department of Institutions & Agencies (Corrections), New Jersey State Prison at Trenton, Inmate Registers, 1894-1975
	CBUCL009	Burlington County Clerk's Office, Record of Trials, Courts of Oyer and Terminer and General Quarter Sessions, 1887-1937
	CBUCL022	Burlington County Clerk's Office, Record of Indictments and Sentences, 1887-1910
	CBUCL028	Burlington County Clerk's Office, Court of Oyer and Terminer and Court of General Quarter Sessions of the Peace Indictments, 1732-1897, 1913-1947
	CBUCL035	Burlington County Clerk's Office, Minutes of the Courts of Oyer and Terminer and General Quarter Sessions, 1843-1916
	CBUCL038	Burlington County Clerk's Office, Circuit Court/Court of Oyer and Terminer Minute Books, 1837-1890
	CCDCL016	Camden County Clerk's Office, Court of Oyer and Terminer and General Jail Delivery Minutes, 1844-1948
	CCDCL017	Camden County Clerk's Office, Court of Oyer and Terminer and General Jail Delivery Executions, 1869-1873
	CCDCL018	Camden County Clerk's Office, Court of Oyer and Terminer and General Jail Delivery Indictments, 1885-1945
	CCPCL012	Cape May County Clerk's Office, Court of Oyer and Terminer and General Jail Delivery Minutes, 1813-1925

	CCPCL013	Cape May County Clerk's Office, Court of Oyer and Terminer and General Jail Delivery Judgments, Volume 1, 1852-1906
	CCUCL016	Cumberland County Clerk's Office, Court of Oyer and Terminer Case Papers, 1778-1865
	CCUCL018	Cumberland County Clerk's Office, Court of Oyer and Terminer Minutes, Book A, 1798-1837
	CESCL010	Essex County Clerk's Office, Minutes of the Court of Oyer and Terminer, 1827-1935
	CHDCL009	Hudson County Clerk's Office, Court of Oyer and Terminer Lists of Indictments and Indexes, 1884-1924
	CMECL014	Mercer County Clerk's Office, Court of Oyer and Terminer Trial Transcript, State v. Charles Lewis, 1863
	CMECL016	Mercer County Clerk's Office, Court of Oyer and Terminer Minute Book, 1931-1949
	CPACL028	Passaic County Clerk's Office, Court of Oyer and Terminer Indictments, 1910-1919
	CPACL029	Passaic County Clerk's Office, Court of Oyer and Terminer and Quarter Session Minutes [with gaps], 1840-1942
	CSACL003	Salem County Clerk's Office, Records relating to Chancery Court, Court of Oyer and Terminer, and Supreme Court Cases, 1779-1877
	CSACL005	Salem County Clerk's Office, Record of Indictments Pending, Court of Oyer and Terminer, 1854-1865
	CSACL011	Salem County Clerk's Office, Minutes of the Court of Oyer and Terminer, 1869-1953
	CSOCL014	Somerset County Clerk's Office, Court of Oyer and Terminer Minutes, 1836-1926
	CSUCL023	Sussex County Clerk's Office, Minutes of the Circuit Court, Court of Oyer and Terminer, and Court of General Quarter Sessions, 1798-1851
	CWACL013	Warren County Clerk's Office, Minutes of the Courts of Oyer and Terminer and General Quarter Sessions of the Peace, 1825-1941
	SSTSE028	Department of State, Secretary of State's Office, Petitions to the Court of Pardons, 1800-1921
	SSTSE029	Department of State, Secretary of State's Office, Court of Pardons Term Records, 1914-1940

	SSTSE030	Department of State, Secretary of State's Office, Paroles Granted by the Court of Pardons, 1891-1905
	SSTSE031	Department of State, Secretary of State's Office, Miscellaneous Records of the Court of Pardons, 1804-1907
	S52CO009	Governor William Thomas Cahill (1912-1996; served 1970-1974) Counsel's Office, Executive Clemency Files, 1970-1972
	S53CO025	Governor Brendan Thomas Byrne (1924- ; served 1974-1982) Counsel's Office, Executive Clemency Files, 1974-1981
	S54CO005	Governor Thomas Howard Kean (1935- ; served 1982-1990) Counsel's Office, Executive Clemency Files, 1982-1990
	S55CO011	Governor James Joseph Florio (1937- ; served 1990-1994) Counsel's Office, Executive Clemency Files, 1990-1993

Federal Criminal Court Records at the National Archives & Records Admin. (NARA)

NARA Northeast Region (New York)
201 Varick Street, 12th Floor, New York, NY 10014, (212) 401-1620
http://www.archives.gov/northeast/
newyork.archives@nara.gov

Record Type	ARC Identifier	Title	Description
	2674905	Criminal Dockets, compiled 1929 - 1969	Textual Records from the U.S. District Court for the District of New Jersey. Newark Term. (03/03/1911 -)
	2602407	Law Case Files, compiled 1923 - 1938	Textual Records from the U.S. District Court for the District of New Jersey. Trenton Term. (02/14/1913 -)

New Jersey Executions

 http://users.bestweb.net/~rg/execution/NEW%20JERSEY.htm

New Jersey Department of Corrections – Inmate Lookup

 https://www6.state.nj.us/DOC_Inmate/inmatefinder?i=I

Pre-execution Meals   (Approved by Warden)

Calman Cooper #110-139

July 10, 1955

Dinner

Sour cream
Pot cheese
Black bread
Sweet butter
Honey dew melon
Fresh peaches, plums, apricots, cherries, nuts
2 packs Parliment cigarettes, King size

Supper

Roast chicken - cold
Seeded rye bread
Sweet butter
Tomatoes and green salad
Strawberries with cream
2 Pepsi-cola
Coffee
Ice cream
Ripe black olives

Last meals requested by Calman Cooper before electrocution in Sing Sing electric chair. From New York State Archives, RG B0145, Case files of inmates sentenced to electrocution, 1939-1963. Courtesy of the New York State Archives and the New York Department of Corrections.

New Mexico

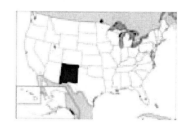

New Mexico Archives and Historical Services Division

1205 Camino Carlos Rey, Santa Fe, NM 87507-5166, (505) 476-7900 www.nmcpr.state.nm.us/
archives/archives_hm.htm
http://www.nmcpr.state.nm.us/archives/gencat_cover.htm
archives@state.nm.us

Record Type	Location (Collection)	Title/Description
	1959-104, file 780-781, Box 20	Reform School Inmates, 1935-38
	1970-006	New Mexico Department of Corrections Records, 1884-[ongoing] As of 1997 collection consists of the records of the New Mexico Penitentiary, the Corrections Department, and its predecessors (1884-1990). Some penitentiary records pertain to county and federal inmates. Include are registers of prisoners, visitors, and parolees; annual reports; correspondence; case files; conduct records; medical records; account books; and intake records that usually include an image of the inmate. Intake records are files by inmate number.
	1970-006, subseries 2.1	Penitentiary of New Mexico Inmate Records
	1970-006, sub-subseries 2.1.2	Inmate Files
	1970-006, sub-subseries 2.1.3	Inmate Intake Records
	1970-006, sub-subseries 2.1.4	Governor's Inmate Notebooks
	1970-006, folder 7239	Governor's Inmate Notebooks, 1884- 1913

	1970-006, folder 17163	Governor's Inmate Notebooks, 1907- 1937
	1970-006, folder 17164	Governor's inmate notebooks, 1937- 1946
	1970-006, folder 17165	Governor's inmate notebooks, 1946- 1955
	1970-006, folder 17166	Governor's inmate notebooks, 1948- 1954
	1959-096, file 212, Box 9	List of Prison Cases Pending
	1970-006, folder 7229	Prison escapee's records, 1913-1928
	1960-043	Records of the United States Territorial and New Mexico District Courts for San Miguel County, 1847-1955. Collection includes record books (1847-1946), case files (1848-1939), and other court material (1889-1955). Record books consist of various dockets (1847-1946), court proceedings record books (1849-1911), and clerk's books (1873-1914). Dockets included criminal (1867-1886), criminal and civil (1847-1850, 1857-1859), judge's (1847-1911), judge's minutes and trial (1892-1894), and judgment and execution (1874-1912) volumes. An index for criminal and civil hearings (1847-1881) is also included. Judge's dockets cover criminal (1847-1850, 1885-1901, 1904, 1908, 1911) trials. Court proceedings record books cover criminal (1881-1907) and criminal and civil (1849-1860, 1866-1881) hearings. Case files consist of criminal cases 2b-6453 (1848-1929. Large gaps may exist between case files.
	1973-017	Records of the United States Territorial and New Mexico District Courts for Rio Arriba County, 1848-1954 (bulk 1848-1912). Collection consists of the territorial and New Mexico district court records for Rio Arriba County, New Mexico (1848-1954). The bulk of the material covers the years 1848-1912. Included are record books (1848-1921), case files (1849-1954), and miscellaneous court records. Records books consist of various dockets (1860-1921) and court proceedings record books (1848-1911). Dockets include criminal (1883-1901, 1901-1909, 1906-1912), judge's criminal (1887-1891, 1899, 1904-1914), and judgment (1891-1905, 1918-1921) volumes. Court proceedings record books cover criminal (1848-1911) hearings. Case files consist of criminal cases 115-1632 (1855-1911). Large gaps may exist between case files. Many case files are unnumbered.

	1974-018	Records of the United States Territorial and New Mexico District Courts for Eddy County, 1891-1935. Collection consists of the territorial and New Mexico district court records for Eddy County, New Mexico (1891-1935). Included are record books (1891-1913), case files (1891-1927), and other court material. Record books include various dockets (1891-1935) and court proceedings record books (1891-1913). Dockets include criminal (1891-1913), civil and criminal (1901, 1902, 1904, 1910), and judgment (1891-1935) volumes. Court proceedings record books include a volume from the Chancery Court (1896-1897). Case files consist of criminal cases 1-1910 (1891-1922). Large gaps may exist between case files. Many case files are unnumbered. Many of the cases after 1912 are not part of this collection.
	1974-019, Box 2	Grant County, N.M., Case Files: Criminal 180-239, 1B-147B, 1899-1914
	1974-019, Box 3	Grant County, N.M., Justice of the Peace Records, 1907-1914, 1904-1905, 1912
	1974-019, Box 4	Grant County, N.M., Case Files: Criminal 149B-6D, Justice of the Peace Records, 1905-1906
	1974-019, Box 5	Grant County, N.M., Case Files: Criminal 7D-106E, Justice of the Peace Records, 1906-1907
	1974-019, Box 6	Grant County, N.M., Case Files: Criminal 207E-239F, Justice of the Peace Records, 1907-1908
	1974-019, Box 8	Grant County, N.M., Case Files: Criminal 1H-320H, Justice of the Peace Records, 1909-1911
	1974-019, Box 9	Grant County, N.M., Case Files: Criminal 1I-271A, Justice of the Peace Records, 1911-1912
	1974-019, Box 10	Grant County, N.M., Case Files: Criminal 272A-629B, Justice of the Peace Records, 1912-1914
	1974-033	Records of the United States Territorial and New Mexico District Court Clerks. Collection consists of the court clerk correspondence for the 1st Judicial District Court, the 3rd Judicial District Court, the 4th Judicial District Court, the 6th Judicial District Court, and the 8th Judicial District Court (1879-1970). The bulk of the correspondence cover the years 1879-1912 and 1960-1970. Collection includes criminal cases for Bernalillo, Chavez, Colfax, Doña Ana, Eddy, Grant, Lincoln, Rio Arriba, San Juan, San Miguel, Santa Fe, Socorro, Taos, Union, and Valencia County District Courts (1853-1962). Criminal and civil cases are arranged alphabetically by county.

	1974-033	Records of the United States Territorial and New Mexico District Court Clerks, Criminal and Civil Case Files, 1864-1962
	1974-033	Doña Ana County District Court (Criminal and Civil Cases), 1890-1908
	1974-033	Bernalillo County District Court (Criminal and Civil Cases), 1876-1962
	1974-033	2nd Judicial District Court - No county indicated (Criminal Case), 1882
	1974-033	Grant County District Court (Criminal Cases), 1883, 1892, 1934
	1974-033	San Miguel County District Court (Criminal and Civil Cases), 1888, 1911
	1974-033	Santa Fe County District Court (Criminal and Civil Cases), 1872-1928
	1974-033	Socorro County District Court (Criminal and Civil Cases), 1868, 1888
	1974-033	Taos County District Court (Criminal and Civil Cases), 1873
	1974-033	3rd Judicial District Court - No county indicated (Criminal Cases), No date, 1864, 1877, 1879
	1974-033	Valencia County District Court (Criminal Cases), 1870, 1894
	1974-038	Records of the United States Territorial and New Mexico District Courts for Grant County. Collection consists of the territorial and New Mexico district court records for Grant County, New Mexico (1868-1937). The bulk of the material covers the years 1874-1912. Included are record books (1868-1919), case files (1868-1937), and other court material. Record books include various dockets (1874-1919) and court proceedings record books (1868-1912). Dockets include criminal (1874-1917) and Chancery Court (1886-1887) volumes. Also included are judges' dockets for criminal (1903-1912) trials. Court proceedings record books include volumes from the Chancery Court (1886-1894). Case files include criminal cases 11-6229 (1870-1933). Large gaps may exist between case files. Many criminal and civil cases are unnumbered.
	1974-038	Records of the United States Territorial and New Mexico District Courts for Grant County, series V, Criminal Case Files.

	1975-005	District Court Cases, Colfax County Criminal Cases #1071-#4543
	1976-007	Records of the United States Territorial and New Mexico District Courts for McKinley County, 1901-1931 (bulk 1901-1915). Collection consists of the territorial and New Mexico district court records for McKinley County, New Mexico (1901-1931). The bulk of the material covers the years 1901-1915. Included are criminal cases 1-154 (1901-1911) and a criminal docket for the 2nd Judicial District. Large gaps may exist between case files.
	1976-014	Records of the United States Territorial and New Mexico District Courts for Taos County. The collection consists of the Territorial and New Mexico District Court records for Taos County, New Mexico (1847-1943). The bulk of the material covers the years 1847-1934. Included are record books (1847-1943), case files (1853-1937), and other court material. Record books include various dockets (1854-1913), court proceedings record books (1847-1911), and an indictment and information book (1934-1943). Dockets include criminal (1854-1859, 1883-1909), judge's (1887-1891), and judgement (1884-1913) volumes. Case files consist of criminal case files 14-1357, 3482 (1855-1905, 1937). Large gaps may exist between case files.
	1976-015	Records of the United States Territorial and New Mexico District Courts for Doña Ana County. Collection consists of the territorial and New Mexico District Court records for Doña Ana County, New Mexico (1851-1961). The bulk of the material covers the years 1851-1950. Included are record books (1851-1913), case files (1852-1950), and other court material. Record books consist of various dockets (1851-1913) and court proceedings record books (1852-1911). Dockets include criminal (1885-1911) and civil and criminal (1852-1856, 1869-1886). Judge's dockets cover criminal (1874-1908) proceedings. Court proceeding books include criminal records (1854-1911). Case files include criminal cases 1-8408 (1852-1950).
	1976-020	Collection consists of the territorial and New Mexico district court records for Mora County, New Mexico (1860-1936). The bulk of the material covers the years 1860-1912. Included are record books (1860-1919) and case files (1863-1936). Record books include various dockets (1867-1911) and court proceedings record books (1863-1911). Dockets include criminal (1880-1885, 1888-1905) and judgment (1874-1875) volumes. Court proceedings record books cover criminal and civil (1863-1888, 1893-1911) hearings. Case files contain criminal cases 1-1577, 2102 (1860-1916, 1936).

	1976-021	Records of the United States Territorial and New Mexico District Courts for Union County. Collection consists of the territorial and New Mexico district court records for Union County, New Mexico (1893-1919). Included are record books (1893-1917) and case files (1894-1919). Record books include various dockets (1894-1912) and court proceedings record books (1893-1913). Dockets consist of criminal (1895-1911), judge's criminal and civil (1896-1909), and judge's trial (1894-1895) volumes. Court proceedings record books cover criminal hearings. Case files include criminal cases 1-649 (1895-1911). Large gaps exist between case files.
	1976-025	Records of the United States Territorial and New Mexico District Courts for Guadalupe County. Collection consists of the territorial and New Mexico district court records for Guadalupe County, New Mexico (1893-1965). Included are record books (1893-1946) and case files (1893-1960). Record books consist of various dockets (1893-1946) and court proceedings record books (1893-1922) hearings. Case files include criminal cases 2-1423 (1897-1942). Two numbering systems exist and many criminal case files are unnumbered. Large gaps may exist between case files.
	1976-031	The collection consists of the Territorial and New Mexico District Court records for Socorro County, New Mexico (1851-1933). The bulk of material covers the years 1851-1919. Included are record books (1851-1919) and case files (1852-1933). Dockets include criminal (1867-1898), judges' (1888-1911), and minutes and motions (1851-1854) volumes. Judges' dockets cover criminal (1888-1889, 1905-1909) and Chancery Court (1896-1897) hearings. Case files include criminal cases 1-3606, 5803 (1852-1911). Large gaps may exist between case files. Many criminal cases are unnumbered.
	1976-034	Collection consists of the territorial and New Mexico district court records for Lincoln County, New Mexico (1870-1957). The bulk of the material covers the years (1870-1912). Included are record books (1873-1912), case files (1870-1929), and other court material. Record books include various dockets (1873-1912), court proceedings record books for criminal cases, and Chancery Court hearings (1889-1897). Dockets include criminal and civil volumes (1873-1911). Case files include criminal cases 1-4720 (1871-1921). Large gaps may exist between case files. Many criminal case files are unnumbered.

	1976-039	Collection consists of the territorial and New Mexico district court records for San Juan County, New Mexico (1887-1954). The bulk of the material covers the years 1887-1914. Included are record books (1887-1926), case files (1887-1954), and other court material. Record books consist of various dockets (1887-1926) and court proceedings record books (1887-1913). Dockets include criminal (1887-1909), judge's (1888-1907, 1912-1914, 1926), and judgment (1887-1909) volumes. Case files include criminal cases 104-1156 (1897-1954). Large gaps may exist between case files. Many criminal and civil case files are unnumbered.
	1978-003	Collection consists of the territorial and New Mexico District Court records for Valencia County, New Mexico (1849-1953). The bulk of the material covers the years 1849-1921. Included are record books (1851-1916), case files (1851-1953), and other court material. Record books include various dockets (1851-1913) and court proceedings record books (1854-1856, 1859-1860, 1889-1909, 1873-1880). Judges' dockets cover criminal (1910-1913) and civil (1910-1911) trials. Case files include criminal cases 1-836, 1646 (1852-1912, 1931). Large gaps may exist between case files.
	1978-021	Collection consists of the records of Luna County, New Mexico (1901-1970). The bulk of the materials cover the years 1901 to 1924. Materials include records of the county clerk (1901-1970, sheriff (1910-1913), and justice of the peace (1901-1919, 1929). Justice of the peace records include criminal case files and coroner's inquests (1904-1914).
	1901-1921	Collection consists of the territorial and New Mexico district court records for Luna County, New Mexico (1901-1921). Included are criminal cases 1-664, 1182 (1901-1916, 1921). Large gaps may exist between case files.
	1978-029	The collection consists of the Territorial and New Mexico District Court records for Torrance County, New Mexico (1904-1942). The bulk of the material covers the years 1905-1916. Included are record books (1905-1941) and case files (1904-1942). Record books consist of various dockets (1905-1941) and court proceedings record books (1905-1911). Dockets include criminal (1906-1911), and judge's civil and criminal (1907-1923, 1936-1941) volumes. Case files include criminal cases 1-379 (1904-1916). Large gaps may exist between case files.

	1979-011	Collection consists of the territorial and New Mexico district court records for Curry County, New Mexico (1909-1945). The bulk of the material covers the years 1909-1917. Includes records books (1909-1915) and case files (1909-1917). Record books include various dockets (1909-1915) and a court proceedings record book (1909-1912). Case files include criminal cases 1-381 (1909-1911). Large gaps may exist between case files.
	1979-016	Collection consists of the territorial and New Mexico district court records for Colfax County, New Mexico (1869-1935). The bulk of the material covers the years, 1869-1913. Included are record books (1869-1911) and case files (1869-1935). Record books include various dockets (1869-1911) and court proceedings record books (1869-1911). Dockets include criminal (1869-1908) and judge's (1875-1891) volumes. Court proceedings record books cover criminal (1902-1907) and civil and criminal (1869-1888) hearings. Case files include criminal cases 3-3533 (1869-1920). Large gaps may exist between case files. Many criminal case files may be unnumbered.
	1979-022	Collection consists of the territorial and New Mexico district court records for Otero County, New Mexico (1899-1951). Included are record books (1899-1911) and case files (1899-1951). Record books include various dockets (1899-1912) and court proceedings record books (1899-1910). Dockets include criminal (1899-1912) and judge's criminal (1904) volumes. Court proceedings record books include criminal hearings (1904-1906). Case files include criminal cases 1-756, 954 (1899-1915). Large gaps may exist between case files. Many criminal case files are unnumbered.
	1979-025	The collection consists of the territorial and New Mexico District Court records for Sierra County, New Mexico (1884-1926). The bulk of the material covers the years 1884-1914. Included are record books (1884-1914) and case files (1884-1926). Record books include various dockets (1888-1910) and court proceedings record books (1884-1914). Dockets include criminal (1888-1893) volumes. Court proceedings record books include three volumes from the Chancery Court (1884-1898). Other record books consist of a criminal register and cost book (1884-1912) and an undated index to a criminal docket. Case files consist of criminal cases 1-1129, 3569 (1884-1911). Large gaps may exist between case files. Many criminal cases are unnumbered.

	1979-032	Collection consists of the territorial and New Mexico district court records for Roosevelt County, New Mexico (1903-1954). Included are record books (1903-1954) and case files (1903-1952). Record books consist of criminal dockets (1904-1913, 1931-1936, 1938-1945), civil and criminal dockets (1910-1916), and court proceedings record books (1904-1912). Case files include criminal cases 1-513, 1146, 7506-8581, 32-460 (1904-1916, 1917, 1934, 1940-1949). Many criminal and civil case files are unnumbered, and several changes in the numbering system have occurred. Large gaps may exist between case files.
	1979-033	Collection consists of the territorial and New Mexico district court records for Quay County, New Mexico (1903-1921). Included are record books (1903-1912), case files (1903-1921), and other court material. Record books consist of various dockets (1903-1912) and court proceedings record books (1903-1912). Dockets include criminal volumes (1903-1911). Court proceedings record books cover criminal hearings (1903-1906). Case files consist of criminal cases 1-504, 2614 (1889-1911, 1921). Large gaps may exist between case files. Many case files are unnumbered.
	1980-034	Collection consists of the territorial and New Mexico district court records for Chaves County, New Mexico (1890-1937). The bulk of the material covers the years 1891-1914. Included are record books (1891-1914) and case files (1890-1937). Record books consist of criminal dockets (1892-1912) and court proceedings record books (1891-1914). Case files include criminal cases 1-1344 (1890-1913). Large gaps may exist between case files.
	1982-135	Collection consists of the records of the United States Territorial Supreme Court for New Mexico (1846-1912) and the records of the New Mexico State Supreme Court (1912-1978). The bulk of the material consists of case files from the New Mexico territorial period (1846-1912). Also included are court records (1863-1978), and administrative reports (1959-1978). Case files contained in the collection are cases 1-1483 (1846-1912). Some of the later cases are not part of this collection.
	1985-089	As of 1997 collection consists of the records of the New Mexico Public Defender Department (1976-1994). Included are correspondence, administrative files, primary mission records, and felony case files. Case files consist of cases 1-727 (1987).

| | 1978-029 | The collection consists of the Territorial and New Mexico District Court records for Torrance County, New Mexico (1904-1942). The bulk of the material covers the years 1905-1916. Included are record books (1905-1941) and case files (1904-1942). Record books consist of various dockets (1905-1941) and court proceedings record books (1905-1911). Dockets include criminal (1906-1911) and judge's civil and criminal (1907-1923, 1936-1941) volumes. Case files include criminal cases 1-379 (1904-1916). Large gaps may exist between case files. Most cases after 1912 are not part of this collection. |

Federal Criminal Court Records at the National Archives & Records Admin. (NARA)

NARA Rocky Mountain Region (Denver)
Denver Federal Center, Bldgs 46, 48, Denver, CO 80225, (303) 407-5740
http://www.archives.gov/rocky-mountain/
denver.archives@nara.gov

Record Type	ARC Identifier	Title	Description
	1079766	Criminal Docket, compiled 1891 - 1911	Textual Records from the New Mexico. District Court (5th Judicial District) (1889 -)
	1102923	Criminal Docket, compiled 1910 - 1910	Textual Records from the New Mexico. District Court (7th Judicial District) (1909 -)
	1067699	Criminal Dockets, compiled 1887 - 1911	Textual Records from the New Mexico. District Court (4th Judicial District) (1887 -)
	890251	Civil and Criminal Case Files, compiled 1866 - 1911	Textual Records from the New Mexico. District Court (1st Judicial District) (1851 -)
	981020	Civil and Criminal Case Files, compiled 1895 - 1911	Textual Records from the New Mexico. District Court (2nd Judicial District) (1851 -)
	1103575	Criminal Dockets, compiled 1912 - 1949	Textual Records from the U.S. District Court for the District of New Mexico. (01/06/1912 - ca. 9999)
	990837	Civil and Criminal Dockets, compiled 1883 - 1904	Textual Records from the New Mexico. District Court (2nd Judicial District) (1851 -)
	1089779	Criminal Docket, compiled 1904 - 1911	Textual Records from the New Mexico. District Court (6th Judicial District) (1904 -)

	778067	Criminal Case Files, compiled 1912 - 1953	Textual Records from the U.S. District Court for the District of New Mexico. (01/06/1912 - ca. 9999)
	894290	Criminal Dockets, compiled 1881 - 1911	Textual Records from the New Mexico. District Court (1st Judicial District) (1851 -)
	894365	Judge's Civil and Criminal Docket, compiled 1894 - 1911	Textual Records from the New Mexico. District Court (1st Judicial District) (1851 -)
	1067456	Combined Civil and Criminal Docket, compiled 1889 - 1900	Textual Records from the New Mexico. District Court (3rd Judicial District) (1851 -)
	1067465	Criminal Dockets, compiled 1877 - 1911	Textual Records from the New Mexico. District Court (3rd Judicial District) (1851 -)
	894476	Registers of Civil and Criminal Actions, compiled 1886 - 1888	Textual Records from the New Mexico. District Court (1st Judicial District) (1851 -)
	1040736	Criminal Dockets, compiled 1895 - 1912	Textual Records from the New Mexico. District Court (2nd Judicial District) (1851 -)
	876990	Criminal Case Files, compiled 1847 - 1865	Textual Records from the New Mexico. District Court (1st Judicial District) (1851 -)
	1079907	Criminal Case Files, compiled 1904 - 1911	Textual Records from the New Mexico. District Court (6th Judicial District) (1904 -)
	1065767	Criminal Case Files, compiled 1890 - 1911	Textual Records from the New Mexico. District Court (3rd Judicial District) (1851 -)
	1078532	Criminal Case Files, compiled 1891 - 1912	Textual Records from the New Mexico. District Court (5th Judicial District) (1889 -)
	898715	Criminal Case Files, compiled 1874 - 1889	Textual Records from the New Mexico. District Court (1st Judicial District) (1851 -)
	1065782	Civil and Criminal Case Files, compiled 1851 - 1897	Textual Records
	1067654	Criminal Case Files, compiled 1887 - 1910	Textual Records from the New Mexico. District Court (4th Judicial District) (1887 -)
	1102844	Criminal Case Files, compiled 1910 - 1910	Textual Records from the New Mexico. District Court (7th Judicial District) (1909 -)

	990745	Bankruptcy, Civil, and Criminal Case Files, compiled 1866 - 1904	Textual Records from the New Mexico. District Court (2nd Judicial District) (1851 -)
	2674835	Criminal Case Files, compiled 1967 - 1971	Textual Records from the U.S. District Court for the District of New Mexico. (01/06/1912 - ca. 9999)
	2674836	Records Relating to Criminal Judgments and Orders, compiled 1950 - 1953	Textual Records from the U.S. District Court for the District of New Mexico. (01/06/1912 - ca. 9999)
	4116415	Criminal Case Files, compiled 1974 - 1983	Textual Records from the U.S. District Court for the District of New Mexico. (01/06/1912 - ca. 9999)

New Mexico Executions

 http://users.bestweb.net/~rg/execution/NEW%20MEXICO.htm

New Mexico Department of Corrections – Offender Lookup

 http://corrections.state.nm.us/offenders/search.php

New York

New York State Archives
Cultural Education Center
Albany, NY 12230, (518) 474-8955
http://www.archives.nysed.gov/aindex.shtml
archref@mail.nysed.gov

Record Type	Location	Author	Title/Description
![]	B0143	Sing Sing Prison	Inmate admission registers, 1842-1971 (bulk 1842-1852, 1865-1971) Quantity: 76.1 cu. ft. (149 volumes)
![]	B0147	Sing Sing Prison	Admission registers for prisoners to be executed, 1891-1946. Quantity: 0.5 cu. ft. (2 volumes)
![]	B0145	Sing Sing Prison	Case files of inmates sentenced to electrocution, 1939-1963. Quantity: 19 cu. ft.
![]	B0068	Auburn Prison	Registers of male inmates discharged, 1817-1949. Quantity: 6 cu. ft. (8 volumes)
![]	21832	New York (State). Dept. of Correction	Inmate execution files, 1930-1963. Quantity: 3.5 cu. ft. (ca. 250 case files)
![]	B0097	Clinton Correctional Facility	Inmate record cards, [ca. 1914-1975] Quantity: 28 cu. ft.
![]	A1505	Dannemora State Hospital	Inmate data cards, 1900-1972. Quantity: 9 cu. ft.
![]	A1502	Dannemora State Hospital	Inmate commitment files, [ca. 1900-1961] Quantity: 5 cu. ft.
![]	21833	New York (State). Dept. of Correctional Services. Central Depository	Inmate summary cards, ca. 1890-1987 (bulk 1940-1980). Quantity: ca. 20 cu. ft. (ca. 100,000 index cards)
![]	A0505	Fishkill Correctional Facility	Records, 1858-1975. Quantity: 33 cu. ft.

	B0082	New York (State). Board of Parole	Auburn Prison inmate parole files, 1918-1955. Quantity: 117 cu. ft.
	B0130	Elmira Reformatory	Register of men returned for violation of parole, 1907-1948. Quantity: 2 cu. ft.
	A2088	New York House of Refuge	Inmate admission registers, 1882-1932. Quantity: 1 cu. ft. (3 volumes) Quantity: Copies: 1 microfilm reel; 35mm
	A2069	New York House of Refuge	Parole registers, 1882-1933. Quantity: 1 cu. ft. (3 volumes) Quantity: Copies: 2 microfilm reels; 35mm
	A2087	New York House of Refuge	Register of inmates admitted and discharged, 1859-1882. Quantity: .2 cu. ft. (1 volume) Quantity: Copies: 1 microfilm reel; 35mm
	A2064	New York House of Refuge	Inmate case histories, 1824-1935. Quantity: 70 cu. ft. (106 volumes) Quantity: Copies: 47 microfilm reels; 35mm
	B0064	Auburn Prison	Parole Board ledgers of applicants to be considered for parole, 1924-1935, 3 cu. ft. (3 volumes)
	B0075	Auburn Prison	Parole Board register of inmates paroled, 1893-1926, 0.7 cu. ft. (2 volumes)
	B0136	Elmira Reformatory	Biographical register of men returned for parole violations, 1913-1937. Quantity: 10 cu. ft. (10 volumes)
	B1862	Elmira Reformatory	Discharge registers, 1909-1931. Quantity: 0.2 cu. ft. (2 volumes)
	A0604	New York (State). Governor	Registers of discharges of convicts by commutation of sentences, 1883-1916, 20 cubic feet (25 volumes and 9 rolls)
	B0141	Elmira Reformatory	Biographical registers and receiving blotters, 1879-1957. Quantity: 211 cu. ft (170 volumes)
	B0139	Elmira Reformatory	Index to inmate consecutive numbers, 1877-1947
	A0603	New York (State). Governor	Registers of commitments to prisons, 1842-1908. Quantity: 30 cu. ft. (32 volumes)
	B0042	New York (State). Dept. of State	Executive pardons, 1799-1846, 1856-1931

	14610	New York (State). Dept. of Correctional Services.	Inmate case files, 1894-1995 (bulk ca. 1925-1992]) 5,071 cu. ft. Inmate case files for the following correctional facilities: Adirondack, Albion, Attica, Auburn, Bayview, Bedford Hills, Buffalo, Bushwick, Camp Gabriels, Clinton, Colilns, Coxackie, Downstate, Eastern, Edgecombe, Elmira, Fishkill, Fulton, Great Meadow, Green Haven, Greene, Groveland, Hudson, Lincoln, Lynn Mountain, Mt. McGregor, Mid-Orange, Mid-State, Orleans, Otisville, Parkside, Queensboro, Rochester, Sullivan, Taconic, Wallkill, Wende, Western House, Woodbourne, & Wyoming

NYC Municipal Archives

31 Chambers Street, Room 103, New York, NY, (212) 788-8577
http://www.nyc.gov/html/records/html/collections/home.shtml

Record Type	Title	Description
	Court Records 1684-1966 (Indictments, case files, and docket books.)	The Municipal Archives has the most comprehensive collection of records pertaining to the administration of criminal justice in the English-speaking world. There is a record, at least in summary form, of every felony prosecution in Manhattan from 1684 to 1966. For the period after 1790, there are indictment papers and case files for every felony arrest. Every misdemeanor and violation is recorded in docket books that date back to 1800. The major series are New York County Court of General Sessions, Minutes of the Sessions, 1684-1920; indictment files, 1790-1938 (also identified as District Attorney indictment papers); Police Court/Magistrate's Court docket books, 1799-1930; papers filed in dismissed cases, 1807-1856; Court of Special Sessions, calendar of prisoners, 1829-1839. Kings County Criminal Court indictment records 1894-1965 (with gaps); Kings County Special Sessions (Bastardy proceedings) 1926-1936; Richmond County Special Sessions (Bastardy proceedings) 1899-1939.
	Murder, Inc. Files	Files created by Burton Turkus, NYC District Attorney, in his attempt to prosecute NYC criminals. Another part of the same original collection can be found at John Jay College of Criminal Justics, Sealy Library, Special Collections Department

	Bertillon Card Collection	A collection of about 3,000 cards containing photos and measurements of NYC convicted felons. Named after Aphonse Bertillon, who created a series of measurements (pre-fingerprints) to distinguish one person from another.
	District Attorney Records, 1895-1971 (Closed case files, docket books, newspaper clippings, investigations, correspondence.)	The Municipal Archives holdings of records created by the District Attorneys of the five counties are closely related to (and often identical to), many of the criminal court series. The New York County District Attorney collection is the most extensive. It consists of closed case files, 1895 through 1966 and the related "record of cases," docket books which serve as an index to the closed cases. Other series include the newspaper clipping scrapbooks, 1882-1940 (with gaps), and official correspondence, 1898-1937. The 1943-1955 Carlo Tresca and the 1936 "Lucky" Luciano closed case files are maintained as separate collections with their own finding guide. The Kings County District Attorney holdings comprise closed case files 1940-1945; and 1965-1971. The "Murder Inc." investigative files from the 1940's are maintained as a separate collection with its own finding guide. The Bronx County District Attorney collection consists of closed cases from 1967 through 1971 and the Queens County District Attorney case files date from 1971.

John Jay College of Criminal Justice, Sealy Library

899 10th Avenue, NY, NY 10019, (212) 237-8246
http://www.lib.jjay.cuny.edu
libinfo@jjay.cuny.edu

Record Type	Title	Description
	Trial Transcripts of the County of New York, Court of General Sessions 1883-1927	A collection of about 3,000 Manhattan criminal court trials. All files are on microfilm which one can borrow via Inter-Library Loan
	Burton Turkus Files	Files created by NYC District Attorney, Burton Turkus, in his attempt to bring NYC gangsters to justice in the 1940s. Another part of this original collection is located at the NYC Municipal Archives at 31 Chambers Street, Manhattan. For more info, see: http://www.lib.jjay.cuny.edu/crimeinny/trials/

	Papers of Lewis E. Lawes 1883 - 1947, Warden of Sing Sing Prison, 1920 - 1941	Collection includes personal papers, Sing Sing publications: Star of Hope (1899-19032) and Sing Sing Bulletin (1917-1918), photos, and information about the 'Black Shee' football team.

New York Public Library, Special Collections

42nd Street @ 5th Avenue, New York, NY

Record Type	Title	Description
	Committee of Fourteen records, 1905-1932	The Committee of Fourteen was founded in 1905 as a citizens' association dedicated to the abolition of saloons that provided rooms for prostitution (called "Raines Law hotels".) By 1911 most of the saloons had closed up and the Committee's focus turned to the suppression of commercialized vice in New York City with an emphasis on prostitution. By the time the Committee was dissolved in 1932, the focus included crime prevention as well. Collection includes reports of vice investigations. Tenement House correspondence, 1905, 1911-1932, relates to actions taken against infringements of the law against solicitation or prostitution. Investigators' reports, 1905-1932, contain information collected by the Committee's undercover investigators. Also, files of cases, 1914-1932, brought before the Women's Court.

Columbia University Library, Rare Book & Manuscript Library

Butler Library, 6th Floor, 535 West 114th Street, New York, NY 10027,
http://www.columbia.edu/cu/lweb/indiv/rbml/
rbml@libraries.cul.columbia.edu

Record Type	Title	Description
	Lillian D. Wald Papers 1895-1936.	Papers concerning both the administration of the Henry Street Settlement and Wald's involvement in numerous philanthropic and liberal causes. Her office files trace the foundation and growth of the Henry Street Settlement from 1895 until 1933. Many materials regarding NYC prostitution (See p.59 of collection finding aid: http://www.columbia.edu/cu/libraries/inside/projects/findingaids/scans/pdfs/46_WA-WE_03.pdf)

Federal Criminal Court Records at the National Archives & Records Admin. (NARA)

NARA Northeast Region (New York)

201 Varick Street, 12th Floor, New York, NY 10014, (212) 401-1620

http://www.archives.gov/northeast/

newyork.archives@nara.gov

Record Type	ARC Identifier	Title	Description
	278376	Criminal Case Files, compiled 1790 - 1912	Textual Records from the U.S. Circuit Court for the Southern District of New York. (04/09/1814 - 01/01/1912)
	583516	Criminal Case Files, compiled 1865 - 1978	Textual Records from the U.S. District Court for the Eastern District of New York. (1865 -)
	582173	Criminal Case Files, compiled 1845 - 1977	Textual Records from the U.S. District Court for the Southern District of New York. (1814 -)

New York Executions

http://users.bestweb.net/~rg/execution/NEW%20YORK.htm

New York Department of Corrections – Inmate Search

http://nysdocslookup.docs.state.ny.us/

North Carolina

North Carolina Office of Archives and History

109 E Jones St, Raleigh, NC 27601-1023, (919) 807-7310
www.history.ncdcr.gov/
http://www.history.ncdcr.gov/search/query.htm
http://mars.archives.ncdcr.gov/BasicSearch.aspx
archives@ncmail.net

Record Type	Location (Mars ID)	Title/Description
	286.102.1	Inmate Register, County Home, 1914-1961
	52.2	Death Row Inmate Parole, 1933-1977, Jacket (Capital Case) File
	52	Probation/Parole Record Group
	53	Prisons Record Group
	127	Correction Record Group
	201.16	Alamance County, Minute Docket, Superior Court. Superior courts were established in each county in 1806, replacing the district superior courts that had functioned since 1778. These courts were clothed with original and appellate civil and criminal jurisdiction, as well as actions in equity. Criminal jurisdiction extended to serious felonies, such as murder, rape, larceny, house breaking, assault and battery, riot, forgery and the like)
	201.31	Alamance County, Criminal Action Papers. Criminal case files from magistrates courts, Court of Pleas and Quarter Sessions, Superior Court and, in some counties, other inferior courts, arranged chronologically. In most counties, also includes executions issued supplementary to criminal actions.

	203.16	Alexander County, Minute Docket, Superior Court.
	203.31	Alexander County, Criminal Action Papers.
	204.16	Alleghany County, Minute Docket, Superior Court.
	204.31	Alleghany County, Criminal Action Papers.
	205.16	Anson County, Minute Docket, Superior Court.
	205.31	Anson County, Criminal Action Papers.
	206.16	Ashe County, Minute Docket, Superior Court.
	206.31	Ashe County, Criminal Action Papers.
	207.16	Avery County, Minute Docket, Superior Court.
	207.31	Avery County, Criminal Action Papers.
	209.16	Beaufort County, Minute Docket, Superior Court.
	209.31	Beaufort County, Criminal Action Papers.
	210.16	Bertie County, Minute Docket, Superior Court.
	210.31	Bertie County, Criminal Action Papers.
	211.16	Bladen County, Minute Docket, Superior Court.
	211.31	Bladen County, Criminal Action Papers.
	212.16	Brunswick County, Minute Docket, Superior Court.
	212.31	Brunswick County, Criminal Action Papers.

	213.16	Buncombe County, Minute Docket, Superior Court.
	213.31	Buncombe County, Criminal Action Papers.
	214.16	Burke County, Minute Docket, Superior Court.
	214.31	Burke County, Criminal Action Papers.
	215.16	Bute County, Minute Docket, Superior Court.
	215.31	Bute County, Criminal Action Papers.
	216.16	Cabarrus County, Minute Docket, Superior Court.
	216.31	Cabarrus County, Criminal Action Papers.
	217.16	Caldwell County, Minute Docket, Superior Court.
	217.31	Caldwell County, Criminal Action Papers.
	218.16	Camden County, Minute Docket, Superior Court.
	218.31	Camden County, Criminal Action Papers.
	219.16	Carteret County, Minute Docket, Superior Court.
	219.31	Carteret County, Criminal Action Papers.
	220.16	Caswell County, Minute Docket, Superior Court.
	220.31	Caswell County, Criminal Action Papers.
	221.16	Catawba County, Minute Docket, Superior Court.
	221.31	Catawba County, Criminal Action Papers.

	222.16	Chatham County, Minute Docket, Superior Court.
	222.31	Chatham County, Criminal Action Papers.
	223.16	Cherokee County, Minute Docket, Superior Court.
	223.31	Cherokee County, Criminal Action Papers.
	224.16	Chowan County, Minute Docket, Superior Court.
	224.31	Chowan County, Criminal Action Papers.
	225.16	Clay County, Minute Docket, Superior Court.
	225.31	Clay County, Criminal Action Papers.
	226.16	Cleveland County, Minute Docket, Superior Court.
	226.31	Cleveland County, Criminal Action Papers.
	227.16	Columbus County, Minute Docket, Superior Court.
	227.31	Columbus County, Criminal Action Papers.
	228.16	Craven County, Minute Docket, Superior Court.
	228.31	Craven County, Criminal Action Papers.
	229.16	Cumberland County, Minute Docket, Superior Court.
	229.31	Cumberland County, Criminal Action Papers.
	230.16	Currituck County, Minute Docket, Superior Court.
	230.31	Currituck County, Criminal Action Papers.

	231.16	Dare County, Minute Docket, Superior Court.
	231.31	Dare County, Criminal Action Papers.
	232.16	Davidson County, Minute Docket, Superior Court.
	232.31	Davidson County, Criminal Action Papers.
	233.16	Davie County, Minute Docket, Superior Court.
	233.31	Davie County, Criminal Action Papers.
	235.16	Duplin County, Minute Docket, Superior Court.
	235.31	Duplin County, Criminal Action Papers.
	236.16	Durham County, Minute Docket, Superior Court.
	236.31	Durham County, Criminal Action Papers.
	237.16	Edgecombe County, Minute Docket, Superior Court.
	237.31	Edgecombe County, Criminal Action Papers.
	238.16	Forsyth County, Minute Docket, Superior Court.
	238.31	Forsyth County, Criminal Action Papers.
	239.16	Franklin County, Minute Docket, Superior Court.
	239.31	Franklin County, Criminal Action Papers.
	240.16	Gaston County, Minute Docket, Superior Court.
	240.31	Gaston County, Criminal Action Papers.

	241.16	Gates County, Minute Docket, Superior Court.
	241.31	Gates County, Criminal Action Papers.
	242.16	Glasgow County, Minute Docket, Superior Court.
	242.31	Glasgow County, Criminal Action Papers.
	243.16	Graham County, Minute Docket, Superior Court.
	243.31	Graham County, Criminal Action Papers.
	244.103.8	Granville County, Criminal Actions Concerning Slaves and Free Persons of Color, 1764-1876
	245.16	Greene County, Minute Docket, Superior Court.
	245.31	Greene County, Criminal Action Papers.
	246.16	Guilford County, Minute Docket, Superior Court.
	246.31	Guilford County, Criminal Action Papers.
	247.16	Halifax County, Minute Docket, Superior Court.
	247.31	Halifax County, Criminal Action Papers.
	248.16	Harnett County, Minute Docket, Superior Court.
	248.31	Harnett County, Criminal Action Papers.
	249.16	Haywood County, Minute Docket, Superior Court.
	249.31	Haywood County, Criminal Action Papers.
	250.16	Henderson County, Minute Docket, Superior Court.

	250.31	Henderson County, Criminal Action Papers.
	251.16	Hertford County, Minute Docket, Superior Court.
	251.31	Hertford County, Criminal Action Papers.
	252.16	Hoke County, Minute Docket, Superior Court.
	252.31	Hoke County, Criminal Action Papers.
	253.16	Hyde County, Minute Docket, Superior Court.
	253.31	Hyde County, Criminal Action Papers.
	254.16	Iredell County, Minute Docket, Superior Court.
	254.31	Iredell County, Criminal Action Papers.
	255.16	Jackson County, Minute Docket, Superior Court.
	255.31	Jackson County, Criminal Action Papers.
	256.16	Johnston County, Minute Docket, Superior Court.
	256.31	Johnston County, Criminal Action Papers.
	257.16	Jones County, Minute Docket, Superior Court.
	257.31	Jones County, Criminal Action Papers.
	258.16	Lee County, Minute Docket, Superior Court.
	258.31	Lee County, Criminal Action Papers.
	259.16	Lenoir County, Minute Docket, Superior Court.

	259.31	Lenoir County, Criminal Action Papers.
	260.16	Lincoln County, Minute Docket, Superior Court.
	260.31	Lincoln County, Criminal Action Papers.
	261.16	Macon County, Minute Docket, Superior Court.
	261.31	Macon County, Criminal Action Papers.
	262.16	Madison County, Minute Docket, Superior Court.
	262.31	Madison County, Criminal Action Papers.
	263.16	Martin County, Minute Docket, Superior Court.
	263.31	Martin County, Criminal Action Papers.
	264.16	McDowell County, Minute Docket, Superior Court.
	264.31	McDowell County, Criminal Action Papers.
	265.16	Mecklenburg County, Minute Docket, Superior Court.
	265.31	Mecklenburg County, Criminal Action Papers.
	266.16	Mitchell County, Minute Docket, Superior Court.
	266.31	Mitchell County, Criminal Action Papers.
	267.16	Montgomery County, Minute Docket, Superior Court.
	267.31	Montgomery County, Criminal Action Papers.
	268.16	Moore County, Minute Docket, Superior Court.

	268.31	Moore County, Criminal Action Papers.
	269.16	Nash County, Minute Docket, Superior Court.
	269.31	Nash County, Criminal Action Papers.
	270.16	New Hanover County, Minute Docket, Superior Court.
	270.31	New Hanover County, Criminal Action Papers.
	271.16	Northampton County, Minute Docket, Superior Court.
	271.31	Northampton County, Criminal Action Papers.
	272.16	Onslow County, Minute Docket, Superior Court.
	272.31	Onslow County, Criminal Action Papers.
	273.16	Orange County, Minute Docket, Superior Court.
	273.31	Orange County, Criminal Action Papers.
	274.16	Pamlico County, Minute Docket, Superior Court.
	274.31	Pamlico County, Criminal Action Papers.
	275.16	Pasquotank County, Minute Docket, Superior Court.
	275.31	Pasquotank County, Criminal Action Papers.
	276.16	Pender County, Minute Docket, Superior Court.
	276.31	Pender County, Criminal Action Papers.
	277.16	Perquimans County, Minute Docket, Superior Court.

	277.31	Perquimans County, Criminal Action Papers.
	278.16	Person County, Minute Docket, Superior Court.
	278.31	Person County, Criminal Action Papers.
	279.16	Pitt County, Minute Docket, Superior Court.
	279.31	Pitt County, Criminal Action Papers.
	280.16	Polk County, Minute Docket, Superior Court.
	280.31	Polk County, Criminal Action Papers.
	281.16	Randolph County, Minute Docket, Superior Court.
	281.31	Randolph County, Criminal Action Papers.
	282.16	Richmond County, Minute Docket, Superior Court.
	282.31	Richmond County, Criminal Action Papers.
	283.16	Robeson County, Minute Docket, Superior Court.
	283.31	Robeson County, Criminal Action Papers.
	284.16	Rockingham County, Minute Docket, Superior Court.
	284.31	Rockingham County, Criminal Action Papers.
	285.16	Rowan County, Minute Docket, Superior Court.
	285.31	Rowan County, Criminal Action Papers.
	286.16	Rutherford County, Minute Docket, Superior Court.

	286.31	Rutherford County, Criminal Action Papers.
	287.16	Sampson County, Minute Docket, Superior Court.
	287.31	Sampson County, Criminal Action Papers.
	288.16	Scotland County, Minute Docket, Superior Court.
	288.31	Scotland County, Criminal Action Papers.
	289.16	Stanly County, Minute Docket, Superior Court.
	289.31	Stanly County, Criminal Action Papers.
	290.16	Stokes County, Minute Docket, Superior Court.
	290.31	Stokes County, Criminal Action Papers.
	291.16	Swain County, Minute Docket, Superior Court.
	291.31	Swain County, Criminal Action Papers.
	292.16	Surry County, Minute Docket, Superior Court.
	292.31	Surry County, Criminal Action Papers.
	293.16	Transylvania County, Minute Docket, Superior Court.
	293.31	Transylvania County, Criminal Action Papers.
	294.16	Tryon County, Minute Docket, Superior Court.
	294.31	Tryon County, Criminal Action Papers.
	296.16	Tyrrell County, Minute Docket, Superior Court.

	296.31	Tyrrell County, Criminal Action Papers.
	297.16	Union County, Minute Docket, Superior Court.
	297.31	Union County, Criminal Action Papers.
	299.16	Wake County, Minute Docket, Superior Court.
	299.31	Wake County, Criminal Action Papers.
	300.16	Warren County, Minute Docket, Superior Court.
	300.31	Warren County, Criminal Action Papers.
	301.16	Washington County, Minute Docket, Superior Court.
	301.31	Washington County, Criminal Action Papers.
	302.16	Watauga County, Minute Docket, Superior Court.
	302.31	Watauga County, Criminal Action Papers.
	303.16	Wayne County, Minute Docket, Superior Court.
	303.31	Wayne County, Criminal Action Papers.
	304.16	Wilkes County, Minute Docket, Superior Court.
	304.31	Wilkes County, Criminal Action Papers.
	305.16	Wilson County, Minute Docket, Superior Court.
	305.31	Wilson County, Criminal Action Papers.
	306.16	Yadkin County, Minute Docket, Superior Court.

	306.31	Yadkin County, Criminal Action Papers.
	307.31	Yancey County, Criminal Action Papers.

Federal Criminal Court Records at the National Archives & Records Admin. (NARA)

NARA Southeast Region
5780 Jonesboro Road, Morrow, Georgia 30260, (770) 968-2100
www.archives.gov/southeast/
atlanta.archives@nara.gov

Record Type	ARC Identifier	Title	Description
	2737754	Criminal Case Files, compiled 1957 - 1980	Textual Records from the U.S. District Court for the Middle District of North Carolina. Greensboro Term. (03/02/1927 -)
	2618814	Index Cards to Criminal Case Files for the Eastern District of North Carolina, compiled 1952 - 1981	Textual Records from the U.S. District Court for the Eastern District of North Carolina. Raleigh Term. (08/09/1894 -)
	2540321	Criminal Dockets, compiled 1906 - 1984	Textual Records from the U.S. District Court for the Eastern District of North Carolina. Wilson Term. (10/07/1914 - ?)
	2789486	Criminal Dockets, compiled 1956 - 1979	Textual Records from the U.S. District Court for the Middle District of North Carolina. Greensboro Term. (03/02/1927 -)
	2843376	Criminal Trial Docket, compiled 1813 - 1872	Textual Records from the U.S. Circuit Court for the Eastern District of North Carolina. (06/04/1872 - 02/17/1887)
	2867037	Magistrate Criminal Case Dockets, compiled 1971 - 1992	Textual Records from the U.S. District Court for the Eastern District of North Carolina. New Bern Term. (06/04/1872 -)
	733760	Criminal Case Files, compiled 1895 - 1980	Textual Records from the U.S. District Court for the Eastern District of North Carolina. Raleigh Term. (08/09/1894 -)

	2524709	Criminal Dockets, compiled 1944 - 1947	Textual Records from the U.S. District Court for the Western District of North Carolina. Shelby Term. (12/24/1924 - ?)
	2542462	Criminal Dockets, compiled 1895 - 1985	Textual Records from the U.S. District Court for the Eastern District of North Carolina. Raleigh Term. (08/09/1894 -)
	2524685	Criminal Case Files, compiled 1941 - 1947	Textual Records from the U.S. District Court for the Western District of North Carolina. Shelby Term. (12/24/1924 - ?)
	2568915	Criminal Case Files, compiled 1872 - 1983	Textual Records from the U.S. District Court for the Middle District of North Carolina. Greensboro Term. (03/02/1927 -)
	2555901	Criminal Minutes, compiled 1807 - 1878	Textual Records from the U.S. Circuit Court for the Eastern District of North Carolina. (06/04/1872 - 02/17/1887)
	2581229	Criminal Dockets, compiled 1868 - 1985	Textual Records from the U.S. District Court for the Eastern District of North Carolina. Wilmington Term. (06/04/1872 -)
	2637943	Criminal Calendars, compiled 1919 - 1925	Textual Records from the U.S. District Court for the Eastern District of North Carolina. Raleigh Term. (08/09/1894 -)
	2540319	Criminal Minutes, compiled 1873 - 1964	Textual Records from the U.S. District Court for the Western District of North Carolina. Asheville Term. (06/04/1872 -)
	2555902	Criminal Minutes, compiled 1904 - 1957	Textual Records from the U.S. District Court for the Middle District of North Carolina. Wilkesboro Term. (03/02/1927 - ?)
	2568916	Criminal Case Files, compiled 1898 - 1982	Textual Records from the U.S. District Court for the Eastern District of North Carolina. New Bern Term. (06/04/1872 -)
	2568920	Criminal Case Files, compiled 1865 - 1983	Textual Records from the U.S. District Court for the Eastern District of North Carolina. Wilmington Term. (06/04/1872 -)
	2568921	Criminal Case Files, compiled 1921 - 1983	Textual Records from the U.S. District Court for the Eastern District of North Carolina. Wilson Term. (10/07/1914 - ?)
	2568912	Criminal Case Files, compiled 1927 - 1956	Textual Records from the U.S. District Court for the Middle District of North Carolina. Salisbury Term. (03/02/1927 - ?)
	2637952	Criminal Calendars, compiled 1896 - 1921	Textual Records from the U.S. District Court for the Eastern District of North Carolina. New Bern Term. (06/04/1872 -)

	2591958	Criminal Minutes, compiled 1928 - 1947	Textual Records from the U.S. District Court for the Western District of North Carolina. Bryson City Term. (04/25/1928 -)
	2540320	Criminal Dockets, compiled 1928 - 1956	Textual Records from the U.S. District Court for the Eastern District of North Carolina. Durham Term. (05/10/1928 - 06/28/1935)
	2133288	Criminal Dockets, compiled 1927 - 1956	Textual Records from the U.S. District Court for the Middle District of North Carolina. Rockingham Term. (03/02/1927 - ?)
	2524696	Criminal Dockets, compiled 1928 - 1946	Textual Records from the U.S. District Court for the Western District of North Carolina. Bryson City Term. (04/25/1928 -)
	2524703	Criminal Minutes, compiled 1944 - 1947	Textual Records from the U.S. District Court for the Western District of North Carolina. Shelby Term. (12/24/1924 - ?)
	2439858	Criminal Dockets, compiled 1872 - 1891	Textual Records from the U.S. Circuit Court for the Western District of North Carolina. Asheville Term. (06/04/1872 - 12/31/1911)
	2591962	Index Cards to Criminal Case Files, compiled 1968 - 1982	Textual Records from the U.S. District Court for the Eastern District of North Carolina. Wilmington Term. (06/04/1872 -)
	2789489	Magistrate Criminal Case Dockets, compiled 1971 - 1975	Textual Records from the U.S. District Court for the Eastern District of North Carolina. Raleigh Term. (08/09/1894 -)
	2568913	Criminal Case Files, compiled 1927 - 1946	Textual Records from the U.S. District Court for the Middle District of North Carolina. Rockingham Term. (03/02/1927 - ?)
	2568917	Criminal Case Files, compiled 1872 - 1983	Textual Records from the U.S. District Court for the Western District of North Carolina. Statesville Term. (06/04/1872 -)
	2439854	Criminal Dockets, compiled 1872 - 1946	Textual Records from the U.S. District Court for the Western District of North Carolina. Asheville Term. (06/04/1872 -)
	2555904	Criminal Minutes, compiled 1938 - 1956	Textual Records from the U.S. District Court for the Middle District of North Carolina. Rockingham Term. (03/02/1927 - ?)
	3242450	Criminal Final Record Book, compiled 1900 - 1912	Textual Records from the U.S. District Court for the Eastern District of North Carolina. Wilmington Term. (06/04/1872 -)
	3242444	Criminal Final Record Book, compiled 1900 - 1907	Textual Records from the U.S. District Court for the Eastern District of North Carolina. Elizabeth City Term. (06/04/1872 -)

	2568922	Criminal Case Files, compiled 1927 - 1956	Textual Records from the U.S. District Court for the Middle District of North Carolina. Winston-Salem Term. (03/02/1927 -)
	2568923	Criminal Case Files, compiled 1872 - 1901	Textual Records from the U.S. Circuit Court for the Western District of North Carolina. Statesville Term. (06/04/1872 - 12/31/1911)
	2568924	Criminal Case Files, compiled 1798 - 1897	Textual Records from the U.S. Circuit Court for the Eastern District of North Carolina. Raleigh Term. (02/17/1887 - 01/01/1912)
	2637965	Criminal Calendar, compiled 1923 - 1926	Textual Records from the U.S. District Court for the Western District of North Carolina. Asheville Term. (06/04/1872 -)
	2568919	Criminal Case Files, compiled 1927 - 1956	Textual Records from the U.S. District Court for the Middle District of North Carolina. Wilkesboro Term. (03/02/1927 - ?)
	2555907	Criminal Minutes, compiled 1938 - 1957	Textual Records from the U.S. District Court for the Middle District of North Carolina. Salisbury Term. (03/02/1927 - ?)
	2524718	Criminal Dockets, compiled 1909 - 1985	Textual Records from the U.S. District Court for the Eastern District of North Carolina. New Bern Term. (06/04/1872 -)
	2385482	Criminal Case Files, compiled 1872 - 1980	Textual Records from the U.S. District Court for the Western District of North Carolina. Asheville Term. (06/04/1872 -)
	3242379	Criminal Minutes Court Blotter , compiled 1989 - 1991	Textual Records from the U.S. District Court for the Eastern District of North Carolina. Elizabeth City Term. (06/04/1872 -)
	2555891	Criminal Minutes, compiled 1872 - 1909	Textual Records from the U.S. Circuit Court for the Western District of North Carolina. Greensboro Term. (06/04/1872 - 12/31/1911)
	2555908	Criminal Minutes, compiled 1872 - 1906	Textual Records from the U.S. Circuit Court for the Western District of North Carolina. Statesville Term. (06/04/1872 - 12/31/1911)
	2542580	Criminal Dockets, compiled 1872 - 1928	Textual Records from the U.S. District Court for the Western District of North Carolina. Statesville Term. (06/04/1872 -)
	2542579	Criminal Dockets, compiled 1927 - 1956	Textual Records from the U.S. District Court for the Middle District of North Carolina. Salisbury Term. (03/02/1927 - ?)
	2555890	Criminal Minutes, compiled 1880 - 1902	Textual Records from the U.S. Circuit Court for the Western District of North Carolina. Charlotte Term. (06/19/1878 - 12/31/1911)

	2524697	Criminal Dockets, compiled 1869 - 1897	Textual Records from the U.S. Circuit Court for the Eastern District of North Carolina. Raleigh Term. (02/17/1887 - 01/01/1912)
	2439878	Criminal Dockets, compiled 1878 - 1968	Textual Records from the U.S. District Court for the Western District of North Carolina. Charlotte Term. (06/19/1878 -)
	2439880	Criminal Dockets, compiled 1899 - 1985	Textual Records from the U.S. District Court for the Eastern District of North Carolina. Elizabeth City Term. (06/04/1872 -)
	2579371	Criminal Dockets, compiled 1905 - 1976	Textual Records from the U.S. District Court for the Eastern District of North Carolina. Washington Term. (03/03/1905 - 04/21/1992)
	2568918	Criminal Case Files, compiled 1905 - 1975	Textual Records from the U.S. District Court for the Eastern District of North Carolina. Washington Term. (03/03/1905 - 04/21/1992)
	2568914	Criminal Case Files, compiled 1928 - 1945	Textual Records from the U.S. District Court for the Western District of North Carolina. Bryson City Term. (04/25/1928 -)
	2637942	Criminal Calendars, compiled 1904 - 1925	Textual Records from the U.S. District Court for the Western District of North Carolina. Wilkesboro Term. (02/23/1903 - 03/02/1927)
	2637954	Criminal Calendars, compiled 1894 - 1927	Textual Records from the U.S. District Court for the Western District of North Carolina. Greensboro Term. (06/04/1872 - 03/02/1927)
	2524689	Criminal Case Files, compiled 1915 - 1981	Textual Records from the U.S. District Court for the Eastern District of North Carolina. Fayetteville Term. (06/07/1924 -)
	2637956	Criminal Calendars, compiled 1895 - 1929	Textual Records from the U.S. District Court for the Western District of North Carolina. Charlotte Term. (06/19/1878 -)
	2555898	Criminal Minutes, compiled 1938 - 1957	Textual Records from the U.S. District Court for the Middle District of North Carolina. Durham Term. (06/24/1936 -)
	2555886	Criminal Minutes, compiled 1880 - 1932	Textual Records from the U.S. District Court for the Western District of North Carolina. Charlotte Term. (06/19/1878 -)
	2568935	Criminal Minutes, compiled 1928 - 1947	Textual Records from the U.S. District Court for the Western District of North Carolina. Bryson City Term. (04/25/1928 -)
	2439896	Criminal Dockets, compiled 1929 - 1968	Textual Records from the U.S. District Court for the Eastern District of North Carolina. Fayetteville Term. (06/07/1924 -)

	2439895	Criminal Dockets, compiled 1872 - 1955	Textual Records from the U.S. District Court for the Middle District of North Carolina. Greensboro Term. (03/02/1927 -)
	2579375	Criminal Dockets, compiled 1903 - 1956	Textual Records from the U.S. District Court for the Middle District of North Carolina. Wilkesboro Term. (03/02/1927 - ?)
	2637937	Criminal Calendars, compiled 1898 - 1913	Textual Records from the U.S. District Court for the Eastern District of North Carolina. Wilmington Term. (06/04/1872 -)
	2618763	Criminal Orders, compiled 1955 - 1981	Textual Records from the U.S. District Court for the Eastern District of North Carolina. Wilmington Term. (06/04/1872 -)
	2521090	Criminal Case Files, compiled 1896 - 1982	Textual Records from the U.S. District Court for the Western District of North Carolina. Charlotte Term. (06/19/1878 -)
	2555884	Criminal Minutes, compiled 1872 - 1899	Textual Records from the U.S. Circuit Court for the Western District of North Carolina. Asheville Term. (06/04/1872 - 12/31/1911)
	2439874	Criminal Dockets, compiled 1879 - 1902	Textual Records from the U.S. Circuit Court for the Western District of North Carolina. Charlotte Term. (06/19/1878 - 12/31/1911)
	2555935	Criminal Minutes, compiled 1872 - 1925	Textual Records from the U.S. District Court for the Western District of North Carolina. Statesville Term. (06/04/1872 -)
	2524693	Criminal Case Files, compiled 1928 - 1957	Textual Records from the U.S. District Court for the Middle District of North Carolina. Durham Term. (06/24/1936 -)
	2618765	Criminal Orders, compiled 1979 - 1986	Textual Records from the U.S. District Court for the Eastern District of North Carolina. Elizabeth City Term. (06/04/1872 -)
	2439899	Criminal Dockets, compiled 1872 - 1909	Textual Records from the U.S. Circuit Court for the Western District of North Carolina. Greensboro Term. (06/04/1872 - 12/31/1911)
	2540318	Criminal Minutes, compiled 1938 - 1957	Textual Records from the U.S. District Court for the Middle District of North Carolina. Winston-Salem Term. (03/02/1927 -)
	2524692	Criminal Case Files, compiled 1899 - 1982	Textual Records from the U.S. District Court for the Eastern District of North Carolina. Elizabeth City Term. (06/04/1872 -)
	2555895	Criminal Minutes, compiled 1873 - 1957	Textual Records from the U.S. District Court for the Middle District of North Carolina. Greensboro Term. (03/02/1927 -)

	2568925	Criminal Case Files, compiled 1904 - 1910	Textual Records from the U.S. Circuit Court for the Eastern District of North Carolina. Wilmington Term. (02/17/1887 - 01/01/1912)
	2524714	Criminal Dockets, compiled 1872 - 1899	Textual Records from the U.S. Circuit Court for the Western District of North Carolina. Statesville Term. (06/04/1872 - 12/31/1911)
	2629264	Criminal Calendars, compiled 1928 - 1933	Textual Records from the U.S. District Court for the Eastern District of North Carolina. Elizabeth City Term. (06/04/1872 -)
	2579368	Criminal Dockets, compiled 1927 - 1956	Textual Records from the U.S. District Court for the Middle District of North Carolina. Winston-Salem Term. (03/02/1927 -)
	2591966	Index Cards to Criminal Case Files, compiled 1951 - 1982	Textual Records from the U.S. District Court for the Eastern District of North Carolina. Fayetteville Term. (06/07/1924 -)
	2674567	Criminal Final Record Book, compiled 1899 - 1916	Textual Records from the U.S. District Court for the Eastern District of North Carolina. Raleigh Term. (08/09/1894 -)
	2674562	Criminal Final Record Book, compiled 1872 - 1894	Textual Records from the U.S. District Court for the Western District of North Carolina. Greensboro Term. (06/04/1872 - 03/02/1927)
	2642367	Criminal Final Record Book, compiled 1878 - 1916	Textual Records from the U.S. District Court for the Western District of North Carolina. Charlotte Term. (06/19/1878 -)
	2679371	Index to Criminal Case Files, compiled 1867 - 1895	Textual Records from the U.S. Circuit Court for the Eastern District of North Carolina. Raleigh Term. (02/17/1887 - 01/01/1912)
	2674565	Criminal Final Record Book, compiled 1906 - 1914	Textual Records from the U.S. District Court for the Eastern District of North Carolina. New Bern Term. (06/04/1872 -)
	2679369	Index to Criminal Case Files, compiled 1897 - 1924	Textual Records from the U.S. District Court for the Western District of North Carolina. Asheville Term. (06/04/1872 -)
	2715052	Index to Criminal Case Files, compiled 1875 - 1923	Textual Records from the U.S. District Court for the Western District of North Carolina. Statesville Term. (06/04/1872 -)
	2679360	Index to Criminal Case Files, compiled 1910 - 1925	Textual Records from the U.S. District Court for the Western District of North Carolina. Wilkesboro Term. (02/23/1903 - 03/02/1927)
	2642369	Criminal Final Record Book, compiled 1872 - 1914	Textual Records from the U.S. District Court for the Western District of North Carolina. Asheville Term. (06/04/1872 -)

Executions in North Carolina

 http://users.bestweb.net/~rg/execution/NO%20CAROLINA.htm

North Department of Corrections – Offender Lookup

 http://webapps6.doc.state.nc.us/opi/offendersearch.do?method=view

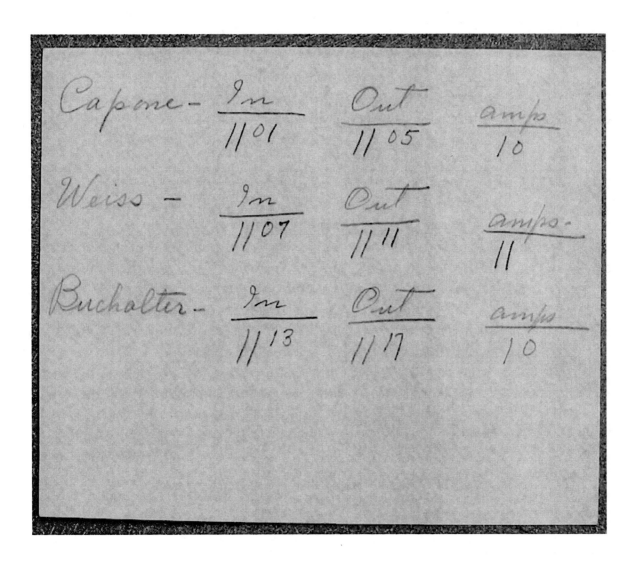

Amount of electiricty used to electrocute Louis Capone, Emanuel Weiss and Louis "Lepke" Buchalter in Sing Sing's electric chair. From New York State Archives, RG B0145, Case files of inmates sentenced to electrocution, 1939-1963. Courtesy of the New York State Archives and the New York Department of Corrections.

North Dakota

North Dakota State Archives and Historical Reseqrch Library

612 East Boulevard Avenue, Bismark, ND, (701) 328-2091
http://history.nd.gov/archives/index.html
archives@state.nd.us

State Historical Society of North Dakota

http://history.nd.gov/

Record Type	Location	Author	Title/Description
	Series 31255	ND State Penitentiary	Inmate case files, 1885-1950s. Consists of documents concerning sentencing, commitment, and discharge of inmates; correspondence; medical reports; parole reports; notes; vouchers; and identification papers.
	Series 31256	ND State Penitentiary	Inmate case files index, 1891-1971.
	Series 30360	ND State Penitentiary	Inmate census schedules, 1920-1955.
	Series 30366	ND State Penitentiary	Mug shot books, 1892-1917.
	Series 30966	ND State Penitentiary	Consists of a record of inmate offenses or violations and punishment administered by Penitentiary officials.
	Series 31431	ND State Penitentiary	North Dakota State Penitentiary discharge record, 1885-1923. Records inmate discharges and pardons.
	Series 30361	ND State Penitentiary	North Dakota State Penitentiary inmate record, 1885-1923.
	Series 30943	ND State Penitentiary	Board of Pardons case record, 1895-1925, 1929-1938. Consists of a record of Board of Pardons actions on pardon applications.

	Series 30184	North Dakota. Governor.	Board of Pardons criminal case files, 1889-1908. Consists of correspondence, indictments, transcripts of testimony, court proceedings, and applications.

Federal Criminal Court Records at the National Archives & Records Admin. (NARA)

NARA Central Plains Region (Kansas City),
400 West Pershing Road, Kansas City, MO 64108, (816) 268-8000
http://www.archives.gov/central-plains/kansas-city/
kansascity.archives@nara.gov

Record Type	ARC Identifier	Title	Description
	583191	Criminal Case Files, compiled 1890 - 1961	Textual Records from the U.S. District Court for the Southeastern (Fargo) Division of the District of North Dakota. (04/26/1890 -)
	583192	Criminal Case Files, compiled 1957 - 1960	Textual Records from the U.S. District Court for the Southwestern (Bismarck) Division of the District of North Dakota. (04/26/1890 -)
	1801233	Criminal Case Files, compiled 1863 - 1881	Textual Records from the U.S. Territorial Court for the First (Vermillion) District of the District of Dakota. (1861 - 1889)
	1145987	Criminal Case Files, compiled 1927 - 1960	Textual Records from the Department of the Interior. Bureau of Indian Affairs. Pine Ridge Agency. (09/17/1947 - 09/09/9999)
	283682	Distsrict of North Dakota: Fargo: Criminal Cases, compiled 1890 - 1957	Photographs and other Graphic Materials and Textual Records from the U.S. District Court for the Southeastern (Fargo) Division of the District of North Dakota. (04/26/1890 -)

Federal Criminal Court Records at the National Archives & Records Admin. (NARA)

NARA Rocky Mountain Region (Denver)
Denver Federal Center, Bldgs 46, 48, Denver, CO 80225, (303) 407-5740
http://www.archives.gov/rocky-mountain/
denver.archives@nara.gov

Record Type	ARC Identifier	Title	Description
	1126764	Criminal Dockets, compiled 1902 - 1931	Textual Records from the U.S. District Court for the Northwestern (Devil's Lake) Division of the District of North Dakota. (04/26/1890 - 1948)
	3955401	Criminal Case Files, compiled 1976 - 1979	Textual Records from the U.S. District Court for the Southwestern (Bismarck) Division of the District of North Dakota. (04/26/1890 -)
	3974971	Criminal Case Files, compiled 1978 - 1979	Textual Records from the U.S. District Court for the Southeastern (Fargo) Division of the District of North Dakota. (04/26/1890 -)

North Dakota Executions

http://users.bestweb.net/~rg/execution/NO%20DAKOTA.htm

North Dakota Supreme Court – Online Case Lookup

http://www.ndcourts.gov/publicsearch/contactsearch.aspx

North Dakota Depatment of Corrections: Inmate Lookup

http://www.nd.gov/docr/offenderlkup/index.asp

Charles Kraushaar

late of the County of Cook, on the **twenty third**

in the year of our Lord, one thousand nine hundred and thirty   th

County of Cook, in the State of Illinois aforesaid, feloniously, burg

forcibly,

did break and enter a certain building, to-wit:

dwelling house of Albert H. Miller

there situate, with intent the personal goods, chattels, money and

Albert H. Miller, of Mary H. Miller and of

four rings each being of the value of one dol
the United States of America

of the personal goods, chattels, money and pr
Miller

three rings each being of the value of one do
the United States of America
one bracelet of the value of two dollars law:
States of America and
one watch of the value of ten dollars lawful
States of America

IL Supreme Court case #22297: The People v. Kraushaar, 357 Ill. 463 (1934) about
Charles Kraushaar, brother-in-law of Belva Gaertner, a true-life murderess and
role model for the character Velma in the Broadway musical and movie 'Chicago.'
Found in Record Group 901.001 (Case Files of the Illinois Supreme Court) held at
the Illinois State Archives, Springfield, IL.

Ohio

Ohio State Archives and Historical Reseqrch Library

Ohio Historical Center, 1982 Velma Ave. Columbus, OH 43211
http://www.ohiohistory.org/resource/statearc/
email: http://www.ohiohistory.org/contact.html

Record Type	Location (OCLC #)	Author	Title/Description
	ocm36373646	Ohio Penitentiary (Columbus, Ohio)	Account book for convict labor, 1891-1911. Contains records of convict labor listing company utilizing the labor and amount paid.
	ocm36595174	Ohio State Reformatory	Account ledgers, 1896-1924.
	Series 1002 AV	Ohio Penitentiary (Columbus, Ohio)	Bertillon cards with photographs [graphic], 1888-1919. Individual cards for each prisoner include front and profile photographs, height, age, weight, color of hair, state of birth, and several Bertillon system measurements
	ocm36373653	Ohio Penitentiary (Columbus, Ohio)	Bertillon record, 1887-1923. Contains records of convicts admitted to the penitentiary. Each entry includes prisoner's serial number, name, county of conviction, admission date, length of sentence, crime, age, height, weight, complexion, forehead description, nose description, chin description, eye color, hair color, birthplace, occupation, any previous imprisonments, marital status, name and address of nearest friend or relative, any distinguishing features, etc.
	ocm36373680	Ohio Penitentiary (Columbus, Ohio)	First hearing register, 1967-1989. Contains records of prisoners' first hearings. Each record includes prisoner's number, name, date received, and term served.

	ocm36373667	Ohio Penitentiary (Columbus, Ohio)	Court record, 1891-1917. Contains records of offenses committed by prisoners while in prison. Each record includes prisoner's name, crime, term, serial number, county, receipt date, and earliest possible release date. Each entry includes date, name of guard reporting the offense, case number, offense, name of presiding deputy, punishment administered, and remarks.
	ocm36373673	Ohio Penitentiary (Columbus, Ohio)	Criminal record, 1815-1818. Contains records of cases involving criminals who served time at the Ohio Penitentiary. Each handwritten entry includes date, name of accused, crime, narrative description of case, court costs, county, and sentence imposed.
	ocm36373674	Ohio Penitentiary (Columbus, Ohio)	Deputy warden's directory of inmate admissions, 1870-1907. Lists admissions to the penitentiary. Each entry includes inmate's serial number, name, length of term, age, whether or not a tobacco user, physical condition, occupation, date received, county of residence, crime, date of expiration of full term, date of expiration of short term, discharge date, and remarks.
	ocm36373675	Ohio Penitentiary (Columbus, Ohio)	Discharge records and applications for restoration of citizenship, 1896-1936. Contains records of discharges and applications for restoration of citizenship from former prisoners. Each discharge record includes date, prisoner's name, court of sentencing, date of sentencing, length of sentence, number of previous terms of imprisonment, etc. Each application for restoration of citizenship includes convict's name, date of sentencing, court of sentencing, crime committed, length of sentence, place of residence, amount of time since discharge, signatures of witnesses to convict's conduct, judge's signature, date of application, and prisoner's address.
	ocm36373685	Ohio Penitentiary (Columbus, Ohio)	Index to register of prisoners, 1913-1973. Contains index to prisoners. Each entry includes prisoner's name, serial number, and county of residence.

	ocm36373676	Ohio Penitentiary (Columbus, Ohio)	Duplicate register of prisoners received and discharged, 1930- 1936. Contains records of prisoners received and discharged. Each receipt entry includes date, receipt number, name, serial number, length of prison term, county of residence, and remarks. Each discharge entry includes date, discharge number, serial number, county of residence, and reason for discharge.
	ocm36373688	Ohio Penitentiary (Columbus, Ohio)	List of men electrocuted at the Ohio Penitentiary, 1897-1941. Lists prisoners electrocuted at the Ohio Penitentiary. Each entry includes prisoner's name, serial number, date received, county of conviction, and date of electrocution.
	ocm36373695	Ohio Penitentiary (Columbus, Ohio)	Pardon record, 1882-1924. Contains records of prisoners' pardons. Each record includes governor's name, term of court, county, year, prisoner's name, crime, length of sentence, condition of pardon, date of pardon, and pertinent signatures.
	ocm36373699	Ohio Penitentiary (Columbus, Ohio)	Penitentiary post office record, 1881-1905. Contains records of the penitentiary post office. Each entry includes date, prisoner's number, name, cell number, county of residence, length of term, any alias used, remarks, and shop of employment.
	V 920 Sm58	Ohio Penitentiary (Columbus, Ohio)	Photographs of executed prisoners and of the death house, 1885-1963. Individual photographs of executed prisoners with each prisoner's name, home county, date of execution, and the crime for which the prisoner was executed.
	Series 6548	Ohio Penitentiary (Columbus, Ohio)	Prisoner transfers from old to new prison, 1831-1834.
	ocm36373702	Ohio Penitentiary (Columbus, Ohio)	Record of escaped prisoners, 1834-1935. Lists prisoners who escaped from the penitentiary. Each record includes prisoner's name, serial number, crime, sentence length, county of conviction, receiving date, term of court in which convicted, register number where case was recorded, page number of register, and method of escape.

	ocm36373700	Ohio Penitentiary (Columbus, Ohio)	Prisoners' register [microform], 1829-1973. Between 1829 to October 1913 the record consists of one-line entries on three consecutive double-page spreads. The first two pages list name, length of term, crime, serial number, county, term of court, when received, time out, and when and how discharged. The second pair of pages lists name, age, nativity, occupation, height, eye and hair color, complexion, general appearance, and marks and scars. The third double page spread lists name, habits (liquor), residence of relatives, statement of property, and education. From October 1913 onward the record consists of one-line entries on a two page spread. The two pages list serial number, name, age, race, term, crime, county, term of court, when received, maximum time, minimum time, and when and how discharged.
	ocm36373704	Ohio Penitentiary (Columbus, Ohio)	Record of persons sentenced to be executed, 1885-1968. Contains records of persons sentenced to be executed at the penitentiary. Not all sentences were carried out. Each record includes prisoner's name, serial number, county of conviction, date prisoner was received, recording register, register page number, name of person or persons the prisoner was convicted of murdering, and date of execution set by trial court. If applicable, record might include execution dates set by other courts, dates of stays of execution, institution granting stay of execution, date of granting of new trial, who granted new trial, date execution occurred, and time of execution.
	ocm36373705	Ohio Penitentiary (Columbus, Ohio)	Register of anthropometric descriptions, 1897-1920. Contains anthropometric (physical) descriptions of prisoners, probably based on the Bertillon system. Each entry includes date, serial number, name, height, length of outstretched arms, trunk size, length of head, width of head, length of right ear, length of left foot, length of left middle finger, length of left little finger, color of left eye, forehead description, nose description, age, birthplace, beard color, hair color, complexion, weight, and remarks.

	ocm36373706 Series 1532	Ohio Penitentiary (Columbus, Ohio)	Register of arrivals, 1865-1905. One-line entries across two pages list date received, name, serial number, age when vaccinated, length of sentence, crime, county, and remarks.
	ocm37438744	Ohio Penitentiary (Columbus, Ohio)	Register of identification, 1910-[1937?]. Contains register of identification of prisoners. Each entry includes prisoner's name, serial number, name of recipient of identification, and remarks.
	ocm37382578	Ohio Penitentiary (Columbus, Ohio)	Visitors' registers, 1944-1949. Contains registers of visitors to the prison listing date, visitor's name, address, surname of prisoner being visited, prisoner's serial number, and relationship between visitor and prisoner. See Prisoners' register (State Archives Series 1536) for more information about the prisoners.
	LGR MIC136	Jefferson County (Ohio). Clerk of Courts	Criminal action case files [microform], 1877-1952. Docket of criminal cases assigned for trial in common pleas court.
	bjh01909	Jefferson County (Ohio). Clerk of Courts	Criminal action case files [microform], 1886-1887, 1889-1891, 1894, 1913, 1932-1952. Docket of criminal cases assigned for trial in common pleas court.
	ocm32405179	Jefferson County (Ohio). Clerk of Courts	Criminal action case files : records, 1886-1952.
	LGR MIC 1, 2	Jefferson County (Ohio). Clerk of Courts	Criminal action case files (scattered) [microform], 1877-1955. Docket of criminal cases assigned for trial in common pleas court.
	Series 4898	Delaware County (Ohio). Clerk of Courts.	Common Pleas criminal docket, 1853-1860, 1854-1880. Collects in one section defendant and charge. May include all actions in the case, final disposition of the case, and costs.
	Series 5280	Union County (Ohio). Probate Court.	Criminal appearance docket, 1877-1881. Collects in one section defendant, case number, charges, plea, summary of all actions in the case showing final disposition.

	LGR 0173	Mahoning County (Ohio). Probate Court.	Criminal appearance docket, 1877-1906. Record of criminal appearance, showing attorneys' names, case number, parties, kind of action, date and cost bill, findings, judgements, orders, and decrees.
	Series 5169	Fayette County (Ohio). Probate Court.	Criminal appearance docket, 1882-1918. Docket of criminal cases for appearance in probate court, showing case number, names of attorneys and defendant, offense charged, date transcript from magistrate's court filed, date affidavit of information filed, date warrant for arrest filed, date warrant returned, and record of court findings and sentence.
	Series 4962	Delaware County (Ohio). Probate Court.	Criminal appearance docket, 1886-1928. Collects in one section defendant, case number, charges, plea, summary of all actions in the case showing final disposition.
	LGR 0166	Mahoning County (Ohio). Court of Common Pleas.	Criminal appearance docket, 1906-1933. Collects in one section defendant, case number, charge, attorney, amount of bond, bondsman, and judge; summarizing all actions in the case and indexing original entry in order book by volume and page.
	Series 6541	Mount Vernon (Ohio). Municipal Court.	Criminal appearance docket, 1972-1975. Collects in one section defendant, case number, charges, plea, summary of all actions in the case showing final disposition.
	bjh01910	Jefferson County (Ohio). Clerk of Courts.	Criminal appearance docket [microform], 1896-1906, 1926-1946. Docket of criminal cases tried before common pleas court.
	ocm36643944 Series 1523	Ohio State Reformatory	Parole record, 1893-1922. Contains parole records listing parole number, inmates' name, serial number, admission date, county of conviction, crime, minimum sentence, maximum sentence, number of months served, parole date, check list of monthly report dates, date due for final release, name of employer or relative, address of employer or relative, and remarks.

	LGR MIC136	Jefferson County (Ohio). Clerk of Courts.	Criminal appearance docket [microform], 1904-1906, 1926-1946. Docket of criminal cases tried before common pleas court.
	ocm35597813 Series 1551	Boys' Industrial School (Lancaster, Ohio)	Parole record, 1928-1955 (bulk 1928-1934, 1953-1955).
	ocm36109431	London Prison Farm (Ohio)	Parole and inmate index, 1908-1948. Indexes Prisoners' register (State Archives Series 1609). Each entry includes prisoner's name, prison number or parole number, and serial number.
	ocm37438736	Ohio Adult Parole Authority	Pardon and Parole Commission minutes, Ohio State Reformatory [microform], 1923-1955. Contains minutes of the Pardon and Parole Commission that concern the Ohio State Reformatory. Minutes list prisoners discharged, paroled, and returned for paroleviolations. Each entry includes prisoner's serial number, name, county of conviction, and action taken.
	ocm37438733	Ohio Adult Parole Authority	Pardon and Parole Commission minutes, Ohio Penitentiary [microform], 1923-1955. Contains minutes of the Pardon and Parole Commission that concern the Ohio Penitentiary. Minutes list prisoners discharged, paroled, and returned for parole violations. Each entry includes prisoner's serial number, name, county of conviction, and action taken.
	ocm37438731	Ohio Adult Parole Authority	Pardon and Parole Commission minutes, London Prison Farm [microform], 1925-1955. Contains minutes of the Pardon and Parole Commission concerning the London Prison Farm. Minutes list prisoners discharged, paroled, and returned for parole violations. Each enty includes prisoner's serial number, name, county of conviction, and action taken.
	ocm34021522	Ohio. Office of the Governor.	Pardon applications, 1865-1915. Contains pardon applications listing convict's name, crime, and application date. Also contains letters supporting or opposing pardons. Some applications include certificate of pardon if pardon was granted. Most of these pardon applications were rejected.

	ocm34021524	Ohio. Office of the Governor.	Pardon papers, 1817-1922. Contains pardons issued by Ohio governors and related materials such as applications and petitions for pardon. Each certificate of pardon includes prisoner's name, date of conviction, county of conviction, crime, length of sentence, date of pardon, and governor's signature.
	ocm35154363	Ohio. Board of Clemency.	Pardon record, 1917-1929. Contains applications for pardons. Each entry includes convict's name, serial number, crime, date of conviction, county, sentence, date of application, action taken, and remarks.
	ocm34021528	Ohio. Office of the Governor.	Pardon records, 1838-1984. Contains applications for pardons and commutations. The most complete entries include prisoner's name, identification number, institution, crime, county of conviction, date of conviction, sentence, application filing information, supporting statements, governor's action, and justification.

Federal Criminal Court Records at the National Archives & Records Admin. (NARA)

NARA Great Lakes Region (Chicago),
7358 South Pulaski Road, Chicago, IL 60629-5898, (773) 948-9001
http://www.archives.gov/great-lakes/
chicago.archives@nara.gov

Record Type	ARC Identifier	Title	Description
	1105351	Criminal Case Files, compiled 1912 - 1977	Textual Records from the U.S. District Court for the Eastern (Cleveland) Division of the Northern District of Ohio. (06/08/1878 -)
	1089044	Criminal Case Files, compiled 1888 - 1969	Textual Records from the U.S. District Court for the Eastern (Columbus) Division of the Southern District of Ohio. (02/04/1880 -)
	1127007	Criminal Case Files, compiled 1880 - 1898, documenting the period 1850 - 1898	Textual Records from the U.S. Circuit Court for the Western (Cincinnati) Division of the Southern District of Ohio. (02/04/1880 - 01/01/1912)

	1105220	Criminal Case Files, compiled 1888 - 1968	Textual Records from the U.S. District Court for the Western (Cincinnati) Division of the Southern District of Ohio. (02/04/1880 -)
	1105494	Criminal Case Files, compiled 1917 - 1969	Textual Records from the U.S. District Court for the Western Division of the Southern District of Ohio. Dayton Term. (03/04/1907 -)
	2765894	Criminal Case Files, compiled 1912 - 1977	Textual Records from the U.S. District Court for the Eastern (Cleveland) Division of the Northern District of Ohio. (06/08/1878 -)
	1105498	Criminal Case Files, compiled 1920 - 1969	Textual Records from the U.S. District Court for the Western (Toledo) Division of the Northern District of Ohio. (06/08/1878 -)
	1126952	Criminal Case Files, compiled 1880 - 1892, documenting the period 1877 - 1892	Textual Records from the U.S. Circuit Court for the Eastern (Columbus) Division of the Southern District of Ohio. (02/04/1880 - 01/01/1912)

Ohio Executions

 http://users.bestweb.net/~rg/execution/OHIO.htm

Ohio Department of Rehabilitation and Correction – Offender Search

 http://www.drc.ohio.gov/OffenderSearch/Search.aspx

Charles Kraus

7595 Name *Charles Kraushaar*

ASSIGNMENT

Received *September 7, 1933*

Sentence *1 - Life*

County *Cook*

Crime *Burglary*   Term of Court

Color *White*

Hair *Ch. Dk Grey* Eyes *Haz Gr Sl.*

Height *5 5¼* Build *Med.*

Religion *Lutheran*

Profanity *No*

Smoke *No*

Age *59*

Nativity *Ill.*

Weight *155*

Education *H.H.S.*

Drink *Yes*

Chew *No*

Associates *None*

Parents Living *No*

Left Home What Age *17*

Married *Yes*

Wife Living *Yes*

Hereditary Disease *None*

Condition of Heart *Good*

Condition of Lungs *Good*

Occupation *Carpenter*

Working when arrested on present charge *Yes*

How long before if not

Name and address of

Parents or family } Wife } *Ethel Kraushaar 812 Eastwood Ave*

Correspondents   *Chicago Ill.*

Father born in *Germany*

Mother born in *Ill.*

Children

How long have you lived in the United States?

Are you a Naturalized Citizen?

Have you taken out 1st Papers?

Are you an Alien?

Joliet Prison admission record for Charles Kraushaar. Found at Illinois State Archives, Springfield, IL.

Oklahoma

Oklahoma Department of Corrections

http://www.doc.state.ok.us/

Record Type	
![icon]	The Dept. of Corrections has all prison records for state prisons from 1907 onward

Oklahoma State Archives and Record Management

Dept. of Libraries, 200 NE 18th St, Oklahoma City, OK 73105
(800) 522-8116, (405) 522-3579
http://www.odl.state.ok.us/oar/
http://www.odl.state.ok.us/oar/archives/index.htm
http://www.odl.state.ok.us/oar/governors/home.htm
http://catalog.odl.state.ok.us/
email: http://www.odl.state.ok.us/oar/contacts/index.html

Record Type	Location	Title/Description
![icon]		Court of Criminal Appeals Case Mades A00001 through A18214. Oklahoma. Supreme Court, 1907 - 1972, multiple holdings available
![icon]	29-1-4 R36	Court of Criminal Appeals Case Files 73-1 through 73-471. Oklahoma. Supreme Court, 1973, multiple holdings available
![icon]	29-1-4 R36 T8	Court of Criminal Appeals Case Files 74-1 through 74-843. Oklahoma. Supreme Court, 1974, multiple holdings available
![icon]		Court of Criminal Appeals Case Files 75-1 through 75-814. Oklahoma. Supreme Court, 1975, multiple holdings available
![icon]		Court of Criminal Appeals Case Files 76-1 through 76-979. Oklahoma. Supreme Court, 1976, multiple holdings available

		Court of Criminal Appeals Case Files 77-1 through 77-893. Oklahoma. Supreme Court, 1977, multiple holdings available
		Court of Criminal Appeals Case Files 78-1 through 78-700. Oklahoma. Supreme Court, 1978, multiple holdings available
		Court of Criminal Appeals Case Files 79-1 through 79-746. Oklahoma. Supreme Court, 1979, multiple holdings available
	19-20 R37 T19 S4, S5	Pardons and Paroles. #b 00001 - 32921. Oklahoma. Office of the Secretary of State, 1906 multiple holdings available
	19-20 R37 T20 S1	Pardons and Paroles. #b 32922-47459. Oklahoma. Office of the Secretary of State, 1906 multiple holdings available
	19-20 R37 T20 S2	Pardons and Paroles. #b 47460-49897. Oklahoma. Office of the Secretary of State, 1906
	19-20 R37 T20 S3	Pardons and Paroles. #b 49895-59669. Oklahoma. Office of the Secretary of State, 1906
	19-20 R37 T20 S3, S4	Pardons and Paroles. #b 59700-77850. Oklahoma. Office of the Secretary of State, 1906
	19-20 R37 T20 S2	Pardons and Paroles. #b 35391-44200. Oklahoma. Office of the Secretary of State, 1906

Oklahoma Supreme Court Records

 http://oklegal.onenet.net/sample.basic.html

also http://www.findlaw.com/11stategov/ok/okca.html

Federal Criminal Court Records at the National Archives & Records Admin. (NARA)

NARA Southwest Region (Fort Worth)

501 West Felix Street, Building 1, Fort Worth, TX 76115-3405, Phone: 817-831-5620

http://www.archives.gov/southwest/

ftworth.archives@nara.gov

Record Type	ARC Identifier	Title	Description
	731292	Criminal Return Dockets, compiled 1915 - 1973	Textual Records from the U.S. District Court for the Western District of OKlahoma. Office of the U.S. Magistrate Judge. (1968 -)
	731294	Criminal Dockets, compiled 1928 - 1957	Textual Records from the U.S. District Court for the Western District of Oklahoma. (06/16/1906 -)
	650898	Criminal Case Files, compiled 1907 - 1981	Textual Records from the U.S. District Court for the Western District of Oklahoma. (06/16/1906 -)
	650901	Criminal Orders, compiled 1938 - 1984	Textual Records from the U.S. District Court for the Western District of Oklahoma. (06/16/1906 -)
	3371091	Criminal Record Books, compiled 11/16/1907 - 1950	Textual Records from the U.S. District Court for the Eastern District of Oklahoma. (06/16/1906 -)
	3371097	Records of Proceedings in Criminal Cases, compiled 1916 - 1970	Textual Records from the U.S. District Court for the Eastern District of Oklahoma. (06/16/1906 -)
	783831	Criminal Case Files, compiled 1907 - 1911	Textual Records from the U.S. Circuit Court for the Western District of Oklahoma. Guthrie Term. (06/16/1906 - 01/01/1912)
	649435	Criminal Case Files, compiled 1925 - 1979	Textual Records from the U.S. District Court for the Northern District of Oklahoma. (02/16/1925 -)
	650900	Criminal Writ Execution Docket, compiled 1911 - 1925	Textual Records from the U.S. District Court for the Western District of Oklahoma. (06/16/1906 -)
	650193	Index to Judgments, compiled 1908 - 1947	Textual Records from the U.S. District Court for the Western District of Oklahoma. (06/16/1906 -)

	650196	Judgment Dockets, compiled 1908 - 1969	Textual Records from the U.S. District Court for the Western District of Oklahoma. (06/16/1906 -)
	3371066	Index to Judgments, compiled 1911 - 1941	Textual Records from the U.S. District Court for the Eastern District of Oklahoma. (06/16/1906 -)
	3371090	Criminal Minutes, compiled 1912 - 1940	Textual Records from the U.S. District Court for the Eastern District of Oklahoma. (06/16/1906 -)
	650229	Card Index to Plaintiffs and Defendants, compiled 1907 - 1983	Textual Records from the U.S. District Court for the Western District of Oklahoma. (06/16/1906 -)
	650904	Index to Criminal Defendants, compiled ca. 1907 - ca. 1983	Textual Records from the U.S. District Court for the Western District of Oklahoma. (06/16/1906 -)
	3371094	Criminal Dockets, compiled 1908 - 1965	Textual Records from the U.S. District Court for the Eastern District of Oklahoma. (06/16/1906 -)
	783827	Criminal Docket, compiled 1908 - 1911	Textual Records from the U.S. Circuit Court for the Western District of Oklahoma. Guthrie Term. (06/16/1906 - 01/01/1912)
	649479	Criminal Dockets, compiled 1925 - 1945	Textual Records from the U.S. District Court for the Northern District of Oklahoma. (02/16/1925 -)
	650902	Criminal Dockets, compiled 1907 - 1956	Textual Records from the U.S. District Court for the Western District of Oklahoma. (06/16/1906 -)
	650899	Criminal Indictment Records, compiled 1907 - 1916	Textual Records from the U.S. District Court for the Western District of Oklahoma. (06/16/1906 -)
	650903	Index to Defendants in Criminal Cases, compiled ca. 1907 - ca. 1957	Textual Records from the U.S. District Court for the Western District of Oklahoma. (06/16/1906 -)
	3371095	Criminal Case Files, compiled 1907 - 1982	Textual Records from the U.S. District Court for the Eastern District of Oklahoma. (06/16/1906 -)

Current Court Case Lookup

 http://www1.odcr.com/search.php

Oklahoma Executions

 http://users.bestweb.net/~rg/execution/OKLAHOMA.htm

Oklahoma Department of Corrections Offender Lookup

 http://docapp065p.doc.state.ok.us/servlet/page?_pageid=395&_dad=portal30&_schema=PORTAL30

List of California prisons where Charles Kraushaar served time.
Courtesy of California State Archives, Sacramento, CA

Oregon

Oregon State Archives and Record Management

800 Summer St. NE, Salem OR 97310, (503) 373-0701
http://arcweb.sos.state.or.us/
reference.archives@state.or.us

Record Type	Title	Description
	Convict Record	1915-1921, 1 vol., Arrangement: chronological Includes: name, county, date arrived, sentence, how realesed, date released, time served, crime, nativity, age, skin color, height, weight, eyes, hair color. Preceded with an index of names; appendix contains alphabetical list of prisoners confined prior to 12-15-1915 and in cutsody post ca. 1921.
	Daily Inmate Totals Registers	1896 - 1925, 3 boxed volumes, Arrangement: chronological
	Inmate Admissions and Discharges	1889 - 1974, 7 vols., Arrangement: chronological Daily Admissions and Discharges, 1906 - 1917, 2 volumes; "Record of Prisoners Received or Released", 1914-1949, 3 boxed volumes; Record of Prisoners Received or Released-Surnames C-E, 1894-1974, 1 boxed volume; "Discharged Convict Register, 1889-1916, 1 volume (Includes record of escaped convicts, 1898-1913).
	Inmate Case Files	1853 - 1920, 38.5 cu. ft., Arrangement: numerical by case number; 1853 - 1920, (bulk of case files cover the date span of 1890 - 1920; highest inmate number is 8154; more complete starting at #2200) 38 cu. ft.; 1927, 1983 (one item), Roy De Autremont case file (3 photos and 1 negative) .25 cu. ft.
	Inmates Received and Average Time Served Calendars	1901-1921, 2 vols., Arrangement: chronological Recorded by biennium; includes parole violations (box 18).

	Visitor Registers	1910 - 1931, 5 vols., Arrangement: chronological
	Inmate Commitment Journal	1857 - 1878, 1 vol., Arrangement: chronological Penitentiary Inmate Registers (Great Registers, inmate #'s 230 - 16754), 1854 - 1946, 9 volumes; Prisoner Register (alpha arranged), 1881 - 1894, 1 volume; Rogues Gallery Register (alphabetical, thereunder chronological), 1891 - 1898, 1 volume; Federal Prisoner Roll (arranged chronologically by quarter), 1889 - 1905, 1 volume.
	Inmate Description and History Registers	1887 - 1922, 5 vols., Arrangement: chronological 1916 - 1922 (#'s 7500 - 8531), 1 volume; 1887 - 1895 (#-s 1943 - 3428), 4 volumes (boxed).
	Inmate Disciplinary Journals	1905 - 1929, 3 vols., Arrangement: chronological 1905 - 1923, 1 loose leaf binder (arranged alphabetically by inmate surname); 1908 - 1921, 1 volume; 1925 - 1929, 1 volume (boxed).
	Inmate Indexes	1854 - 1946, 4 cu. ft. / 16 vols., Arrangement: chronological 1854 - 1946, 8 volumes (inmate #'s 1 - 18678); 1854 - 1932, 4 cu. ft., Inmate Index Cards (number-to-name cross reference) (visit the Historical Records Index to search names from this series); 1895 - 1899, 1 volume (record of inmates during the administration of A. N. Gilbert); 1907 - 1910, 5 volumes (inmate #'s 3040 - 6249); 1909 - 1919, 1 volume (alpha by surname); 1915 - 1922, 1 volume (indexed by surname); 1924 - 1929, 1 volume (numerical by inmate number)
	Inmate Isolation and Segregation Logs	1955 - 1969, 4 cu. ft. / 21 vols., Arrangement: chronological Isolation and Segregation Logs, 1955 - 1969, 4 cu. ft.; Segregation and Isolation Unit Activity Logs, 1957 - 1963, 21 volumes (in 2 boxes).
	Inmate Labor Ledgers	1889 - 1912, 2 vols., Arrangement: chronological Inmate Labor Ledger (totals of inmates furnishing labor and hours worked reported quarterly for North Western Foundry, Oregon State Stove Works, and Lowenburg & Going Co. Also includes number of men working for Asylum Building Fund and Reform School Fund), 1889 - 1912, 1 volume; Petty Account Ledger - Convict Labor (alpha index by institution or company), 1912, 1 volume.
	Inmate Merit Award Register	1878 - 1890, 1 vol., Arrangement: chronological Arranged by numbers corresponding to entries in Great Register and includes information on days awarded, awarded conduct, amounts paid, crime committed, date of discharge.

	Inmate Record	1916-1917, 1 vol., Arrangement: chronological "Private Book" of Charles A Murphy, warden of Oregon State Penitentiary. Records all inmates leaving the institution since November 21, 1916 and inmates received as of August 7, 1917.
	Inmate Registers	1854-1946, 12 vols., Arrangement: chronological Penitentiary Inmate Registers (Great Registers, inmate #'s 230 - 16754), 1854 - 1946, 9 volumes; Prisoner Register (alpha arranged), 1881 - 1894, 1 volume; Rogues Gallery Register (alphabetical, thereunder chronological), 1891 - 1898, 1 volume; Federal Prisoner Roll (arranged chronologically by quarter), 1889 - 1905, 1 volume.
	Pardons and Commutations Register	1886 - 1915, vol., Arrangement: chronological
	Parole Board Actions	1915 - 1947, .25 cu. ft. / 26 vols., Arrangement: chronological 1915 - 1938, 7.5 cu. ft. (26 boxed volumes); 1933 -1943, 1 volume; 1940 - 1947, .25 cu. ft.
	Parole Board Registers	1905 -1937, 3 vols., Arrangement: n/a "Indeterminate Record", 1905-1927, 2 volumes "Record of Men on Parole", 1930 - 1937, 1 volume.

County Files

Record Type	Location (Repository)	County/Title/Description
	Baker County Courthouse, Clerk's Lower Vault, Back Room	Baker County Circuit Court Case Files / Criminal [Case Files], no. 500-2399, 1960-1983 (36 cu.ft.);
	Baker County Courthouse, Clerk's Lower Vault, Front Room:	Baker County Circuit Court Case Files /Criminal [Case Files], drawer no. 1-71, 1865-1948 (24 cu.ft.); no. 1-499, 1948-1960 (5 cu.ft.); Criminal Cases [Circuit Court Case Files], 1931-1946 (.35 cu.ft.);
	Baker County Courthouse, Trial Court Records Dept.	Baker County Circuit Court Case Files / Criminal Index [Convictions-Circuit Court Case Files Index], 1928-1988 (1 volume); Criminal Judgment Roll Index, vol. 1, 1865-1971 (1 volume);
	Baker County Courthouse, Clerk's Lower Vault, Back Room:	Baker County Justice Court Case Files / Criminal Trans. from J.P. Court [Transcripts from Justice of the Peace to Circuit Court], 1911-1925 (.30 cu.ft.).

	Baker County Courthouse, Clerk's Lower Vault, Back Room:	Baker County Prisoner Registers / Jail Register, 1892-1904 (1 volume); [Jail Register-with index], 1902-1931 (1 volume); Register of Prisoners [with index], vol. 1, 1890-1902 (1 volume).
	Oregon State Archives	Benton County Circuit Court Case Files / Circuit Court Case Files, no. 1-11147, 1852-1937 (110 cu.ft.); Circuit Court Case Files Indexes, no. 1-8457, 1851-1926 (2 volumes)
	Benton County Courthouse, Room 106	Benton County Circuit Court Case Files / Civil Files and Criminal Files [Circuit Court Case Files], no. 11148-43000, 1937-1983 (181 inches microfiche)
	Benton County Historical Museum	Benton County Justice Court Dockets / Docket Justice Court Precinct # 2, 1874-1880 (1 volume); Justice Court Journal [District 10, Philomath], 1896-1916 (1 volume); Justice Court Kings Valley [Record], 1894-1916 (1 volume); Justice Court Philomath, 1872-1900 (1 volume); 1889-1895 (1 volume); Small Claims Docket [Justice Court], 1922-1948 (1 volume).
	Benton County Courthouse, Clerk's Vault	Benton County Prisoner Registers / [Jail Register], 1892-1908 (1 volume); Jail Register, vol. 2-3, 1952-1966 (2 volumes); [Register of Prisoners Confined in the County Jail], 1886-1952 (1 volume).
	Clackamas County Courthouse, Court File Room	Clakamas County Circuit Court Case Files / Circuit Court Criminal Case Files], no. 81.1-81.1245, 1981 (11 reels of microfilm); no. 81.13-83.941, 1981-1983 (20 inches of microfilm jackets); Civil and Criminal [Circuit Court Case Files, no. 76.7.1-83.12.364, 1976-1983 (41 feet of microfilm jackets); Crim Civil Domestic [Circuit Court Criminal, Civil, and Domestic Case Files], no. 10000-31600, 1919-1939 (242 reels of microfilm)
	Oregon State Archives	Clakamas County Justice Court Case Files / Justice Court Case Records [Upper Molalla and Lower Molalla Precincts], 1859-1876 (.10 cu.ft.).
	Clackamas County Sheriff's North Station Building, Lobby Exhibit Case	Clakamas County Prisoner Registers / [Jail Register], 1891-1925 (1 volume); [Jail Register and Mug Book-includes photographs-with index], 1929-1964 (1 volume).
	Oregon State Archives	Clatsop County Circuit Court Case Files / Misc. Court Records [Miscellaneous Circuit Court Records-includes civil, criminal, divorce, and juvenile cases], 1920-1923 (.35 cu.ft.)

	Oregon State Archives	Clatsop County Justice Court Case Files / Justice Court Case File, 1852 (.05 cu.ft.); Justice Court Process Records [Cases Files-Astoria Precinct], 1846-1918 (5.75 cu.ft.).
	Clatsop County Courthouse, Clerk's Old Lower Vault	Clatsop County Justice Court Case Files / Elections [Justice Court Documents-Astoria Precinct], 1878 (.05 cu.ft.); Justice Ct. Prior to 1880 [Court-Astoria Precinct], 1877-1880 (1 cu.ft.).
	Clatsop County Jail, Upstairs Elevator Lobby, Cabinet 2	Clatsop County Prisoner Registers / Old Booking Ledgers [Jail Register], vol. 1-7, 1888-1967 (7 volumes).
	Columbia County Courthouse Annex, Vault	Columbia County Circuit Court Case Files / [Circuit Court Case Files], no. 5552-30180, 1924-1983 (339 reels of microfilm); 1969-1982 (36 inches of aperture cards); General Index [to mining, judgments, complaints, divorce, insane, and guardianships], 1941-1945 (1 volume); Index to Circuit Court Case Files, 1854-1973 (2 volumes); [Index to Circuit Court Case Files], 1973-1987 (3 volumes).
	Columbia County Courthouse, Basement Vault	Columbia County Justice Court Case Files / [Case Files-Justice Court], ca.1930-1941 (3 cu.ft.); [Criminal Cases-Justice Court], vol. 18, 1932 (.10 cu.ft.); Transcripts from Justice Court [includes some circuit court records], 1913-1917 (1 cu.ft.).
	Columbia County Courthouse, Historical Society Museum	Columbia County Prisoner Registers / Jail Register, 1892-1938 (1 volume).
	Columbia County Sheriff's Office Bldg, Evidence Locker	Columbia County Prisoner Registers / Jail Docket, 1939-1960 (1 volume).
	Coos County Courthouse, Criminal Court Office	Coos County Circuit Court Case Files / General Criminal Index, 1853-1978 (1 volume);
	Coos County Courthouse, Old Jail Storage	Coos County Circuit Court Case Files / [Circuit-Court Case Files-includes criminal case files], no. 4950-10171, 78CR0001-78CR0559, 1960-1978 (24 reels of microfilm); Criminal [Circuit Court Case Files], no. 2464-2749, 1931-1935 (2 cu.ft.); Out of Order Large Files [Circuit Court Criminal Case Files], 1931-ca.1940 (1 cu.ft.).
	Coos County Courthouse, Clerk's Vault	Coos County Circuit Court Case Files / Index to Criminal Cases [Circuit Court and Justice Court], 1854-1936 (1 volume).

	Coos County Courthouse, Clerk's Downstairs Archives	Coos County Justice Court Case Files / Bound-over for Justice Court [3rd District Case Records], 1929-1940 (.25 cu.ft.); Justice Court Criminal Transcripts [various districts], no. 1-1231, 1932-1936 (1 cu.ft.); Justice Court Transcripts [includes related documents], 1870-1920 (1 cu.ft.).
	Coos County Historical Society	Coos County Prisoner Registers / [Jail Register], 1893-1896 (1 volume).
	Crook County Courthouse, Clerk's Vault	Crook County Circuit Court Case Files / Old State Cases [Circuit Court Criminal Case Files], 1909-1917 (.30 cu.ft.); State Cases [Circuit Court Criminal Case Files], 1913-1919 (.20 cu.ft.)
	Crook County Courthouse, Clerk's Vault	Crook County Justice Court Case Files / Justice Transcripts [Court], 1898-1918 (.35 cu.ft.).
	Crook County Courthouse, Trial Court Downstairs Vault	Crook County Justice Court Case Files / [Justice Court Case Files-Prineville Precinct No. 1], 1927-1930, 1934-1940 (2.10 cu.ft.).
	Crook County Road Department Yard, Records Storage Unit 4	Crook County Justice Court Case Files / [Justice Court Case Records], 1903-1910 (.05 cu.ft.); Justice Transcripts [District No. 1], 1885-1905 (.10 cu.ft.).
	Crook County Archives Center, Trial Court Storage Cage	Crook County Prisoner Registers / Record of Accused Persons [Booking and Jail Register], 1947-1956 (1 volume).
	Oregon State Sheriffs' Association Museum	Crook County Prisoner Registers / Jail Register Crook County, 1892-1954 (1 volume).
	Curry County Courthouse, State Courts Civil-Domestic-Probate Office	Curry County Circuit Court Case Files / Circuit Court Cases [Files-Felony], 1961-1983 (9 reels of microfilm)
	Curry County Courthouse, Clerk's Office Vault	Curry County Justice Court Case Files / Justice Court [Case Files], 1935-1940 (.10 cu.ft.).
	Coos/Curry Counties Trial Court Storage (North Bend)	Curry County Justice Court Case Files / Justice Ct. [Court Case Files-5th District], 1929-1940 (1 cu.ft.).
	Curry County Historical Society Museum	Curry County Prisoner Registers / [Jail Register], 1892-1967 (1 volume).
	Deschutes County Justice Building Basement, Court Archives	Deschutes County Justice Court Case Files / Justice Docket [Bend Precinct], 1917-1919 (1 volume); Justice Docket Small Claims [Bend District-with index], 1926-1936 (1 volume).

	Deschutes County Justice Building Basement, Court Archives	Deschutes County Circuit Court Case Files / [Circuit Court Case Files-boxed], no. 4600-10639, 1935-1959 (71 cu.ft.); [Circuit Court Case Files-open shelves], no. 10640-35797, 1959-1983 (388 cu.ft.); Circuit Court Records [Case Files], no. 130-438, ca.1911-ca.1920 (4 reels of microfilm);
	Deschutes County Justice Building, Main Floor Lobby Exhibit Case	Deschutes County Justice Court Case Files / Justice Docket [Bend Precinct-with index], vol. 1-2, 1921-1922 (2 volumes); [Justice Docket-Criminal], 1924 (1 volume).
	Douglas County Courthouse, Clerk's Archives	Douglas County Circuit Court Case Files / Circuit Court Index Direct, vol. 1-5, 1852-1978 (5 reels of microfilm); Circuit Court Index Indirect, vol. 1-5, 1852-1978 (5 reels of microfilm)
	Douglas County Courthouse, Clerk's Archives	Douglas County Justice Court Case Files / Yoncalla Justice of the Peace Filings [also includes Drain justice district records], 1922-1938 (1.20 cu.ft.).
	Douglas County Museum of History and Natural History, Research Library	Douglas County Justice Court Case Files / Calapooia District Justice Court [Case Files], 1884-1935 (3.50 cu.ft.).
	Douglas County Justice Building, Sheriff's Office, Detective Area Storage Room	Douglas County Prisoner Registers / Jail Register [with index], vol. 2-3, 1931-1950 (2 volumes); [Prisoner Records], 1949-1954 (1 volume); Tax Sale Record [actually serves as a prisoner register], 1949-1952 (1 volume).
	Douglas County Museum of History and Natural History, Research Library	Douglas County Prisoner Registers / Jail Register, 1954-1962 (1 volume); 1962-1972 (1 volume).
	Oregon State Archives	Gilliam County Circuit Court Case Files / Circuit Court Case Files, no. 4-3517, 1885-1930 (39 cu.ft.); Circuit Court Case Index [copy-in reference library], 1893-1912 (1 volume)
	Gilliam County Courthouse, Trial Clerk's Office	Gilliam County Circuit Court Case Files / General Index Register and Circuit Court Docket, vol. 1-2, 1909-1983 (2 volumes).
	Gilliam County Courthouse, Lower Vault	Gilliam County Justice Court Case Files / City of Condon Recorders Court Case Files [Ex-officio Justice of the Peace], 1905-1909 (.30 cu.ft.); Justice Court Records Historical Save [Justice Transcripts-trifolded], 1885-1905 (.40 cu.ft.).

	Gilliam County Court-house, Lower Vault	Gilliam County Prisoner Registers / Jail Record Gilliam County, 1925-1976 (1 volume).
	Oregon State Archives	Grant County Circuit Court Case Files / Civil and Criminal Files [Circuit Court Case], no. 223-2197, 1870-1906 (22 cu.ft.); Unnumbered Civil and Criminal Files [Circuit Court Case], 1871-1905 (1 cu.ft.);
	Grant County Courthouse, Basement Vault	Grant County Circuit Court Case Files / JR [Judgment Roll-Circuit Court Case Files-includes criminal, law, and equity cases], no. JR1885-JR3336, 1930-1942 (16 cu.ft.); no. JR 6261-JR8712, 1975-1981 (22 cu.ft.)
	Grant County Courthouse, Basement Vault	Grant County Justice Court Case Files / Justice Court [Case Files], 1906-1908 (.20 cu.ft.); Old Transcripts [includes justice court transcripts], 1904 (.20 cu.ft.); Reports of Co. Engineer [includes Justice Court Transcripts], ca.1890-ca.1899 (.25 cu.ft.); Transcripts [Circuit and Justice Court-includes related documents], ca.1875-ca.1900 (.35 cu.ft.).
	Grant County Criminal Justice Facility, Storage Closet	Grant County Prisoner Registers / Jail Register, 1892-1893 (1 volume); vol. 2, 1937-1952 (1 volume); vol. 3, 1957-1969 (1 volume).
	Oregon State Sheriffs' Association Museum	Grant County Prisoner Registers / Register of Prisoners [includes photographs of some prisoners and county officials in the front and back of volume-with index], vol. 1, 1888-1957 (1 volume).
	Harney County Court-house, Clerk's Office	Harney County Circuit Court Case Files / County Court Cases [Files], 1921-1927 (.30 cu.ft.).
	Harney County Courthouse, Clerk's Basement Records Room	Harney County Justice Dockets / Justice Docket [Harney District No.1-with index], 1890-1917 (1 volume); Justice's Docket [Burns District-with index], 1938-1946 (1 volume); Justice's Docket for Burns District, 1919-1927 (1 volume); S.E. Ledger [Andrews District Justice Docket], 1940-1953 (1 volume); Small Claims Docket [Burns District Justice Court-with index], 1923-1955 (1 volume).
	Harney County Sheriff's Office	Harney County Prisoner Registers / Jail Register Harney County, 1922-1959 (1 volume).
	Oregon State Archives	Hood River County Circuit Court Case Files / Criminal [Circuit Court Case Files], no. 1-215, 1909-1930 (.50 cu.ft.)

	Hood River County Courthouse, Small Jury Room	Hood River County Circuit Court Case Files / Probate [District & Circuit Court-Case Files-includes circuit court criminal, probate, and mental commitment case files], 1982 (1 reel of microfilm)
	Hood River County Courthouse, Trial Court Office	Hood River County Circuit Court Case Files / Criminal Cases [Circuit Court Case Files], no. CR83.001-CR84.132, 1983-1984 (1 CD-ROM disc); Criminal Records [Circuit Court Case Files], no. 1171-2414, 1974-1982 (2 CD-ROM discs).
	Hood River County Business Admin. (Dean) Bldg., County Archives	Hood River County Circuit Court Case Files / Circuit Court Case Files Criminal, no. 216-1172, 1930-1977 (10 cu.ft.).
	Oregon State Archives	Hood River County Justice Court Case Files / Justice Court Transcripts, ca.1900-1940 (.25 cu.ft.); Letters [includes justice court writs and warrants], 1911-1914 (.05 cu.ft.).
	Oregon State Archives	Jackson County Circuit Court Case Files / [Circuit Court Case Files-Criminal], 1860-1912 (3.25 cu.ft.)
	Jackson County Justice Building Basement, Court Archives	Jackson County Circuit Court Case Files / [Index to State vs. Criminal-Cases], 1862-1912 (1 reel of microfilm); [Old Criminal Records-Circuit Court Case File Index], 1909-1946 (1 reel of microfilm)
	University of Oregon, Knight Library, Special Collections	Jackson County Justice Court Case Files / Justice Court Papers, 1858-1916 (.50 cu.ft.).
	Oregon Historical Society	Jackson County Justice Court Case Files / Mss. 1264 Jackson County [Justice Court Transcripts], 1902-1907, 1914-1915 (.50 cu.ft.); Mss. 1264 Jackson County Justice of the Peace Case Files, 1858-1870 (1.50 cu.ft.).
	Record Masters of Southern Oregon	Jackson County Prisoner Registers / Deeds [serves as prisoner numerical register with mug shots-78A.60], vol. 64, ca.1920 (1 volume); [Jail Registers-78A.17], 1960-1965 (.40 cu.ft.); Lord Rochester Clothes [County Jail Inmate Mug Shots-78A.37], ca.1934-n.d. (1 volume); Register of Prisoners [with index-78A.60], vol. 2, 1929-1934 (1 volume).
	Southern Oregon Historical Society, Research Library	Jackson County Prisoner Registers / Register of Prisoners [MS 906], vol. 1, 1886-1929 (1 volume).

	Jefferson County Courthouse, Trial Court Basement Archives	Jefferson County Circuit Court Case Files / County Court Cases [Files], 1946-1960 (.25 cu.ft.).
	Jefferson County Public Works Department Office, Vault	Jefferson County Circuit Court Case Files / Circuit, Justice, & County Court Records [includes a variety of case related records], 1915-1945 (2.50 cu.ft.); Judges [Miscellaneous Circuit, Justice, and County Court Records], ca.1922-ca.1927 (.50 cu.ft.).
	Jefferson County Public Works Department Office, Vault	Jefferson County Justice Court Case Files / Circuit, Justice, & County Court Records [includes a variety of interfiled case related records], 1915-1945 (2.50 cu.ft.); Judges [Miscellaneous Circuit, Justice, and County Court Records], ca.1922-ca.1927 (.50 cu.ft.).
	Jefferson County Public Works Department Office, Vault	Jefferson County Prisoner Registers / Jail Register [with index], 1929-1931 (1 volume); Jefferson County Jail Record [Alphabetical Cards-includes register information], ca.1950-ca.1974 (.75 cu.ft.).
	Josephine County Courthouse, Trial Court Civil Unit Office	Josephine County Circuit Court Case Files / [Circuit Court Case Files], no. 4049-9734, 50.001-79.1770, 1928-1979 (307 reels of microfilm); Index to Register of Actions and Judgment Roll Docket, 1909-1984 (7 volumes); vol. 4-6, 1934-1970 (3 reels of microfilm); [Register of Actions-with index to case files], vol. 1-2, 1889-1908 (1 reel of microfilm).
	Josephine County Courthouse, Clerk's Vault	Josephine County Justice Court Case Files / Transcripts from Justice Court [Old and New], 1877-1911 (1 cu.ft.); Transcripts from Justice Court to Appear in Circuit Court, 1909-1914 (.35 cu.ft.).
	Josephine County Historical Society Library	Josephine County Justice Court Case Files / [Justice Court Case Files-Merlin District], 1935 (.05 cu.ft.).
	Josephine County Historical Society Booth Street Storage Unit	Josephine County Prisoner Registers / [Jail Register], vol. 1, 1892-1940 (1 volume); Jail Register [with index], vol. 2-3, 1940-1966 (2 volumes).
	Klamath County Courthouse, Room 222	Klamath County Circuit Court Case Files / Criminal Tapes [Circuit Court Criminal Case Files], 1929-1983 (73 reels of microfilm)

	Klamath County Courthouse, Room 17, Court Basement Storage Cage	Klamath County Circuit Court Case Files / Criminal [Circuit Court Case Files], 1983 (4 cu.ft.); Defendant Index Dissolution, 1983-1987 (.80 cu.ft.); Register of Actions Criminal [also indexes case files], vol. 8-9, 1923-1965 (2 volumes); [Register of Criminal Actions-also indexes case files], vol. 10-21, 1966-1983 (12 volumes); Register of Criminal Actions Index [also indexes case files], 1923-1949 (1 volume).
	Klamath County Courthouse, Room 17, Court Basement Storage Cage	Klamath County Justice Court Dockets / Justice Court Register of Action [Linkville District-with index], vol. 3, 1932-1935 (1 volume).
	Klamath County Museum	Klamath County Justice Court Dockets / Criminal Docket [Justice Court-Linkville-includes small claims-with index], 1917-1925 (1 volume); Justice Docket Criminal [Linkville District-with index], 1918 (1 volume); Justice Docket [Linkville District Criminal-with index], 1907-1921 (9 volumes)
	Klamath County Jail, Second Floor Archives Room	Klamath County Prisoner Registers / [Board Account of Prisoners], 1925-1933 (1 volume); Jail Docket, vol. 2-9, 1927-1969 (8 volumes); Jail Register, 1893-1926 (1 volume).
	Lake County Courthouse, Clerk's Basement South Storage Room	Lake County Circuit Court Case Files / Box [Circuit Court Case Files], ca.1875-1916 (24 cu.ft.)
	Lake County Courthouse, Circuit Court Basement West Storage Room	Lake County Circuit Court Case Files / Circuit Court Case Files [includes some older cases], no. 267-9190, 1913-1981 (110 cu.ft.); [Circuit Court Orders], 1959-1967 (.10 cu.ft.); Circuit Ct. Orders [Court], 1972-1981 (.20 cu.ft.);
	Lake County Courthouse, Circuit Court Basement East Storage Room	Lake County Circuit Court Case Files / Circuit Court Case Index Direct, 1875-1983 (2 volumes)
	Lake County Courthouse, Circuit Court Basement West Storage Room	Lake County Justice Court Case Files / Criminal Cases [South Lakeview District Justice Court Case Files], 1929-1930 (.15 cu.ft.)
	Oregon State Archives	Lake County Prisoner Registers / Jail Register, 1894-1952 (1 volume).

	Lake County Courthouse, Sheriff's Department Office	Lake County Prisoner Registers / Register of Prisoners, 1952-1991 (1 volume).
	Oregon State Archives	Lane County Circuit Court Case Files / Aggravated Murder Cases [Circuit Court Files-includes Elizabeth Diane Downs case], 1975, 1982-1985 (1.50 cu.ft.); Circuit Court Case Files, no. 1-3000, 1853-1900 (31 cu.ft.);
	Lane County Courthouse, Court Archives	Lane County Circuit Court Case Files / [Circuit Court Case Files-includes probate cases from 1979-1983], no. 43882-102160, 71.0001-83.10100, 1953-1983 (1511 reels of microfilm); Circuit Court Case Files, no. 1-43881, 1854-1953 (351 reels of microfilm); [Circuit Court Name Index-includes probate], 1978-1982 (11 sheets of microfiche)
	Oregon State Archives	Lane County Justice Court Case Files / Justice Court Transcripts, ca.1855-ca.1929 (.20 cu.ft.).
	Lane County Historical Museum, Archives	Lane County Justice Court Case Files / [Justice Court Case Files], 1866, 1891-1892, 1922 (.05 cu.ft.).
	Lane County Historical Museum, Archives	Lane County Prisoner Registers / Del. Taxes [serves as record of prisoners], 1929 (1 volume); Jail Register City Jail Eugene [includes prisoners arrested in Lane County], ca.1930 (1 volume); Record Criminal Cases [includes prisoner information], vol. B-C, 1929-1942 (2 volumes); Register of Prisoners, 1902-1929 (2 volumes).
	Lincoln County Courthouse, Trial Court Office:	Lincoln County Circuit Court Case Files / Index to Circuit Court Cases, 1893-1965 (4 volumes); Microfilm [Circuit Court Case Files], no. 18142-22038, 1959-1961 (13 inches of microfiche).
	Lincoln County Law Library, Trial Court Warehouse	Lincoln County Circuit Court Case Files / [Book of Circuit Court-Case Files-title varies], reel 2-42, 1968-1983 (41 reels of microfilm); [Circuit Court Case Files], no. 22039-48395, 1961-1982 (ca.260 cu.ft.); 1983 (ca.40 cu.ft.).
	Lincoln County Community Corrections Building, County Archives	Lincoln County Circuit Court Case Files / [Book of Circuit Court -Case Files], reel 2-37, 1968-1982 (36 reels of microfilm); Old Circuit Court [Civil Case Files-includes some district court], 1970-1973 (1 cu.ft.).
	Lincoln County Public Service Building, Trial Court Main Storage Room	Lincoln County Circuit Court Case Files / Index to Circuit Court Journal [also indexes case files], vol. 1-2, 1893-1978 (2 volumes);

	Lincoln County Public Service Building, Trial Court Storage Room 7	Lincoln County Circuit Court Case Files / [Circuit Court Case Files], no. 1-18141, 1893-1959 (276 cu.ft.).
	Lincoln County Community Corrections Building, County Archives	Lincoln County Justice Court Case Files / Justice Court [Miscellaneous Documents], 1911-1922 (.10 cu.ft.).
	Lincoln County Corrections Facility, Central Stores Room	Lincoln County Prisoner Registers / Jail Register [with index], 1893-1968 (6 volumes).
	Oregon State Archives	Linn County Circuit Court Case Files / Index to Papers in Circuit Court Direct [Case File], 1854-1935 (2 volumes)
	Linn County Courthouse, Circuit Court Office, File Room	Linn County Circuit Court Case Files / [Circuit Court Case Files], no. 1-43110, 1861-1974 (561 reels of microfilm); no. 43111-83.1976, 1974-1983 (16.50 feet of microfiche).
	Linn County Courthouse, Circuit Court Office, Counter	Linn County Circuit Court Case Files / Index [Circuit Court Case File and Journal Index], 1875-1985 (10 inches of microfiche)
	Oregon State Archives	Linn County Justice Court Dockets / Justice Court Dockets [District 1-Criminal], no. 3001-9399, 1926-1941 (1.70 cu.ft.); Justice of Peace Docket, 1858-1866 (1 volume); Justice of Peace Record [with index], 1859-1862 (1 volume); Register of Justices of the Peace [lists historical justices and constables], 1890-1972 (1 volume).
	Linn County Sheriff's Main Office Building, Records Section Office	Linn County Prisoner Registers / Jail Register, vol. A, 1891-1939 (1 volume).
	Linn County Sheriff's Main Office Building, Support Services Lieutenant's Office	Linn County Prisoner Registers / Jail Register, vol. 2, 1940-1959 (1 volume).
	Linn County Sheriff's Office Archives	Linn County Prisoner Registers / Jail Register, vol. 3-4, 1952-1967 (2 volumes).
	Oregon State Archives	Malheur County Circuit Court Case Files / Criminal Court [Circuit Court Case Files], no. 1-249, 1887-1930 (2.60 cu.ft.); Index to Circuit Court Journal [also indexes case files], vol. A-B, 1887-1930 (2 volumes)

	Malheur County Courthouse, Trial Court Basement Civil Records Storage Room	Malheur County Circuit Court Case Files / [Circuit Court Civil Case Files], no. 4191-10544, 1931-1966 (95 cu.ft.); no. 12511-14859, ca.1971-ca.1978 (24 reels of microfilm); Criminal [Circuit Court Case Files], no. 1665-1924, 1969-1972 (10 inches of aperture cards).
	Malheur County Courthouse, Trial Court Basement Criminal Records Storage Room	Malheur County Circuit Court Case Files / [Circuit Court Criminal Case Files], no. 250-3383, 1930-1983 (53 cu.ft.); Index to Circuit Court Journal [also indexes case files], vol. C-I , 1930-1984 (7 volumes).
	Malheur County Courthouse, Justice Court Basement Storage Area	Malheur County Justice Court Dockets / Justice Docket [McDermitt District-with index], 1937-1957 (1 volume).
	Malheur County Justice Court Office	Malheur County Justice Court Dockets / Justice Docket [Ontario District-with index], 1895-1898 (1 volume); [Justice Docket-Ontario District-with index], 1905-1911 (1 volume).
	Malheur County Courthouse, Sheriff's Basement Storage Room	Malheur County Prisoner Registers / Jail Register [with index], vol. 4-5, 1953-1968 (2 volumes).
	Oregon State Archives	Marion County Circuit Court Case Files / Circuit Court Case Files [does not include divorce cases], no. 4-15339, 1848-1921 (285 cu.ft.); Circuit Court Cases Indirect [Index], 1952-1970 (.80 cu.ft.); Index to Circuit Court Cases Direct, 1908-1935 (.50 cu.ft.); Index to Circuit Court Cases Indirect, 1908-1962 (1.40 cu.ft.); Index to Circuit Court Direct [Case Files], 1963-1970 (.40 cu.ft.);
	Marion County Courthouse, Circuit Court Vault	Marion County Circuit Court Case Files / CC [Circuit Court Case Files], no. 1-74727, 1848-1971 (980 reels of microfilm); [Defendant Index Circuit Court-to case files], 1910-1984 (8 reels of microfilm)
	Oregon State Archives	Marion County Justice Court Case Files / Justice Court Case Files, 1855-1925 (1 cu.ft.); Prohibition Records [includes search warrants issued by justice courts], 1923-1925, 1927-1931 (.25 cu.ft.);
	Marion County Archives	Marion County Justice Court Case Files / Justice Ct. Criminal Information Miscellaneous [Court], 1931-1938 (.35 cu.ft.)
	Marion County Jail, Visiting Lobby Display Case	Marion County Prisoner Registers / Jail Register], 1927-1967 (1 volume).

	Marion County Historical Society Museum	Marion County Prisoner Registers / [Jail Register], 1891-1921 (1 volume); Register of Prisoners [with index], vol. A, 1884-1896 (1 volume).
	Morrow County Courthouse, Basement Vault	Morrow County Circuit Court Case Files / Vault Index Circuit Court Papers, vol. 3-5, ca.1885-1985 (3 volumes).
	Morrow County Courthouse, Circuit Court Office	Morrow County Circuit Court Case Files / Cir. Ct. Index [Circuit Court-indexes case files no.1-4240], 1885-1955 (1 binder).
	Umatilla County Courthouse, Trial Court Criminal Office, Room 209, Public Research Area Cabinet	Morrow County Circuit Court Case Files / Morrow County [Circuit Court Case Files], no. 1-4240, 1885-1955 (51 reels of microfilm).
	Umatilla County Records Storage Building, Trial Court Front Records Storage Area	Morrow County Circuit Court Case Files / Morrow County Circuit Court [Case Files-title varies], no. 4241-7425, 1955-1983 (45 cu.ft.).
	Morrow County Courthouse, Clerk's Vault	Morrow County Justice Court Case Files / [Justice Court Case Files], 1898-1931 (.20 cu.ft.).
	Morrow County Courthouse, Basement Vault	Morrow County Justice Court Case Files / Clerk Save [Justice Court Case Files], 1904-1924 (.10 cu.ft.).
	Morrow County Sheriff's Department Building, Sheriff's Private Office Storage Cabinet	Morrow County Prisoner Registers / [Jail Register], 1892-1969 (1 volume).
	Multnomah County Courthouse, Room 131, Circuit Court File Viewing Room	Multnomah County Circuit Court Case Files / Circuit Court Indexes, 1976-1987 (1 binder of microfiche).

	Multnomah County Courthouse, Room 131, Circuit Court File Room	Multnomah County Circuit Court Case Files / [Circuit Court Case Files-includes civil and domestic relations cases-also includes criminal cases beginning in 1976], no. 263000-424451, 70.10.0001-83.69164, 1960-1983 (178 feet of microfiche); [Circuit Court Case Files-includes civil and domestic relations cases-also includes criminal cases until 1931], no. 1-100093, 1A-49335A, 100101-262999, 1855-1960 (3769 reels of microfilm); [Circuit Court Criminal Case Files], no. C46000-C60905, 1965-ca.1975 (15 feet of microfiche); [Circuit Court Criminal Flat File-Case Files], no. C16429-C46819, 1931-1965 (198 reels of microfilm); Circuit Court Index [Plaintiff and Defendant], 1874-1979 (70 reels of microfilm).
	Oregon State Archives	Multnomah County Justice Court Dockets / Justice Court Dockets, 1859-1862 (2 volumes); Justice Court Dockets [Albina Precinct], 1891 (1 volume); Justice Court Dockets [Couch Precinct], 1872-1883 (2 volumes); Justice Court Dockets [East Portland Precinct], 1866-1882, (4 volumes); Justice Court Dockets [Madison Precinct], 1871-1874 (1 volume); Justice Court Dockets [Morrison Precinct], 1872-1876, 1878-1883 (4 volumes); Justice Court Dockets [North Portland Precinct], 1877-1881 (2 volumes); Justice Court Dockets [Recorders Court, Morrison Precinct, and North Portland Precinct], 1863-1874 (1 volume); Justice Court Dockets [South Portland Precinct], 1882-1883 (1 volume); Justice Court Dockets [Washington Precinct], 1868-1871 (1 volume).
	Multnomah County Courthouse, Room B13, District Court Basement Archives	Multnomah County Justice Court Dockets / [Criminal Docket-Justice and District Court], vol. 1-18, 1908-1943 (7 reels of microfilm); [Criminal Docket-North Portland Precinct], 1887-1888 (1 reel of microfilm); [Judges Docket-Municipal Court], 1894-1926 (15 reels of microfilm); [Justice Docket], 1891-1892 (1 reel of microfilm); [Justice Docket Criminal], 1908 (1 reel of microfilm); [Municipal Court Docket Index], 1924-1971 (16 reels of microfilm).

	City of Portland Archives	Multnomah County Justice Court Dockets / Criminal Docket Recorders Court [with index], 1863-1864 (1 volume); riminal Docket [Recorders Court-with index], 1865 (1 volume); Criminal Record [Recorders Court Journal], 1867-1868 (1 volume); Docket Indexes [Municipal Court], 1912-1926 (38 volumes); Judge's Docket Municipal Court, 1893-1894 (1 volume); Judges Docket Police Court [Municipal Court beginning in 1893], 1886-1908 (10 volumes); Justice Docket City of St. Johns [with index], 1907-1911 (1 volume); vol. 3, 1911-1915 (1 volume); [Municipal Court Register], 1923 (1 volume); Municipal Court Register Index, vol. 4-5, 7, 1895-1900, 1905-1907 (3 volumes); Municipal Court Register [with index], vol. 1-2, 1893-1895 (2 volumes); Original Record Municipal Court, 1925 (2 volumes); Police Court Docket], 1884-1890 (1 volume); Police Court Docket State Cases, 1887-1903 (2 volumes); Police Court Record [title varies], 1871-1889 (10 volumes); Record [Police Court Docket-Ordinance Violation and Other Crimes], vol. 2-3, 1872-1876 (2 volumes); Record [Recorders Court Journal], 1868-1870 (1 volume); Records [Recorders and Police Court Journal], 1867-1871 (2 volumes); Witness Docket Police Court, 1886-1891 (1 volume).
	Oregon Historical Society	Multnomah County Justice Court Dockets / Mss. 1714 Criminal Docket [Justice Docket-North Portland Precinct], 1883-1885, 1894 (2 volumes); Mss. 1714 [Justice Docket-Couch Precinct], 1882-1886 (2 volumes); Mss. 1714 [Justice Docket-East Portland Precinct], 1882-1908 (17 volumes); Mss. 1714 [Justice Docket-Madison Precinct], 1880-1886 (3 volumes); Mss. 1714 [Justice Docket-Morrison Precinct], 1880-1886 (4 volumes); Mss. 1714 [Justice Docket-Northeast Portland Precinct], 1882-1886 (4 volumes); Mss. 1714 [Justice Docket-North Portland Precinct], 1880-1890, 1893-1894 (8 volumes); Mss. 1714 [Justice Docket-South Portland Precinct], 1884-1902 (5 volumes); Mss. 1714 [Justice Docket-Western Precinct], 1880-1886 (2 volumes); Mss. 1714 Record [Justice Docket-Albina Precinct], 1885-1893 (4 volumes).
	Oregon State Archives	Multnomah County Prisoner Registers / Jail Register, 1882-1918 (11 volumes); Prisoners Receipt, 1917 (1 volume).

	Yeon Building, Multnomah County Records Management Office	Multnomah County Prisoner Registers / Jail Docket, 1918-1972 (4 reels of microfilm).
	Oregon Historical Society	Multnomah County Prisoner Registers / Mss. 1275B Prisoner Record, 1896-1899 (1 volume); Mss. 1275B Record of Criminals [includes photographs-with index], 1929-1941 (3 volumes).
	Oregon State Archives	Polk County Circuit Court Case Files / Circuit Court Case Exhibits, 1861-1925 (1.20 cu.ft.); Circuit Court Case Files [excludes divorce cases], ca.1854-ca.1912 (27 cu.ft.); Circuit Court Case Files Index, 1862-1909 (1 volume)
	Polk County Courthouse, Circuit Court Records Office	Polk County Circuit Court Case Files / [Circuit Court Case Files], no. 1-32800, 1846-1983 (25 feet of microfilm jackets).
	Polk County Courthouse, Circuit Court Cell Block A Records Storage Room	Polk County Circuit Court Case Files / [Circuit Court Vault Index], no. 1-279, 1846-1856 (2 reels of microfilm).
	Polk County Public Works Department Complex, Building 12, Circuit Court Records Storage Cage	Polk County Circuit Court Case Files / [Circuit Court Reg.-Case Files], no.7458-15971, 1931-ca.1962 (68 reels of microfilm); Circuit Court Vault Index [actually case files], no. 534-3747, 1865-1909 (39 reels of microfilm).
	Polk County Historical Society Museum, Archives	Polk County Circuit Court Case Files / Index to Circuit Court Cases, 1870-1875 (1 volume).
	Oregon State Archives	Polk County Justice Court Case Files / Justice Court Case Records [District no. 1], 1893-1896 (.05 cu.ft.); Justice Court Case Records [District no. 2], 1892-1897 (.10 cu.ft.); Justice Court Case Records [District no. 3], 1892-1899 (.35 cu.ft.); Justice Court Case Records [District no. 4], 1896 (.05 cu.ft.); Justice Court Case Records [District no. 5], 1892-1905 (.25 cu.ft.); Justice Court Case Records [District no. 7], 1924-1925 (.15 cu.ft.).
	Polk County Public Works Department Complex, Building 12, North Loft	Polk County Justice Court Case Files / DA Files [includes justice court case documents], ca.1928-1940 (ca.1 cu.ft.); Justice Court Case Files [includes 2nd, 5th, and West Salem districts], ca.1925-1940 (2 cu.ft.).
	Oregon Historical Society	Polk County Justice Court Case Files / Mss. 1276 Justice Court Case Papers, 1861-1881 (.05 cu.ft.).

	Oregon State Archives	Sherman County Circuit Court Case Files / [Circuit Court Case Files], no. 2250-4468, 1933-1985 (25 cu.ft.).
	Sherman County Courthouse, Clerk's Vault	Sherman County Circuit Court Case Files / [Circuit Court Case Files], no. 1-2249, 1889-1933 (29 cu.ft.).
	Sherman County Courthouse, Jury Room	Sherman County Circuit Court Case Files / Index to Circuit Court Case Files, vol. 1-2, 1889-1989 (2 volumes).
	Sherman County Court, Clerk's Vault	Sherman County Justice Court Case Files / Justice Court [Case Files-District no. 2], 1923-1932 (.25 cu.ft.); [Miscellaneous Justice Court Documents], ca.1916-ca.1923 (.50 cu.ft.); T [Justice Court Transcripts], 1892-1910 (.15 cu.ft.); Transcripts of Judgments [includes Justice Court], 1934-1940 (.05 cu.ft.).
	Sherman County Courthouse, Sheriff's Office	Sherman County Prisoner Records / Jail Register, 1891-2003 (1 volume).
	Oregon State Archives	Tillamook County Circuit Court Case Files / Circuit Court Case Files [Criminal-alphabetical arrangement], 1871-1904 (.75 cu.ft.); Circuit Court Case Files, no. 580-3925, 1904-1927 (23.50 cu.ft.); Indictments [Circuit Court], 1922-1962 (1.10 cu.ft.); Miscellaneous Circuit Court Orders, 1951-1969 (.25 cu.ft.);
	Tillamook County Courthouse, Trial Court Large Basement Storage Room	Tillamook County Circuit Court Case Files / [Circuit Court Case Files], no. 8141-9915, 1948-1953 (14 reels of microfilm); no. 9916-9999, 1953 (1.50 cu.ft.); no. 10.000-23.290, 1953-1983 (245 cu.ft.); Roll [Circuit Court Case Files], no. 3927-8140, 1926-1948 (45 reels of microfilm).
	Tillamook County Courthouse, Trial Court Office	Tillamook County Circuit Court Case Files / Circuit Court General Index [to case files and dockets], vol. 2-6, 1910-1983 (5 volumes); Index to Plaintiffs and Defendants, ca.1868-ca.1910 (1 volume).
	Tillamook County Pioneer Museum	Tillamook County Justice Court Case Files / Justice Docket Third District [includes some loose case records], 1915-1920 (1 volume).
	Tillamook County Justice Facility, Jail Storage Room	Tillamook County Prisoner Registers / Register of Persons Charged [no. 1414-3186], vol. 1-3, 1946-1950 (3 volumes); [Register of Persons Charged-no. 3187-3946], vol. 4-5, 1950-1952 (2 volumes); [Register of Persons Charged-no. 3947-9858], 1952-1958 (1 volume).

	Umatilla County Courthouse, Trial Court Criminal Office	Umatilla County Circuit Court Case Files / [Court Microfilm Records-includes circuit court civil, criminal and probate case files as well as district court case files-not comprehensive], ca.1863-ca.1997 (ca.600 reels of microfilm); [Court Microfilm Records Indexes-to circuit court civil and criminal, probate, and district court case files-not comprehensive], ca.1863-ca.1997 (4 binders); Vault Index to Criminal Actions, vol. 2, ca.1953-1985 (1 volume).
	Umatilla Cty Records Storage Building, Trial Court Front Room	Umatilla County Circuit Court Case Files / Criminal [Circuit Court Case Files-title varies], ca.1930-ca.1955 (33 cu.ft.); Defendant's Index, vol. 1, ca.1915-1955 (1 volume)
	Umatilla Cty Records Storage Building, Trial Court Back Room	Umatilla County Circuit Court Case Files / Judgement Rolls [Circuit Court Case Files], 1863-1948 (63 reels of microfilm).
	Oregon State Archives	Umatilla County Justice Court Case Files / Misc. [Justice Court Case Files-Freewater District], 1915, 1925 (.05 cu.ft.); Misc. [Justice Court Case Files-Pendleton District], 1909-1920 (.05 cu.ft.); Misc. [Justice Court Case Files-Stanfield District], 1913-1914 (.05 cu.ft.).
	Umatilla County Courthouse, Basement Vault	Umatilla County Justice Court Case Files / Commitment [Justice Court Commitment After Conviction Records-Pendleton Precinct], ca.1928-ca.1938 (.15 cu.ft.)
	Umatilla County Courthouse, Records Office Research Room	Umatilla County Prisoner Registers / [Jail Register], 1892-1908 (1 volume); Jail Register [with index], 1928-1970 (3 volumes); [Register of Prisoners-with index], 1902-1927 (1 volume); Register of Prisoners [with index], vol. 1, 1885-1895 (1 volume).
	Joseph Building, Attic, Section 1 Storage Area	Union County Circuit Court Case Files / Circuit Court [Case Files], no. 1-15203, 1865-1946 (134.35 cu.ft.); no. 24201-27750, 1977-1982 (63 cu.ft.).
	Joseph Building, Trial Court Civil Records Office, Resource Room	Union County Circuit Court Case Files / Defendants Index to Judgment Roll, vol. 1-3, 1864-1986 (3 volumes)
	Union County Law Enforcement Services Building, Microfilm Storage Room	Union County Circuit Court Case Files / [Circuit Court Case Files], no. 1-24294, 1865-1977 (ca.210 reels of microfilm); Circuit Court Records [Case Files], no. 25237-26455, ca.1978-ca.1980 (13 inches of microfilm jackets).

	Joseph Building, Trial Court Attic Archives Room	Union County Justice Court Case Files / Justice of the Peace Transcript Criminal Cases, 1908-1923 (1 cu.ft.); Transcripts of Judgement [Justice Court], 1865-1896 (.50 cu.ft.).
	Joseph Building, County Archives	Union County Justice Court Case Files / Transcript of Executions [Justice Court], 1872-1920 (.25 cu.ft.).
	Union County Law Enforcement Services Building, Sheriff's Office Exhibit Case	Union County Prisoner Registers / Record of Prisoners, vol. 1-3, 1885-1947 (3 volumes).
	Union County Law Enforcement Services Building, Basement Storage Room	Union County Prisoner Registers / Record of Prisoners, vol. 4, 1947-1967 (1 volume).
	Wallowa County Courthouse, Clerk's Vault	Wallowa County Circuit Court Case Files / Cases Criminal Indictments, no. 1-45, 1917-1922 (.35 cu.ft.); Criminal Cases [Justice and Circuit Court Case Files], 1924-1936 (.25 cu.ft.); Index to Judgment Roll Defendant, vol. 1-2, 1887-1983 (2 volumes)
	Wallowa County Courthouse, Attic	Wallowa County Circuit Court Case Files / Criminal Circuit Court [Case Files], no. 1030-1152, 1978-1983 (.60 cu.ft.)
	Wallowa County Courthouse, Clerk's Vault	Wallowa County Justice Court Case Files / Criminal Cases [Justice and Circuit Court Case Files], 1924-1936 (.25 cu.ft.); Transcripts Justice Court Criminal, 1923-1939 (.10 cu.ft.).
	Wallowa County Courthouse, Clerk's Vault	Wallowa County Prisoner Registers / Register of Prisoners [vol. A with index], vol. A-B, 1888-1991 (2 volumes).
	Oregon State Archives	Wasco County Circuit Court Case Files / Circuit Court Criminal Case Files, ca.1851-1963 (23 cu.ft.); U.S. District Court Case Files [Criminal] 1853-1865 (.20 cu.ft.)
	Wasco County Courthouse, Clerk's Vault	Wasco County Circuit Court Case Files / [Circuit Court Civil Case Files], no. 814-6429, 1910-1943 (78 cu.ft.); Indictments [Circuit Court], 1900-1915 (.15 cu.ft.).
	Wasco County Courthouse, Basement County Archives	Wasco County Circuit Court Case Files / Index to Circuit Court Cases, no. 1-626, n.d. (1 volume).
	Wasco County Courthouse, Trial Court Room 307	Wasco County Circuit Court Case Files / Criminal [Circuit Court Case Files], 1961-1983 (18 inches of microfiche)

	Wasco County Courthouse, Trial Court Jury Room	Wasco County Circuit Court Case Files / Criminal Index [to Circuit Court Case Files], ca.1963-1989 (1 volume); Index to Circuit Court Cases [Case Files and Registers], ca.1900-1959 (1 volume); vol. 2-4, 1959-1989 (3 volumes); Index to Circuit Court Cases [Files], vol. 1-3, 1854-1969 (3 volumes).
	Wasco Cty Court-house, Trial Court Basement Vault A	Wasco County Circuit Court Case Files / Criminal [Circuit Court Case Files], 1961-1983 (26 inches of micro-film jackets).
	Oregon State Archives	Wasco County Justice Court Case Files / Justice Court Criminal Case Files, 1862-1916 (7 cu.ft.); Recorder's Court Case Files [Civil and Criminal], ca.1897-ca.1905, 1912 (.75 cu.ft.).
	Wasco County Courthouse, Basement County Archives	Wasco County Justice Court Case Files / Justice Court Criminal Cases [Files-The Dalles District], 1936-1938 (.25 cu.ft.).
	Wasco County Courthouse, Basement Old Jail Room H2	Wasco County Prisoner Registers / Jail Register, 1892-1929 (1 volume); vol. 3-4, 1943-1970 (2 volumes).
	Wasco County Courthouse, Second Floor Lobby Exhibit Case	Wasco County Prisoner Registers / Description of Prisoners [Register-includes photographs-with index], vol. 1, 1901-1953 (1 volume).
	Wasco County Courthouse, Basement County Archives	Wasco County Prisoner Registers / Jail Register, vol. 2, 1929-1943 (1 volume).
	Oregon State Archives	Washington County Circuit Court Case Files / Circuit Court Criminal Case Files, no. 7134-8901, 1920-1930 (8.75 cu.ft.); Circuit Court Criminal Cases [Files-with gaps], 1845-1906 (1 cu.ft.)
	Walnut Street Center Building, Second Floor Circuit Court Archives	Washington County Circuit Court Case Files / Circuit Court Criminal [Case Files], no. 8746-21403, 1931-1981 (141 cu.ft.); 82.0001-83.1122, 1982-1983 (29 cu.ft.); Misdemeanor [Circuit Court Case Files], no. D001-D17366, 1958-1965 (26 cu.ft.)
	Washington County Justice Services Building, Records Vault	Washington County Circuit Court Case Files / [Index to Criminal Case Files], n.d.-1982 (1 reel of microfilm)
	Washington Cty Justice Services Building, Criminal Records Rm	Washington County Circuit Court Case Files / State Criminal Index [Case File], n.d.-1982 (1 volume).

	Oregon State Archives	Washington County Justice Court Case Files / County Court Records [Justice Court-Case Records-reel no. 6], 1859-1870 (1 reel of microfilm); Justice Court Case Records [includes various precincts], 1845-1889 (.50 cu.ft.).
	Walnut Street Center Complex, Building E, County Historical Records Vault	Washington County Justice Court Case Files / C.C. State Cases Pending J.P. Transcripts [includes justice court documents], 1893-1917 (.35 cu.ft.).
	Walnut Street Center Complex, Building E, County Historical Records Vault	Washington County Prisoner Registers / [Index to Jail Record], ca.1938-ca.1962 (1 volume); Jail Record, vol. 2, 1925-1937 (1 volume); Jail Register, 1928-1946 (1 volume); [Jail Register-includes meals], 1955-1958 (1 volume); Parole Record [County Jail-includes parolee reports and some photographs], 1912-1920 (1 volume); Register of Prisoners, vol. 1, 1884-1891 (1 volume); Wash. Co. Jail Big Book [Washington County Jail Register-unbound], 1958-1964 (1 volume); 1962-1971 (1 volume); Washington County Jail Record [Big Book-unbound], 1938-1962 (1 volume).
	Washington County Historical Museum	Washington County Prisoner Registers / Jail Register, 1892-1927 (1 volume); [Prisoner Jail Register], 1892-1927 (1 reel of microfilm).
	Wheeler County Court-house, Clerk's Vault	Wheeler County Circuit Court Case Files / File Case Criminal [Circuit Court], 1899-ca.1906 (.15 cu.ft.)
	Wheeler County Courthouse, Trial Court Second Floor Records Storage Room	Wheeler County Circuit Court Case Files / Civil [Circuit Court Case Files-also includes some criminal case files and some case files from 1899-1935], no. 1213-2435, 1935-1976 (16 cu.ft.); Criminal [Circuit Court Case Files], no. 13.C-194.C, 1967-1983 (4 cu.ft.)
	Wheeler County Courthouse, Clerk's Vault	Wheeler County Justice Court Case Files / Misc. [Miscellaneous Court Documents-includes indictments, undertakings, complaints, bonds, and related records from circuit, county, justice, and probate courts], ca.1904-ca.1948 (.15 cu.ft.).
	Wheeler Cty Court-house, Sheriff's Office	Wheeler County Prisoner Registers / Jail Record, 1935-1942 (1 volume).
	Oregon State Archives	Yamhill County Circuit Court Case Files / Circuit Court Case Index, 1857-1861 (1 volume); Circuit Court Trial Transcripts, 1880-1943 (5.50 cu.ft.); Index Circuit Court [indexes case files and bench docket], vol. 1, 1857-1894 (1 volume)

	Yamhill County 4th Street Archives	Yamhill County Circuit Court Case Files / Index Circuit Court [indexes case files and journals], vol. 3, 1941-1970 (1 volume)
	Yamhill County Courthouse, Trial Court Exhibit Closet	Yamhill County Circuit Court Case Files / Direct Index Circuit Court [indexes case files and journals], vol. 2-3, 1894-1979 (2 volumes)
	Yamhill County Courthouse, Trial Court Office Break Room	Yamhill County Circuit Court Case Files / Circuit Court [Case Files], no. 12070-17649, 1938-ca.1948 (34 reels of microfilm); no. 17650-38899, 810001-831660, ca.1948-1983 (100 inches of microfilm jackets); Direct Index Circuit Court [indexes case files and journals], vol. 2-3, 1894-1979 (19 sheets of microfilm jackets)
	Oregon State Archives	Yamhill County Justice Dockets / Justice Court Docket [Criminal-Lafayette District], 1866-1880 (1 volume); Justice Court Docket [Criminal-Lafayette District-with index], 1869-1879 (1 volume)
	Yamhill County 4th Street Archives	Yamhill County Justice Dockets / Justice of the Peace Civil & Criminal Dockets [Criminal Docket-District no. 4], 1937-1940 (1 volume); Justice of the Peace Civil & Criminal Dockets [Proceedings in Justice Court-District no. 4], 1935-1937 (1 volume).
	Yamhill County Jail, Administrative Sergeant's Office	Yamhill County Prisoner Registers / Jail Record, 1888-1895 (1 volume); Register of Prisoners [Jail Record], 1891-1977 (2 volumes).
	Yamhill County Museum	Yamhill County Prisoner Registers / Jail Register, 1891-1948 (1 volume).

Federal Criminal Court Records at the National Archives & Records Admin. (NARA)

NARA Pacific Alaska Region (Seattle),
6125 Sand Point Way NE, Seattle, WA 98115-7999, (206) 336-5134
http://www.archives.gov/pacific-alaska/seattle/
seattle.archives@nara.gov

Record Type	ARC Identifier	Title	Description
	568042	Civil, Criminal, and Admiralty Case Files, compiled 1859 - 1923	Textual Records from the U.S. District Court for the District of Oregon. (03/03/1859 -)
	571877	Criminal Dockets, compiled 1907 - 1912	Textual Records from the U.S. District Court for the District of Oregon. (03/03/1859 -)

	572595	Criminal Dockets, compiled 1907 - 1970	Textual Records from the U.S. District Court for the District of Oregon. (03/03/1859 -)
	571108	Civil and Criminal Case Files, compiled 1923 - 1963	Textual Records from the U.S. District Court for the District of Oregon. (03/03/1859 -)
	567746	Civil and Criminal Case Files, compiled 1870 - 1911	Textual Records from the U.S. Circuit Court for the District of Oregon. (03/03/1863 - 01/01/1912)
	567805	Criminal Case Files, compiled 1955 - 1971	Textual Records from the U.S. District Court for the District of Oregon. (03/03/1859 -)

Oregon Executions

http://users.bestweb.net/~rg/execution/OREGON.htm

Oregon Department of Corrections – Offender Search

http://docpub.state.or.us/OOS/intro.jsf

B.   That is stuff he bought himself. He committed for the contract
then we took it into our outfit. Now we are trying to sell it and get a
smaller one. You never know what he was making until we look into those
things. I build the plant, get the stuff, and everything and he is a part-
ner and all he is is a lot of headaches. Yeah, got another headache.
First thing I do when I go back the other day I go up....are you listening?

M.   I'm listening.

B.   So I go up for a hearing for the license so they take it under
advisement. So I had to go up to get nine S___ of B_____ to make an appearance. Bawled the J____ out of them, granted the license for liquor
and gambling. Getting It Tuesday. I get the license, get a call from the
C.,.A. in Washington an order to cease building immediately or they will
indict us criminally. ███████████████████ they got an OK to go ahead
right after you left a week ago. ....

M.   Yeah.

Wire-tapped conversation between Bugsy Siegel and Meyer Lansky regarding the
building of the Flamingo Hotel in Las Vegas. From Bugsy Siegel's FBI file, available
online at: http://foia.fbi.gov/foiaindex/siege.htm

Pennsylvania

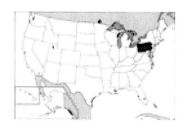

Pennsylvania State Archives
350 North Street, Harrisburg, PA 17120, (717) 783-3281
http://www.portal.state.pa.us/portal/server.pt/community/state_archives/2887
ra-statearchives@state.pa.us

Record Type	Location	Title/Description
	Manuscript Group 197	Allegheny County Work House: Discharge Description Dockets, 1873-1971
	Manuscript Group 197	Allegheny County Work House: Prison Register Books, 1869-1951
	Manuscript Group 197	Allegheny County Work House: Registers to Include all Prisoners Who Have Been tried and Sentenced to Hard Labor or Otherwise, 1869-1971
	RG-15, Series 15.51	Eastern State Penitentiary: Admission and Discharge Books, 1844-1888
	RG-15, Series 15.56	Eastern State Penitentiary: Convict Reception Registers, 1842-1850, 1857-1861, 1866-1873, 1882-1929
	RG-15, Series 15.57	Eastern State Penitentiary: Descriptive Registers, 1829-1903
	RG-15, Series 15.59	Eastern State Penitentiary: Discharge Books, 1830-1858
	RG-15, Series 15.58	Eastern State Penitentiary: Discharge Descriptive Dockets, 1873-1934
	RG-15, Series 15.64	Eastern State Penitentiary: Population Records Indices, 1900's
	RG-15, Series 15.65	Eastern State Penitentiary: Reception Description List, 1879-1884

	RG-15, Series 15.90	PA Industrial Reformatory at Huntingdon: Biographical and Descriptive Registers, 1889-1932
	RG-15, Series 15.92	PA Industrial Reformatory at Huntingdon: Physician's Record of Prisoners, 1889-1910
	RG-15, Series 15.98	PA Industrial Reformatory at Huntingdon: Register of Prisoners, 1889-1925
	RG-15, Series 15.120	Western State Penitentiary: Admission and Discharge Books, 1872-1900
	RG-15, Series 15.123	Western State Penitentiary: Convict Description and Receiving Dockets, 1872-1957
	RG-15, Series 15.124	Western State Penitentiary: Convict Docket, 1826-1859
	RG-15, Series 15.127	Western State Penitentiary: Descriptive Books, 1826-1873
	RG-15, Series 15.129	Western State Penitentiary: Descriptive Registers, 1826-1876
	RG-15, Series 15.130	Western State Penitentiary: Discharge Descriptive Dockets, 1873-1957
	RG-15, Series 15.133	Western State Penitentiary: Discharge Descriptive Dockets, 1873-1957
	RG-15, Series 15.135	Western State Penitentiary: Record of County and Federal Prisoners, 1857-1870
	RG-15, Series 15.10	Copper Printing Plates of Prison Inmate Images, Undated. (16 items) Sixteen copper printing plates containing portrait images of prison inmates. The images are identified only by inmate number.
	RG-15, Series 15.16	Bureau of Pardons: Calendars Summarizing Each Case to be Considered, 1893, 1894, 1898, 1943-1969. (11 cartons) Calendars provide summaries of cases considered by the Board of Pardons. Information provided is date hearing scheduled, inmate name, inmate number, county and court where sentenced, crime committed, sentence imposed, date application was filed, # of previous arrests and convictions, a description of the crime committed, and a record of the inmate's behavior while imprisoned.

	RG-15, Series 15.17	Clemency File, 1874-1900, 1906-1907, 1948-1962. (70 cartons, 3 boxes) Summary sheets, correspondence, petitions, court transcripts, newspaper notices, copies of death warrants, and pardon proclamations relating to clemency granted to inmates by the Governor and the Board of Pardons.
	RG-15, Series 15.18	Commutation and Parole Books, 1907-1932. (3 volumes) Recommendations sent to the Governor by the Board of Pardons for granting commutation or parole.
	RG-15, Series 15.19	Commutation Lists of Prisoners, 1964-1965. (1 folder) Lists of the names of inmates whose sentences were commuted under Governor William Warren Scranton's administration. Information provided is name of inmate, inmate number, and date sentence commuted.
	RG-15, Series 15.20	Commutations, 1967. (3 folders) Records of commutations issued under Governor Raymond P. Shafer. Information provided is name of inmate, inmate number, crime for which sentenced, date of commutation, and date discharged.
	RG-15, Series 15.21	Death Warrants File, 1874-1899. (21 boxes, 1 volume) Microfilm Rolls #454-466 Records of death warrants issued. Information provided is name of warden, name of inmate, nature of crime, name of court in which convicted and place where tried, period authorized for the execution to occur, method of execution imposed, date of conviction, and date of execution.
	RG-15, Series 15.22	Discharge Books, 1871-1923. (11 volumes) Indexed internally, alphabetically by surname of inmate prior to 1906 and by institution from 1906. Orders issued by Governors authorizing discharge of prisoners under the provisions of the Act approved May 21, 1869 and subsequent amending legislation. Information provided is date of release order, name of prisoner, name of correctional facility where confined.
	RG-15, Series 15.22	Minute Books, 1898-1901, 1939-1970. (7 volumes) Minutes of the meetings of the Board of Pardons. Information provided is date of meeting, names of those present, names of inmates considered for pardons, description of the discussion, and description of business transacted.
	RG-15, Series 15.25	Pardon Books, 1874-1934. (23 volumes) Applications made to, and proclamations issued by, the Board of Pardons. The applications volumes provide brief narrative case histories and recommendations for pardons or commutations and whether the pardons or commutations were granted.

	RG-15, Series 15.26	Pardons, 1967. (1 folder) Records of pardons issued under Governor Raymond P. Shafer. Information provided is name of inmate, inmate number, crime for which sentenced, date of pardon, and date discharged.
	RG-15, Series 15.27	Parole and Respite Books, 1910-1942. (2 volumes) Records of paroles and respites granted by the Governor under the provisions of the Act of 1909 and subsequent acts and of paroles revoked. Information provided is name of warden, name of penitentiary, name of inmate paroled or respited, crime for which sentenced, penalty imposed, date parole or respite was issued, period of respite in capital cases, and reason for a revocation of parole.
	RG-15, Series 15.28	Record Books of Capital Cases, 1894-1969. (2 volumes) Information provided is name of inmate, inmate number, county, date warrant issued. date of execution, date certificate of execution filed and remarks that general provide dates of applications to Pardon Board, issuance of new warrants, and commutations.
	RG-15, Series 15.29	Record of Respites and Execution Warrants, 1886-1893, 1948-1956, 1965, 1967. (1 volume, 5 folders) Records of respites and execution warrants issued. Information provided is date respite or execution warrant was issued, name of inmate, inmate number, crime for which sentenced, name of institution where incarcerated, and period during which execution was to be carried out.
	RG-47	Bedford County – Board of County Commissioners: Record of Prisoners, 1899-1931.
	RG-47 ,LC104	Berks County – Clerk of Courts: Criminal Records, 1845-1903. 3 rolls
	RG-47, LC24	Berks County – Clerk of Courts: Constables' and Justices' Returns (transcripts), 1895-1937. 50 rolls.
	RG-47, LRGP139	Carbon County – Sheriff' Office: Prison Registers, 1922-1990. 1 roll.
	RG-47, LRGP59	Fayette County – Clerk of Courts: Criminal Court Dockets, 1965-1983. 15 rolls.
	RG-47 , LC84	Lancaster County – Clerk of Courts: Criminal Case Files, 1902-1948. 134 rolls.
	RG-47, LC21	Lehigh County – Clerk of Courts: Criminal Case Papers, 1812-1877. 21 rolls.
	RG-47, LR429	Lycoming County – Clerk of Courts: Miscellaneous Civil and Criminal Records, 1843-1932. 1 roll.
	RG-47, LC105	Schuylkill County – Clerk of Courts: Criminal Session Docket Books, 1824-1956. 22 rolls

	RG-47, LRGP123	Washington County – Clerk of Courts: Court of Quarter Sessions Criminal Files, 1782-1827. 5 rolls.
	RG-47, LRGP138	Washington County – Clerk of Courts: Court of Quarter Sessions Criminal Files, 1828-1863. 10 rolls
	RG-47, LRGP151	Washington County – Clerk of Courts: Court of Quarter Sessions Criminal Files, 1864-1874. 4 rolls
	RG-47, LRGP156	Washington County – Clerk of Courts: Court of Quarter Sessions Criminal Files, 1874-1879. 4 rolls
	RG-81	Records of the Board of Probation and Parole

Federal Criminal Court Records at the National Archives & Records Admin. (NARA)

NARA Mid Atlantic Region (Philadelphia)

900 Market Street, Philadelphia, PA, 19107-4292, (215) 606-0100

http://www.archives.gov/midatlantic/

philadelphia.archives@nara.gov

Record Type	ARC Identifier	Title	Description
	278938	Criminal Case Files, compiled 1791 - 1883	Textual Records from the U.S. Circuit Court for the Eastern District of Pennsylvania. (04/20/1818 - 01/01/1912)
	279067	Criminal Case Files, compiled 1791 - 1970	Textual Records from the U.S. District Court for the Eastern District of Pennsylvania. (04/20/1818 - 03/03/1901)
	572204	Criminal Case Files, compiled 1842 - 1978	Textual Records from the U.S. District Court for the Western District of Pennsylvania. Pittsburgh Term. (05/26/1824 -)
	572205	Criminal Case Files, compiled 1924 - 1958	Textual Records from the U.S. District Court for the Western District of Pennsylvania. Erie Term. (07/28/1866 -)
	895431	Criminal Dockets, compiled 1867 - 1958	Textual Records from the U.S. District Court for the Western District of Pennsylvania. Erie Term. (07/28/1866 -)
	824584	Record of Criminal Cases, compiled 02/1860 - 11/1871	Textual Records from the U.S. District Court for the Eastern District of Pennsylvania. (04/20/1818 - 03/03/1901)

	572150	Criminal Case Files, compiled 1901 - 1983	Textual Records from the U.S. District Court for the Middle District of Pennsylvania. Scranton Term. (03/02/1901 -)
	895386	Dockets for Miscellaneous Criminal Proceedings , compiled 1927 - 1976	Textual Records from the U.S. District Court for the Middle District of Pennsylvania. Harrisburg Term. (03/02/1901 -)
	2791187	Judgment Dockets, compiled 1902 - 1932	Textual Records from the U.S. District Court for the Middle District of Pennsylvania. Scranton Term. (03/02/1901 -)
	2790506	Pardons, compiled 1835 - 1866	Textual Records from the U.S. Circuit Court for the Eastern District of Pennsylvania. (04/20/1818 - 01/01/1912)
	2770229	Criminal Dockets, compiled 1789 - 1989	Textual Records from the U.S. District Court for the Eastern District of Pennsylvania. (04/20/1818 - 03/03/1901)
	2771434	Criminal Dockets, compiled 1843 - 1979	Textual Records from the U.S. District Court for the Western District of Pennsylvania. Pittsburgh Term. (05/26/1824 -)
	587050	Abstracts of Criminal Case Files, compiled ca. 1930 - ca. 1940, documenting the period 1791 - 1825	Textual Records from the U.S. District Court for the Eastern District of Pennsylvania. (04/20/1818 - 03/03/1901)
	2848760	Judgment Dockets, compiled 1869 - 1906	Textual Records from the U.S. Circuit Court for the Western District of Pennsylvania. Erie Term. (07/28/1866 - 01/01/1912)
	2842859	Index to Criminal Case Files , compiled 1924 - 1958	Textual Records from the U.S. District Court for the Western District of Pennsylvania. Erie Term. (07/28/1866 -)
	2806018	Index for Criminal Proceedings, compiled 1924 - 12/31/1958	Textual Records from the U.S. District Court for the Middle District of Pennsylvania. Scranton Term. (03/02/1901 -)
	2794682	Criminal Return Dockets, compiled 1901 - 1926	Textual Records from the U.S. District Court for the Middle District of Pennsylvania. Office of U.S. Commissioners. (1901 - 1968)

	2771686	Judgment Indexes and Dockets, compiled 1795 - 1956	Textual Records from the U.S. District Court for the Eastern District of Pennsylvania. Philadelphia Term. (03/03/1901 -)
	2771420	Criminal Dockets, compiled 1901 - 1959	Textual Records from the U.S. District Court for the Middle District of Pennsylvania. Harrisburg Term. (03/02/1901 -)
	2774947	Indexes to Criminal Dockets, compiled 1928 - 1972	Textual Records from the U.S. District Court for the Eastern District of Pennsylvania. Philadelphia Term. (03/03/1901 -)
	2843344	Records in Proceedings in Criminal Cases, compiled 1924 - 1951	Textual Records from the U.S. District Court for the Western District of Pennsylvania. Erie Term. (07/28/1866 -)

Eastern State Penitentiary – Research Service for Inmates Incarcerated Before 1940

 http://www.easternstate.org/history/genealogy.php

Pennsylvania Executions

 http://users.bestweb.net/~rg/execution/PENNSYLVANIA.htm

Pennsylvania Department of Corrections – Offender Search

 http://www.phmc.state.pa.us/bah/dam/rg/ys/r15ysd.htm#15.51

http://caselaw.lp.findlaw.com/scripts/getcase.pl?court=us&vol=319&invol=427

FindLaw   SUPREME COURT

View enhanced case on Westlaw
  KeyCite this case on Westlaw
Cases citing this case: Supreme Court
Cases citing this case: Circuit Courts

http://laws.findlaw.com/us/319/427.html

U.S. Supreme Court

BUCHALTER v. PEOPLE OF THE STATE OF NEW YORK, 319 U.S. 427 (1943)

319 U.S. 427

BUCHALTER

v.

PEOPLE OF STATE OF NEW YORK

WEISS

v.

SAME.

CAPONE

v.

SAME.

Nos. 606, 610, 619.
Argued May 7-10, 1943.
Decided June 1, 1943.

Messrs. J. Bertram Wegman and I. Maurice Wormser, both of New York City, for petitioner Buchalter.

Messrs. Arthur Garfield Hays and John Schulman, both of New York City, for petitioner Weiss.

Mr. Sidney Rosenthal, of New York City, for petitioner Capone. [319 U.S. 427, 428] Mr. Solomon A. Klein, of Brooklyn, N.Y., for respondent.

U.S. Supreme Court case involving Louis "Lepke" Buchalter. Found online at: http://www.findlaw.com/casecode/supreme.html

Rhode Island

Rhode Island Historical Society

121 Hope Street, Providence, RI, (401) 273-8107
http://www.rihs.org/
http://isis.minisisinc.com/RIHS/prototype2/index.htm

Record Type	Title/Description
	State Workhouse: Records of commitment, workhouse building, 1871-1936
	State Workhouse: Intake / release ledgers, workhouse building, 1895-1968
	State Workhouse: Miscellaneous, workhouse building, 1885-1929, including a visitor register, 1916-1924; and two discharge books, 1885-1896 and 1918-1924
	State Workhouse: State Prison and County Jail, 1839-1943

Rhode Island Judicial Records Center Archives

5 Hill Street, Pawtucket? RI 02860, (401) 721-2640
http://www.courts.state.ri.us/records/forms.htm

Record Type	Title/Description
	Criminal Cases: 1671-1900
	District Court Criminal Cases: 1st Division up to 1900
	District Court Criminal Cases: 2nd Division up to 1993
	District Court Criminal Cases: 3rd Division up to 1993

	District Court Criminal Cases: 4th Division up to 1998
	District Court Criminal Cases: 5th Division up to 1990
	District Court Criminal Cases: 6th Division up to 1993
	District Court Criminal Cases: 7th Division up to 1990
	District Court Criminal Cases: 8th Division up to 1990
	Superior Court Criminal Cases: Providence County: 1984 to 1995
	Superior Court Criminal Cases: Kent County: 1986 to 1993
	Superior Court Criminal Cases: Newport County: 1986 to 1995
	Superior Court Criminal Cases: Washington County: 1986 to 1995
	Providence County Superior Criminal: Prior to 1984 (stored offsite)
	District Court – 2nd Division Criminal: 1994-1996 (stored offsite)
	District Court – 3rd Division Criminal: 1994-1996 (stored offsite)
	District Court – 6th Division Criminal: 1994-1995 (stored offsite)

Federal Criminal Court Records at the National Archives & Records Admin. (NARA)

NARA Northeast Region (Boston)

Frederick C. Murphy Federal Center, 380 Trapelo Road, Waltham, MA, 02452-6399

(781) 663-0130

http://www.archives.gov/northeast/

waltham.archives@nara.gov

Record Type	ARC Identifier	Title	Description
	592855	Criminal Case Files, compiled 1893 - 1978	Textual Records from the U.S. District Court for the District of Rhode Island. (1790 -)
	278236	Case Files, compiled 11/1790 - 12/1911	Textual Records from the U.S. Circuit Court for the District of Rhode Island. (1790 - 01/01/1912)

Rhode Island Executions

 http://users.bestweb.net/~rg/execution/RHODE%20ISLAND.htm

Rhode Island Department of Corrections – Inmate Search

http://www.doc.ri.gov/inmate_search/index.php

Adult Criminal Information Database

http://courtconnect.courts.state.ri.us/pls/ri_adult/ck_public_qry_main.cp_main_idx

Photocopy made at NARA's Pacific Region (San Francisco)
Form #1153
Revised 12-9-66

MEDICAL CENTER FOR FEDERAL PRISONERS
Springfield, Missouri

REPORT OF ADVERSE BEHAVIOR

PATIENT'S NAME: COHEN   REG. NO. 14738-H   STATUS: Medical

QUARTERS: 1-2   PLACE OF OFFENSE: Out going mail DATE: 9-9-1967   TIME: 1:00 AM

BEHAVIOR COMPLAINT: Vuglar reference to the East Gate Mail Censor. Evidence enclosed.

STATEMENT OF REPORTING OFFICER: On 9-8-1967 I returned a letter to the above named

inmate for using profanity in his letter. This is not the first time letters have

been returned to this inmate for using profanity in them.

(Use reverse side, if necessary)

SIGNED: KENNETH L. GREEN S.O.
Name and Title

CORRECTIONAL SUPERVISOR'S COMMENTS: The above inmate has had letters returned to him by
the officers who have inspected his letters for some time. This is not the first
time he has referred to him them in this manner, and apparently he has gained no
insight into his problems by having them returned, hence the report.

PATIENT'S QUARTERS FOLLOWING REPORT: 1-2   SIGNED: J. W. Blatchford
Correctional Supervisor

WARD PHYSICIAN'S COMMENTS:
(Use reverse side, if necessary)
PATIENT'S STATEMENT: The original letter that I sent out used the expression, "God damned
money" referring to the money that my sister is being robbed of. She has been robbed a number of times and I was telling her not to worry about, "The God damned money. These letters
xxxxx were in explanation of the first one.

BEHAVIOR COMMITTEE'S COMMENT: Patient was given returned letters in I-2 Strong Section with
an explanation that such letters--with profanity or slurring remarks about personnel--will
not be sent out of the institution. (Copies of letters attached).

BEHAVIOR COMMITTEE'S ACTION: Warned and reprimanded.

DATE: 9-11-67   CHAIRMAN: Chief Corr. Suprv. C. C. Holt

COMMITTEE MEMBERS: Corr. Suprv. B. J. O'Mara; Mr. B. W. Wright, Chief, Acting, C&P.

Report of Adverse Behavior for Mickey Cohen. Found in Alcatraz
inmate case file at the National Archives, San Bruno, CA.

South Carolina

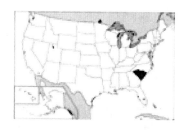

South Carolina Department of Archives and History

South Carolina Archives and History Center
8301 Parklane Road, Columbia, SC 29223, (803) 896-6100
http://scdah.sc.gov/
email: http://archives.sc.gov/contactus.htm

Record Type	Location (Record Group/ Series)	Author	Title/Description
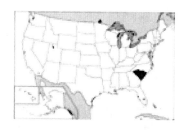	132000 / .S 132003	Central Correctional Institution (S.C.)	Commitments of prisoners, 1900-1964, 28.00 cubic ft.
	132000 / .S 132008	Central Correctional Institution (S.C.)	Record of deaths, discharges, escapes, pardons, and paroles, 1867-1965, 10.00 volume(s)
	132000 / .S 132075	South Carolina. Dept. of Corrections. --Division of Administrative Operations	Inmate records and paroles ledger books, 1954-1970, 2.00 volume(s)
	166000 / .S 166029	South Carolina. Office of the Governor	Register of petitions for pardon, parole, and commutation, 1901-1914, 3.00 volume(s)
	166000 / .S 166046	South Carolina. Office of the Governor	Indeterminate sentence law parole orders, 1927-1939 0.33 cubic ft.
	000002 / .L 02068	Aiken County (S.C.). County Council	Poor House records, 1886-1925, 1.00 volume
	128000 / .S 128003	South Carolina. Confederate Home Commission - Confederate Home	Inmate records, 1909-1957, 2.00 volumes, 2.00 microfilm reels
	132000 / .S 132075	South Carolina. Dept. of Corrections. --Division of Administrative Operations	Inmate records and paroles ledger books, 1954-1970, 2.00 volumes

	000002 / .L 02073	Aiken County (S.C.). County Council	Paroles, 1943-1960, 2.00 volumes
	000004 / .L 04167	South Carolina. Court of General Sessions (Anderson County)	Pardons, paroles, and commutations, 1851-1914, 0.33 cubic ft.
	000008 / .L 08044	South Carolina. Court of General Sessions (Berkeley County)	Pardons, paroles, and commutations, 1921-1944, 0.33 cubic ft.
	000011 / .L 11047	South Carolina. Court of General Sessions (Cherokee County)	Pardons, paroles, and commutations, 1912-1953, 0.00 cubic ft.
	000013 / .L 13070	South Carolina. Court of General Sessions (Chesterfield County)	Pardons, paroles, and commutations (recorded copy), 1897-1944, 1.00 volume
	000014 / .L 14117	South Carolina. Court of General Sessions (Clarendon County)	Pardons, paroles, and commutations, 1898-1950, 0.00 cubic ft.
	000017 / .L 17027	South Carolina. Court of General Sessions (Dillon County)	Pardons, paroles, and commutations (recorded copy), 1910-1926, 1.00 volume
	000021 / .L 21019	South Carolina. Court of General Sessions (Florence County)	Pardons, paroles, and commutations (recorded copy), 1897-1915, 1.00 volume
	000026 / .L 26073	South Carolina. Court of General Sessions (Horry County)	Pardons, paroles, and commutations, 1882-1932, 0.16 cubic ft.
	000026 / .L 26074	South Carolina. Court of General Sessions (Horry County)	Pardons, paroles, and commutations (recorded copy), 1895-1932, 1.00 volume
	000028 / .L 28198	South Carolina. Court of General Sessions (Kershaw County)	Pardons, paroles, and commutations, 1897-1902, 0.33 cubic ft.
	000030 / .L 30168	South Carolina. Court of General Sessions (Laurens County)	Pardons, paroles, and commutations, 1802-1896, 0.00 cubic ft.
	000032 / .L 32162	South Carolina. Court of General Sessions (Lexington County)	Pardons, paroles, and commutations (recorded copy), 1896-1945, 1.00 volume
	000032 / .L 32303	South Carolina. Court of General Sessions (Lexington County)	Pardons, paroles, and commutations, 1925, 0.00 cubic ft.

	000036 / .L 36103	South Carolina. Court of General Sessions (Newberry County)	Pardons, paroles, and commutations (recorded copy), 1897-1949, 1.00 volume
	000040 / .L 40061	South Carolina. Court of General Sessions (Richland County)	Pardons, paroles, and commutations, 1924-1932, 0.33 cubic ft.
	000042 / .L 42167	South Carolina. Court of General Sessions (Spartanburg County)	Pardons, paroles, and commutations, 1901-1904, 0.00 cubic ft.
	000044 / .L 44202	South Carolina. Court of General Sessions (Union County)	Pardons, paroles, and commutations (recorded copy), 1896-1963, 1.00 volume
	000045 / .L 45087	South Carolina. Court of General Sessions (Williamsburg County)	Pardons, paroles, and commutations (recorded copy), 1896-1914 0.16 cubic ft.
	000046 / .L 46101	South Carolina. Court of General Sessions (York County)	Pardons, paroles, and commutations (recorded copy), 1898-1919 1.00 microfilm reel

Note: Hundreds of sets of criminal court records can be found by searching on the key words 'criminal journals' and 'criminal dockets in the title field of the Archives' online catalog found at the Archives' website:

http://rediscov.sc.gov/scar/default.asp?include=wordsearch.htm

To narrow down the results, type in the name of the county in the Creator field.

Federal Criminal Court Records at the National Archives & Records Admin. (NARA)

NARA Southeast Region

5780 Jonesboro Road, Morrow, Georgia 30260, (770) 968-2100

www.archives.gov/southeast/

atlanta.archives@nara.gov

Record Type	ARC Identifier	Title	Description
	1076572	Criminal Case Files, compiled 1966 - 1981	Textual Records from the U.S. District Court for the Columbia Division of the District of South Carolina. (03/18/1966 -)
	1076577	Criminal Case Files, compiled 1866 - 1965	Textual Records from the U.S. District Court for the Charleston Division of the Eastern District of South Carolina. (06/26/1926 - 03/18/1966)
	1076582	Criminal Case Files, compiled 1866 - 1965	Textual Records from the U.S. District Court for the Greenville Division of the Western District of South Carolina. (06/26/1926 - 03/18/1966)
	1943546	Criminal Dockets, compiled 1954 - 1976	Textual Records from the U.S. District Court for the Columbia Division of the District of South Carolina. (03/18/1966 -)
	2839369	Index to Criminal Case Files, compiled 1873 - 1907	Textual Records from the U.S. Circuit Court for the District of South Carolina. Charleston Term. (02/1907 - 01/01/1912)
	2839419	Index to Criminal Case Files, compiled 1866 - 1895	Textual Records from the U.S. District Court for the Eastern District of South Carolina. (02/21/1823 - 03/03/1915)
	1943544	Criminal Dockets, compiled 1868 - 1965	Textual Records from the U.S. District Court for the Greenville Division of the Western District of South Carolina. (06/26/1926 - 03/18/1966)
	1661882	Criminal Case Files, compiled 1867 - 1911	Textual Records from the U.S. Circuit Court for the District of South Carolina. Charleston Term. (02/1907 - 01/01/1912)
	1943551	Criminal Dockets, compiled 1954 - 1965	Textual Records from the U.S. District Court for the Columbia Division of the Eastern District of South Carolina. (06/26/1926 - 03/18/1966)
	2838794	Criminal Minutes, compiled 1873 - 1911	Textual Records from the U.S. Circuit Court for the District of South Carolina. Charleston Term. (02/1907 - 01/01/1912)

	1943549	Criminal Dockets, compiled 1884 - 1966	Textual Records from the U.S. District Court for the Charleston Division of the Eastern District of South Carolina. (06/26/1926 - 03/18/1966)
	2839422	Index to Criminal Case Files, compiled 1922 - 1941	Textual Records from the U.S. District Court for the Greenville Division of the Western District of South Carolina. (06/26/1926 - 03/18/1966)

Note: there are 1,800 other criminal case files for South Carolina listed in the National Archives ARC database. To find these, type in the defendant's name in the search field at: http://www.archives.gov/research/arc/

South Carolina Executions

http://users.bestweb.net/~rg/execution/RHODE%20ISLAND.htm

South Carolina Department of Corrections – Inmate Search

https://sword.doc.state.sc.us/incarceratedInmateSearch/

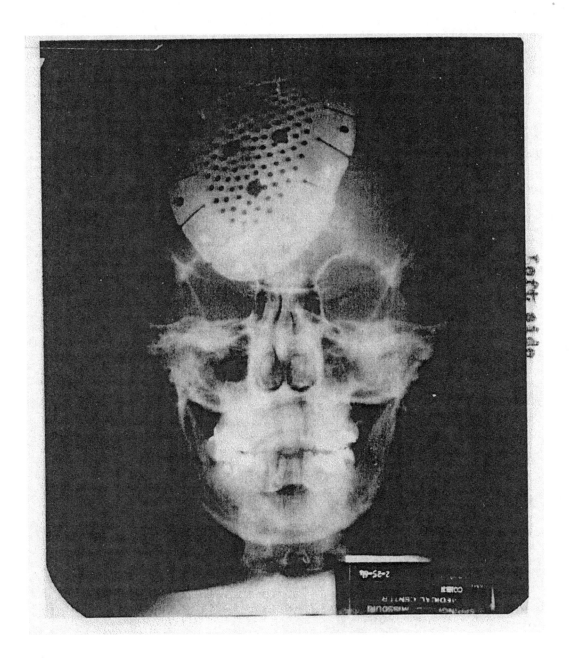

X-ray of Mickey Cohen showing metal plate placed inside his head after he was hit with an iron rod while incarcerated at the U.S. Penitentiary in Atlanta. Found in the Alcatraz inmate case file at the National Archives, San Bruno, CA.

South Dakota

South Dakota State Archives

900 Governors Drive, Pierre, SD; (605) 773-3804
http://www.sdhistory.org/arc/archives.htm
archref@state.sd.us

Record Type	Title/Description
![]	Prisoner Case Files, 1878-1959. Restricted; permission must be obtained from the SD Department of Corrections.
![]	Penitentiary Parole Files, 1906-1940
![]	Criminal case files for Union and Roberts Counties

Note: All counties other than Union and Roberts Counties maintain all of their own criminal case files.

Federal Criminal Court Records at the National Archives & Records Admin. (NARA)

NARA Rocky Mountain Region (Denver)
Denver Federal Center, Bldgs 46, 48, Denver, CO 80225, (303) 407-5740
http://www.archives.gov/rocky-mountain/
denver.archives@nara.gov

Record Type	ARC Identifier	Title	Description
![]	3535516	Criminal Case Files, compiled 1974 - 1981	Textual Records from the U.S. District Court for the Southern (Sioux Falls) Division of the District of South Dakota. (02/27/1890 -)

	3533794	Criminal Case Files, compiled 1979 - 1981	Textual Records from the U.S. District Court for the Central (Pierre) Division of the District of South Dakota. (02/27/1890 -)
	3532442	Criminal Case Files, compiled 1979 - 1981	Textual Records from the U.S. District Court for the Western (Rapid City) Division of the District of South Dakota.

Federal Criminal Court Records at the National Archives & Records Admin. (NARA)

NARA Central Plains Region (Kansas City),
400 West Pershing Road, Kansas City, MO 64108, (816) 268-8000
http://www.archives.gov/central-plains/kansas-city/
kansascity.archives@nara.gov

Record Type	ARC Identifier	Title	Description
	1145987	Criminal Case Files, compiled 1927 - 1960	Textual Records from the Department of the Interior. Bureau of Indian Affairs. Pine Ridge Agency. (09/17/1947 - 09/09/9999)
	583185	Criminal Case Files, compiled 1890 - 1963	Textual Records from the U.S. District Court for the Western (Deadwood) Division of the District of South Dakota. (02/27/1890)
	583170	Criminal Case Files, compiled 1895 - 1963	Textual Records from the U.S. District Court for the Northern (Aberdeen) Division of the District of South Dakota. (11/03/1893 -)
	583182	Criminal Case Files, compiled 1891 - 1963	Textual Records from the U.S. District Court for the Central (Pierre) Division of the District of South Dakota. (02/27/1890 -)
	583178	Criminal Case Files, compiled 1890 - 1963	Textual Records from the U.S. District Court for the Southern (Sioux Falls) Division of the District of South Dakota. (02/27/1890 -)

South Dakota Executions

 http://users.bestweb.net/~rg/execution/SO%20DAKOTA.htm

South Dakota Department of Corrections – Inmate Search

Not Available

Tennessee

Tennessee State Library and Archives

403 7th Avenue North, Nashville; TN; (605) 773-3804
http://www.tennessee.gov/tsla/history/military/pension128.htm
http://www.youseemore.com/tsla/ Catalog
http://state.tn.us/tsla/Collections.htm
reference.tsla@state.tn.us

Record Type	Location	Author	Title/Description
	RG 25	Department of Corrections	Tennessee State Penitentiary Records, 1831-1922
	RG 261	Department of Corrections	Board of Probation and Paroles Records, 1940-1967
	RG 280	Department of Corrections	Board of Pardons and Paroles: Inmate Pardon Records, 1938-1962
	RG 31	State Courts	Chancery Courts: 7th Division, Part II (Davidson County), Opinion Books, 1941-1967
	RG 191	State Supreme Court	Clerk's Records, 1810-1955
	RG 307	State Supreme Court	Records, 1793-1820
	RG 170	State Supreme Court	Trial Cases, 1796-1955
	RG 164	State Supreme Court	Trial Dockets, 1817-1936
		County Courts	http://state.tn.us/tsla/preservation/microfilmindex.htm Look for Circuit Court records

		Governors Office	http://tennessee.gov/tsla/history/govpapers/ gplist.htm Pardon papers are divided up in various Governors' papers

Federal Criminal Court Records at the National Archives & Records Admin. (NARA)

NARA Southeast Region

5780 Jonesboro Road, Morrow, Georgia 30260, (770) 968-2100

www.archives.gov/southeast/

atlanta.archives@nara.gov

Record Type	ARC Identifier	Title	Description
	654956	Law, Equity, and Criminal Case Files, compiled 1798 - 1887	Textual Records from the U.S. Circuit Court for the District of Tennessee. Nashville Term. (01/31/1797 - 04/29/1802)
	733759	Criminal Case Files, compiled 1803 - 1980	Textual Records from the U.S. District Court for the Nashville Division of the Middle District of Tennessee. (03/04/1923 -)
	654955	Criminal Case Files, compiled 1867 - 1905	Textual Records from the U.S. Circuit Court for the Western District of Tennessee. Memphis Term. (01/26/1864 - 06/20/1878)
	733761	Criminal Case Files, compiled 1905 - 1979	Textual Records from the U.S. District Court for the Western (Memphis) Division of the Western District of Tennessee. (06/20/1878 -)
	722103	Case Files, compiled 1924 - 1976	Textual Records from the U.S. Court of Appeals for the Sixth Circuit. (1948 -)
	1102936	Criminal Case Files, compiled 1900 - 1979	Textual Records from the U.S. District Court for the Southern (Chattanooga) Division of the Eastern District of Tennessee. (06/11/1880 -)
	2517311	Criminal Dockets, compiled 1925 - 1958	Textual Records from the U.S. District Court for the Winchester Division of the Eastern District of Tennessee. (11/27/1940 -)
	2517312	Criminal Dockets, compiled 1903 - 1956	Textual Records from the U.S. District Court for the Northeastern (Greenville) Division of the Eastern District of Tennessee. (02/07/1900 -)
	1089770	Criminal Case Files, compiled 1898 - 1973	Textual Records from the U.S. District Court for the Northern (Knoxville) Division of the Eastern District of Tennessee. (06/11/1880 -)

	1489290	Criminal Case Files, compiled 1880 - 1981	Textual Records from the U.S. District Court for the Eastern (Jackson) Division of the Western District of Tennessee. (06/20/1878 -)
	2642024	Index of Criminal Cases, compiled 1893 - 1974	Textual Records from the U.S. District Court for the Southern (Chattanooga) Division of the Eastern District of Tennessee. (06/11/1880 -)
	2642019	Index of Criminal Cases, compiled 1967 - 1981	Textual Records from the U.S. District Court for the Nashville Division of the Middle District of Tennessee. (03/04/1923 -)
	2580180	Criminal Minutes, compiled 1936 - 1960	Textual Records from the U.S. District Court for the Northeastern (Cookeville) Division of the Middle District of Tennessee. (02/13/1909 -)
	1102989	Criminal Case Files, compiled 1925 - 1978	Textual Records from the U.S. District Court for the Columbia Division of the Middle District of Tennessee. (03/04/1923 -)
	2406696	Criminal Dockets, compiled 1878 - 1973	Textual Records from the U.S. District Court for the Nashville Division of the Middle District of Tennessee. (03/04/1923 -)
	2881570	Index of Bankruptcy, Civil, and Criminal Case Files, compiled 1957 - 1992	Textual Records from the U.S. District Court for the Southern (Chattanooga) Division of the Eastern District of Tennessee. (06/11/1880 -)
	1102950	Criminal Case Files, compiled 1912 - 1969	Textual Records from the U.S. District Court for the Northeastern (Cookeville) Division of the Middle District of Tennessee. (02/13/1909 -)
	2573315	Criminal Minutes, compiled 1941 - 1954	Textual Records from the U.S. District Court for the Southern (Chattanooga) Division of the Eastern District of Tennessee. (06/11/1880 -)
	2573318	Criminal Minutes, compiled 1897 - 1909	Textual Records from the U.S. District Court for the Eastern (Jackson) Division of the Western District of Tennessee. (06/20/1878 -)
	2406659	Criminal Dockets, compiled 1909 - 1970	Textual Records from the U.S. District Court for the Northeastern (Cookeville) Division of the Middle District of Tennessee. (02/13/1909 -)
	2517323	Criminal Dockets, compiled 1864 - 1963	Textual Records from the U.S. District Court for the Western (Memphis) Division of the Western District of Tennessee. (06/20/1878 -)

	2642025	Index of Criminal Cases, compiled 1888 - 1929	Textual Records from the U.S. District Court for the Northern (Knoxville) Division of the Eastern District of Tennessee. (06/11/1880 -)
	1138229	Criminal Case Files, compiled 1925 - 1977	Textual Records from the U.S. District Court for the Winchester Division of the Eastern District of Tennessee. (11/27/1940 -)
	2600976	Criminal Minutes, compiled 1938 - 1962	Textual Records from the U.S. District Court for the Nashville Division of the Middle District of Tennessee. (03/04/1923 -)
	2406665	Criminal Dockets, compiled 1881 - 1969	Textual Records from the U.S. District Court for the Southern (Chattanooga) Division of the Eastern District of Tennessee. (06/11/1880 -)
	2517304	Criminal Dockets, compiled 1864 - 1957	Textual Records from the U.S. District Court for the Northern (Knoxville) Division of the Eastern District of Tennessee. (06/11/1880 -)
	2642028	Index of Criminal Cases, compiled 1864 - 1898	Textual Records from the U.S. Circuit Court for the Northern (Knoxville) Division of the Eastern District of Tennessee. (06/11/1880 - 01/01/1912)
	2573325	Criminal Minutes, compiled 1889 - 1896	Textual Records from the U.S. District Court for the Western (Memphis) Division of the Western District of Tennessee. (06/20/1878 -)
	2573321	Criminal Minutes, compiled 1854 - 1861	Textual Records from the U.S. District Court for the Eastern District of Tennessee. (04/29/1802 - 06/11/1880)
	2517318	Criminal Dockets, compiled 1925 - 1967	Textual Records from the U.S. District Court for the Columbia Division of the Middle District of Tennessee. (03/04/1923 -)
	2658456	Criminal Orders, compiled 1953 - 1960	Textual Records from the U.S. District Court for the Nashville Division of the Middle District of Tennessee. (03/04/1923 -)
	1103003	Criminal Case Files, compiled 1905 - 1980	Textual Records from the U.S. District Court for the Northeastern (Greenville) Division of the Eastern District of Tennessee. (02/07/1900 -)
	1489297	Criminal Dockets, compiled 1880 - 1963	Textual Records from the U.S. District Court for the Eastern (Jackson) Division of the Western District of Tennessee. (06/20/1878 -)
	2600998	Criminal Minutes, compiled 1938 - 1961	Textual Records from the U.S. District Court for the Columbia Division of the Middle District of Tennessee. (03/04/1923 -)

	2658454	Criminal Orders, compiled 1953 - 1960	Textual Records from the U.S. District Court for the Northeastern (Cookeville) Division of the Middle District of Tennessee. (02/13/1909 -)
	2573323	Criminal Minutes, compiled 1864 - 1886	Textual Records from the U.S. Circuit Court for the Northern (Knoxville) Division of the Eastern District of Tennessee. (06/11/1880 - 01/01/1912)
	2642021	Index of Criminal Cases, compiled 1928 - 1941	Textual Records from the U.S. District Court for the Northeastern (Greenville) Division of the Eastern District of Tennessee. (02/07/1900 -)
	2838491	Criminal Final Records, compiled 1880 - 1906	Textual Records from the U.S. District Court for the Eastern (Jackson) Division of the Western District of Tennessee. (06/20/1878 -)
	2838466	Criminal Final Records, compiled 1872 - 1906	Textual Records from the U.S. Circuit Court for the Western (Memphis) Division of the Western District of Tennessee. (06/20/1878 - 01/01/1912)
	2838472	Criminal Final Records, compiled 1881 - 1903	Textual Records from the U.S. Circuit Court for the Southern (Chattanooga) Division of the Eastern District of Tennessee. (1880 - 01/01/1912)
	2838503	Criminal Final Records, compiled 1879 - 1909	Textual Records from the U.S. Circuit Court for the Middle District of Tennessee. (01/18/1839 - 02/13/1909)
	2838505	Criminal Final Records, compiled 1879 - 1914	Textual Records from the U.S. District Court for the Middle District of Tennessee. Nashville Term. (02/13/1909 - 03/04/1923)
	2838479	Criminal Final Records, compiled 1906 - 1911	Textual Records from the U.S. District Court for the Southern (Chattanooga) Division of the Eastern District of Tennessee. (06/11/1880 -)
	2838485	Criminal Final Records, compiled 1909 - 1914	Textual Records from the U.S. District Court for the Northeastern (Cookeville) Division of the Middle District of Tennessee. (02/13/1909 -)
	2838497	Criminal Final Records, compiled 1871 - 1899	Textual Records from the U.S. Circuit Court for the Northern (Knoxville) Division of the Eastern District of Tennessee. (06/11/1880 - 01/01/1912)

	2838482	Criminal Final Records, compiled 1909 - 1911	Textual Records from the U.S. Circuit Court for the Northeastern (Cookville) Division of the Middle District of Tennessee. (02/13/1909 - 01/01/1912)
	2838502	Criminal Final Records, compiled 1897 - 1915	Textual Records from the U.S. District Court for the Northern (Knoxville) Division of the Eastern District of Tennessee. (06/11/1880 -)
	2838487	Criminal Final Records, compiled 1906 - 1912	Textual Records from the U.S. District Court for the Northeastern (Greenville) Division of the Eastern District of Tennessee. (02/07/1900 -)

Tennessee Executions

http://users.bestweb.net/~rg/execution/SO%20DAKOTA.htm

Tennessee Department of Corrections – Archived Records

http://www.tennessee.gov/correction/public/archive&sentence.html

Tennessee Department of Corrections – Inmate Search

Not Found

Texas

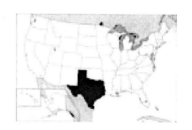

Texas State Library and Archives Commission

Lorenzo De Zavala State Archives & Library Building
Capitol Complex, 1201 Brazos St., Austin, TX, (512) 463-5455
http://www.tsl.state.tx.us/arc/index.html
archinfo@tsl.state.tx.us

Record Type	Location	Author	Title/Description
		Texas. Dept. of Criminal Justice.	Convict record ledgers, 1849-1954 (indexes date 1849-1970), 29.95 cubic ft. (21.75 cubic ft. for the ledgers, 8.2 cubic ft. for the indexes) (29 convict ledgers, 10 indexes, also on 20 reels of microfilm)
		Texas. Dept. of Criminal Justice.	Conduct registers, 1855-[ca. 1976] (bulk 1877-1945), 33.4 cubic ft. (60 ledgers)
		Texas. Dept. of Criminal Justice.	Miscellaneous convict ledgers, 1849-1869, 1884-1885, 1897-1970, 4.44 cubic ft. (23 volumes)
		Texas. Dept. of Criminal Justice.	Escape record, 1851-1943, 0.22 cubic ft. (one ledger)
		Texas. Dept. of Criminal Justice.	Record of United States prisoners, 1874-1883, fractional cubic ft.
		Texas. Dept. of Criminal Justice.	Photographs, [ca. 1911-ca. 1985], undated (bulk [ca. 1965-ca. 1980]), 25.07 cubic ft.
		Texas. Dept. of Criminal Justice.	Topical photographs, 1920, [ca. 1955-ca. 1985], undated (bulk [ca. 1965-ca. 1980]), 3.6 cubic ft.
		Texas. Dept. of Criminal Justice.	Topical photographs, [ca. 1911-ca. 1985], undated (bulk [ca. 1960-ca. 1980]), 7.74 cubic ft.

		Texas. Dept. of Criminal Justice.	Unit photographs, 1933-[ca. 1985], undated (bulk [ca. 1955-ca. 1980]), 9.12 cubic ft.
		Texas. Dept. of Criminal Justice.	Slides and miscellaneous photographic media, [ca. 1962-ca. 1985], undated, 4.08 cubic ft.
		Texas. Dept. of Criminal Justice.	Scrapbooks, 1911, [ca. 1940-ca. 1980], undated, 0.53 cubic ft.
	1990/134-1 Thru 6	Texas. Board of Pardons and Paroles	Board of Pardon Advisors pardon books, 1898-1930
	2-1/70 Thru 72, 77 Thru 79, 82 Thru 89	Texas. Secretary of State	Pardon registers and reward proclamations, 1870-1938
		Secretary of State	Executive record books, 1835-1917. [microform]
		Texas. Court of Criminal Appeals	Court of Criminal Appeals centralized court case files (part I: through file number 25006), 1909-1975. These records contain the most thorough documentation of the cases heard before the court. They consist of case files containing copies of documents filed with the Texas Court of Criminal Appeals. 3,238 cubic ft.
		Texas. Secretary of State. Statutory Documents Section.	Secretary of State executive clemency records, 1840, 1845-2006. These records, include executive record books, clemency proclamations, indexes to clemency proclamations, applications for pardons and other forms of executive clemency, and registers of applications for pardons. 110.68 cubic ft., 168 reels of microfilm (originals), 22 reels of microfilm (duplicates)

		Texas. Court of Criminal Appeals	Court of Criminal Appeals records, 1892-2008. The Texas Court of Criminal Appeals is the highest criminal court in the state, holding the same position in the area of state criminal law that the Supreme Court holds in civil law. The Court of Criminal Appeals has appellate jurisdiction in all criminal cases (both felonies and misdemeanors). These records document the activities of the court. They consist of minutes, opinions, orders, dockets, indexes, account books, correspondence, press releases, and case files that may include transcripts, briefs, exhibits, statements, memoranda, motions, warrants, questionnaires, writs, photographs, videotapes, audio cassettes, and floppy discs, dating 1892-2008. 4,311 cubic ft.

Federal Criminal Court Records at the National Archives & Records Admin. (NARA)

NARA Southwest Region (Fort Worth)
501 West Felix Street, Building 1, Fort Worth, TX 76115-3405, Phone: 817-831-5620
http://www.archives.gov/southwest/
ftworth.archives@nara.gov

Record Type	ARC Identifier	Title	Description
	566223	Criminal Case Files, compiled 1896 - 1975	Textual Records from the U.S. District Court for the Fort Worth Division of the Northern District of Texas. (06/11/1896 -)
	566530	Criminal Case Files, compiled 1929 - 1973	Textual Records from the U.S. District Court for the Lubbock Division of the Northern District of Texas. (05/26/1928 -)
	572729	Criminal Case Files, compiled 1906 - 1973	Textual Records from the U.S. District Court for the Del Rio Division of the Western District of Texas. (06/09/1906 -)
	572708	Criminal Case Files, compiled 1919 - 1977	Textual Records from the U.S. District Court for the Pecos Division of the Western District of Texas. (02/05/1913 -)

	573384	Criminal Case Files, compiled 1879 - 1977	Textual Records from the U.S. District Court for the Marshall Division of the Eastern District of Texas. (07/27/1962 -)
	2660716	Records of Jury Verdicts in Criminal Proceedings, compiled 1902 - 1926	Textual Records from the U.S. District Court for the Laredo Division of the Southern District of Texas. (03/11/1902 -)
	573389	Criminal Case Files, compiled 1917 - 1977	Textual Records from the U.S. District Court for the Paris Division of the Eastern District of Texas. (03/01/1889 -)
	2658200	Dockets of Terminated Criminal Cases, compiled 1909 - 1911	Textual Records from the U.S. District Court for the Brownsville Division of the Southern District of Texas. (03/11/1902 -)
	572664	Criminal Case Files, compiled 1867 - 1976	Textual Records from the U.S. District Court for the Austin Division of the Western District of Texas. (02/21/1857 -)
	573062	Criminal Case Files, compiled 1879 - 1977	Textual Records from the U.S. District Court for the San Antonio Division of the Western District of Texas. (02/24/1879 -)
	563137	Criminal Case Files, compiled 1908 - 1973	Textual Records from the U.S. District Court for the Houston Division of the Southern District of Texas. (03/11/1902 -)
	3834470	Index to Criminal Minutes, compiled 1913? - 1927?	Textual Records from the U.S. District Court for the Pecos Division of the Western District of Texas. (02/05/1913 -)
	2660711	Criminal Minutes, compiled 1926 - 1954	Textual Records from the U.S. District Court for the Laredo Division of the Southern District of Texas. (03/11/1902 -)
	2546036	Criminal Minutes, compiled 1926 - 1954	Textual Records from the U.S. District Court for the Houston Division of the Southern District of Texas. (03/11/1902 -)
	2565526	Records of Sentences in Criminal Cases, compiled 1909 - 1927	Textual Records from the U.S. District Court for the Houston Division of the Southern District of Texas. (03/11/1902 -)
	563083	Criminal Case Files, compiled 1879 - 1973	Textual Records from the U.S. District Court for the Dallas Division of the Northern District of Texas. (06/18/1896 -)
	564437	Criminal Case Files, compiled 1879 - 1976	Textual Records from the U.S. District Court for the Abilene Division of the Northern District of Texas. (06/11/1896 -)
	573087	Criminal Case Files, compiled 1879 - 1977	Textual Records from the U.S. District Court for the Waco Division of the Western District of Texas. (03/11/1902 -)

	576380	Criminal Case Files, compiled 1903 - 1971	Textual Records from the U.S. District Court for the Texarkana Division of the Eastern District of Texas. (03/02/1903 -)
	567788	Criminal Case Files, compiled 1905 - 1977	Textual Records from the U.S. District Court for the Brownsville Division of the Southern District of Texas. (03/11/1902 -)
	563138	Criminal Case Files, compiled 1879 - 1977	Textual Records from the U.S. District Court for the San Antonio Division of the Western District of Texas. (02/24/1879 -)
	572814	Criminal Case Files, compiled 1886 - 1977	Textual Records from the U.S. District Court for the El Paso Division of the Western District of Texas. (06/03/1884 -)
	564570	Criminal Case Files Relating to Juvenile Offenders, compiled 1948 - 1973	Textual Records from the U.S. District Court for the Amarillo Division of the Northern District of Texas. (02/14/1908 -)
	567870	Criminal Case Files, compiled 1913 - 1976	Textual Records from the U.S. District Court for the Corpus Christi Division of the Southern District of Texas. (05/29/1912 -)
	3834473	Criminal Term Docket, compiled 1922 - 1927	Textual Records from the U.S. District Court for the Pecos Division of the Western District of Texas. (02/05/1913 -)
	2660730	Bankruptcy, Criminal, and Law Subpoena Dockets, compiled 1907 - 1945	Textual Records from the U.S. District Court for the Victoria Division of the Southern District of Texas. (04/18/1906 -)
	3725288	Criminal Term Dockets, compiled 1872 - 1918	Textual Records from the U.S. District Court for the Austin Division of the Western District of Texas. (02/21/1857 -)
	574272	Criminal Case Files, compiled 1878 - 1977	Textual Records from the U.S. District Court for the Tyler Division of the Eastern District of Texas. (02/24/1879 -)
	2660744	Criminal Minutes, compiled 1935 - 1954	Textual Records from the U.S. District Court for the Victoria Division of the Southern District of Texas. (04/18/1906 -)
	568061	Criminal Case Files, compiled 1899 - 1974	Textual Records from the U.S. District Court for the Laredo Division of the Southern District of Texas. (03/11/1902 -)
	574367	Criminal Case Files, compiled 1901 - 1976	Textual Records from the U.S. District Court for the Sherman Division of the Eastern District of Texas. (02/19/1901 -)

	3778818	Criminal Term Dockets, compiled 1886 - 1917	Textual Records from the U.S. District Court for the El Paso Division of the Western District of Texas. (06/03/1884 -)
	2658257	Criminal Minutes, compiled 1931 - 1954	Textual Records from the U.S. District Court for the Corpus Christi Division of the Southern District of Texas. (05/29/1912 -)
	568095	Criminal Case Files, compiled 1866 - 1969	Textual Records
	568064	Criminal Case Files, compiled 1908 - 1938	Textual Records from the U.S. District Court for the Victoria Division of the Southern District of Texas. (04/18/1906 -)
	573248	Criminal Case Files, compiled 1898 - 1972	Textual Records from the U.S. District Court for the Beaumont Division of the Eastern District of Texas. (02/08/1897 -)
	2658353	Criminal Minutes, compiled 1927 - 1955	Textual Records from the U.S. District Court for the Southern District of Texas. Galveston Term. (03/11/1902 -)
	566719	Criminal Case Files, compiled 1900 - 1970	Textual Records from the U.S. District Court for the San Angelo Division of the Northern District of Texas. (06/11/1896 -)
	2660717	Records of Sentences in Criminal Cases, compiled 1902 - 1926	Textual Records from the U.S. District Court for the Laredo Division of the Southern District of Texas. (03/11/1902 -)
	566745	Criminal Case Files, compiled 1917 - 1973	Textual Records from the U.S. District Court for the Wichita Falls Division of the Northern District of Texas. (02/26/1917 -)
	3778819	Criminal Dockets, compiled 1891 - 1968	Textual Records from the U.S. District Court for the El Paso Division of the Western District of Texas. (06/03/1884 -)
	2658201	Index to Criminal Dockets, compiled ca. 1907 - ca. 1939	Textual Records from the U.S. District Court for the Brownsville Division of the Southern District of Texas. (03/11/1902 -)
	2660745	Criminal Dockets, compiled 1907 - 1955	Textual Records from the U.S. District Court for the Victoria Division of the Southern District of Texas. (04/18/1906 -)
	2660696	Civil, Criminal, Equity, and Law Dockets, compiled 1918 - 1945	Textual Records from the U.S. District Court for the Laredo Division of the Southern District of Texas. (03/11/1902 -)
	3778820	Index to Defendants, compiled 1887 - 1892	Textual Records from the U.S. District Court for the El Paso Division of the Western District of Texas. (06/03/1884 -)

	2658259	Records of Judgments in Criminal Cases, compiled 1915 - 1931	Textual Records from the U.S. District Court for the Corpus Christi Division of the Southern District of Texas. (05/29/1912 -)
	3730471	Criminal Dockets, compiled 1906 - 1957	Textual Records from the U.S. District Court for the Del Rio Division of the Western District of Texas. (06/09/1906 -)
	2565521	Indexes to Criminal Dockets, compiled ca. 1908 - ca. 1954	Textual Records from the U.S. District Court for the Houston Division of the Southern District of Texas. (03/11/1902 -)
	3783838	Criminal Docket Sheets, compiled 1968 - 1983	Textual Records from the U.S. District Court for the Midland Division of the Western District of Texas. (12/18/1967 -)
	2658365	Final Record Books, compiled 1867 - 1911	Textual Records from the U.S. District Court for the Southern District of Texas. Galveston Term. (03/11/1902 -)
	2658258	Criminal Dockets, compiled 1913 - 1954	Textual Records from the U.S. District Court for the Corpus Christi Division of the Southern District of Texas. (05/29/1912 -)
	2660715	Criminal Dockets, compiled 1899 - 1984	Textual Records from the U.S. District Court for the Laredo Division of the Southern District of Texas. (03/11/1902 -)
	564560	Criminal Case Files, compiled 1912 - 1973	Textual Records from the U.S. District Court for the Amarillo Division of the Northern District of Texas. (02/14/1908 -)
	3783839	Criminal Case Files, compiled 1968 - 1991	Textual Records from the U.S. District Court for the Midland Division of the Western District of Texas. (12/18/1967 -)
	2658202	Criminal Dockets, compiled 1868 - 1954	Textual Records from the U.S. District Court for the Brownsville Division of the Southern District of Texas. (03/11/1902 -)
	2658260	Records of Sentences in Criminal Cases, compiled 1915 - 1931	Textual Records from the U.S. District Court for the Corpus Christi Division of the Southern District of Texas. (05/29/1912 -)
	2660718	Criminal Final Record Book, compiled 1916 - 1917	Textual Records from the U.S. District Court for the Laredo Division of the Southern District of Texas. (03/11/1902 -)
	3725292	Criminal Dockets, compiled 1891 - 1962	Textual Records from the U.S. District Court for the Austin Division of the Western District of Texas. (02/21/1857 -)
	2660728	Admiralty, Criminal, Civil, Equity, and Law Dockets, compiled 1918 - 1941	Textual Records from the U.S. District Court for the Victoria Division of the Southern District of Texas. (04/18/1906 -)

![icon]	2660719	Index to Criminal Cases, compiled ca. 1899 - ca. 1912	Textual Records from the U.S. District Court for the Laredo Division of the Southern District of Texas. (03/11/1902 -)
![icon]	2660747	Records of Sentences in Criminal Cases, compiled 1907 - 1926	Textual Records from the U.S. District Court for the Victoria Division of the Southern District of Texas. (04/18/1906 -)
![icon]	2660746	Records of Judgments in Criminal Cases, compiled 1909 - 1933	Textual Records from the U.S. District Court for the Victoria Division of the Southern District of Texas. (04/18/1906 -)
![icon]	2660714	Index to Criminal Dockets, compiled ca. 1907 - ca. 1942	Textual Records from the U.S. District Court for the Laredo Division of the Southern District of Texas. (03/11/1902 -)
![icon]	2658356	Criminal Dockets, compiled 1866 - 1955	Textual Records from the U.S. District Court for the Southern District of Texas. Galveston Term. (03/11/1902 -)
![icon]	2658361	Records of Sentences in Criminal Cases, compiled 1903 - 1926	Textual Records from the U.S. District Court for the Southern District of Texas. Galveston Term. (03/11/1902 -)

Texas Executions

 http://users.bestweb.net/~rg/execution/TEXAS.htm

Texas Department of Criminal Justice – Offender Information Search

 http://168.51.178.33/webapp/TDCJ/index2.htm

Utah

Utah Division of Archives and Records Service

Research Center, 300 South Rio Grande, Salt Lake City, UT 84104, (801) 533-3535
http://archives.utah.gov/
http://archives.utah.gov/research/guides/index.html
email: http://historyresearch.utah.gov/question.htm

Record Type	Location (Series)	Author	Title/Description
	80388	Deptartment of Corrections, Inmate Services	Prison commitment registers, 1875-
		Deptartment of Corrections, Inmate Services	Inmate jackets, 1875-[ongoing]. Files include commitment papers, admittance and assessment records (face sheet),Parole Board results, incident reports, contracts, treatment plans, pre-release agreements, detainers, disciplinary reports, educational and work records, correspondence, CCC reports, and presentence investigations. <612.0> microfilm reels and <96.0> microfiche.
	11886	State Prison	Criminal physical description book, 1904-1914
	16982	State Prison	Prisoner received and released record book, 1889-
	832	State Prison	Publications, 1957-
	804	State Prison	Visitors register, 1946-1952
	134	Attorney General's Office	Criminal actions registers, 1896-1899

	3591	Attorney General's Office	District attorney criminal case reports, 1900, 1913
	80134	Board of Pardons	Criminal history case files, 1960-
	14829	Board of Pardons	Hearings tapes, 1982-
	332	Board of Pardons	Minutes, 1896-
	328	Board of Pardons	Prisoners Pardon Application Files, 1892-1949
	330	Board of Pardons	Schedule of proceedings, 1896-1918
	22678	Attorney for the Territory	Criminal register of actions, 1889-1891
	20697	Circuit Court (First Circuit)	Criminal registers of actions, 1978-
	22967	Circuit Court (Seventh Circuit)	Registers of actions, 1978-1985
	7719	Logan Municipal Court	Criminal index, undated
	5386	Logan Municipal Court	Criminal registers of actions, 1919-1980
	5391	Logan Municipal Court	Judgment docket books, 1919-1939
	5390	Logan Municipal Court	Minute books, 1921-1942
	83989	Provo City Court	Criminal registers of actions, 1919-1922; 1929-1937
	84058	Provo City Court	Judgment docket book, 1933-1955
	9581	Provo City Court	Judgment roll, 1923-1927
	83988	Provo City Court	Minutes, 1924-1927
	4860	Salt Lake City City Court	Criminal case docket books, 1909-1958

	5364	Salt Lake City City Court	Criminal case minute books, 1902-1958
	1620	Salt Lake City City Court	Criminal and civil sampled case files, 1916-1957
	3258	Salt Lake City City Court	Transcripts, 1924-1955
	25011	Territorial Courts: District Court (1st District)	Case files, 1851-1856; 1865
	7571	Territorial Courts: District Court (1st District)	Civil and criminal case blotters, 1890-1891
	1520	Territorial Courts: District Court (1st District)	Criminal case administrative records, 1881-1896
	1526	Territorial Courts: District Court (1st District)	Grand jury dockets, 1883-1886
	1525	Territorial Courts: District Court (1st District)	Grand jury minutes, 1886-1893
	1527	Territorial Courts: District Court (1st District)	Grand jury reports, 1895-1896
	10035	Territorial Courts: District Court (1st District)	Minute books, 1851-1896
	1529	Territorial Courts: District Court (1st District)	North division criminal case files, 1878-1891
	21018	Territorial Courts: District Court (1st District)	Plaintiff index, 1878-1890
	1521	Territorial Courts: District Court (1st District)	South Division Criminal Case Files, 1875-1895
	24553	Territorial Courts: District Court (2nd District)	Criminal case index, 1889-1892
	25022	Territorial Courts: District Court (2nd District)	Criminal information record book, 1898-1926
	24346	Territorial Courts: District Court (2nd District)	Criminal registers of action, 1886-1897
	24071	Territorial Courts: District Court (2nd District)	Final case records, 1888-1889
	24247	Territorial Courts: District Court (2nd District)	General indexes, 1852-1896

	24554	Territorial Courts: District Court (2nd District)	Judgment index, 1890-1896
	24129	Territorial Courts: District Court (2nd District)	Judgement Record, 1888-1895
	5319	Territorial Courts: District Court (2nd District)	Minute books, 1852-1896
	3811	Territorial Courts: District Court (3rd District)	Attorney's roll book, 1895
	3243	Territorial Courts: District Court (3rd District)	Case file index, 1871-1896
	9802	Territorial Courts: District Court (3rd District)	Case files, 1851-1896
	20011	Territorial Courts: District Court (3rd District)	Civil and criminal registers of action, 1870-1871
	3834	Territorial Courts: District Court (3rd District)	Criminal case docket book, 1890
	22664	Territorial Courts: District Court (3rd District)	Criminal registers of action, 1882-1896
	1635	Territorial Courts: District Court (3rd District)	Grand jury minute books, 1878-1896
	4576	Territorial Courts: District Court (3rd District)	Salt Lake County docket book, 1897-1900
	6836	Territorial Courts: District Court (3rd District)	Territorial criminal case files, 1882-1896
	1649	Territorial Courts: District Court (3rd District)	Territorial Minute Books, 1858-1896
	3928	Territorial Courts: District Court (3rd District)	US Commissioner criminal case record book, 1890-1895
	4662	Territorial Courts: District Court (3rd District)	US Commissioner criminal case docket book, 1889-1895
	4878	Territorial Courts: District Court (3rd District)	U.S. Commissioner W.C. Jennings civil and criminal docket book, 1894-1895
	4879	Territorial Courts: District Court (3rd District)	U.S. Commissioner Harmel Pratt's criminal docket book, 1889-1892

	17825	Territorial Courts: District Court (4th District)	Civil and criminal registers of action, 1878-1896
	1629	Territorial Courts: District Court (4th District)	Criminal case files, 1889-1895
	17462	Territorial Courts: District Court (4th District)	Criminal registers of action, 1889-1895
	1630	Territorial Courts: District Court (4th District)	Grand jury reports, 1892-1894
	24808	Territorial Courts: District Court (4th District)	Judgment index, 1878-1892
	5062	Territorial Courts: District Court (4th District)	Minute Books, 1878-1896
	1666	Territorial Courts: District Court (4th District)	Plaintiff's Index, 1880-ca. 1895
	5069	Territorial Courts: District Court (4th District)	U.S. Commissioner A.C. Bishop's Weber county criminal docket book, 1891-1893
	24058	Territorial Courts: District Court (4th District)	U.S. Commissioner M.A. Breeden's Weber county docket book, 1892
	3671	Territorial Courts: District Court (4th District)	U.S. Commissioner Cache County docket books, 1887-1898
	24057	Territorial Courts: District Court (4th District)	U.S. Commissioner Valentine Gideon's Weber county docket books, 1893-1895
	24059	Territorial Courts: District Court (4th District)	U.S. Commissioner B. Ternes' Weber county docket book, 1892-1895
	83336	Territorial Courts: District Court (5th District)	Information and indictment record book, 1920-1942
	83443	Territorial Courts: District Court (5th District)	Judgment docket books, 1895-
	83338	Territorial Courts: District Court (5th District)	Juror and witness fee book, 1896-1958
	82944	Statehood Courts: District Court (1st District: Box Elder County)	Court orders, 1899-1938
	11797	Statehood Courts: District Court (1st District: Box Elder County)	Criminal Case Files, 1850-

	3688	Statehood Courts: District Court (1st District: Box Elder County)	Minute books, 1896-
	6252	Statehood Courts: District Court (1st District: Box Elder County)	Records, 1981-1987
	3676	Statehood Courts: District Court (1st District: Cache Cty)	Civil and criminal case index, 1895-1923
	1570	Statehood Courts: District Court (2nd District: Davis Cty)	Davis and Weber County case files, 1907-1909
	4681	Statehood Courts: District Court (2nd District: Davis Cty)	Minutes, 1896-
	21007	Statehood Courts: District Court (2nd District: Weber Cty)	Appeals to the District Court, 1903-1907
	17463	Statehood Courts: District Court (2nd District: Weber Cty)	Criminal case indexes, 1879-1947
	1569	Statehood Courts: District Court (2nd District: Weber Cty)	Exhibits, 1903-
	1586	Statehood Courts: District Court (2nd District: Weber Cty)	Findings of fact and conclusions of law case books, 1896-1903
	17809	Statehood Courts: District Court (2nd District: Weber Cty)	Grand jury reports, 1914, 1917
	1588	Statehood Courts: District Court (2nd District: Weber Cty)	Information and indictment record books, 1898-1963
	1582	Statehood Courts: District Court (2nd District: Weber Cty)	Judgment dockets index, undated
	1407	Statehood Courts: District Court (2nd District: Weber Cty)	Minutes, 1896-1961
	21023	Statehood Courts: District Court (2nd District: Weber Cty)	Probate Court index, 1851-1899
	21032	Statehood Courts: District Court (2nd District: Weber Cty)	Transcript of judgment Book A, undated
	1663	Statehood Courts: District Court (3rd District: Salt LakeCty)	Abstracts of judgment books, 1889-1963
	17603	Statehood Courts: District Court (3rd District: Salt LakeCty)	Briefs and opinions records, undated
	1626	Statehood Courts: District Court (3rd District: Salt LakeCty)	Civil and criminal blotters, 1876-1917

	14158	Statehood Courts: District Court (3rd District: Salt Lake Cty)	Court case indexes, 1977-1988
	1471	Statehood Courts: District Court (3rd District: Salt Lake Cty)	Criminal Case Files, 1896-1969
	13126	Statehood Courts: District Court (3rd District: Salt Lake Cty)	Criminal case files and registers of action index, 1916-1975
	3253	Statehood Courts: District Court (3rd District: Salt Lake Cty)	Criminal registers of actions, 1896-1974
	5607	Statehood Courts: District Court (3rd District: Salt Lake Cty)	Exhibits, 1899-1959, 1972
	23983	Statehood Courts: District Court (3rd District: Salt Lake Cty)	Grand jury records, 1903, 1907
	3257	Statehood Courts: District Court (3rd District: Salt Lake Cty)	Information and indictment record books
	1650	Statehood Courts: District Court (3rd District: Salt Lake Cty)	Minute Books, 1896-1967
	6381	Statehood Courts: District Court (3rd District: Salt Lake Cty)	Miscellaneous case files, 1940-1992
	14157	Statehood Courts: District Court (3rd District: Salt Lake Cty)	Miscellaneous civil and criminal file registers of action, 1925-1977
	7712	Statehood Courts: District Court (4th District: Juab County)	Criminal case files, 1892-
	18185	Statehood Courts: District Court (4th District: Juab County)	Criminal registers of actions, 1895-1985
	1397	Statehood Courts: District Court (4th District: Juab County)	Minute books, 1896-1985
	19504	Statehood Courts: District Court (4th District: Utah County)	Minutes, 1896-1969
	3589	Statehood Courts: District Court (4th District: Utah County)	Trial transcript, 1930-
	24549	Statehood Courts: District Court (5th District: Beaver County)	Case indexes, 1896-
	24338	Statehood Courts: District Court (5th District: Beaver County)	Criminal case files, 1896-
	24378	Statehood Courts: District Court (5th District: Beaver County)	Criminal registers of actions, 1896-

	24546	Statehood Courts: District Court (5th District: Beaver County)	General indexes to action, 1896-
	1394	Statehood Courts: District Court (5th District: Beaver County)	Minute books, 1906-1949
	83445	Statehood Courts: District Court (5th District: Millard County)	Criminal registers of action, 1896-1982
	18186	Statehood Courts: District Court (5th District: Millard County)	Judgment record books, 1893-1963
	1406	Statehood Courts: District Court (5th District: Millard County)	Minute Books, 1896-1948
	83438	Statehood Courts: District Court (5th Dist: Washington Cty)	Probate court minute books, 1854-1963
	23738	Statehood Courts: District Court (5th Dist: Washington Cty)	Minutes, 1896
	23737	Statehood Courts: District Court (5th Dist: Washington Cty)	Register of actions, 1895-1899
	18264	Statehood Courts: District Court (6th Dist: Garfield County)	Orders and decrees, 1896
	18270	Statehood Courts: District Court (6th Dist: Garfield County)	Registers of action, 1896-1966
	18230	Statehood Courts: District Court (6th District: Piute County)	Civil and criminal registers of action, 1896-1953
	20909	Statehood Courts: District Court (6th District: Piute County)	Indictment Records, 1899-1925
	6107	Statehood Courts: District Court (6th District: Piute County)	Judgment records index, undated
	21849	Statehood Courts: District Court (6th Dist: Sanpete County)	Judgment record book, 1896-1945
	21850	Statehood Courts: District Court (6th Dist: Sanpete County)	Minute books, 1896-1941
	17547	Statehood Courts: District Court (6th District: Sevier County)	Blotter, 1902-1906
	6945	Statehood Courts: District Court (6th District: Sevier County)	Criminal case files, 1943-
	7062	Statehood Courts: District Court (6th District: Sevier County)	Daily court case files, 1896-

18224	Statehood Courts: District Court (6th District: Sevier County)	Registers of actions, 1896-1948
18226	Statehood Courts: District Court (6th District: Wayne County)	Court case index, 1896-1966
7	Statehood Courts: District Court (6th District: Wayne County)	Criminal case files, 1896-
13446	Statehood Courts: District Court (6th District: Wayne County)	Judgment record books, 1896-1983
18225	Statehood Courts: District Court (6th District: Wayne County)	Registers of action, 1896-1957
4031	Statehood Courts: District Court (7th District: Wayne County)	Criminal case files, 1896-
21842	Statehood Courts: District Court (7th District: Wayne County)	Criminal registers of actions, 1896-1987
14179	Statehood Courts: District Court (7th District: Wayne County)	Judgment dockets, 1896-
14180	Statehood Courts: District Court (7th District: Wayne County)	Minute books, 1896-1978
21843	Statehood Courts: District Court (7th District: Emery County)	Criminal registers of actions, 1896-1976
23834	Salt Lake City Justice Court	Jeter Clinton's criminal docket books, 1867-1874
4629	Salt Lake City Justice Court	Criminal court day books, 1890-1897
4671	Salt Lake City Justice Court	Criminal docket books, 1890-1902
4630	Salt Lake City Justice Court	Criminal fines and forfeiture account books, 1891-1897
4625	Salt Lake City Justice Court	Forfeitures index books, 1890-1897
4885	Salt Lake City Justice Court	Minute books, 1880-1889
12022	Salt Lake City Justice Court	Miscellaneous offense docket books, 1890-1902
4618	Salt Lake City Justice Court	Miscellaneous offenses indexes, 1891-1899

	14893	Beaver County Probate Court	Record books, 1856-1897
	9642	Box Elder County Probate Court	Civil and criminal case files, 1856, 1873
	82970	Box Elder County Probate Court	Record books, 1856-1877
	17493	Cedar County Probate Court	Minutes, 1859-1862
	25012	Davis County Probate Court	Minute books, 1854-1872
	17477	Iron County Probate Court	Minutes, 1853-1868
	373	Salt Lake County Probate Court	Civil and Criminal Case Files, 1852-1887
	3944	Salt Lake County Probate Court	Civil and criminal case docket books, 1852-1887
	3939	Salt Lake County Probate Court	Civil and criminal case minute book, 1860-1884
	17693	Sanpete County Probate Court	Minutes, 1852-1896
	14650	Tooele County Probate Court	Minute books, 1859-1888
	1422	Tooele County Probate Court	Records Books, 1859-1892
	3168	Washington County Probate Court	Civil and criminal records books, 1859-1886
	1593	Weber County Probate Court	Civil and criminal case files, 1852-1877
	83901	Weber County Probate Court	Civil and criminal case registers of actions, 1868-1887
	4638	Salt Lake City City Attorney	Attorney David M. Haigh's docket book, 1904-1905
	80388	Department of Corrections	Photographs: Prison Commitment Registers, 1875-
	83497	Ogden Police Department	Mug shots, 1902-1960

	10396	State Prison	Inmate identification photos, 1890-1925; 1950-1968
	10398	State Prison	Inmate photographs, 1940-1954
	10413	State Prison	Inmate and prison glass plate negatives, 1900, 1930
	13938	State Prison	Executions records, 1854-
	24073	Beaver County Justice of the Peace	Justice court docket, 1881-1894; 1897-1903
	4589	Bingham Canyon City	Justice of the Peace criminal dockets, 1912-1915, 1927-1929, 1938-1951, 1955-1956
	17941	Cache County Justice of the Peace: Logan Precinct	Combined civil and criminal docket book, 1914-1915
	5388	Cache County Justice of the Peace: Logan Precinct	Complaints and summons, 1917-1919
	5379	Cache County Justice of the Peace: Logan Precinct	Criminal case docket books, 1894-1919
	3685	Cache County Justice of the Peace: Logan Precinct	Docket books, 1890-1910
	22331	Clearfield Justice of the Peace	Justice docket, 1924-
	22332	Davis Justice of the Peace	Justice dockets, 1891-1913; 1916-1930
	22333	Farmington Justice of the Peace	Justice dockets, 1908-1913; 1925-1929
	21885	Manti Justice of the Peace	Criminal docket, 1873-1892
	83339	Millard County Justice of the Peace: Abraham Precinct	Docket book, 1902-1928
	83340	Millard County Justice of the Peace: Delta Precinct	Docket books, 1922-1969
	83341	Millard County Justice of the Peace: Fillmore Precinct	Docket books, 1901-1938

	83342	Millard County Justice of the Peace: Flowell Precinct	Docket books, 1927-1941
	83344	Millard County Justice of the Peace: Kanosh Precinct	Docket books, 1942-1970
	83345	Millard County Justice of the Peace: Meadow Precinct	Docket book, 1940-1952
	83347	Millard County Justice of the Peace: Scipio Precinct	Docket books, 1912-1942; 1961-1964
	5369	Park City Justice of the Peace	Criminal case docket books, 1886-1953
	19026	Piute County Justice of the Peace: Junction Precinct	Justice Docket, 1907-1932; 1949-1963
	19027	Piute County Justice of the Peace: Marysvale Precinct	Justice Docket, 1920-1928; 1933-1948
	23523	Tooele County Justice of the Peace	Ophir and Tooele City precinct docket book, 1876-1890
	9578	Utah County Justice of the Peace	Civil and criminal docket book, 1873-1892
	5036	Utah County Justice of the Peace	County attorney's criminal docket book, 1905-
	5035	Utah County Justice of the Peace	Criminal case dockets, 1885-1896
	5077	Weber County Justice of the Peace	Docket books, 1880-1901
	5070	Weber County Justice of the Peace	Judge Terme's criminal docket books, 1896-1898
	5336	Weber County Justice of the Peace	Judge Wandleigh's docket book, 1901-1903
	9628	Weber County Justice of the Peace	Uintah Justice Precinct docket book, 1870-1893
	4607	Bingham Canyon County	Police arrest register, 1908-1917, 1932-1938
	5384	Cache County County Sheriff	Commitment orders record book, 1888-1909
	3699	Cache County County Sheriff	Jail prisoner's register, 1888-1912

	83453	Millard County County Sheriff	Summons and arrest book, 1909-1926
	4101	Ogden Police Department	Glass plate negatives of documents, 1911-1913
	5368	Park City Public Safety	Arrests registers, 1892-1904, 1930-1942, 1962
	85234	Provo Police Department	Case files, 1968-1975
	83985	Provo Police Department	Commitment orders register, 1903-1908
	83986	Provo Police Department	Complaint log book, 1925-1926
	85118	St. George Police Department	Incident reports, 1892-
	4628	Salt Lake City City Attorney	Police court dockets, 1896-1898
	4612	Salt Lake City Police Department	Arrest blotters, 1892-1893
	4611	Salt Lake City Police Department	Arrest registers, 1891-1899
	4617	Salt Lake City Police Department	Book of drunks index, 1891-1902
	4639	Salt Lake City Police Department	Criminal record books, 1871-1878
	4658	Salt Lake City Police Department	Criminal register, 1892-1897
	4925	Salt Lake City Police Department	Publications, 1928-
	238	Secretary of State	Board of Pardons minutes, 1969-1974
	397	Secretary of State	Pardons granted record books, 1880-1921
	1470	Utah Supreme Court	Case files, 1870-
	1455	Utah Supreme Court	Civil and criminal case index, 1935-1956

	1513	Utah Supreme Court	Civil and criminal docket books, 1973-1977
	1460	Utah Supreme Court	Docket books, 1924-1974
	1487	Utah Supreme Court	Opinions, 1886-
	1461	Utah Supreme Court	Record of opinions index, undated
	1473	Utah Supreme Court	Recorded arguments, 1952-1958; 1962-1977
	1484	Utah Supreme Court	Rehearing petitions, 1907-1920

Federal Criminal Court Records at the National Archives & Records Admin. (NARA)

NARA Rocky Mountain Region (Denver)

Denver Federal Center, Bldgs 46, 48, Denver, CO 80225, (303) 407-5740

http://www.archives.gov/rocky-mountain/

denver.archives@nara.gov

Record Type	ARC Identifier	Title	Description
	1116870	Combined Bankruptcy, Civil, and Criminal Case Files, compiled 1896 - 1931, documenting the period 1880 - 1931	Textual Records from the U.S. District Court for the District of Utah. (1896 -)
	1122072	Register of Actions in Criminal Cases, compiled 1893 - 1895	Textual Records from the U.S. Territorial Court for the District of Utah. Ogden Term. (1859 - 1896)
	1123474	Criminal Order Books, compiled 1938 - 1948	Textual Records from the U.S. District Court for the District of Utah. (1896 -)
	1121486	Criminal Case Files, compiled 1931 - 1969	Textual Records from the U.S. District Court for the District of Utah. (1896 -)
	2679310	Criminal Case Files, compiled 1966 - 1969	Textual Records from the U.S. District Court for the District of Utah. (1896 -)
	1123469	Judgment Docket, compiled 1896 - 1914	Textual Records from the U.S. District Court for the District of Utah. (1896 -)

Utah Executions

 http://users.bestweb.net/~rg/execution/UTAH.htm

Utah Department of Corrections – Offender Search

 http://corrections.utah.gov/contentservices/offendersearch.asp

BILLY GRAHAM

RECEIVED

SEP 12 1966

U. S. BOARD OF PAROLE

September 9, 1966

Dear Mr. Shore:

I have recently learned of Mickey Cohen's pitiful physical condition and am moved to ask that you take this into full consideration when the question of his parole comes up late this year.

I have known Mickey ever since 1949 when I was preaching in Los Angeles. I am fully aware of his past record; but as he has been crippled for life by the beating he received at the hands of another inmate in the Atlanta penitentiary, I believe the ends of both justice and mercy would be served by giving him a medical parole.

This request is made on humanitarian grounds and with, at the same time, a full appreciation of the requirements of justice.

Trusting that you can give favorable consideration to this request, I am

Sincerely yours,

Billy Graham

Mr. Joseph N. Shore
Parole Executive
United States Department of Justice
United States Board of Parole
Washington, D.C. 20537

A letter from Reverend Billy Graham in to the United States Board of Parole, with an endorsement for Mickey Cohen. Found in the Alcatraz inmate case file for Mickey Cohen at the National Archives, San Bruno, CA.

Vermont

Vermont State Archives and Records Administration

1078 Route 2, Middlesex, Montpelier, Vt. 05633-7701, 802-828-3700

http://vermont-archives.org/

http://vermont-archives.org/research/database/series.asp (Catalog)

archives@sec.state.vt.us

Record Type	Location	Title	Description
	PRA-092	Jail register for county of Grand Isle, 1877-1965	Registers include the names of all prisoners, residence, time of commitment, for what cause, by what authority, descriptions of prisoners, including age, occupation, place of birth, height, eye color, hair color, complexion, additional identifying features, and the date of discharge, and by which authority, or the time and manner of escapes.
	PRA-093	Jail register for county of Rutland, Town of Rutland, 1877-1906.	Registers include the names of all prisoners, residence, time of commitment, for what cause, by what authority, descriptions of prisoners, including age, occupation, place of birth, height, eye color, hair color, complexion, additional identifying features, and the date of discharge, and by which authority, or the time and manner of escapes.
	PRA-084	Office of the Attorney General: Cases and investigations, 1907-1913.	Included are detective reports which document investigations of murders, illegal selling and drinking of liquor, gambling, prison escapes, larceny, arson and anarchists.
	PRA-070	Rutland Municipal Court. Court dockets, 1873-1907.	Series consists of civil and criminal court dockets from Rutland Municipal Court.

	A-091	Vermont. County Court (Caledonia County): County and Superior Court records, 1797-1969, bulk 1797-1913.	Series consists of registers, counterfeit money, writs, dockets, recognizances, discharge commissions, accounts, and maps. The records include: Criminal Recognizances, 1864-1871, Recognizances Criminal Cases, 1876-1900,
	PRA-084	Vermont. Office of the Attorney General.Cases and investigations, 1907-1913.	Series consists of correspondence, case files, and reports related to various criminal cases and investigations led by the Office of the Attorney General. Included are detective reports which document investigations of murders, illegal selling and drinking of liquor, gambling, prison escapes, larceny, arson and anarchists.
	A-153	VT Governor (1894-1896: Woodbury) Governor Urban A. Woodbury records, 1894-1896.	Series consists of correspondence with various departments, boards, commissions and constituents. Included are some petitions for pardon.
	A-181	VT Governor (1969-1973 : Davis) Governor Deane C. Davis records, 1969-1972.	The records include correspondence, memos, reports, proclamations, appointments, oaths, executive orders, and pardons.
	A-184	VT Governor (1977-1985: Snelling) Governor Richard A. Snelling records, 1977-1985.	The records include executive orders, appointments, proclamations, pardons, publications, photographs, and reports.
	A-185	VT Governor (1985-1991 : Kunin) Governor Madeleine M. Kunin records, 1985-1991.	The records include executive orders, appointments, proclamations, pardons, schedules and supporting material, speeches, reviews of legislative bills, commissioners' goals and objectives, and commissioners' weekly reports.
	A-187	VT Governor (1991-2003 : Dean) Governor Howard Dean records, 1991-2003.	The records include executive orders, appointments, proclamations, pardons, correspondence, memos and reports.
	A-189	VT Governor. Vermont governor's executive records, 1791-1977.	Series consists of governors' pardons, proclamations, appointments, and executive orders.
	A-239	VT Office of Secretary of State. Reports and returns by town and county officers, 1800-1882.	The records include petitions for pardon 1833, and statements regarding persons prosecuted sent to the secretary of state by town jailkeepers, town treasurers, and states' attorney from circa 1860 to 1880.

Federal Criminal Court Records at the National Archives & Records Admin. (NARA)

NARA Northeast Region (Boston)

Frederick C. Murphy Federal Center, 380 Trapelo Road, Waltham, MA, 02452-6399

(781) 663-0130

http://www.archives.gov/northeast/

waltham.archives@nara.gov

Record Type	ARC Identifier	Title	Description
	595372	Case Files, compiled 11/1791 - 10/1906	Textual Records from the U.S. District Court for the District of Vermont. (1791 -)
	595562	Case Files, compiled 1792 - 1869	Textual Records from the U.S. Circuit Court for the District of Vermont. (1791 - 01/01/1912)
	592864	Criminal Case Files, compiled 1906 - 1979	Textual Records from the U.S. District Court for the District of Vermont. (1791 -)

Vermont Executions

 http://users.bestweb.net/~rg/execution/VERMONT.htm

Vermont Department of Corrections – Inmate Locator

 http://doc.vermont.gov/offender-locator/

From *Meyer Harris Cohen* May 1st – 1963
Michael. Mickey. Cohen
To *atty General, Robert Kennedy*
(Name)   (Address)

1

Dear Sir.

It is apparent to all that you have propounded the practice of fair play. And in my once again seeing you here at the Atlanta Penitentiary Some days ago. And during our conversation. Your complete dedication and feeling for your fellow man. And equal justice for all. Couldn't help but to be noticed by not only myself. but also by many others. And I can't help but feel that in just consideration you will acknowledge this letter as having proper cause and merit.

Since you have been in office it has been the good fortune of 40 or so individuals to receive pardons or commutations of Sentences. I think this is highly commendable and should give heart to many incarcerated men such as myself that true humanity exsists in the thinking processes of our New Frontiers administration.

With all propriety I ask you to correct what I feel along with many, many, others in official capacity. And also in our Countrys Federal Prison service to be an extremely severe and unjust Sentence for violating the United States income tax laws. This as the essential and basic purpose of my letter.

Mr Kennedy, While the comparison may be considered mute or of a different nature. I would

2

like to bring to your attention Sir. the fact that three men all considered 1. 2. 3. in notoriety in American jurisprudence together did not receive the amount of time I was given for practically the same offence. They were Albert Anastasia (1 year) Frank Costello (5 years) and finally Al Capone (8 years) – Total of fourteen years. Same type of offense. And I am sitting here doing fifteen years. "And mind you sir" I started serving this Sentence at Alcatraz. Which did not happen to any other person of noteriety at the start of there Sentence.

Letter from Mickey Cohen to Robert Kennedy, Jr., U.S. Attorney General. Found in Alcatraz inmate file at the National Archives, San Bruno, CA

Virginia

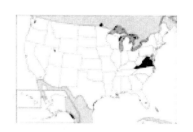

Virginia State Archives and Records Administration

The Library of Virginia, 800 East Broad St., Richmond, VA 23219, (804) 692-3500

http://www.lva.virginia.gov/

http://ajax.lva.lib.va.us/F/?func=file&file_name=find-b-clas05&local_base=CLAS05 Catalog

http://lva1.hosted.exlibrisgroup.com/F Catalog

email : http://www.lva.lib.va.us/whatwedo/archemailform.asp

Record Type	Location	Author	Title/Descirption
	30769	Virginia Penitentiary	Inmate index cards for felons, 1914, 1919, 1921-1949. Each index card includes the prisoner name, prisoner number, alias, race, fingerprint classification, crime, term, date and place received, date term expires, jail time, criminal history, measurements (hat, shoe, collar, coat, and pants), previous address, names and addresses of immediate family.
	40350	Virginia Penitentiary	Index cards for jail men, 1917-1965 (bulk 1919-1949). These records are housed in 17 index card boxes and are arranged alphabetically by prisoner name. Each index card includes the following information: name of prisoner, race, camp number, report number, place of conviction, date put in jail, sentence, fine, good time allowed, date received, date discharged, punishments, escape/recapture and remarks.
	41991	Virginia Penitentiary	Inmate photographs (negatives and interpositives), 1914, 1934-1961.
	38213	Virginia Parole Board	Dockets, 1942-1979

Note: Many county records found when searching for subject 'prisoners virginia' at: http://lva1.hosted.exlibrisgroup.com/F Catalog

Library of Virginia

800 East Broad Street, Richmond, Virginia 23219-8000, (804) 692.3500

County and City Records at the Library of Virginia:

http://www.lva.virginia.gov/whatwehave/local/county_formation/index.htm

Federal Criminal Court Records at the National Archives & Records Admin. (NARA)

NARA Mid Atlantic Region (Philadelphia)

900 Market Street, Philadelphia, PA, 19107-4292, (215) 606-0100

http://www.archives.gov/midatlantic/

philadelphia.archives@nara.gov

Record Type	ARC Identifier	Title	Description
	1112229	Criminal Order Books, compiled 09/22/1938 - 12/30/1954	Textual Records from the U.S. District Court for the Norfolk Division of the Eastern District of Virginia. (02/03/1871 -)
	1168976	Criminal Order Books, compiled 10/03/1938 - 12/1988	Textual Records from the U.S. District Court for the Richmond Division of the Eastern District of Virginia. (02/03/1871 -)
	593085	Criminal Case Files, compiled 1906 - 1944	Textual Records from the U.S. District Court for the Parkersburg Division of the Northern District of West Virginia. (01/22/1901 - 01/14/1983)
	570404	Criminal Case Files, compiled 1847 - 1960	Textual Records from the U.S. District Court for the Norfolk Division of the Eastern District of Virginia. (02/03/1871 -)
	593068	Criminal Case Files, compiled 1908 - 1976	Textual Records from the U.S. District Court for the Charlottesville Division of the Western District of Virginia. (06/30/1902 -)
	572258	Criminal Case Files, compiled 1941 - 1978	Textual Records from the U.S. District Court for the Newport News Division of the Eastern District of Virginia. (06/13/1938 -)
	593070	Criminal Case Files, compiled 1883 - 1967	Textual Records from the U.S. District Court for the Harrisonburg Division of the Western District of Virginia. (02/03/1871 -)
	593069	Criminal Case Files, compiled 1871 - 1971	Textual Records from the U.S. District Court for the Danville Division of the Western District of Virginia. (02/03/1871 -)

	572296	Criminal Case Files, compiled 1867 - 1912	Textual Records from the U.S. Circuit Court for the Richmond Division of the Eastern District of Virginia. (02/03/1871 - 01/01/1912)
	570402	Criminal Case Files, compiled 1878 - 1969	Textual Records from the U.S. District Court for the Richmond Division of the Eastern District of Virginia. (02/03/1871 -)
	572301	Criminal Case Files, compiled 1871 - 1911	Textual Records from the U.S. Circuit Court for the Norfolk Division of the Eastern District of Virginia. (02/03/1871 - 01/01/1912)
	2279474	Criminal Order Books, compiled 12/24/1960 - 12/30/1986	Textual Records from the U.S. District Court for the Abingdon Division of the Western District of Virginia. (02/03/1871 -)
	2279469	Index of Criminal Cases, compiled 1871 - 1892	Textual Records from the U.S. District Court for the Abingdon Division of the Western District of Virginia. (02/03/1871 -)
	593071	Criminal Case Files, compiled 1871 - 1983	Textual Records from the U.S. District Court for the Lynchburg Division of the Western District of Virginia. (02/03/1871 -)
	593072	Criminal Case Files, compiled 1925 - 1984	Textual Records from the U.S. District Court for the Roanoke Division of the Western District of Virginia. (06/30/1902 -)
	571616	Criminal Case Files, compiled 1872 - 1984	Textual Records from the U.S. District Court for the Alexandria Division of the Eastern District of Virginia. (02/03/1871 -)
	1112228	Criminal Dockets, compiled 1890 - 1956	Textual Records from the U.S. District Court for the Norfolk Division of the Eastern District of Virginia. (02/03/1871 -)
	719857	Criminal Dockets, compiled 1871 - 1953	Textual Records from the U.S. District Court for the Danville Division of the Western District of Virginia. (02/03/1871 -)
	593067	Criminal Case Files, compiled 1871 - 1984	Textual Records from the U.S. District Court for the Abingdon Division of the Western District of Virginia. (02/03/1871 -)
	593073	Criminal Case Files, compiled 1904 - 1984	Textual Records from the U.S. District Court for the Big Stone Gap Division of the Western District of Virginia. (04/22/1904 -)
	1168975	Criminal Dockets, compiled 1909 - 1988	Textual Records from the U.S. District Court for the Richmond Division of the Eastern District of Virginia. (02/03/1871 -)
	2771972	Criminal Docket, compiled 1871 - 1894	Textual Records from the U.S. Circuit Court for the Lynchburg Division of the Western District of Virginia. (02/03/1871 - 01/01/1912)

	1691938	Criminal Docket, compiled 1941 - 1954	Textual Records from the U.S. District Court for the Newport News Division of the Eastern District of Virginia. (06/13/1938 -)
	1112702	Criminal Docket, compiled 1890 - 1906	Textual Records from the U.S. Circuit Court for the Norfolk Division of the Eastern District of Virginia. (02/03/1871 - 01/01/1912)
	1112694	Criminal Return Dockets, compiled 1900 - 1956	Textual Records from the U.S. District Court for the Norfolk Division of the Eastern District of Virginia. Office of U.S. Commissioners. (1896 - 1968)
	1403789	Criminal Dockets, compiled 1871 - 1911	Textual Records from the U.S. Circuit Court for the Richmond Division of the Eastern District of Virginia. (02/03/1871 - 01/01/1912)
	2771583	Criminal Dockets, compiled 1912 - 1978	Textual Records from the U.S. District Court for the Alexandria Division of the Eastern District of Virginia. (02/03/1871 -)
	2771967	Criminal Dockets, compiled 1908 - 1941	Textual Records from the U.S. District Court for the Lynchburg Division of the Western District of Virginia. (02/03/1871 -)
	2279471	Criminal Dockets, compiled 1908 - 1978	Textual Records from the U.S. District Court for the Abingdon Division of the Western District of Virginia. (02/03/1871 -)
	2279472	Criminal Indictments, com-piled 1873 - 1934	Textual Records from the U.S. District Court for the Abingdon Division of the Western District of Virginia. (02/03/1871 -)
	2774959	Criminal Docket, compiled 1909 - 1933	Textual Records from the U.S. District Court for the Charlottesville Division of the Western District of Virginia. (06/30/1902 -)
	1168998	Criminal Return Docket, compiled 1871 - 1873	Textual Records from the U.S. Circuit Court for the Richmond Division of the Eastern District of Virginia. Office of U.S. Commissioners. (02/03/1871 - 1896)
	2774963	Criminal Dockets, compiled 1872 - 1889	Textual Records from the U.S. Circuit Court for the Danville Division of the Western District of Virginia. (02/03/1871 - 01/01/1912)
	2774958	Criminal Dockets, compiled 1909 - 1962	Textual Records from the U.S. District Court for the Roanoke Division of the Western District of Virginia. (06/30/1902 -)
	2774961	Criminal Dockets, compiled 1907 - 1948	Textual Records from the U.S. District Court for the Big Stone Gap Division of the Western District of Virginia. (04/22/1904 -)

| | 2771964 | Criminal Dockets, compiled 1871 - 1959 | Textual Records from the U.S. District Court for the Harrisonburg Division of the Western District of Virginia. (02/03/1871 -) |

Virginia Executions

 http://users.bestweb.net/~rg/execution/VIRGINIA.htm

Virginia Department of Corrections – Inmate Locator

 http://www.vadoc.virginia.gov/offenders/locator/index.cfm

POLICE DEPARTMENT
CITY OF NEW YORK

NUMBER OF PICTURES IN GALLERY
42491

RECORD

Spier

ALIAS

Arrested 7-28-16, N.Y.C. Forgery. On 8-14-16,
sentence suspended. Judge May. Det Reif and Hemendinger
7th ch

NYPD "Yellow Sheet" (Police report) found in folder of the
Grand Jury case file for the author's ancestor. Courtesy of the
New York City Municipal Archives, Manhattan.

Washington

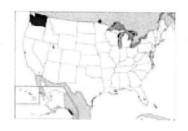

Washington State Archives and Records Administration

1129 Washington Street SE Olympia, WA, 98504-0238, (360) 586-1492
http://www.secstate.wa.gov/archives/
archives@secstate.wa.gov

Record Type	Location	Title	Title/Description
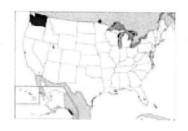	AR129-9-46	Corrections Department, Pine Lodge Corrections Center, Inmate Identification Cards, 1978-1989	Index cards prepared by the corrections center to identify each inmate. Includes inmate number, a photo, sentencing and crime data, and other information. Arranged alphabetically.
	AR129-8-1	Corrections Department, McNeil Island Penitentiary, 1977-1990	Includes files on inmate programs, inmate marriages, extended family visits, and and an incomplete collection of Federal inmate index cards (1912-83), which contain a summary of the particulars on each inmate.
	AR129-5-4	Corrections Department, Penitentiary, Commitment Registers, 1877-1961	A record of each prisoner's admission and stay, including personal data. Gives name, alias, residence, physical condition, social background, crime, date of admission, sentence, date of discharge, remarks on prison behavior, and other personal data. Arranged chronologically.
	AR129-5-23	Corrections Department, Penitentiary, Convict Index, 1878-1956	An index to convicts incarcerated at the State Penitentiary in Walla Walla. Lists Convict Number and other information on each prisoner. Arranged alphabetically
	AR129-5-9	Corrections Department, Penitentiary, Inmate Cards, 1920-1980	Cards prepared on each inmate of the Penitentiary. Includes a photo of the inmate and details of his work record, sentence, release and infractions. Arranged by inmate number. Incomplete.

	AR129-5-5	Corrections Department, Penitentiary, Convict Record, 1877-1932	Record of inmates admitted to the State Penitentiary. Shows name, alias, residence, place convicted, crime, sentence, physical condition, and date of discharge, parole or escape. Arranged chronologically. The 1877-87 volume was for the first Territorial Penitentiary at Seatco (now Bucoda). Individual names searchable on Archives' website: http://www.digitalarchives.wa.gov/Default.aspx
	AR129-5-6	Corrections Department, Penitentiary, Inmate Execution Files, 1904-1999	Files of those inmates executed at the State Penitentiary at Walla Walla. Includes official papers, correspondence, photos, descriptions, summaries of crimes, death certificates, and other documents. Arranged by inmate number. Includes a list of all inmates executed.
	AR129-5-7	Corrections Department, Penitentiary, Inmate Files, 1886-1920	Files on each inmate admitted into the Penitentiary during this period. Typically, the files include a photo of the inmate, a fact sheet on his/her crime and sentence, physical description, correspondence, parole or pardon papers, and other filings pertaining to the inmate's stay at the Penitentiary. Arranged by inmate number. Indexes available. Individual names searchable on Archives' website: http://www.digitalarchives.wa.gov/Default.aspx
	AR129-5-37	Corrections Department, Penitentiary, Parole Index, 1907-1922	An index to prisoners paroled. Shows name, number, and date of parole. Arranged alphabetically.
	AR129-5-35	Corrections Department, Penitentiary, Parole Record, 1898-1921	A record of prisoners paroled from the State Penitentiary. Shows name of prisoner, number, date of parole, and date parole revoked. Arranged chronologically.
	AR129-5-36	Corrections Department, Penitentiary, Paroles and Discharges, 1901-1935	A record of prisoners paroled and discharged from the Penitentiary. Shows name, number, sentence served, date of discharge, and other information. Arranged chronologically.

	AR129-5-38	Corrections Department, Penitentiary, Prisonor Register and Statistics, 1910-1944	A record of admissions, release, and parole at the State Penitentiary in Walla Walla. Shows name of prisoner, number, date received, date released, nature of crime, and other data. Arranged chronologically.
	AR129-5-8	Inmate Mug Shots, 1893-1962	This collection consists of mug shots of Washington State Penitentiary inmates as they were admitted. In some cases includes information about the crime committed, a summary of the inmate's stay and a statement by the inmate concerning the crime. Arranged by inmate number. Includes an index volume.
	AR27-1-15	Supreme Court, Index to Cases, 1854-1969	Index to the journals of the Supreme Court and General Index to cases. Indexed by both plaintiff and defendant, showing name, case number and date.

Record Type	Author / Title
	Adams County Government - Superior Court Journal 1890-1964
	Adams County Government - Justice of the Peace Court Dockets 1889-1970
	Adams County Government - Criminal Case Files 1889-1980
	Adams County Government - Justice of the Peace Court Dockets 1960-1964
	Asotin County Government - Territorial Criminal Case Files 1885-1889
	Attorney General, State - Attorney General, Departmental Correspondence 1891-1995
	Attorney General, State - Attorney General, Case Files, Criminal Justice and Corrections 1985-2003
	Auburn Municipal Government - Criminal Dockets 1914-1949
	Bellingham Municipal Government - Justice Court Dockets 1908-1952

	Benton County Government - Criminal Case Files 1906-1954
	Benton County Government - Criminal Appearance Docket 1906-1945
	Bothell Municipal Government - Criminal Justice Dockets 1948-1962
	Bremerton Municipal Government - Police Court Dockets 1902-1927
	Camas Municipal Government - Camas Precinct Justice Court Criminal Case Files 1930-1934
	Camas Municipal Government - Camas Police Court Criminal Complaint Register 1942-1946
	Cashmere Municipal Government - Justice Court Dockets 1891-1960
	Cathlamet Municipal Government - Police Court Dockets 1907-1981
	Centralia Municipal Government - Police Court Criminal Complaints 1925-1925
	Chelan County Government - Criminal Case Files 1902-1977
	Chelan County Government - Criminal Journals 1902-1978
	Chelan County Government - Criminal Appearance Dockets 1902-1963
	Chelan County Government - Court Room Journals 1900-1966
	Chelan County Government - District Court Criminal Dockets 1904-1950
	Chelan County Government - General Index to Case Files 1900-1973
	Chelan County Government - Court Journals Index 1900-1909
	Chelan Municipal Government - Justice Court Dockets 1936-1938
	Cheney Municipal Government - Criminal Justice Dockets 1946-1950

	Clallam County Government - Clerk's Docket and Fee Book 1889-1901
	Clallam County Government - Criminal Case Index 1914-1983
	Clallam County Government - Justice Court Dockets, Forks Precinct 1927-1973
	Clallam County Government - Police Court Dockets, Forks 1953-1976
	Clallam County Government - Justice Court Docket, Civil and Criminal 1860-1919
	Clallam County Government - Criminal Case Files 1890-1989
	Clallam County Government - Justice Court Civil Dockets, Port Angeles 1921-1960
	Clallam County Government - Justice Criminal Docket, Port Angeles 1921-1940
	Clallam County Government - Police Court Docket, Port Angeles 1937-1939
	Clallam County Government - Miscellaneous Court Documents 1863-1944
	Clallam County Government - Superior Court Journals 1892-1948
	Clallam County Government - Appearance Docket - Criminal 1890-1979
	Clallam County Government - Superior Court Final Record 1889-1908
	Clark County Government - Camas Precinct Justice Court Docket 1953-1958
	Columbia County Government - Territorial Criminal Case Files 1877-1915
	Columbia County Government - Journals 1878-1889
	Columbia County Government - Superior Court Journals 1891-1975
	Cowlitz County Government - Trial Dockets 1934-1981

	Cowlitz County Government - Longview Precinct Justice Court Documentation 1925-1966
	Cowlitz County Government - Superior Court Index 1892-1976
	Cowlitz County Government - Dungan Precinct Justice Court Docket 1945-1946
	Cowlitz County Government - Lower Coweeman Precinct Justice Court Dockets 1946-1955
	Cowlitz County Government - Appearance Docket and Fee Book 1883-1976
	Cowlitz County Government - Miscellaneous Court Records 1873-1983
	Douglas County Government - Criminal Case Files 1894-1986
	Douglas County Government - Prosecuting Attorney Information Notices 1894-1898
	Douglas County Government - Criminal Appearance and Fee Docket 1903-1956
	Douglas County Government - Criminal Court Calendar 1911-1926
	Douglas County Government - Bar Dockets 1888-1905
	Elma Municipal Government - Elma Precinct Justice Court Dockets 1909-1972
	Finance, Budget and Business, Department of - Department of Finance, Budget and Business, Budget Files 1935-1947
	Franklin County Government - Witness Registers 1902-1969
	Franklin County Government - Miscellaneous Papers 1891-1967
	Franklin County Government - Criminal Case Files 1890-1990
	Franklin County Government - Criminal Appearance Dockets 1909-1983
	Garfield County Government - Territorial Criminal Case Files 1883-1890

	Goldendale Municipal Government - Justice Court Dockets 1883-1948
	Governors, State - Governor Dixy Lee Ray, Indian Tribal Affairs Files 1957-1988
	Governors, State - Governor Clarence D. Martin, Legal Files 1933-1940
	Governors, Territorial - Governor John H. McGraw, Prosecuting Attorney Reports 1894-1897
	Grant County Government - Appeals from Lower Courts 1909-1981
	Grant County Government - Criminal Case Files 1909-1986
	Grant County Government - Criminal Bar Docket 1909-1930
	Grant County Government - Record of Cases 1909-1911
	Grant County Government - Superior Court Blotter 1910-1933
	Grays Harbor County Government - Superior Court Trial Docket 1893-1908
	Grays Harbor County Government - Criminal Dockets 1927-1959
	Grays Harbor County Government - Criminal Case Files 1950-1960
	Grays Harbor County Government - Criminal Docket 1921-1939
	Grays Harbor County Government - Miscellaneous Filings 1869-1976
	House of Representatives - Representative Marlin Appelwick's Papers 1983-1998
	House of Representatives - House Corrections Committee, Issue Files 1981-1996
	Institutions, Department of - Institutions Department, Central Files, Administration, General Correspondence and Subject Files 1955-1971
	Island County Government - Criminal Case Files 1926-1987

	Island County Government - Final Record 1890-1911
	Island County Government - Territorial Justice Court Case Files 1860-1891
	Island County Government - Justice Docket 1889-1960
	Island County Government - Territorial District Court Docket and Fee Book 1853-1854
	Island County Government - Territorial Justice Court Record 1858-1888
	Issaquah Municipal Government - Police Justice Docket 1965-1965
	Issaquah Municipal Government - Police Court Docket 1892-1946
	Jefferson County Government - Territorial District Court Dockets 1859-1890
	Jefferson County Government - Territorial District Court Journal 1853-1890
	Jefferson County Government - Territorial District Court Calendar 1868-1890
	Jefferson County Government - Territorial District Court Case Index 1854-1880
	Jefferson County Government - Territorial District Court Case Files 1853-1889
	Jefferson County Government - Superior Court Docket 1889-1893
	Jefferson County Government - Civil and Criminal Case Files 1890-1928
	Jefferson County Government - Superior Court Journal 1892-1975
	Jefferson County Government - Criminal Case Files 1926-1993
	Jefferson County Government - Superior Court Final Record 1910-1922
	Jefferson County Government - Justice Court Docket, Civil and Criminal 1927-1929

	Jefferson County Government - Justice Court Docket, Civil and Criminal and Traffic 1907-1938
	Jefferson County Government - Justice Court Docket, Criminal and Traffic 1943-1972
	Jefferson County Government - Justice Court Docket, Criminal 1954-1962
	Jefferson County Government - Police Court Docket, Port Townsend 1958-1962
	Jefferson County Government - Probate Court Journal 1857-1973
	Jefferson County Government - Territorial District Court Final Record 1877-1889
	Judicial Council - Judicial Council, General Files 1957-1988
	Kalama Municipal Government - Justice Court Documentation 1903-1964
	King County Government - Juvenile Index 1959-1978
	King County Government - Justice Dockets 1909-1955
	King County Government - Statements of Facts (Criminal) 1870-1968
	King County Government - Journals 1889-1909
	King County Government - Miscellaneous Bound Records 1871-1889
	King County Government - Final Records 1854-1891
	King County Government - Fee Books 1901-1903
	King County Government - Criminal Court Record Books 1891-1895
	King County Government - Criminal Justice Dockets 1951-1960
	King County Government - Criminal Dockets 1963-1970

	King County Government - Criminal Case Files 1889-1972
	King County Government - Criminal Case Final Records 1887-1889
	King County Government - Criminal Transfer Calendar 1944-1945
	King County Government - Criminal Trial Calendars--District and Justice Courts 1924-1964
	King County Government - Criminal Case Final Records 1891-1895
	King County Government - Criminal Dockets 1890-1897
	King County Government - Criminal Index 1890-1977
	King County Government - Criminal Docket 1966-1967
	King County Government - Justice Dockets 1890-1906
	King County Government - Criminal Justice Docket 1960-1960
	King County Government - Justice Dockets 1939-1942
	King County Government - Case Files 1867-1889
	Kitsap County Government - Dockets 1915-1950
	Kitsap County Government - Superior Court Minute Books 1893-1970
	Kitsap County Government - Witness Claim Book 1905-1910
	Kitsap County Government - Justice Court Criminal Case Files 1931-1942
	Kitsap County Government - Criminal Docket 1966-1969
	Kitsap County Government - Trial Dockets 1894-1905

	Kitsap County Government - Justice Docket 1883-1909
	Kitsap County Government - Justice Dockets 1942-1945
	Kitsap County Government - Justice Dockets 1909-1936
	Kitsap County Government - Justice Docket 1916-1937
	Kitsap County Government - Justice Docket 1931-1935
	Kitsap County Government - Justice Dockets 1889-1947
	Kitsap County Government - Criminal Dockets 1947-1966
	Kitsap County Government - Justice Dockets 1915-1931
	Kitsap County Government - Justice Dockets 1905-1919
	Kitsap County Government - Criminal Dockets 1919-1967
	Kitsap County Government - Justice Docket 1938-1942
	Kitsap County Government - Criminal Dockets 1944-1967
	Kitsap County Government - Criminal Dockets 1967-1974
	Kitsap County Government - Index to Appearance Docket, Criminal 1973-1978
	Kitsap County Government - Justice Docket 1945-1949
	Kittitas County Government - Criminal Court Calendar 1891-1901
	Kittitas County Government - Minute Books 1923-1981
	Kittitas County Government - Territorial District Court Journals 1878-1890

	Kittitas County Government - Territorial District Court Calendars 1887-1889
	Kittitas County Government - Criminal Case Files 1889-1989
	Kittitas County Government - Criminal Appearance Docket 1904-1982
	Kittitas County Government - Judgment Transcripts 1887-1913
	Klickitat County Government - Territorial Criminal Case Files 1882-1889
	Klickitat County Government - Territorial Appearance Docket 1880-1889
	Klickitat County Government - Bar Dockets 1881-1890
	Klickitat County Government - Mug Books 1930-1961
	Klickitat County Government - Clerk's Final Record 1880-1958
	Klickitat County Government - Clerk's Minute Book 1911-1955
	La Conner Municipal Government - Justice Court Records 1886-1962
	Leavenworth Municipal Government - Criminal Justice Court Dockets 1908-1944
	Legislative Council - Legislative Council, Committee Reports 1943-1970
	Lewis County Government - Criminal Case Files 1969-1972
	Lewis County Government - Justice Court Criminal Docket 1922-1922
	Lewis County Government - Criminal Case Files 1914-1922
	Lewis County Government - Centralia Precinct Justice Court Criminal Case Files 1951-1955
	Lincoln County Government - Criminal Case Files 1927-1979

	Lincoln County Government - Territorial Criminal Case Files 1885-1889
	Lincoln County Government - Superior Court Dockets 1914-1979
	Long Beach Municipal Government - Long Beach Precinct Justice Court Dockets 1903-1955
	Mabton Municipal Government - Justice Court Cost Bill Book 1917-1923
	Mabton Municipal Government - Justice Court Criminal Dockets 1923-1953
	Mason County Government - Shelton Precinct Justice Court Case Files 1933-
	Mason County Government - Shelton Precinct Justice Court Case File Index 1950-1954
	Mason County Government - Justice Court Dockets 1892-1993
	Northwest Region Special Collections - Frontier Justice Project 1853-1889
	Okanogan County Government - Robert J. Murray (Judge), Papers 1961-1971
	Okanogan County Government - Prosecuting Attorney's Files 1949-1958
	Okanogan County Government - Criminal Case Files 1902-1924
	Okanogan County Government - Criminal Court Calendar 1890-1906
	Okanogan County Government - Justice Dockets 1888-1970
	Olympia Municipal Government - Criminal Record 1948-1953
	Pacific County Government - Civil and Criminal Case Files 1878-1889
	Pacific County Government - Justice Dockets 1963-1992
	Pacific County Government - Appearance Docket and Fee Book 1872-1892

	Pacific County Government - South Bend Precinct Justice Court Dockets 1906-1963
	Pasco Municipal Government - Justice Court Traffic Case Files 1946-1960
	Pierce County Government - Criminal Docket 1962-1965
	Pierce County Government - Territorial District Court Dockets 1882-1889
	Pierce County Government - Criminal Execution Docket 1893-1902
	Pierce County Government - Justice Court Dockets 1913-1962
	Pierce County Government - Justice Dockets 1948-1962
	Pierce County Government - Criminal Justice Dockets 1952-1954
	Pierce County Government - Criminal Justice Dockets 1950-1953
	Pierce County Government - Criminal Justice Dockets 1957-1963
	Pierce County Government - Criminal Dockets 1952-1974
	Pierce County Government - Superior Court Journals 1889-1977
	Pierce County Government - Appearance Docket and Fee Books 1864-1966
	Pierce County Government - Superior Court Criminal Appearance Docket and Fee Books 1892-1961
	Pierce County Government - Territorial District Court and Superior Court Case Files 1854-1961
	Pierce County Government - Superior Court Defendant Index 1890-1896
	Pierce County Government - Superior Court Plaintiff Index 1891-1896
	Pierce County Government - Clerk's Witness Books 1894-1965

	Pierce County Government - Clerk's Minutes of Presiding Court 1959-1974
	Pierce County Government - Superior Court Criminal Docket 1892-1892
	Pierce County Government - Superior Court Fee Books 1892-1898
	Pierce County Government - Superior Court Criminal Judgment and Sentence Records 1911-1950
	Pierce County Government - Record of Bonds 1887-1946
	Port Townsend Municipal Government - Police Court Docket 1911-1953
	Puyallup Municipal Government - Police Court Dockets 1928-1952
	Raymond Municipal Government - Superior and Police Court Case Files 1909-1940
	San Juan County Government - Civil and Criminal Case Files 1886-1944
	San Juan County Government - Justice Court Criminal Docket, Friday Harbor 1890-1929
	San Juan County Government - Justice Court Docket 1891-1967
	San Juan County Government - Miscellaneous Court Documents 1886-1975
	San Juan County Government - Court Journal 1885-1977
	San Juan County Government - Court Orders, Criminal Cases 1974-1976
	San Juan County Government - Police Court Docket - Friday Harbor 1940-1960
	San Juan County Government - Criminal Case Files 1975-1989
	Secretary of State and Territory - Secretary of State, Archives, Frontier Justice Project, Overview 1853-1889
	Secretary of State and Territory - Frontier Justice Project 1852-1889

	Sedro Woolley Municipal Government - Municipal Court Records 1891-1977
	Senate - Senate Judiciary Committee, Issue Files 1970-1993
	Senate - Senator Phil Talmadge's Papers 1983-1993
	Skagit County Government - Territorial District Court Case Files 1878-1889
	Skagit County Government - Civil and Criminal Case Files 1889-1936
	Skagit County Government - Criminal Case Files 1927-1966
	Skagit County Government - Criminal Case Files, Sampled 1968-2005
	Skagit County Government - Criminal Dockets 1927-1975
	Skagit County Government - Civil and Criminal Journals 1885-1923
	Skagit County Government - Territorial District Court Final Record 1878-1889
	Skagit County Government - Criminal Case Index 1927-1981
	Skagit County Government - Justice Court Docket 1892-1982
	Skamania County Government - Cascades Precinct Justice Court Case Files 1935-1950
	Skamania County Government - North Bonneville Municipal Court Case Files 1935-1938
	Skamania County Government - Justice Court Documentation 1923-1930
	Snohomish County Government - Justice Court Civil and Criminal Docket, Everett Precinct 1903-1907
	Snohomish County Government - Justice Court Criminal Docket, Snohomish Precinct 1944-1972
	Snohomish County Government - Police Court Docket, Edmonds 1949-1959

	Snohomish County Government - Justice Court Docket, Various Precincts 1891-1967
	Snohomish County Government - Justice Court Criminal Docket, Everett Precinct 1908-1969
	Snohomish County Government - Justice Court Criminal and Traffic Docket, Mukilteo and Lake Stevens 1967-1970
	Snohomish County Government - Justice Court Docket, Snohomish Precinct 1890-1942
	Snohomish County Government - Justice Court Criminal and Traffic Docket, Everett 1967-1969
	Snohomish County Government - Justice Court Receipt Books, Everett Precinct 1961-1963
	Snohomish County Government - Territorial District Court Case Files 1876-1889
	Snohomish County Government - Civil and Criminal Case Files 1889-1923
	Snohomish County Government - Criminal Case Files 1937-1958
	Snohomish County Government - Criminal Case Files, Sampled 1919-1995
	Snohomish County Government - Criminal Appearance Docket 1893-1971
	Snohomish County Government - Civil and Criminal Case Index 1890-1979
	Snohomish County Government - Mug Books 1921-1983
	Snohomish County Government - Superior Court Journals 1890-1951
	Social and Health Services, Department of - Social and Health Services Department, Juvenile Rehabilitation Reports 1968-1979
	South Bend Municipal Government - Criminal Dockets 1922-1969
	Spokane County Government - Justice Docket Books 1889-1970
	Spokane County Government - Superior Court Journals 1879-1935

	Spokane County Government - Superior Court Minute Books 1893-1901
	Spokane County Government - Superior Court Dockets 1889-1945
	Spokane County Government - Indexes, Civil, Criminal 1887-1974
	Spokane Municipal Government - Case Files 1899-1979
	Springdale Municipal Government - Police Docket 1892-1910
	State Boards, Commissions and Councils - Uniform Law Commission, General Files and Commercial Code Working Files 1939-1997
	Thurston County Government - District Court Case Files 1852-1889
	Thurston County Government - Criminal Court Calendar 1891-1910
	Thurston County Government - Criminal Case Files 1900-1992
	Thurston County Government - Olympia Precinct Justice Court Dockets 1891-1963
	Thurston County Government - Justice Court Dockets -
	Thurston County Government - Tumwater Precinct Justice Court Docket 1922-1955
	Thurston County Government - Appearance Docket and Fee Book 1854-1978
	Thurston County Government - Yelm Precinct Justice Court Dockets 1927-1965
	Thurston County Government - Tenino Precinct Justice Court Dockets 1921-1966
	Thurston County Government - Superior Court Docket 1923-1932
	Thurston County Government - Superior Court Index 1854-1978
	Thurston County Government - Criminal Docket 1866-1972

	Thurston County Government - Final Record of Criminal Cases 1860-1872
	Vader Municipal Government - Court Records 1906-1978
	Wahkiakum County Government - Criminal Justice Court Dockets 1891-1947
	Walla Walla County Government - Territorial District Court Civil/Criminal Case Files 1860-1889
	Walla Walla County Government - Superior Court Case Files 1860-1930
	Walla Walla County Government - Criminal Dockets 1953-1963
	Whatcom County Government - Criminal Case Files, Sampled 1986-1996
	Whatcom County Government - Territorial District Court Order Book 1854-1859
	Whatcom County Government - Territorial District Court Journal 1883-1889
	Whatcom County Government - Criminal Appearance Docket 1897-1973
	Whatcom County Government - Justice Court Criminal Docket, Bellingham Precinct 1904-1972
	Whatcom County Government - Justice Court Docket, New Whatcom Precinct 1891-1898
	Whatcom County Government - Criminal Case Files 1951-1986
	Whatcom County Government - Criminal Court Docket 1895-1917
	Whatcom County Government - Criminal Court Minute Book 1987-1987
	Whatcom County Government - Superior Court Journal - Civil and Criminal 1889-1949
	Whatcom County Government - Court Calendar 1887-1898
	Whatcom County Government - Criminal Case Index 1897-1944

	Whatcom County Government - Justice Court Docket 1873-1972
	Whatcom County Government - Territorial District Court Case Files 1883-1889
	White Salmon Municipal Government - Justice Court Dockets 1895-1957
	Whitman County Government - Superior Court Criminal Journals 1904-1938
	Whitman County Government - Territorial Criminal Case Files 1862-1889
	Woodland Municipal Government - Justice Court Criminal Dockets 1960-1969
	Yakima County Government - Criminal Files Index 1882-1977
	Yakima County Government - Court Journals, Criminal 1907-1951
	Yakima County Government - Appearance Dockets 1882-1975
	Yakima County Government - Superior Court Minute Books 1869-1951
	Yakima County Government - Criminal Case Files 1882-1975
	Yakima County Government - Sheriff's Criminal Docket 1921-1931
	Yakima County Government - Criminal Appearance Dockets 1882-1971
	Yakima County Government - Justice Dockets -
	Corrections, Department of - Corrections Department, Penitentiary, Centralia Massacre Convict Files 1920-1939
	Corrections, Department of - Corrections Department, Penitentiary, Inmate Files 1886-1920
	Corrections, Department of - Corrections, Penitentiary, Conditional Pardon Record 1899-1921

	Federal Records - Federal Records, Office of the Secretary of the Interior, Territorial Papers, Washington Territory 1854-1902
	Governors, State - Governor Louis F. Hart, Legal Files 1919-1924
	Governors, State - Governor Roland H. Hartley, Legal Files 1925-1932
	Governors, State - Governor Clarence D. Martin, Legal Files 1933-1940
	Governors, State - Governors' Office, Clemency and Pardon Case Files 1919-2003
	Governors, State - Governor John Spellman, Clemency Case Files 1978-1984
	Governors, State - Governor Gary Locke, Clemency and Pardon Files 1996-2004
	Governors, State - Governor Christine Gregoire Administration, Clemency and Pardon Board Hearing Files 2005-2007
	Governors, State - Governors' Office, Card Index to Pardons and Clemency Actions 1889-1960
	Governors, State - Governors' Office, Clemency, Pardon, Parole, Commutation and Reprieve Registers 1902-1965
	Governors, State - Governor Elisha P. Ferry, Legal Files 1889-1894
	Governors, State - Governor John H. McGraw, List of Pardons Submitted to the Legislature 1895-1895
	Governors, State - Governor John R. Rogers, Private Secretary's Correspondence File 1898-1901
	Governors, Territorial - Governor William A. Newell, Pardon Files 1881-1884
	Governors, Territorial - Governor Eugene Semple, Pardon Files 1889-1889
	Governors, Territorial - Governor Miles Moore, Pardon Files 1889-1889
	Governors, Territorial - Governor Elisha P. Ferry, Petitions for Pardon of Arthur Floweree 1874-1877

District Court Records

 http://www.secstate.wa.gov/archives/FrontierJusticeGuidestotheDistrictCourt
.aspx

Federal Criminal Court Records at the National Archives & Records Admin. (NARA)

NARA Pacific Alaska Region (Seattle),
6125 Sand Point Way NE, Seattle, WA 98115-7999, (206) 336-5134
http://www.archives.gov/pacific-alaska/seattle/
seattle.archives@nara.gov

Record Type	ARC Identifier	Title	Description
	567959	Civil, Criminal, and Admiralty Case Files, compiled 1890 - 1928	Textual Records from the U.S. District Court for the Seattle Division of the Western District of Washington. (03/02/1905 -)
	567675	Civil, Criminal, and Admiralty Case Files, compiled 1890 - 1911	Textual Records from the U.S. Circuit Court for the Seattle Division of the Western District of Washington. (03/02/1905 - 01/01/1912)
	572104	Criminal Dockets, compiled 1890 - 1911	Textual Records from the U.S. Circuit Court for the Spokane Division of the Eastern District of Washington. (03/02/1905 - 01/01/1912)
	567519	Criminal Case Files, compiled 1929 - 1965	Textual Records from the U.S. District Court for the Spokane Division of the Eastern District of Washington. (03/02/1905 -)
	572263	Criminal Dockets, compiled 1890 - 1950	Textual Records from the U.S. District Court for the Walla Walla Division of the Eastern District of Washington. (03/02/1905 - ca. 1951)
	567677	Civil, Criminal, and Admiralty Case Files, compiled 1890 - 1911	Textual Records from the U.S. Circuit Court for the Tacoma Division of the Western District of Washington. (03/02/1905 - 12/31/1911)
	567109	Criminal Case Files, compiled 1927 - 1970	Textual Records from the U.S. District Court for the Yakima Division of the Eastern District of Washington. (03/02/1905 -)
	572385	Criminal Dockets, compiled 1890 - 1956	Textual Records from the U.S. District Court for the Spokane Division of the Eastern District of Washington. (03/02/1905 -)

	569566	Civil, Criminal, Admiralty, and Bankruptcy Case Files, compiled 1890 - 1939	Textual Records from the U.S. District Court for the Tacoma Division of the Western District of Washington. (03/02/1905 -)
	567604	Criminal Case Files, compiled 1929 - 1971	Textual Records from the U.S. District Court for the Seattle Division of the Western District of Washington. (03/02/1905 -)
	572774	Criminal Dockets, compiled 1913 - 1947	Textual Records from the U.S. District Court for the Bellingham Division of the Western District of Washington. (ca. 1909 - ca. 1969)
	572200	Criminal Dockets, compiled 1907 - 1956	Textual Records from the U.S. District Court for the Yakima Division of the Eastern District of Washington. (03/02/1905 -)
	572084	Criminal Dockets, compiled 1907 - 1911	Textual Records from the U.S. Circuit Court for the Tacoma Division of the Western District of Washington. (03/02/1905 - 12/31/1911)
	567052	Criminal Case Files, compiled 1929 - 1965	Textual Records from the U.S. District Court for the Tacoma Division of the Western District of Washington. (03/02/1905 -)
	567585	Criminal Case Files, compiled 1913 - 1947	Textual Records from the U.S. District Court for the Bellingham Division of the Western District of Washington. (ca. 1909 - ca. 1969)
	572876	Criminal Case Files, compiled 1913 - 1947	Textual Records from the U.S. District Court for the Bellingham Division of the Western District of Washington. (ca. 1909 - ca. 1969)
	572692	Criminal Dockets, compiled 1890 - 1966	Textual Records from the U.S. District Court for the Seattle Division of the Western District of Washington. (03/02/1905 -)

Washington State Executions

http://users.bestweb.net/~rg/execution/WASHINGTON.htm

Washington State Department of Corrections – Offender Locator

http://www.doc.wa.gov/offenderinfo/default.aspx

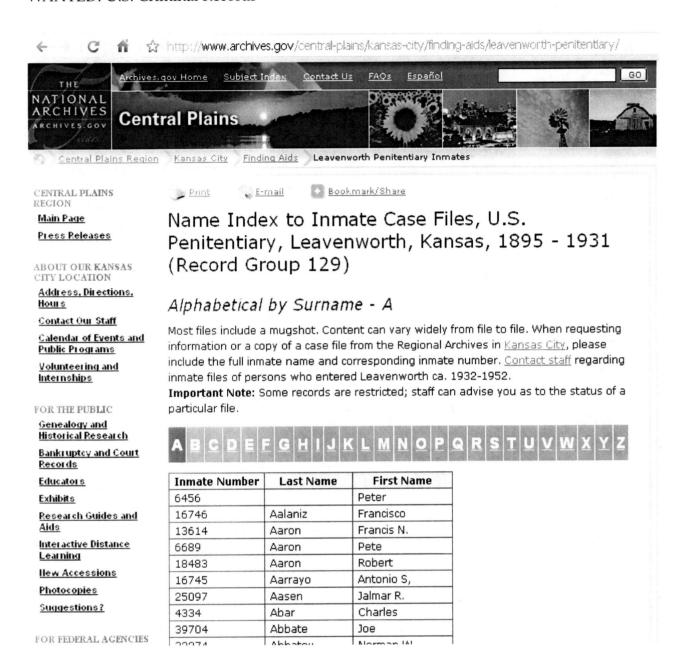

Index to Leavenworth Prison inmate case files, 1895-1931. Files
held at the National Archives in Kansas City, MO.

West Virginia

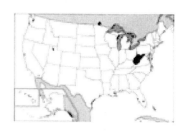

West Virginia State Archives and Records Administration

1900 Kanawha Boulevard, E.; Charleston, WV 25305-0300, (304) 558-0230
http://www.wvculture.org/HiStory/wvsamenu.html
No email; all requests must be made in writing

Record Type	Location	Title/Description
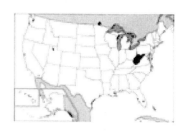	AR-1804	Department of Corrections. Penitentiary records, ca. 1890-1930. / Note: Privacy laws apply to these records. According to the Department of Corrections, open access to these records is prohibited for 70 years from the time of their creation. During that 70 year period, staff may check records for information which may have appeared in other sources, such as newspaper accounts. This information includes crime, dates, county, etc., but not internal Corrections' material. 143 cu. ft.
	AR-1892	Corrections. / Penitentiary prisoner records, including fingerprint cards, declaration cards, case files, list of inmate executions, 1890s-1975. 100 cu. ft.
	AR-1561-1586	Secretary of State's Office. Pardon and parole records, 1865-1925, 11 ft.
	AR-1587-1590	Secretary of State's Office. / Convict records [n.d.], 20 in.
	AR-1769 Box 2	Governor's Office. / Rewards for arrest and conviction of persons and escaped prisoners, 1864-1922;
	AR-1769 Box 5	Secretary of State's Office. / o Series 40: West Virginia Penitentiary records o Series 41: West Virginia Medium Security Prison records o Series 42: West Virginia State Prison for Women records

County Court Records

 http://www.wvculture.org/history/countrec.html

Federal Criminal Court Records at the National Archives & Records Admin. (NARA)

NARA Mid Atlantic Region (Philadelphia)
900 Market Street, Philadelphia, PA, 19107-4292, (215) 606-0100
http://www.archives.gov/midatlantic/
philadelphia.archives@nara.gov

Record Type	ARC Identifier	Title	Description
	593080	Criminal Case Files, compiled 1938 - 1969, documenting the period 1934 - 1969	Textual Records from the U.S. District Court for the Fairmont Division of the Northern District of West Virginia. (06/29/1938 - 11/11/1977?)
	593085	Criminal Case Files, compiled 1906 - 1944	Textual Records from the U.S. District Court for the Parkersburg Division of the Northern District of West Virginia. (01/22/1901 - 01/14/1983)
	593088	Criminal Case Files, compiled 1887 - 1981	Textual Records from the U.S. District Court for the Wheeling Division of the Northern District of West Virginia. (01/22/1901 -)
	593086	Criminal Case Files, compiled 1907 - 1917	Textual Records from the U.S. District Court for the Philippi Division of the Northern District of West Virginia. (02/11/1907 - ca. 1934)
	593079	Criminal Case Files, compiled 1918 - 1977	Textual Records from the U.S. District Court for the Elkins Division of the Northern District of West Virginia. (08/22/1914 -)
	593077	Criminal Case Files, compiled 1834 - 1986	Textual Records from the U.S. District Court for the Clarksburg Division of the Northern District of West Virginia. (01/22/1901 -)
	593083	Criminal Case Files, compiled 1936 - 1943	Textual Records from the U.S. District Court for the Southern District of West Virginia. Lewisburg Term. (03/23/1912 -)
	593084	Criminal Case Files, compiled 1888 - 1945	Textual Records from the U.S. District Court for the Martinsburg Division of the Northern District of West Virginia. (01/22/1901 -)

	561851	Criminal Dockets, compiled 01/1908 - 03/1944	Textual Records from the U.S. District Court for the Parkersburg Division of the Northern District of West Virginia. (01/22/1901 - 01/14/1983)
	593081	Criminal Case Files, compiled 1896 - 1982	Textual Records from the U.S. District Court for the Huntington Division of the Southern District of West Virginia. (01/22/1901 -)
	593076	Criminal Case Files, compiled 1903 - 1981	Textual Records from the U.S. District Court for the Charleston Division of the Southern District of West Virginia. (01/22/1901 -)
	593075	Criminal Case Files, compiled 1915 - 1982	Textual Records from the U.S. District Court for the Bluefield Division of the Southern District of West Virginia. (01/22/1901 -)
	593074	Criminal Case Files, compiled 1941 - 1978	Textual Records from the U.S. District Court for the Beckley Division of the Southern District of West Virginia. (06/29/1938 -)
	612524	Judgment Dockets, compiled 1909 - 1976	Textual Records from the U.S. District Court for the Clarksburg Division of the Northern District of West Virginia. (01/22/1901 -)
	2771759	Criminal Docket, compiled 1903 - 1925	Textual Records from the U.S. District Court for the Addison Division of the Southern District of West Virginia. (01/31/1903)
	2771762	Criminal Docket, compiled 1922 - 1941	Textual Records from the U.S. District Court for the Southern District of West Virginia. Lewisburg Term. (03/23/1912 -)
	2788695	Criminal Docket, compiled 1908 - 1920	Textual Records from the U.S. District Court for the Philippi Division of the Northern District of West Virginia. (02/11/1907 - ca. 1934)
	2788676	Criminal Docket, compiled 1908 - 1955	Textual Records from the U.S. District Court for the Clarksburg Division of the Northern District of West Virginia. (01/22/1901 -)
	2788736	Criminal Dockets, compiled 1877 - 1952	Textual Records from the U.S. District Court for the Wheeling Division of the Northern District of West Virginia. (01/22/1901 -)
	2788749	Criminal Docket, compiled 1931 - 1941	Textual Records from the U.S. District Court for the Fairmont Division of the Northern District of West Virginia. (06/29/1938 - 11/11/1977?)
	2788727	Criminal Dockets, compiled 1908 - 1910	Textual Records from the U.S. Circuit Court for the Philippi Division of the Northern District of West Virginia. (02/11/1907 - 01/01/1912)
	2771763	Criminal Dockets, compiled 1889 - 1907	Textual Records from the U.S. Circuit Court for the Charleston Division of the Southern District of West Virginia. (01/22/1901 - 01/01/1912)

	2771751	Criminal Dockets, compiled 1901 - 1967	Textual Records from the U.S. District Court for the Charleston Division of the Southern District of West Virginia. (01/22/1901 -)
	2788681	Criminal Dockets, compiled 1908 - 1910	Textual Records from the U.S. Circuit Court for the Clarksburg Division of the Northern District of West Virginia. (01/22/1901 - 01/01/1912)
	2771754	Criminal Dockets, compiled 1911 - 1963	Textual Records from the U.S. District Court for the Huntington Division of the Southern District of West Virginia. (01/22/1901 -)
	2788689	Criminal Dockets, compiled 1908 - 1942	Textual Records from the U.S. District Court for the Martinsburg Division of the Northern District of West Virginia. (01/22/1901 -)
	2774964	Criminal Dockets, compiled 04/1902 - 09/1902	Textual Records from the U.S. Circuit Court for the Huntington Division of the Southern District of West Virginia. (01/22/1901 - 01/01/1912)
	2788766	Criminal Dockets, compiled 1908 - 1911	Textual Records from the U.S. Circuit Court for the Parkersburg Division of the Northern District of West Virginia. (01/22/1901 - 01/01/1912)
	2788741	Criminal Docket, compiled 1908 - 1911	Textual Records from the U.S. Circuit Court for the Wheeling Division of the Northern District of West Virginia. (01/22/1901 - 01/01/1912)
	2788744	Criminal Dockets, compiled 1915 - 1938	Textual Records from the U.S. District Court for the Elkins Division of the Northern District of West Virginia. (08/22/1914 -)

West Virginia Executions

http://users.bestweb.net/~rg/execution/WEST%20VIRGINIA.htm

West Virginia State Department of Corrections – Offender Search

http://www.wvdoc.com/wvdoc/OffenderSearch/tabid/117/Default.aspx

Wisconsin

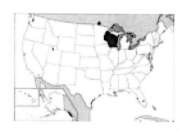

Wisconsin Historical Society

816 State Street, Madison, WI 53706-1417, (608) 264-6460

http://arcat.library.wisc.edu/

email: http://wisconsinhistory.org/libraryarchives/reference_form.asp?program=ar

Record Type	Location	Author	Title
	Kenosha Series 80	Kenosha County (Wis.). Sheriff.	Jail registers, 1900-1919, 1921-1976.
	La Crosse Series 34	La Crosse (Wis.). Police Justice.	Criminal docket, 1862-1941.
	Waukesha Series 17	Waukesha County (Wis.). Sheriff.	County jail register, 1901-1904.
		Wisconsin. Dept. of Corrections.	Inmate related data files-primary information [electronic resource], 1983-[ongoing]
		Wisconsin. Dept. of Justice. Division of Legal Services.	Closed case files, 1885-1976, 1980-1985; 1994-2004.
		Wisconsin. Dept. of Justice. Division of Legal Services.	Inmate complaints, 1973-1991.
		Wisconsin. Division of Community Corrections.	Case number assignment log--electronic [electronic resource], 1992-[ongoing]
		Wisconsin. Division of Community Corrections.	Case number assignment log--paper, 1962-1992.

	Series 2383	Wisconsin. Division of Corrections.	Case records of parolees and inmates of correctional institutions [microform], 1943-1950.
	Series 1387	Wisconsin Industrial Home for Women.	Inmate case history books, 1921-1925.
	Series 1399	Wisconsin Industrial Home for Women.	Medical officer's records of inmates, 1922-1927.
		Wisconsin Resource Center (Winnebago, Wis.)	Inmate's permanent WRC record, 1983-[ongoing]
	Series 2177	Wisconsin School for Boys.	Inmate admission record, 1897-1899.
	Series 2178	Wisconsin School for Boys.	Inmate case file summaries, 1943-1948.
	Series 2176	Wisconsin School for Boys.	Inmate case history books, 1860-1950.
	Series 311	Wisconsin School for Girls.	Inactive case files (Institutional series), 1875-1959.
	Series 1381	Wisconsin School for Girls.	Inmate case history books, 1875-1926.
	Series 1383	Wisconsin School for Girls	Inmate record book, 1926-1939.
	Series 1989/179	Wisconsin. State Board of Control.	Parole record, 1909, 1911, 1913, 1914, 1916.
	Series 1376	Wisconsin State Prison.	Bertillon record [microform], 1894-1923.
	Series 1377	Wisconsin State Prison.	Classified bertillon record [microform], 1894-1901.
	Series 1395	Wisconsin State Prison.	Index to prisoner's record [microform], 1850-1897.
	Series 1379	Wisconsin State Prison.	Inmate conduct records [microform], 1854-1946.
	Series 1380	Wisconsin State Prison.	Parole record [microform], 1909-1932.
	Series 1392	Wisconsin State Prison.	Prisoner's descriptive record [microform], 1870-1889.

	Series 1391	Wisconsin State Prison.	Register [microform], 1850-1874.
		Wisconsin State Reformatory.	Case files, 1927-1940.
	Series 1390	Wisconsin State Reformatory.	Inmate case history books [microform], 1898-1954.
	Series 2786	Wisconsin State Reformatory	Inmate recreation log, 1953-1954.
	Series 2787	Wisconsin State Reformatory	Record of paroles, 1916-1926.
	Series 2782	Wisconsin State Reformatory.	Record of prisoner conduct, 1898-1908.
	Series 2084	Wisconsin. Division of Corrections.	Case files [microform], 1940-1951.
		Wisconsin. Division of Corrections.	Institutionalized adult case files, 1955-1967.
	Series 2082	Wisconsin State Prison.	Case files, 1933-1940.
	Series 1380	Wisconsin State Prison.	Parole record [microform], 1909-1932.
	Series 2420	Wisconsin State Prison.	Parole register, 1907-1958.
		Wisconsin State Reformatory.	Case files, 1927-1940.
	Series 1390	Wisconsin State Reformatory.	Inmate case history books [microform], 1898-1954.
	Series 2783	Wisconsin State Reformatory.	Parole histories, 1899-1916.
		Wisconsin State Reformatory.	Record of paroles, 1916-1926.
	Series 2243	Wisconsin. Governor.	Index to pardon dockets, 1837-1970.
	Series 95	Wisconsin. Governor.	Pardon dockets, 1868-1972.
	Milwaukee Series 47	Wisconsin. Governor.	Criminal case files, 1930-1938.

	Series 326	Wisconsin. Secretary of State.	Pardons, 1866-1978.

Local Records (e.g. Court Records) Available at Area Research Centers (Libraries)

 http://www.wisconsinhistory.org/libraryarchives/arcnet/

Federal Criminal Court Records at the National Archives & Records Admin. (NARA)

NARA Great Lakes Region (Chicago),
7358 South Pulaski Road, Chicago, IL 60629-5898, (773) 948-9001
http://www.archives.gov/great-lakes/
chicago.archives@nara.gov

Record Type	ARC Identifier	Title	Description
	1127035	Criminal Case Files, compiled 1858 - 1862, documenting the period 1849 - 1862	Textual Records from the U.S. Circuit Court for the District of Wisconsin. Milwaukee Term. (05/29/1858 - 06/30/1870)
	1089746	Criminal Case Files, compiled 1870 - 1969, documenting the period 1862 - 1969	Textual Records from the U.S. District Court for the Eastern District of Wisconsin. Milwaukee Term. (06/30/1870 -)
	1107005	Criminal Case Files, compiled 1870 - 1968	Textual Records from the U.S. District Court for the Western District of Wisconsin. Madison Term. (06/30/1870 -)
	1105818	Criminal Case Files, compiled 1886 - 1889, documenting the period 1871 - 1889	Textual Records from the U.S. District Court for the Western District of Wisconsin. LaCrosse Term. (08/05/1886 -)
	722104	Case Files, compiled 1945 - 1980	Textual Records from the U.S. Court of Appeals for the Seventh Circuit. (1948 -)

Kenosha County Sheriff's Department – Inmate Locator

 http://www.kccjs.org/jail/inmate_search/index.html

Milwaukee County Sheriff's Department – Inmate Locator

 http://www.inmatesearch.mkesheriff.org/

Wyoming

Wyoming State Archives Historical Society

2301 Central Avenue, Cheyenne, WY 82002, (307) 777-7826
http://wyoarchives.state.wy.us/
wyarchive@state.wy.us

Record Type	Location	Author	Title/Description
	N/A	Laramie County Sheriff	Criminal Case Files, 1939-1940 / Files may contain picture, arrest card, criminal history and correspondence. Note: Some information may be restricted.
	N/A	Laramie County Sheriff	Index to Prisoners , 1930-1976 / Index to individuals listed in prison calendars/registers.
	N/A	Laramie County Sheriff	Jail Registers, 1916-1968 / Monthly lists of prisoners boarded by the county. Tables List name, number of days boarded, and sometimes, crime and cost of boarding prisoners. Some volumes contain names of federal prisoners held by the county.
	N/A	Laramie County Sheriff	Prison Calendars/Registers, 1881-1989 / Record of individuals arrested and jailed by the sheriff. Information includes name, place of residence, prisoner number, physical description, criminal charge, date of arrest, name of sentencing officer, date of discharge, and brief remarks on discharge. Additional comments may be made about a person's occupation, ethnicity or mental condition. Note: Some information may be restricted.
	N/A	Laramie County Sheriff	Visitor Register, 1971-1974 / Record of visitors to jail inmates. Information includes name of visitor, date, prisoner receiving visitor, and visitor's address and relationship to prisoner.

	N/A	Laramie County Clerk of the District Court	Criminal Index, 1884-1956 / Index to names in criminal appearance dockets and District Court Journal.
	N/A	Laramie County Clerk of the District Court	Criminal Appearance Docket - Federal, 1869-1889 / Register of records filed in individual cases. Entries list name of defendant, date and type of record filed, and filing fee.
	N/A	Laramie County Clerk of the District Court	Criminal Transcript Record, 1889-1889 / Information and inventory of pertinent records of Justice of the Peace case files which were transferred over to District Court.
	N/A	Laramie County Clerk of the District Court	Criminal Trial Dockets, 1869-1876, 1891-1920 / Criminal trial dockets record the progress of criminal cases. Entries list case number, name of plaintiff, and charge and note the proceedings or actions taken on a specific day.
	N/A	Laramie County Clerk of the District Court	Criminal Case Files, 1868-1983 / Case files contain various records presented or issued in individual cases. File contents may include criminal complaint, subpoenas, warrant, transcript, indictment, evidence, judgments, and supreme court appeal.
	N/A	Laramie County Clerk of the District Court	Supreme Court Case Files, 1886, 1911 / Records of criminal cases reviewed by the Wyoming Supreme Court.
	N/A	Laramie County Clerk of the District Court	Indictment Record Index, 1890-1907 / Index to names in Indictment Record.
	N/A	Laramie County Clerk of the District Court	Indictment Record, 1890-1907 / Formal written statements charging one or more persons with an offense, as framed by the prosecuting attorney and found by the grand jury.

	N/A	Laramie County Clerk of the District Court	District Court Journals, 1868-1992 / Daily record of all filings and proceedings in civil and criminal courts. Early volumes also record criminal proceedings in the federal court.
	N/A	Laramie County Clerk of the District Court	Federal District Court Journal, 1888-1890 / Daily record of proceedings is U. S. District Court.
	N/A	Laramie County Clerk of the District Court	Minute Books, 1873-1890 / Minute books are a daily record of court activities, including administrative matters, appointment of jurors, and civil and criminal case proceedings. See also District Court Journals.
	N/A	Laramie County Clerk of the District Court	Index to District Court Journals, 1868-1947 / Index to people appearing in District Court Journals.
	N/A	Laramie County Clerk of the District Court	Combined Civil and Criminal Trial Docket, 1875-1877 / Trial dockets record the progress of civil and criminal cases. Information includes names of plaintiff and defendant, case number and sometimes notes on a day's proceedings.
	N/A	Laramie County Clerk of the District Court	Civil and Criminal Bar Dockets, 1881-1900 / Bar dockets are copies of the trial dockets for the use of the bar.
	N/A	Casper Justice of the Peace	Combined Civil and Criminal Docket Books, 1889-1926 / Docket books provide summaries of civil and criminal court proceedings. Information includes names of plaintiff and defendant, nature of charge or complaint, disposition, fine and court costs. Also included are marriages and coroner's inquests.
	N/A	Casper Justice of the Peace	Criminal Docket Books, 1923-1970 / Docket books provide summaries of criminal court proceedings. Information includes name of defendant, criminal charge, plea, disposition, fine, and court costs

	N/A	Casper Justice of the Peace	Criminal Docket Sheets, 1969-1978 / Summaries of criminal court proceedings. Information includes name of defendant, criminal charge, plea, disposition, fine and court costs. Supplementary filings may be attached to docket sheet.
	N/A	Midwest-Edgerton Justice of the Peace	Criminal Docket Sheets, 1977-1978 / Summaries of criminal court proceedings. Information includes name of defendant, offense, judgment, fine and court costs.
	N/A	Midwest-Edgerton Justice of the Peace	Combined Civil and Criminal Docket, 1961-1968 / Docket contains summaries of civil and criminal cases.
	N/A	Midwest-Edgerton Justice of the Peace	Combined Civil and Criminal Docket Sheets, 1970-1975 / Summaries by civil and criminal court proceedings. Information includes names of plaintiff and defendant, offense, judgment and court costs. Traffic tickets and miscellaneous filings may be attached to sheet.
	N/A	Natrona County Court	Criminal Docket Sheets, 1979-1986 / Summaries of criminal court proceedings. Information includes name of defendant, criminal charge, plea, judgment, fine and court costs. Supplementary filings may be attached to docket sheet.
	7704	Secretary of State	Records of Pardons, Paroles, & Discharges; 1890 - 1928
	Multiple	Dept. of Corrections	Closed Probation/Parole Files, 1993, Restricted
	19094	Charities & Reform Board	Records of Parole, 1909-1961, Restricted
	57603	Dept. of Corrections	Parole Records, 1909-1961, Restricted
	7702	Secretary of State	Record of Pardons 1873 - 1917, Volume #1 and Volume #2, 1873-1917
	7704	Secretary of State	Records of Pardons, Paroles, & Discharges; 1890 - 1928, 1890-1928

	24071	Secretary of State	Pardon Record, Vol 1 &2, 1873-1917, Restricted
	24072	Secretary of State	Pardon Record, 1890-1928, Restricted
	Roll 1961-33-73	Pardons Board	Minutes, Book 1, Book 2, Book 3, 1905-1961

Federal Criminal Court Records at the National Archives & Records Admin. (NARA)

NARA Rocky Mountain Region (Denver)
Denver Federal Center, Bldgs 46, 48, Denver, CO 80225, (303) 407-5740
http://www.archives.gov/rocky-mountain/
denver.archives@nara.gov

Record Type	ARC Identifier	Title	Description
	1107096	Civil and Criminal Case Files, compiled 1892 - 1909	Textual Records from the U.S. District Court for the District of Wyoming. Evanston Term. (ca. 1892 -)
	1107106	Criminal Case Files, compiled 1920 - 1920	Textual Records from the U.S. District Court for the District of Wyoming. Evanston Term. (ca. 1892 -)
	1107116	Criminal Case Files, compiled 1911 - 1923	Textual Records from the U.S. District Court for the District of Wyoming. Lander Term. (ca. 1911 -)
	1107439	Criminal Case Files, compiled 1911 - 1920	Textual Records from the U.S. District Court for the District of Wyoming. Sheridan Term. (1910 -)
	292789	Criminal Case Files, compiled 1890 - 1949	Textual Records from the U.S. District Court for the District of Wyoming. (1892 - ?)
	1112598	Criminal Dockets, compiled 1904 - 1954	Textual Records from the U.S. District Court for District of Wyoming. Office of U.S. Commissioners. (07/10/1890 - 1968)
	4105133	Criminal Case Files, compiled 1979 - 1982	Textual Records from the U.S. District Court for the District of Wyoming. (1892 - ?)

Wyoming Executions

 http://users.bestweb.net/~rg/execution/WYOMING.htm

Wyoming Department of Corrections – Inmate Locator

 Not Available

District of Columbia

Historical Society of Washington, DC

801 K Street, NW, Washington, DC, 20001, (202) 383-1850

www.historydc.org

info@historydc.org

Record Type	Location	Author	Title/Description
	MS 0169	District of Columbia. Jail.	The District of Columbia Jail Register, 1858-1861. / Contains information on about 1750 prisoners admitted to the "common prison of Washington County" from February 1858 to May 1861. Information provided in the ledger includes date committed, prisoner's name, by whom committed, offense, date discharged, by whom discharged, witnesses, days in jail, and jail fees. Crimes include malicious mischief, assault and battery, larceny, highway robbery, false pretenses, arson, fraud, kidnapping, keeping a bawdy house, harboring a slave, bestiality, false swearing, stabbing with a bayonet, voting illegally, selling lottery tickets, selling obscene books, passing counterfeit money, poisoning, illegitimacy, and "uttering treasonable sentiments."

Federal Criminal Court Records at the National Archives & Records Admin. (NARA)

NARA

700 Pennsylvania Ave NW, Washington, DC 20004, (202) 357-5400

http://www.archives.gov/

Record Type	ARC Identifier	Title	Description
	563696	Criminal Minutes, compiled 1863 - 1949	Textual Records from the U.S. District Court for the District of Columbia. (1936 -)

	559862	Criminal Docket Books, compiled 04/06/1863 - 03/1980	Textual Records from the U.S. District Court for the District of Columbia. (1936 -)
	560977	Municipal Court Judgements, compiled 1928 - 1966	Textual Records from the U.S. District Court for the District of Columbia. (1936 -)
	561966	Grand Jury Dockets, compiled 11/15/1924 - 1971	Textual Records from the U.S. District Court for the District of Columbia. (1936 -)
	300251	Index to Criminal Cases and Dockets, compiled ca. 1938 - ca. 1991	Textual Records from the U.S. District Court for the District of Columbia. (1936 -)
	559640	Criminal Case Files, compiled 1863 - 1992	Textual Records from the U.S. District Court for the District of Columbia. (1936 -)
	729750	Commitment Papers, compiled 1831 - 1862	Textual Records from the Penitentiary in the District of Columbia
	1137919	Registers of Convicts, compiled 1831 - 1862	Textual Records from the Penitentiary in the District of Columbia
	1137922	Registers of Punishments, compiled 1831 - 1862	Textual Records from the Penitentiary in the District of Columbia
	1142503	Pardon Papers, compiled 1832 - 1862	Textual Records from the Penitentiary in the District of Columbia

District of Columbia Executions

 http://users.bestweb.net/~rg/execution/DC.htm

National / Federal Records

Records at the National Archives & Records Admin. (NARA)

Record Type	ARC Identifier / Location	Title / Description
	580698 / NARA, College Park, MD	Notorious Offenders Files, compiled 1919 - 1975
	URL (see description)	Alphabetical Index of Former Inmates of U.S. Penitentiary, Alcatraz, 1934 - 63: http://www.archives.gov/pacific/archives/san-francisco/finding-aids/alcatraz-alpha.html
	Record Group 129 / NARA San Bruno, CA	Alcatraz Inmate Case Files / These inmate case files represent an artificial grouping of BOP files from many different sites. The complexity of locating and assembling all the files involved records clerks at Federal prisons across the country. It is possible that files were overlooked or otherwise missed during the assembly process.
	URL (see description)	Name Index to Inmate Case Files, 1902 - 1921 / http://www.archives.gov/southeast/finding-aids/atlanta-penitentiary/
	607937 / NARA Morrow, GA	U.S. Penitentiary in Atlanta: Inmate Case Files, compiled 1902 - 1921, documenting the period ca. 1880 - ca. 1922 / These files were created to document all activities related to the inmates' time in prison.
	URL (see description)	Name Index to Inmate Case Files, U.S. Penitentiary, Leavenworth, Kansas, 1895 - 1931 / http://www.archives.gov/central-plains/kansas-city/finding-aids/leavenworth-penitentiary/
	571125 / NARA Kansas City, MO	Leavenworth Inmate Case Files, compiled 07/03/1895 - 06/06/1952 / These files were created to record the institutional life of individual inmates.
	569923 / NARA Kansas City, MO	Leavenworth Inmate Registers, compiled 02/26/1920 - 04/21/1937 / This series was created to record the arrival and release of inmates.
	292110 / NARA Kansas City, MO	Leavenworth: Inmate Case Files, compiled 1895 - 1920 /

	608034 / NARA Seattle, WA	McNeil Island: Records of Prisoners Received, compiled 1875 - 1951 /
	608858 / NARA Seattle, WA	Prisoner Case Files, compiled ca. 1875 - 1920 / These files were created to record the institutional life of individual prisoners to include the progress of prisoners released on parole.
	1074134 / NARA Seattle, WA	Parole Hearing Register, compiled 08/17/1910 - 07/12/1928

Federal Criminal Court Cases Held at the National Archives and Records Administration (NARA)

CHECK CHAPTER FOR STATE WHERE THE TRIAL TOOK PLACE

PACER

Record Type	Location	Description
	URL (see description)	Public Access to Court Electronic Records (PACER) is an electronic public access service that allows users (for a fee) to obtain case and docket information from Federal Appellate, District and Bankruptcy courts, and the U.S. Party/Case Index via the Internet. Links to all courts are provided from this web site. Electronic access is available by registering with the PACER Service Center, the judiciary's centralized registration, billing, and technical support center. Each court maintains its own databases with case information. Because PACER database systems are maintained within each court, each jurisdiction will have a different URL. Accessing and querying information from each service is comparable; however, the format and content of information provided may differ slightly. PACER is a service of the United States Judiciary. The PACER Service Center is run by the Administrative Office of the United States Courts. http://pacer.psc.uscourts.gov/

LoisLaw.com - Public Records, Including Criminal Cases

 http://www.loislaw.com/product/subscriptions/publicrecords.htm

The Library of Congress
James Madison Memorial Building, Room LM101
101 Independence Avenue, SE
Washington, DC 20540-4680, (202) 707-5387 (Reading Room)
http://www.loc.gov/today/pr/2000/00-074.html

Record Type	Title/Description
	Pinkerton Archives: Includes 195 binders on criminal investigations; a large collection of photographs, including criminal "mug shots" of the day. Two-thirds of the binders cover the Pinkerton's greatest activity in criminal work, from 1880 to 1910.

FindLaw.com – U.S. Supreme Court Decisions

 http://www.findlaw.com/casecode/supreme.html

Bureau of Prisons

 http://www.bop.gov/iloc2/LocateInmate.jsp

FBI - Electronic Reading Room

 http://foia.fbi.gov/room.htm

FBI - Famous Cases

 http://www.fbi.gov/libref/historic/famcases/famcases.htm

FBI - Freedom of Information Act (FOIA) Information

http://foia.fbi.gov/foia_instruc.htm

National Inmate Lookup – Vinelink

 https://www.vinelink.com/vinelink/initMap.do

WANTED!

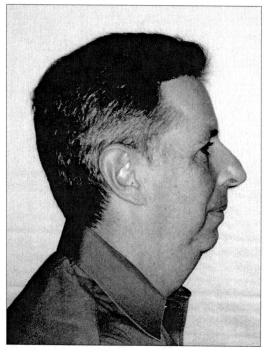

Ron Arons has researched the lives of criminals for more than a decade. His first book, *The Jews of Sing Sing*, based on years of research, provided new insights into the magnitude and scope of Jewish criminality in New York City from the late 1800s through the 1950s.

In 2008 Arons discussed famous Jewish gangsters of Manhattan's Lower East Side on the acclaimed PBS TV series *The Jewish Americans*. In 2005 Mr. Arons received a Lawrence Hackman Research Grant from the New York State Archives for his work with the repository's criminal records.

Mr. Arons has given hundreds of lectures throughout the U.S and around the world on criminal research and various genealogical topics. Mr. Arons earned degrees from Princeton University and the University of Chicago. For more information about Ron, his books and his speaking engagements, visit: www.ronarons.com.

CPSIA information can be obtained at www.ICGtesting.com
Printed in the USA
LVOW06s1724240813

349470LV00003B/21/P